PACIFISTS

CHOCOLATE SOLDIERS

What were you doing
When the drums were calling?
What were you doing
When the bombs were falling?
When you were still young men
And yes, young women too,
What were you doing in the FAU?

Why did you do it
And what did you do?
Thanks to the Quakers
The chocolate makers,
Preachers and teachers
A rat catcher too
Why did you do it?
And what did you do?

Ethiopia
And Greece and China
Islands around the coast
Of Asia Minor
Whitechapel in the blitz
And Finland in the snow
What were you doing there,
We'd like to know

Why did you do it
And what did you do?
Thanks to the Quakers
The chocolate makers,
Actors and doctors
An architect too,
Why did you do it?
And what did you do?

What were you doing
When the drums were calling?
What were you doing
When the bombs were falling?
They said you had to fight,
You said you would not kill.
Fifty years after, would you say that still?
Doctors and nurses, one baronet too
Why did you do it?
And what did you do?

Music: Donald Swann. Lyrics: Sydney Carter and Donald Swann.
Written for BBC programme *Chocolate Soldiers*, 1989.

Pacifists in Action

Lyn Smith

Sessions Book Trust
York, England

ISBN 1 85072 215 3

First Impression: November 1998
Second Impression: January 1999

Printed in 11 on 12½ point Plantin Typeface
from Author's Disk
by Sessions of York
The Ebor Press
York, England

This book is dedicated to the men and women who served in the Friends Ambulance Unit during the Second World War.

One wise man's skill is still worth a world in arms
Euripides (480-406 BC)

Contents

List of Illustrations

Preface

IN 1947, JUST A year after the Friends Ambulance Unit (FAU) World War II had ceased operations, Tegla Davies and his team of researchers produced a comprehensive history of the Unit which at the time received some acclaim. *Pacifists in Action* should be regarded as a complement, rather than an update, of Davies's book. It draws on the direct experience of a wide range of Unit members who explain what they did and why they did it, together with an assessment and evaluation of the impact of war on their pacifism, and the lasting effects of FAU experience on their lives. The accounts are placed within a historical context and themes are signalled throughout. Although some analysis is presented, in the main the voices of the FAU are left to speak for themselves.

Pacifism has been described as '...the most lonely of beliefs, held for the most part in private and sustained in isolation, often in the face of powerful opposition.'[1] This is where the FAU organisation came in good and strong. It provided, not only powerful support and a community with like-minded people, but also opportunities for worthwhile humanitarian service, ranging from hospital work on the Home Front to service right into the heat of war for those who, although refusing to bear arms, sought the risks and danger endured by their service counterparts. As Tegla Davies put it '...The FAU at its best demonstrated the value of a voluntary group within society highly organised for total war.'[2]

The FAU experience should have resonance with those struggling today with challenges in the relief and humanitarian services. Furthermore, it contributes, not only to the history of pacifism in the Second World War, but to that war's historiography. For here we have another dimension of war and a very different perspective with terms such as 'heroism', 'patriotism', 'victory' and 'defeat' given entirely different connotations from those usually accepted. It is also significant at the individual level: how war – the 'locomotive of history' – in its destructive and devastating drive through societies, also impacts on the personal level. For these conscientious objectors, dilemmas and paradoxes abound: the wearing of khaki uniform and close cooperation with the army; how it was war – that most detested phenomenon – which so often provided members with their deepest satisfaction of service and experience. The educative aspect of Unit life is also interesting: how in the post-war era new horizons were sought and new careers taken up, with aims of continuing the humanitarian, cooperative and non-materialistic ethos of the FAU.

This is not the story of a group of saints – although some have been described in this way by their fellows – these were seemingly ordinary young men and women who strove to live up to the high ideals their pacifism imposed. Not all achieved this. Many accepted their short-comings, taking the pragmatic view that they still had something to offer in the humanitarian field, others felt that there was no other choice but to leave for the forces. Given the limitations of space, it has been impossible to cover areas of FAU service in the detail deserved – China, for instance, warrants at least a volume of its own. What I hope emerges is the vast span and impressive nature of FAU wartime service; the contribution it makes to an understanding of the theory and practice of conscientious objection and pacifism in a situation of total war. Most of all, I hope that the spirit of the FAU, encapsulated in its motto 'Go Anywhere, Do Anything' shines through.

I am glad to acknowledge several generous permissions. 'The Pilgrim's Hymn' and 'Kasos', by permission of Alison Smith and the estate of Donald Swann. Sydney Carter himself has kindly granted me permission to use his poem 'My Dancing Doubt'. My thanks are also due to the publishers and individuals who have kindly allowed me to quote from the following works: T.S. Eliot, 'East Coker' from *Four Quartets*, Faber and Faber, London mcmlix. John Keegan, *BBC Reith Lectures*, Programme 1, in *War and Our*

World, Hutchinson 1998. Martin Lidbetter, *Friends Ambulance Unit 1939-1943*, Sessions Book Trust. Caroline Moorhead, *Troublesome People*, Hamish Hamilton, London, 1987.

Research has depended largely on the Anti-War collection of the Imperial War Museum Sound Archive of which the FAU interviews form a part. I would like to thank Margaret Brooks, Keeper of the Sound Archive, for use of the collection and for her support throughout the research and writing of this book. I am very grateful for help provided by the staff of Friends' House Library and for the grant towards publication awarded by Sessions Book Trust. Brian Bone deserves my deep thanks for editing the final proofs with meticulous care and for producing such a splendid index. My thanks to Maurice Broomfield for the cover design. I owe a special debt to Deryck Moore who has steered this book through publication with all the zest, skill and devotion he gave to his wartime 'Big Mac' truck! – thank you Deryck for your unfailing enthusiasm, encouragement and support. A word of thanks also to my husband, Peter, who has lived with the FAU for many years – ever interested, always supportive.

I hope that members of the Friends Relief Service and FAU Post-War/International Service will understand that full accounts of their activities have not been possible; these are touched on only as they impinge on the FAU story. Excellent coverage of both have been given elsewhere.[3]

Finally, I would like to say what a privilege it has been to record and write the FAU story. I hope that Unit members will accept my simple dedication of this book as an indication of the respect and affection I feel for them as well as my gratitude for the way they have shared their memories and deepest thoughts with me. Their generosity in allowing me free use of research materials as well as their poems and photographs is much appreciated, as is the faith they have demonstrated by purchasing their copies in advance, thus facilitating publication. This book took longer to write than originally anticipated and it is my profound regret that several members have not lived to see its publication.

LYN SMITH
October 1998

REFERENCES:

[1] Moorhead, Caroline, *Troublesome People: Enemies of War 1916-1986*, Hamish Hamilton. London 1987, p.xiii.

[2] Davies, A. Tegla, *Friends Ambulance Unit*, Allen and Unwin Ltd. London 1947, p.464.

[3] Bush, Roger (ed) *FAU The Third Generation: Friends Ambulance Unit Post-War Service and International Service, 1946-59*, William Sessions, York, 1998.

Wilson, Roger, *Quaker Relief: An Account of the Relief Work of the Society of Friends, 1940-1948*, Allen and Unwin, London, 1952.

Introduction

'From the earliest days of this war, from the time of the Finnish expedition in 1939, these men have given admirable service. They have served with quiet, self-effacing efficiency and with high courage. I do not think that any fighting soldier would hesitate to pay tribute to these men who, prevented by their principles from bearing arms, have none the less willingly suffered the full dangers and rigours of war while pursuing their humane calling to tending the wounded and sick.'
Basil Nield, MP, House of Commons, 9 November 1945.

*T*HIS TRIBUTE WAS one among many paid to a group of conscientious objectors (COs), not only by politicians at home and officers in the field, but also by countless beneficiaries of their wartime humanitarian service in Britain and throughout the world.

The Friends Ambulance Unit (FAU) – or 'Unit', as it was known – had initially been formed in the First World War. In the autumn of 1914, as the war started, a group of English Quakers decided that although their religious beliefs prevented them from entering the war in a fighting capacity, they could not stand aside in the midst of conflict. Anticipating the need for medical and humanitarian aid that war would create, they offered to serve alongside troops, alleviating the suffering caused by war wherever possible. The FAU began with forty-three and ended with over one thousand men. As it increased in numbers, the more divergent its work became. As well as providing a well organised ambulance service and emergency medical services with the French and British armies in France and Belgium, the Unit also served in hospital ships in the English channel and in the Mediterranean. Civilian relief work was carried out in uninvaded Flanders and hospitals were staffed at home and abroad. Unit members also worked in offices and ploughed and

1

harvested great swaths of England. Although the Unit was disbanded in 1919, its members continued to gather at reunions during the inter-war years.

It was the re-introduction of conscription in 1939 which stimulated the re-formation of the FAU. In April 1939, with war clouds darkening, the news was announced that a limited form of conscription for men between the ages of twenty and twenty-one was to be introduced. Ten years earlier such an announcement would have been considered outrageous: heavy losses and the economic hardship that followed the Great War resulted in a generally held revulsion against war and a rejection of conscription. However, by early 1939, with the failure of the Munich conferences and Hitler's increasing aggression, it was apparent to anyone with a basic awareness of European events that war would surely come. On 26 May 1939, the Military Training Act became law. Like its 1916 counterpart, the Act included a 'conscience clause' which stated that any man who conscientiously objected to war service of a military nature could apply for exemption, then face a tribunal for its judgement of his case. At this stage the Act applied only to men; the Draft Act of 1941 gave the same rights to women when they became liable for compulsory military service. [1]

The news of conscription was received with varying degrees of enthusiasm or dismay by the young men concerned. Some were eager for the changes and excitement war would bring, others were simply resigned or reluctant, seeing no alternative to going off and doing their 'duty.' But there was also a sizeable group of eligible young men who decided that they could not and would not join the fighting, and between 1939 and 1945 more than 67,047 registered as COs – nearly four times as many as in the Great War. [2] Although united in their aversion to violence and war, the COs of the Second World War, as in the First, were divergent both in the bases of their pacifism and the tasks they were prepared to do. Six per cent of COs – the 'absolutists' – requested unconditional exemption from military service and refused to perform any compulsory alternative service even if this meant imprisonment. The great majority accepted conditional exemption and welcomed opportunities to work in agriculture, forestry, coal mining, food distribution, firewatching, medical or relief work – anything, so long as they could keep their distance from military matters. There was also a group who thirsted for action, eager to face the dangers and risks of the fighting zones but contributing in a humanitarian manner; if this meant cooperating with

*the military machine short of bearing arms, so be it. It was in the field
of alternative service, both with civilians as well as with the military,
that the FAU had such an impact.*

*It was Arnold Rowntree and Paul Cadbury, both members of the
well-known Quaker families of chocolate and cocoa manufacturers, who
were instrumental in activating the Unit again.*

Michael Rowntree:

Paul Cadbury, although a business competitor, was a close
friend of my father. Our families holidayed in Anglesey at the same
time and we'd meet up often. It must have been July 1939 when
Paul and his family came to visit us. Conscription had been introduced and it looked quite possible that war was going to break out.
I remember my father – who was a generation older than Paul –
saying to him 'I think the Unit should be revived Paul. *You* do it!'
Tegla Davies described it in his book as Samuel anointing Saul –
one prophet passing on the baton to another – and I think there
was an element of this.[3] An uncle, John Harvey, was also involved
in the original negotiations. He was then connected with the
International Voluntary Service (IVS) which was another, not
entirely Quaker, organisation devoted to international relief work.
He helped Paul in making the initial contacts with government
authorities about the feasibility of re-establishing the Unit, and what
its position would be regarding conscription – that sort of detail.

*Paul Cadbury responded vigorously to Arnold Rowntree's appeal:
he had served with the FAU in France and Belgium throughout the Great
War, working with civilians as well as the war wounded, and he was
determined that young COs of the present generation should have the
same opportunities for humanitarian service in the coming war. Rachel,
his wife, who had also served in the FAU as a Voluntary Aid Detachment
(VAD) in France, backed him wholeheartedly:*

Rachel Cadbury:

I said 'It's alright for Quakers, they can get by, but it's the pacifists who *aren't* Quakers I'm concerned about. They're just as much
pacifist, possibly more so than many Quakers, and they've nobody

Arnold Rowntree and Paul Cadbury – the inspiration behind the World War II Friends Ambulance Unit.

behind them.' It seemed to me that these had nobody to help and understand them. So I told Paul 'that's what the FAU's for; that's one of its missions.' Paul agreed and felt it wasn't fair that Quakers could put their names down as Quakers and get away with it when other keen pacifists couldn't. The good thing was that although I wouldn't say that the work of the FAU in the Great War was well known, it was sufficiently known for the authorities in the second war to realise what young COs *could* do. You could say the way was paved for them by the COs of the Great War.

On 1 September, a letter signed by Paul Cadbury and John Harvey appeared in the Quaker journal The Friend *referring to plans for a training camp for relief and ambulance work then being considered, and asking those Friends interested to forward their names. Three hundred applied in the first few days, giving a clear indication of the demand. It was agreed that numbers had to be strictly limited to begin with and that membership of the first camp should consist of Friends and those who had attended Quaker schools.*

Michael Rowntree:

I think I can regard myself as No 1 in the FAU because two or three days after war was declared in 1939, I went down to Bournville to help Paul Cadbury. I remember sitting in his office in the Cadbury factory feeling much like a spy from the rival firm, going through the applications that had already come in. Paul acted with his customary vigour and panache in getting things going very speedily, and within a fortnight or so of the war starting, he had set up the first training camp for the Unit in Dame Elizabeth Cadbury's Manor Farm at Northfield, Birmingham. Along with half a dozen others I worked at getting Manor Farm ready – cleaning out the Augean stables and suchlike to accommodate the members of the first camp which I joined towards the end of September.

The structure of the FAU was also being laid down, and by 1940 a system of democracy had been worked out which aimed to give a voice for all Unit members in determining policy under the Council. The Unit had been constituted as a Charity with a Council of twenty-four members. Many of these were Great War veterans; they started up the Unit and steered it through its early months. What has been described as the Unit's Magna Carta was ratified by the Council on 2 October 1940. Although various modifications were introduced for meeting new circumstances and demands, it established the form of government for the next six years. A major advance was a new Executive Committee, consisting of seven elected members, meeting every week. This committee became the mainspring of the Unit's administration. Tom Tanner was inaugurated as the committee's first Chairman, and after his tragic death in 1942 Tegla Davies took over the job by common consent.[4] *As the Unit grew, sections were formed, each with its own leader who had to be approved by the committee as well as by those serving with the leader. Weekly meetings were held, and through these the committee dealt with the views, concerns and grievances of the various sections which flowed in through regular reports.*

With the Unit's growth and spread abroad a more complex system became necessary; this meant a development of Head Office staff and, inevitably, increasing bureaucracy. Although some Unit members have voiced complaints, on the whole the democratic principle was maintained and there was a lot of fresh air blown through the HQ in Gordon Square, London, by the men, and later women, who had served abroad returning to do a spell of administrative duties, replacing those seeking a change. In this way the momentum and enthusiasm was retained.

The Executive Committee reported to the Council which met three times a year.

Michael Cadbury:

We would report to them what was going on and the Council members would bring their weight of experience, contacts and wisdom on issues where we were in doubt. Normally they just took our report and said 'Well done, carry on.' But if there were problems we couldn't deal with, their links with local government and other institutions were invaluable, and they'd sort something out. Paul Cadbury was very active during the first two years but gradually, as the Executive Committee gained in experience and confidence, he left it to us.

Increasingly the Unit's elders left matters in the hands of the active members who continued to prove themselves in the field; this gave the Unit the degree of flexibility which was to prove one of its main strengths. The average age was twenty years, although section leaders were often in the thirty-something bracket. Members served on a voluntary basis without guarantee of compensation in the event of injury or death. Board and lodging was provided and certain expenses such as clothing and basic dental and medical treatment. Soon it became clear that a small sum of pocket money was needed and this led to the setting up of the FAU Mutual Assistance Fund (MAF) in September 1941 under which a monthly sum of 25/- (£1.25) was received; this had been raised to 32/6d (£1.62) by the end of the war to meet the increased cost of living.

Throughout the war the Unit refused to accept men and women under direction into the Unit; instead it insisted on retaining its freedom to accept or reject applicants, after interview, according to their conviction and suitability for membership.

In all 5,000 enquired about membership throughout the war and 1,314, including ninety-seven women, actually joined, spreading their humanitarian service throughout Britain and to far-flung places

abroad. [5] *In line with the global reach of the Second World War com-*
pared with the First, the Unit had a far greater international flavour,
with ninety-one members coming from overseas, the majority from the
United States, Canada and New Zealand. According with Paul and
Rachel Cadbury's wishes, the Unit was open to anybody who shared
basic Quaker beliefs that war is inconsistent with the spirit and teaching
of Christ and that the individual should be active in the task of recon-
ciliation between individuals, groups and nations. What the FAU offered
was an outlet for energy, idealism and service for those who believed that
pacifism should show in action just what it is capable of in relieving the
effects of war and demonstrating that there is another path to service.

Who, then, were the young men who applied to the FAU when war
started; and why?

REFERENCES:

(1) Braithwaite, C. *Conscientious Objection to Compulsions Under the Law,*
The Ebor Press, York, 1995, pp.181-184 for details of the changes in
various drafts of the Military Training Act, 1939.

(2) This figure does not include men between the ages of 41 and 51 who
registered provisionally due mainly to liability for service in the Home
Guard. See Braithwaite, C. *ibid.* p.183

(3) Davies, A.Tegla, *Friends Ambulance Unit,* Headley Bros. London,
1947, p.8

(4) Tom Tanner and Peter Hume were lost at sea when the ship *Ceramic*
on which they were travelling to China, was torpedoed and sunk in
the South Atlantic in December 1942.

(5) Apart from the British contingent serving in the FAU, there were forty-
nine Americans, twenty-four Canadians, ten New Zealanders, four
from Eire, two Chinese, one Czech, one Indian, and one South
African; fifty-six more Chinese joined the Unit in China and one
Indian, as associate members. See Davies, A. Tegla *op. cit.* pp.467-
481.

PART ONE

ON THE HOME FRONT

CHAPTER 1

Make Up Your Mind Time

'We utterly deny all outward wars and strife and fightings with outward weapons, for any end, or under any pretence whatsoever. And this is our testimony to the whole world, . . . that the spirit of Christ, which leads us into all Truth, will never move us to fight and war against any man with outward weapons, neither for the kingdom of Christ, nor for the kingdoms of this World.'
Quaker Peace Testimony of 1660, still in force today.

FOR QUAKERS, THE situation facing those liable for military service seemed straightforward enough. Since the Society of Friends was founded under the inspiration of George Fox in the seventeenth century, it has taken an unequivocal stance against violence and war as a means of settling international disputes.

Although the FAU adhered to the Quaker Peace Testimony in spirit, there was considerable argument within the Society of Friends about the active stance it was taking in the Second World War and in fact the FAU, although founded by Friends in both wars, was constitutionally independent of the Society of Friends which held no responsibility for it, nor funded it.

Michael Cadbury:

Friends allowed us to be called the FAU because of the Great War name, but they kept their distance. We didn't work at Friends' House; we had to find our own quarters in Gordon Square nearby. We had links with Yearly Meeting and were allowed to report to it about what we were up to – but an arms length relationship. Later on in the war we worked very closely with the Friends Relief Service (FRS) so the wound had healed by the time the war had got going but initially we were outsiders. Yes, wound is the word – there really was a strain in relations in the early days. A lot of Friends felt hurt that this group of young Bolshie conchies were going to join the war. They gave support to those who went on the land or into prison – that was the Quaker stance. Ours wasn't. In a sense we were letting the side down by being prepared to work with the army and wear khaki uniforms instead of the traditional Quaker grey. We felt we had to. What good was it being trained in ambulance work if you couldn't go into an area where war was raging and there were people to heal? You couldn't get into a war zone without working with the army; Friends didn't want to recognise that. That was a compromise and the Quaker position must not be compromised. Quakers like me thought: yes, it *is* a compromise; we understand the absolute pacifist view, but we can't stand by and do nothing. In some families there were real problems as sons went in different directions. But as time went on and Friends with orthodox views saw what we were achieving, they came behind us very well and the wound healed.

The first training camp at Manor Farm started soon after war's outbreak on 27 September 1939. Of the fifty-eight members all bar a few were Quakers, had close connections with Quakers or had been educated at Quaker schools. During the war, over a thousand young men trained at Manor Farm. As time went by the proportion of non-Friends increased, leading to a far greater diversity of social and religious backgrounds which meant, as many Quakers pointed out, a strengthened and enriched Unit. [1] The sort of young men who chose to enter the FAU were people with individual ideas and views, often idealistic and embracing a broad spectrum: at one end those who were more sympathetic to the FRS stance and resisted service with the army, to those with a strong urge to serve short of bearing weapons, with many keen to get into the very heart of warfare, and who compromised up to the ultimate point short of joining the services.

As for the bases of pacifism, these varied. There is no doubt that religion was the main motive and most Christian denominations were represented, with Methodists, alongside the Quakers, being particularly strong. Political motives were rarer, but certainly present, although these were often masked beneath more overt Christian arguments. Moral and humanitarian drives were very strong and very often these stemmed from experience – direct or otherwise – from the traumas and horrors of the Great War just twenty years in the past. Reared as they had been during the 1930s and living through events such as the Spanish Civil War, as well as witnessing first-hand, as a number had, the nature of Hitler's Germany on holiday or work experience, they found themselves torn by conflicting loyalties and tensions. Therefore, although the decision to be a CO and join the FAU as an active pacifist was made by many with confidence and certainty, others experienced painful dilemmas.

For Quakers, who had imbibed pacifism with their mother's milk the situation seemed straightforward enough:

Michael Rowntree:

Coming from a Quaker background, I suppose one absorbed a lot of pacifism by osmosis as it were. We used to have discussions about peace and war in the family and in the Meeting at York and, of course, at school. I suppose I owed quite a lot to the masters at Bootham, the Quaker public school I attended – people like our headmaster, Donald Gray, who had served in the first FAU. So in a sense it was the build-up of a background in which service of the FAU kind was the normal pattern for someone who had been a birthright Quaker...I suppose it was almost as natural with someone of my background to go into the FAU as someone coming from a military background to go to Sandhurst or to go into the Guards. That's not to say one did it entirely unthinkingly. No, certainly not without questioning.

Michael Cadbury:

I think it's very difficult to pinpoint when one had the actual consciousness of pacifism; one grew up with it as part of one's life. Life is something sacred: things like fox hunting and killing mice were naturally wrong, and to think of killing human beings whatever the justification, was something abhorrent. The Quaker way is getting at the roots of war, the causes, rather than dealing with it when it happens. And when war breaks out, one is faced with the question: do you throw away your principles and join the fighting? Or become an absolutist and refuse to have anything to do with the mess? Or do you try to mend some of the damage? The complexities of the Quaker view can be seen in my family. My brother Kenneth went into the army and did very well: he became a Major and got his MC. Now he was from the same Quaker background but his concern was that Hitler's aggression had gone so far it had to be stood up to and stopped. I took the view that I won't fight by opposing it: I'll enter to try to mend the damage. Another brother, Anthony, was also in the FAU but was more orthodox in his pacifism; he never went abroad or wore khaki.

Duncan Wood:

My mother was a birthright Friend and my father, H.G. Wood, became a rather well known Quaker. My parents became wardens of Woodbrooke, the Quaker college in Birmingham. I think an important part of my background was living as a young child in a Quaker college during the Great War because the atmosphere led me to understand that something dreadful was going on way out there. Looking back on it, I realise that was possibly the foundation of my pacifism. I knew about the COs in that war and that the father of some small companion of mine was in prison and I think I understood that there were people who were against what was going on – not that I understood *what* was going on, just that something awful was happening. At one point my father went out as a sort of chaplain to the FAU which was then operating in France. My mother was terribly anxious as the unit was near the front line. So at least I absorbed the sense of tension and danger, but above all, the feeling of sorrow and anguish and the longing for peace.

During the twenties we were living in some optimism in respect to international affairs. We all welcomed the League of Nations and when I had finished school I spent three months in Geneva to get an impression of the League which, in 1929, was still an institution with considerable prestige and which focused the hopes of a large part of the world. So the spirit of the 1920s simply boosted the anti-war feeling which I had from experiencing the Great War, but it gave a positive and more hopeful conviction that we can live without war. This was all challenged in the thirties with the spread of fascism. By then I was aware of the religious basis of my father's pacifism and only very slowly, not in a flash of conversion, did I accept the religious basis of Quaker pacifism and its central concept of the 'Inner Light.' This is the concept which maintains that within every human being there is a divine spark which, if it is properly tended, can respond to the divinity outside. This means that God is able to enter into us if we let that happen. It means that human beings are remarkable and rather precious. This relates to pacifism in that so remarkable and precious a creature should not be wantonly destroyed. The light is a guiding light which is personified by the life and teaching of Christ; therefore is it conceivable that anyone following that guidance will go to war? I tried to put something like that across at my Tribunal and it was accepted.

Chris Barber was also from a conventional Quaker background, but his decision to apply for conditional exemption and join the FAU was by no means straightforward and his experience points to yet another dilemma young Quakers faced:

Chris Barber:

I was determined to think it out for myself and when war was declared I walked the Lake District mountains, thinking of peace and war and what I should do. Later, whilst living in digs in Birmingham, I continued to work things through for myself – this was during a lonely time of my life; but then I discovered a curate occupying a room below and going through the same process of decision and this helped a bit. By the time my call-up was due, I had applied to join the FAU and was actually training when my Tribunal came up. At my Tribunal, I was careful not to mention that I was a Quaker because I think that Quakers had preferential treatment, especially in the Birmingham area where they were well known. I wanted them to judge me on the basis of my statement:

'I believe that a man's first duty is to his conscience rather than to his country or state. I consider war to be something which is wrong. It is contrary to Christian ideals and although I have great sympathy with the cause for which our country is fighting, I feel I must conscientiously object to taking any part in the propagation of this war. I feel that when there are so many people in this world suffering as a result of the war, my duty lies towards them and I therefore intend to do my utmost to assist them. I would like to do ambulance work under civilian control or some other kind of relief work.'

I felt that by saying one was a Quaker, one was almost trying to take advantage of the situation and I think some who weren't Quakers were given a much tougher time with much more gruelling questioning. But when I was asked what I was doing and said 'the FAU' I was asked whether I was a Quaker and said 'yes.'

Bishop Freddie Temple:

I belonged to the age of upper class English where parents only saw their children for an hour in the evening. Since my father worked in India, even this small portion of my parents' time was usually denied me. I was brought up by a fearful nurse who behaved sweetly in front of my parents but bullied and mistreated me. At the tender age of eight, I was dumped in an equally appalling prep school, then on to Rugby – very fierce and tough in those days – and where visions of my uncle, William Temple, Archbishop of Canterbury, always haunted me.

Very often I would spend my holidays with uncle William, and this is when thoughts of war and pacifism started to come to me. My uncle was pro military action. He left the Labour Party when it refused to back the League of Nations for sanctions against Italy invading Abyssinia. He was a great believer in collective security and wanted us to stop Hitler when he moved into the Ruhr and the Rhine. But although pro military, he also made the interesting point that there must be pacifists amongst us. He used to say 'England is worth fighting for, but only if there are sufficient pacifists in it.' He was very stern with me and once told me 'Of course if you're going to be a pacifist you must be ready not to accept *anything* from the state which is fighting to protect you – no pay, or any sick pay if disabled. If you do this then I will respect and support you.' He always stood for the rights of COs to be heard and not to be bullied or treated unfairly during the war.

So after a bit of havering, I decided to sign on as a CO. By that time ordination was starting to be a flicker in my mind and this made me feel that I just couldn't take part in the fighting and shoot someone. My uncle's support was a tremendous help to me because my parents were both opposed to my decision. My father was a Colonel in the volunteer army in India and instantly became part of the war when it started. During that time I was wondering what I would do. The family was worried about what others would think. So in a sense the FAU was a cop-out. It would have taken more moral courage to have stayed at home. But to be in a front-line hospital unit with no pay, that was alright – 'We don't agree with his argument, but the young do silly things, don't they?' I remember one of my sisters saying to me in 1940 'Of course if the Germans do land in England and turn up in our garden, I would have to shoot you first because I wouldn't know what you might do.'

My tribunal – held in London in the summer of 1940 – was recognised as being rather stiffer than most. In fact it was an ordeal. Being my uncle's nephew meant a lot of publicity. Having taken a very individualistic line and having been honest enough to say that it's alright for some people to be fighting, led to the question 'Well, are you thought to be so much better than others?' This was a valid point. At Balliol, the Master, A.D. Lindsey, used to say to those of us who were thinking of pacifism 'Be sure you're not just wanting others to wash your dirty linen and get their hands soiled on your behalf.

The tribunal's decision was not unanimous: at one stage it looked as though I would be told to join the medical corps rather than the FAU, but the man in favour of my remaining in the Unit won the day 'As he's in, let him stay', he said.

So I approached the Unit from a very individualistic point of view and found it quite difficult in discussions when I argued that it was right for others to fight but not for me. I found several of the Friends – John Bailey was an exception – very wishy-washy in their beliefs. The best Friends did say to me 'Of course we Quakers depend on what we call "convinced Friends" – friends who come into our movement from something else. Birthright Friends tend not to be very strong in argument, more in an attitude to peace, an outlook.' I found this to be so.

Gerald Gardiner:

In 1943 the Government announced that people over a certain age would not be called up. I was then in my fifties and well over that age, but I had always assumed that I would some day be called up and had decided to become a conscientious objector when the time came. I was then a barrister, and with so many young barristers away in the war, I was earning a lot of money. That, plus my pacifist feelings, meant that continuing in my job just didn't seem right. So it was when it was made clear to me that I could stay in my profession that I decided to try to join the FAU. I was accepted into the Unit and I believe that I was the only member of the FAU who was over call-up age and had not gone through the tribunal system.

I was old enough to have experienced the First War. During the years 1914-1918 I was at Harrow and just old enough in 1918 to leave school and join up into the Coldstream Guards Cadet Battalion. It never occurred to me at that age whether it was right or wrong to train for fighting in a war. If your country was at war, then you joined up and there it was. Fortunately for me, I was still training when the Armistice came.

It was through meeting the Sheppards, after the war, that I began to become interested in pacifist ideas. Beryl Sheppard was a beautiful woman and her husband, Dick, was a parson who had served as a chaplain in the war and got an MC for rescuing wounded men under fire. Dick would say that the modern form of warfare wasn't justifiable. He became an incumbent of St. Martins in the Fields after the war. It was a remarkable church because the ordinary Church of England was more women than men, and more old people than young; whereas with Dick Sheppard, the congregations were nearly all young men who had been to the war. I then joined a body called the Peace Pledge Union (PPU) and became a pacifist, as most of his congregation were. My objection was that it was anti-Christian to kill and fight.

I heard about the FAU because I had been in touch with Quakers over a good many issues, particularly capital punishment which they were also against. By the time I joined in 1943, I had heard of the work they were doing at home and abroad. At this time I was a family man, so it meant that my family had to live on the fees I'd earned in the past. I received no money from the FAU although there was a minimum amount provided for those who had nothing at all. The fact that I was much older than others in the Unit tended to make me a sort of senior figure.

Robin Whitworth:

It was when I moved to Manchester with my work as a BBC producer in the mid thirties that I became aware of anti-war feelings. I came from an upper middle class, intellectual family and I had been educated at Eton and Oxford. So Manchester was a great contrast. I saw the unemployment there and began to take life seriously when a young man came to see me for a job. I took him to lunch to a restaurant where you could get a good three course meal for half-a-crown. He couldn't eat it – his stomach had shrunk because he didn't have proper meals. I was so moved by this and all the unemployment that I cut off from all my friends in London. I couldn't talk the same language as them and I couldn't understand why there wasn't a revolution. Then one day in 1935, I saw the headline in the Daily Express 'England on the crest of a trade boom while Hitler tells Germans to tighten their belts.' As if readers would have been comforted to think that England was doing so well while Germans were so distressed. I thought 'This will lead to war, and if there is a war it will be largely our fault.' As I saw it, the Treaty of Versailles was very restrictive in that we would not allow the Germans to trade their way out, which led to terrible unemployment and hardship. Hitler gave them hope and when he found that we would not revise the Treaty of Versailles at all, he decided the only way for Germans to avoid starvation was to fight their way out. And of course the Jews were a useful scapegoat. So if war did come, we would be largely to blame for not trying to make peace while there was a chance.

Then I saw a letter from Dick Sheppard in the papers: would those willing to renounce war send him a postcard saying: 'We say "No" to war.' I did this and went to see him to discuss things. He was a fascinating person: small, round, jovial and friendly. He received me in a most friendly fashion. I found him most inspiring – very charismatic, absolutely convinced and flamingly sincere.

In 1938 I went to Birmingham as Features producer and writer. I'm pretty certain that a producer who was appointed soon after was put there as a snooper to sniff out potential pacifists if war came because it so happened that six of the Birmingham producers were pacifists. I declared my views to him and said that I would offer my resignation if war came. I think he went back with his little notebook in which he had written 'Whitworth: conscientious objector/pacifist, but OK, not dangerous and completely honest.'

When war came, I went to the Regional Director offering my resignation. At that time I was doing some quite successful programmes. He said 'No, don't, we want all opinions expressed in our programmes; you're making a good contribution which is not subversive and which is needed. The BBC want to get rid of COs, but they daren't sack them; if you resign, you let them off the hook and we lose your programmes. Go on doing what you think you should.'

I was then producing a series of programmes called 'Go to it!' the idea being to see how the regions were coping with the war effort. When the Coventry blitz came I was asked to go to Coventry on the following morning and do a thirty minutes programme in the 'Go to it!' series. I rang him up 'Look, you know my position as a conscientious objector; if you want a factual report of what I actually find, I will do it. What I cannot do is specific wartime propaganda.' He said 'We want a true report on what you find.' So of course I went and did it – a thirty minute factual report on the Coventry blitz. In Coventry we found a scene of complete devastation. I knew the city well, but I couldn't recognise it; I couldn't tell which street was which. I simply went and talked to the people about their experiences of the blitz. I went to the cathedral which was completely gutted – it was burning forty-eight hours afterwards. There I met Provost Howard, a very saintly man. He stood there in the ruins saying 'This cathedral will rise again to the glory of

God.' Some worker had stuck up the cross of nails. It was very, very moving. That broadcast is still in the BBC archives.

That programme went all round the world, But it was done within my conscience. It wasn't propaganda. But it certainly boosted British morale because it was such a wonderful story of courage based on truth. The whole series 'Go to it' was based on truth – the truthful reporting of the war effort the British people were making. That raid reinforced my feeling that the world had gone mad. I had my tribunal where I simply told my story. I was told to continue working for the BBC or do ambulance work under civilian control. So I went on broadcasting until the BBC got rid of all their COs. I think I was the last one to go. The most extraordinary thing was that I didn't ever hear a word of disapproval from my colleagues there. Val Gielgud, the head of drama – a very militaristic man who imagined himself a swashbuckling cavalry officer – met me one day and said 'Hello Robin, are you still here?' And he paused and looked me straight in the eye and said: 'If you've got a conviction, you stick to it.' and walked away. I got the impression that he derived strength himself from the fact that I was a conscientious objector.

By this time I had heard about the Quakers and my views were similar. I knew about the FAU and as I had the permission for ambulance service under civilian control, it seemed the thing to join.

Tom Haley:

I was born in Bethnal Green in the East End of London in 1920. My father had a very difficult time finding work, as many did, but when I was about four years old he was able to get a job as a sawyer and remained working in a saw mill for the rest of his working life. My mother was also from an East End family – a very large family from Hoxton which was devastatingly poor. Both my parents had the hardest possible lives with great deprivation. I was a very highly strung and nervous child, always ill until I was about twelve or thirteen. I left school when I was fourteen and got a job with a printer's where I stayed until the war came.

I was very close to my grandfather who lived in Hoxton. He had been gassed in the war and had a leg wound which incapacitated him for the rest of his life. He was a very lovely, jovial and friendly man. He used to tell me stories about the war and what they went through, and how they had to obey senseless orders with no rhyme or reason to them. So I probably got some of my early stirrings of thoughts about war from him. I also had an uncle who had been through the war. He felt that army life was wonderful and had a very enhanced view of the armed forces – all his tales were from a more heroic point of view. I remember very clearly not being able to feel the same way about it as he did, and felt how dreadful it was that suffering was inflicted in such a senseless way. It seemed to me – idealistically I suppose – that there was a better way of settling arguments than seeing who could kill the greatest number of people.

Violence seemed to be the way of life around me and fighting was the way in which you established the pecking order. And fighting *was* enjoyable. I loved boxing and didn't mind getting knocked about a bit because this was all part of the way in which everybody lived. There was a family up the road called Duffield. The man used to get drunk regularly on Sundays and he would call his wife out into the street. She would timidly come out from cooking the dinner, then he would proceed to batter her face in. She would often have a couple of black eyes for the rest of the week until the next hiding came. This was recognised and acceptable behaviour, indicative of the kind of atmosphere in my area at that time. Men used to fight each other outside the pubs when they got drunk. I grew up in an atmosphere where violence was absolutely acceptable. The manly image was vital: you had to be a *man*, you had to punch and be able to fight. All the men in my family were fighters. I was expected to carry this on. But I was not a good fighter and never took to it. Boxing was alright because that's disciplined and you were always protected by rules and those who controlled the YMCA and boys' boxing club which I belonged to.

Also, Mosley and his Blackshirts were very much in evidence in the East End of London. I personally knew many of his recruits and they were absolute thugs. I was utterly appalled as a young man to see men with knuckle-dusters with little claws on each knuckle and razors in cap peaks and other most terrible instruments for inflicting damage on others. I remember vividly a march by Mosley's thugs through some streets near us where the Jews had gathered to confront the Blackshirts. They had marked the road 'They shall not pass.' Well the bloodshed was dreadful: bricks, stones and all sorts of missiles were hurled from both sides. The fighting was beyond description. It was horrible.

But things weren't all bad. There was also a lot of social activities at the nearby Friends' Hall and I took full advantage of these. At this time I had this great feeling for the sanctity of human life and felt that I had to pursue this tremendous feeling that I had within me of the wrongness of war. I remember going to see Father Sarel in St. Matthew's Church where I used to worship. I said 'I feel that the people in the church who bless guns and bless the army when they're going off to war are absolutely wrong. I don't want to go on belonging to the Church of England any longer.' I then started to look around and try to find somebody who had similar ideas. I tried various religious factions but didn't feel that I'd got a home so to speak until I was told about the Quakers who were in charge of Friends' Hall. It was a tremendous relief to know there were others thinking like me, because I thought I was on my own. I thought there was no way in which I could ever get myself out of this impasse and I was utterly miserable, an outcast. It meant so much to me knowing there were a significant minority of people who were prepared to go through anything necessary in order to stand by the principles of the sanctity of human life and the wrong-headed approach of going to war to solve problems. In fact my mother once told me that before she met my father she had met a conscientious objector. 'What is a conscientious objector Mummy?' I said. She answered 'That's a man who is too frightened to go to war so the army won't take him in because they know he'll be no good.' I promptly forgot this until my thoughts were forming when I was about seventeen.

When the war started in 1939, I was eighteen. I knew my call-up was imminent: was I going to join the armed forces or sign on as a conscientious objector? Despite all my feelings against war, the decision was not an easy one to take, but this was make-up-your-mind time! I felt I had to be true to myself. But the difficulty was that I wasn't the only one involved: I was allowing others to fight for me, provide for me and if necessary even die so that I could express myself as a pacifist. How could I allow that? Whatever I did was a compromise. My father was very antagonistic indeed. He relentlessly put forward the opposite point of view and his arguments were not something to be belittled, they were strong, real arguments which I had to cope with. We argued and rowed and this went on day after day whenever we met. We'd argue long into the night and not get enough sleep to do our work the next day. Then one day he said 'Tom, if you register as a conscientious objector, I will never lift up my head again for shame.' Although I didn't like my father and had little respect for him, this was very, very hurtful. A little later he said 'If you can't shed a drop of blood in the protection and defence of your mother and your sisters, I don't see why you should be allowed to share their roof.' At that point I decided I'd have to leave home, and I joined the FAU.

I had two tribunals. I wasn't well educated and fluent at expressing myself and really I gave them nothing to go on except a few mumblings about war not being the right thing to do and the sanctity of human life, that sort of thing. They gave me the RAMC. I appealed against this because the RAMC are taught to use guns. Before I went to my appeal tribunal Charles Haworth, the warden at Friends' Hall, gave me some good advice and I prepared my facts, put my thoughts on paper and when the appeal came up Charles Haworth came along and spoke on my behalf: 'I feel he is one of the finest young men to have passed through my hands; he is absolutely and utterly sincere.' I nearly *died*... he made me feel littler and littler. In the end they gave me exemption provided I stayed in the FAU. That is what I wanted.

Eric Turner:

Growing up as I did in the time after the Great War, stories of the war were really part of childhood. My boyhood friends had fathers who had been in the war and, looking back now, I feel that a lot of the language we used originated from soldiers in the war. My own parents talked about the war a lot, especially my mother, largely through the experiences of her brothers. One uncle I remember vividly because he had been badly gassed and was in and out of the sanitarium in Kinver. Indeed it was from my mother that I first heard the term 'conchie' and this was spoken with great contempt – another term for cowardice. At that time it was part of my perception of things too.

We lived in Kidderminster and were a working class family. My father started his working life as a tramway employee and ended it as a meter reader. I left school at the age of fourteen. My father wanted me to have a better start in life than he had, so I went to work in a solicitor's office as an office boy and general clerk – that's where I spent my working life from 1936 to 1939.

As I entered the working world, the unimaginable possibility of another war was beginning to appear with the rise of Mussolini and, particularly, of Hitler. Those events really cast their shadows. We used to hear older people say 'Oh, there won't be another war.' They still believed the 1914/18 war was the war that had ended war. But those of my generation took it seriously – we felt that some kind of war lay ahead and that we young men would be involved. Until then there had been no doubt about it: if you were called up, you went. But by 1938 I had met a number of people who would not accept that view uncritically. I began to hear of the Peace Pledge Union and War Resisters International (WRI), and I began to realise that conscientious objectors were not the cowards or army dodgers or traitors my family and their friends had thought. So I began to look at the pacifist issue more seriously. I was coming to feel increasingly that fighting in a war and killing was something I could not do. Alongside this, I had a growing religious conviction and putting these two things together, I began to feel that for me there would have to be some other way of responding to the war that was surely coming.

All this came to a head in 1939 with war's outbreak. I didn't have to register until November 1939 but I was clear that I couldn't sit in my job – I felt I ought to do something more directly concerned with the war and share, if possible, something of the disadvantages and hardships that my contemporaries were going through. My boss was a very conservative man, but he was very pleasant about it – this was, you will remember, the 'phoney war' period when people thought it would be over by Christmas. So with another pacifist friend of mine I went to pick sugarbeet at a local farm. Two more unlikely labourers never presented themselves! But we stuck it until the job was finished.

It was largely through a lovely man – Harry Butler, a Quaker – that I heard about the FAU and decided that it was the place I wanted to be. It was a form of service, working for people, it meant involvement with the hardships and other disadvantages of living in a society in wartime. It offered the chance to serve abroad – all this seemed exciting and appealing. So I applied in late 1939 or early 1940.

My application was accepted, but as there was a long queue to get into the training camp, I became a milk roundsman for my local Co-op. I did experience some hostility from my co-workers and customers, but not much. In fact, I could take you to two houses in Kidderminster where I received abuse. One was very under-standable: the woman had young children and was married to a man in the Merchant Navy. One day she looked me in the face and said 'I could spit in your eye.' The other family seemed to know about me. The wife was a real harridan. On one or two occasions she took special pride in coming to the doorstep as I delivered the milk and hurled a stream of abuse at me. I just ignored her; I felt much more for the other woman.

My tribunal came up in Birmingham during the summer of 1940. My application was accepted on condition that I stayed in my present job with the Co-op. I accepted that, not forseeing the problem which occurred when I was called into the FAU in 1941. I was advised by Peter Hume at FAU HQ to negotiate with the Ministry of Labour to join the FAU which I did all through the summer of 1941. When I had no joy, Peter wrote saying 'Let's forget the Ministry of Labour, come and join the 13th training camp on 6 October.' Off I went. It was some months later that the Ministry of Labour tracked me down. I was given another tribunal in which I was heavily grilled about what I was doing in the FAU. Then they granted me permission to stay in the Unit.

The most difficult part, which still upsets me, was the pain and embarrassment I caused my parents in doing what I did. They could not understand, nor could I make them understand, why I wanted to be a conscientious objector. They could not explain it to their friends. This meant that my relationships with my own family, friends and neighbours was much more difficult than going through the tribunal which was a clean and clinical experience compared with the torment I experienced at home. When I think of my parents and my brother and his wife, they must have found it very, *very* hard. In working class communities like ours, it was hard having this odd character who wasn't going along with the rest of the chaps to fight this evil man Hitler. I think it was a great relief for all of us when I went away in the FAU. I think my mother suffered more as I was her youngest child and she was very fond of me... So this was the most painful part for me.

Frank Edmead:

The basis of my pacifism was not specifically religious: it was political, ethical and moral. War seemed to be so pointless and so counter-productive in that it prevented anything happening that it was intended to promote. I had read the standard anti-war authors such as Aldous Huxley and A.A. Milne. These had been recommended by our headmaster who didn't intend that we should all become pacifists but that we should understand every side of the question. Then, when I went to college, I was drawn to others who had the same ideas.

But my decision to be a conscientious objector was not straightforward – far from it! I remember feeling very confused about the Spanish Civil War: did I want to go and take up arms against the fascists or not? It took some time to resolve this. It could be that the dilemmas are greater when the bases of pacifism are political or humanitarian rather than purely religious. I suspect this is so because if you are a religious pacifist, relying on an authoritarian system of belief, that guides you as to what to do. If you accept the New Testament as historical and that Jesus said 'Those who take up the sword shall perish by the sword', then there is no argument. But I was never tempted to think that way. I remember writing in my tribunal statement 'I am not a Christian in the ordinary sense of the word, but I believe that Jesus's ethical teaching is the only working teaching that will produce the right results.' I showed this to my headmaster with whom I was still in touch; he thought this sentence ill-advised as it drew attention to my non-Christianness. But I left it in and it wasn't questioned at all.

My parents were very upset, partly I think for my sake. They both felt that conscientious objectors had a very bad time in the Great War and found it difficult to get work afterwards. My father, coming from a non-intellectual family, had high hopes for me because I was first-generation university; he thought I was ruining my chances. But this just made me more obstinate. So he thought me wrong and misguided as he felt it necessary to stand up to aggression. I don't think he had come up against pacifists before, and if he had it was in a sort of scornful way. So he took it hard, and I would say it took him a long time to get over it – if he ever did. He had been a Chief Petty Officer in the Royal Navy in the First World War.

I joined the FAU in 1943. Talk of the Unit was in the air among pacifists at the time. It was also well known in the public sphere: news of it would get into the newspapers, largely comparing the FAU with COs who weren't so active. I remember how one article contrasted the 'brave FAU men taking convoys up the Burma Road' with those 'cowering behind haystacks.' In fact the whole idea of what the FAU was doing was very attractive to me.

Paul Townsend:

I am one of four children. My father was a dentist, a man of liberal sympathies. He had been in the First World War but didn't have a particularly bad time of it. But certainly, like a lot of people in the thirties, he inclined towards a pacifist view. In the war, the younger of my two brothers – my elder by eight years – objected and went into the Non-Combatant Corps. So there was some kind of pacifist sympathy in the family.

I think temperamentally we all had a horror of violence, not just in the context of war, but any form of violence. I suppose I'm the typical sort of character who is likely to be a pacifist: disapproving of blood sports, capital punishment, corporal punishment and the whole shooting match. I'd like to stress that, because the whole temperament – the whole bundle of sympathies – seems to me to be very important, quite apart from convictions about national and international issues.

I suppose I thought of myself being this way inclined during my teens. I did not, for instance, belong to the Officers' Training Corps. That was something not insisted upon but considered a good thing. Being a prefect, for example, was dependent upon being in the OTC. I'm not talking about a grand public school but an old-fashioned grammar school. So my pacifism springs from what I *am*. But how does one distinguish that from one's upbringing? – in my case a family fairly sympathetic to one taking the pacifist line.

By the time I left school, the war had already started and it was perfectly plain to me what I was going to do. I had one year at university before my call-up. This was Kings' College, London, which had been evacuated to Bristol. I didn't join the university training corps and was allowed to do hospital work in lieu of that. I attended a small group of Fellowship of Reconciliation (FOR) whilst at Bristol and we met once a week and discussed things in a rather eighteen-year-old sort of way and this provided a little bit of mutual support.

Two of my closest friends at Bristol were going into the services. It was always perfectly plain that my views were diametrically opposed to theirs, yet I never felt any disapproval of my views and had no sense of isolation. However, there was uncertainty: I've never been a political animal, not in any sense a person who wants to carry banners or burn them, and, at that time, had a sort of general knowledge of what was going on, but only very slight engagement with the major issues. But quite plainly, being a pacifist in a war where I thought right, if not entirely on one side, was more on one side than another, meant that in a certain sense you felt in an uncertain position all the way through. I suppose everybody – combatant or non-combatant – felt at times in an uncertain position. If, for instance, I had decided to go the other way and had been asked to take part in blanket bombing, presumably I would have had doubts about that. But if you're going along with most people it's perhaps rather easier to accept these doubts, these intellectual inconsistencies. But if you step out of line, then you are aware of the weak points in your position, and then it could be the case that you couldn't take all these problems on board. In my case

I had committed myself to a certain line. The work was useful and I did it.

It was during this first year at university that I was called before my tribunal. I remember very little about it. I was very nervous but was kindly treated. I had heard that the judge was a member of the Magic Circle and I said to myself as I went in 'I must remember that this man is capable of pulling rabbits out of top hats and I must not take the whole thing too seriously.' I was asked a few questions in a most courteous manner and when I mentioned the kind of humanitarian work I was prepared to do, I was granted the necessary conditional exemption.

I had heard about the FAU by this time and had made some enquiries about it. I certainly couldn't have been an absolutist. At least joining the FAU you demonstrated a willingness to be sent anywhere and do anything. I remember my interview for the FAU was conducted by Sandy Parnis, who was the FAU's treasurer – later he became a distinguished civil servant. I remember he asked me if I would regard myself as a christian pacifist. I said, yes, in terms of christian ethics but that I was not in any straight doctrinal sense a believer. I remember him saying in his rather strange voice 'Oh yes, that's alright, I'm not interested in whether you believe in the virgin birth!' Having been accepted and finished university in the summer term, I went to training camp in the autumn of 1942, by which time I was just over nineteen.

Sydney Carter:

I was born in 1915 during the First World War. My father was in the Rifle Brigade; he had a very weak chest so he never went abroad. My mother worked in a jet brooch factory – a lot of black brooches were required at that time. My uncle had been gassed in the war. Actually he was a very merry character and told me some strange things about the war 'It was a mess, boy, but you know sometimes when you'd got a machine gun there and you see them coming, you can't help enjoying it.'

We lived in Islington and I went to the local LCC school. I was clever and got a scholarship to Christ's Hospital. Towards the end of my time there, Hitler was creeping across Europe and you felt 'Oh my God! There may be a war again.' By that time one had found out more about war. I remember, for example, seeing an exhibition of war injuries – terrible things; and we were all reading Aldous Huxley who'd become a pacifist, and Gerald Heard and Auden too.

When the Spanish Civil War broke out, I naturally associated myself with the left-wing government which I thought was just; whereas Franco and his group were a lot of *bastards*. And the question came: could one fight in a war? I felt in a way that a civil war was more the sort of war I could take part in rather than an international war, because you'd be fighting people you really hated and not people you were ordered to hate. What bothered me about any sort of war was that whole lots of people were conscripted to kill people they didn't even know. It was the terrible thing of going over a Niagara under somebody else's control. I wanted to hang on to my liberty to the last bit, whether I was killing or not. And I think that was really the main plank of my pacifism.

Of course once one got interested in pacifism, Quakers popped up left and right. What attracted me to the Quakers was their nerve: for their beliefs, they refused to do all the things you had to do to be a decent member of society. Moreover, they were pacifists, which was pretty insulting too. The only thing I deplored about them was that they weren't too keen on colours – only Quaker grey. Also, their total renunciation of violence didn't fit in with my feelings. I was aware of violent feelings within myself and I think I could possibly fight somebody individually. If somebody came to rape my mother I'd have no trouble at all – if I could stop him, I would. If I had to kill him, I would. Had I been a Greek and the Germans came to my village, I'd have become a freedom fighter or something like that. But here, in England, you had this option. This fatal option, in a way. I say 'fatal' because I'm not sure even now whether it was the right thing or not. But when you felt you were going to be fed into a sausage machine, you feel: to hell with that! I'll bloody well fight for myself on this thing.

So there was a lot of aggression and self defence in being a conchie. Whether that's the same as cowardice, I don't know. But I don't think I was more afraid of death or unwilling to die than anybody in the army. That's to say I was quite often afraid, but went ahead nevertheless.

After Christ's Hospital I went up to Balliol, Oxford and was teaching English history at Frensham Heights school in 1938. We had a lot of German Jewish refugee children there – I remember Claus Moser, now 'Sir', among others. So there was no doubt in my mind about the beastliness of Hitler. People say that they didn't know about the concentration camps. I believed in the existence of the camps and that was one of the things that made it very difficult for me to be a pacifist. When I thought of the appalling things being done! And the persecution of the Jews I thought particularly foul.

I was at Frensham Heights school when war broke out. Time for decision. I decided that I would apply to the FAU. It offered 'arduous and dangerous work under civilian control for those who share the Quaker views on peace and war.' It seemed to stall the question in a way – a sort of compromise you can call it. I wanted to go where the thing was but I wasn't sure that I wanted to be a conchie – I'd much rather have gone as a war correspondent or a doctor if I'd had the qualifications. In a way my decision to be a CO was an act of violence: an old, deep violence. I think in a way I'd been disaffiliated from society – I think partly by the social-class change at Christ's Hospital, changing my accent and feeling that I'd cut the rope that bound me to my parents, and feeling guilty and angry about that. Frensham Heights was a very advanced, liberal school and the staff were very understanding. The head-master had been in the First War and talked to me about the effect of war on him. 'After the war' he said 'a sunset and things like that never meant quite the same thing to me.' Something had been put out of him. Interesting.

Most boys and girls didn't seem to mind much. One girl did though. She told me that she thought I was a coward. I hit her, I slapped her face... Not a pacific thing to do, I agree. I've had a lot of un-pacifist things going on in me that might easily break out. My mother was dead. My father took it quietly. He didn't query what I said. Just listened in silence... I don't know what he thought... I really don't know.

Tony Gibson:

My impressions about the realities of war came first of all from my father's talk about his experiences in the Dardanelles war. He was a young chaplain who tangled with the High Command over the total cock-up with medical facilities at the Suvla Bay landing. He stood up to the general saying 'This is an abominable thing; you've got to do something.' The general was rather surprised by this gangling, angry young cleric, but decided to *do* something. He also took father onto the General Staff and subsequently he marched with General Maude from Kut to Baghdad.

My father was a total oddball: for instance, he blew all his demob money on circulating the whole of the Methodist Conference with copies of Wilson's *Fourteen Points* and Keynes's *Lessons of the Peace*. He was a regular speaker at Hyde Park and the Kingsway Missions. He was obsessed with the League of Nations and once got Attlee to speak on his platform – they had met in Gallipoli where they shared dysentery and used to chat over the latrines. Father was firmly against war and I accepted his views.

The Methodist system was to keep their ministers moving around, so I had few roots. I attended schools for Methodist ministers' sons where I had a hard time, being an oddball myself. I felt much more at home in the sixth form: I took part in the Literary Society and various debates. Once I took the lead in Ibsen's play *Enemy of the People* – I felt very typecast as the eccentric guy who was countering 'the beat of a distant drum.' By the time I got to university, the war in Spain was paramount, and I remember trying to raise money for the war by doing rather crude street theatre. I also wrote, with another chap, a newspaper about unemployment and the dole, and became principle agent for the sale of *Peace News* and the ILP's *New Leader*. I joined the Independent Labour Party which represented for me the guts of the issue. I didn't feel particularly happy with the pure PPU stuff which I thought mainly reactive, not going to the roots of the problem. ILP were on the right lines because they were fully aware of the ineffectiveness of war as an instrument of policy, but at the same time they were trying to change the basis of society so that those we thought warmongers didn't get it all their own way.

I had been to Germany on school exchanges a couple of times – the last in 1938. It was an interesting experience where we obtained some experience of Hitler's regime and the anti-Semitism that went with it first-hand. There was no doubt that it was an abominable regime which had to be opposed, which is why, during the 'phoney war' when we expected invasion, I tried to get together some sort of resistance. This was totally starry-eyed. I had no idea what it entailed, but I was sure that you had to resist. The point was: what was the most effective way of resisting? I had come to the conclusion that you couldn't be effective by behaving as they did. This has been something dominant in my thinking ever since: you have to judge what you're doing on the grounds of whether it corresponds with what you're after. You can't get away with black propaganda and dirty tricks, and gas chambers and concentration camps without, in turn, generating more of it, and not only on the other side, but your own side too. Right the way through I felt I had to find practical ways to express what I felt: 'Right, this is all happening outside my range, but I believe that something small is not only something I can do, but something small has to add up to something big.'

So when the raids started in September 1940 I did a bit of shelter work in Stepney and Poplar. I then heard about the Pacifist Service Unit (PSU) only to be told that I was *it!* Over the next few months we got three sections of ten going which we dispersed around Chadwell. The main thing was going around the shelters in the mornings, taking the buckets of shit and throwing them down manholes and covering the lot with bug powder. Then, in the afternoons we went to houses that had been bombed, rescuing people's possessions. We weren't much use at rescue work or fire fighting, but we were regarded as 'good people.' At the time of Dunkirk when there was talk of 'bloody conchies; what are they doing?' our shelterers said 'Don't you *dare* talk about them, about time *you* started to do something useful!' So it was a rewarding and happy time and we felt ourselves needed.

By 1942 I was feeling at a bit of a loss. I wanted more excitement and I remember sitting on a bus wondering if I ought to volunteer for the RAF. I was always wondering whether I was doing the right thing. At university there was some teetering and at times I found myself on a knife-edge. Anyhow, I decided that I was going to try to get abroad nearer the action. I had always looked down my nose at the FAU in the past. The Unit had a base at the London student's hostel which was known as 'the Conchie Ritz' and we in the PSU were rather toffy-nosed about them as *we* were the ones doing all the action. I had met some of the first group of FAU who had gone out to China and I very much wanted to go. So when things went quiet, I put in for the FAU and they accepted me.

REFERENCES:

[1] Just over half the Unit throughout the war were Quakers. Many non-Quakers joined the Society of Friends at a later stage; others became attenders. It is impossible to get exact figures.

CHAPTER 2

Training: A Very Kindly Community

'The conscientious objector is a pretty individualist character and one of the things we had to do in those early training camps was to break down the individuality of men to make them corporate members. There were one or two awkward cusses who were awkward cusses all the way through, but most fitted in. The spirit of the camp really seemed to work.'

Michael Cadbury

*T*HE HIGH STANDARD *of FAU training in the First World War had been recognised as being vital for the quality of service provided in that war. When the Unit was re-formed, emphasis was once again placed on the importance of training. Manor Farm at Northfield, Birmingham, proved an ideal spot for this. It was the property of Dame Elizabeth Cadbury, situated on the outskirts of the city, surrounded by fields, woods and a large lake – a perfect environment for field work. Tegla Davies aptly described it as the 'nursery' of the Unit and the great majority of members vouch for its importance in creating a sense of identity, providing a home at a time of alienation from a society at war, as well as forging effective units out of the motley intakes of men.*

The first camp was followed by twenty successive camps throughout the war. Members lived simple, spartan lives which were relieved by the hospitality of local Quakers, as Anthony Perry recalls 'I remember the hospitality of Heather Cadbury with real affection: deep soaking hot baths (four persons one after the other in the same water!) and unlimited coffee.'[1] *As time went on, many returned to the Northfield camp to pass on lessons gained from their war experience which meant that modifications and improvements were continually made which contributed to the camps' developments and successes.*

In essence, the training was basic with the emphasis on keeping fit, self sufficiency and gaining basic first aid and home nursing skills. Further training followed in hospitals across the country, as well as mechanical and driving courses where necessary. When opportunities opened for FAU work abroad, then members underwent further specialist training in foreign languages (such as Mandarin and Amharic), tropical medicine or whatever was deemed essential for effective performance.

The intake of men forming the twenty successive camps was diverse: actors, mechanics, teachers, students, carpenters, bank clerks, architects, a barrister, a butcher's boy ' a baronet and rat-catcher too.'[2] *Of course the same mix would be found in the armed services but with the important difference that, despite some vague demarcations of authority, the FAU trained, lived and worked together on terms of equality. This meant that the training camps were important in breaking down barriers of class and forging cohesive, egalitarian units.*

Douglas Turner:

...It was a very simple hierarchy: there was a camp commandant, his assistant and other instructors, then the section leaders and deputy leaders. The leaders were appointed by the camp commandant, which was fair enough, and the deputy leaders by their own section. Some camps had sections of six, but in my camp we were divided into sections of five – six sections of five members – and we duly carried out our leader's wills and whims. Of course going alongside was always our constant questioning and our openness with one another – it was nothing like military discipline at all. But things worked: it was just good acceptable, mutual responsibility with healthy young people really enjoying themselves and getting down to the job with a will.

The Quaker component of the Unit was about one third of total membership when I joined. This was an excellent thing; I think the Unit gained tremendously by opening its doors to all COs who took a similar position. I wasn't a Friend then but, like others, did join the Society as a result of FAU experience. But Friend or otherwise, we had a common bond which in many ways was stronger because of the input from different backgrounds. The FAU gained enormously from its diversity.

Given our varied backgrounds, there was also an admirable lack of class consciousness. This came out strongly when people were chosen for specific tasks or leadership of sections. Very often leaders were appointed from those who'd had practical experience such as men from the blue-collar sections. In my experience there was no feeling of class orientation at all; and if there was, then it was strongly condemned. In fact more often than not we would take the mickey out of university people. This was always appreciated.

We had a lot of fun as well as hard work. There was a very delightful woman, Sister Gibbs, who came along to talk about hospitals and ward work. She was never shy of demonstrating a broken femur by lifting her skirt very high, with the usual comments and sighs from her audience. She enjoyed this just as much as we did. As for our 'practicals' – well God help anybody who suffered from them in any battle condition! In lieu of having no weaponry being fired at us, our instructors used tins filled with stones which they rattled to represent machine-gun fire. We would dive into the undergrowth until the supposed enemy had passed. Had we been under real fire, goodness knows what we would have done. Nevertheless it did give us some imaginary idea of what might happen in such situations. And, of course, some of our members did experience battlefields and were killed.

Following the initial training, I then needed further training for China. So I was sent up to work in Lewisham Hospital for a few weeks and then had a spell in the Failand training centre in Bristol for a mechanics-cum-language course. Then I found myself on an RASC course running in cooperation with the War Department, at Nottingham. This lasted for three weeks during which time we had to wear khaki uniform. We got on very well with the troops. We had a bristling, red-moustached colonel in charge who accepted us willingly, as did the NCOs. They may not necessarily have understood us, and sometimes they envied us: 'No bloody officers, mate? Cor, how do you join your lot?' 'No pay! Blimey mate, you must be *mad*. Whatyer doing this for then?' – that sort of thing. We shared the same canteen and I shall never forget one soldier leaning over and saying 'Oi, are you *really* soldiers?' We assured him we weren't.

Wakey!! Wakey!! Stephen Verney in full cry!

'Thank God for that' he said 'I thought you couldn't have been when I saw you marching down the street all out of step!'

Yes, this initiation into the FAU was really marvellous, and it continued to be so. I can well understand the average soldier feeling very envious towards our set-up. I often wished that my own school friends who went into the services could have experienced such an environment.

Ronald Joynes:

As I joined the first camp, this mainly consisted of Quakers. I wore a Boys Brigade badge on my jacket and when I met Richard Early, the camp commandant, he instantly recognised this, being a member himself, and you could say that henceforth I had friends at court. This meant a lot because I was like a fish out of water among all these public schoolboys and university graduates. But I was fairly good at football and hockey which helped enormously. But really my more humble background never ever mattered – I never felt it a hindrance. In fact having lived in circumstances unknown to most of them, I was able to help in many ways.

Right from the word go we saw ourselves working with the army and used to do drill. This is where my Boys Brigade training came in. It was a great deal of fun because these boys had no intention of behaving like a company of soldiers. They would tease me by obeying my commands to the letter, often with hilarious results. We'd go on route marches singing Ten Green Bottles and Green Grow the Rushes Oh! – quite inspiring it was. In fact we sang these later on our retreat from Greece to cheer ourselves up.

New members of the Unit couldn't understand our insistence on military-orientated rules like folding and looking after kit. One or two found it very difficult to keep their boots clean and in one position. But when we went overseas and lived with the army, several times we had to turn out at very short notice in the dark and unless you had some system, it would have been very hard to know exactly where your boots and jackets were. Many pacifists scoffed at this and I wasn't very popular at times, but I realised early on how important it was if we were to work effectively in war zones. Many didn't realise the importance of having a uniform – it immediately distinguished you. Even though they couldn't tell whether you were a pacifist or not, at least it told them that you were British.

I used to preach the advantage of working with the army and I actually got a section to work with the army in Catterick camp when I returned from overseas. I had approached the director of medical services and we had a little section trained alongside the Armoured Division and in no time at all they felt spurred to outdo the army. I think we wanted to show that although we were pacifists, we weren't to be regarded lightly. I think most, looking back, would appreciate this training although I always used to say 'Don't think you need to ape the army, it isn't necessary; but some of the things do make sense.'

Paul Townsend:

I was just over nineteen when I went to training camp in 1942. One of the amazing things about the Unit was the great friendliness: it's true that I have remained friendly with more Unit people through life than those at school or university and I think this was partly because there were a lot of friendly, creative people who tended to think as one did oneself, which perhaps is not a very good thing, but it made one comfortable. It wasn't just that there is always solidarity in any minority group, it was much more, there was a real sense of community.

The physical training certainly wasn't marine standards, but by my rather decadent standards it was rather tough, partly because many of those involved in training had public school training themselves. Although they hadn't gone the military way themselves, they carried over a certain military ethos: up early, run round the lake, cold showers, marches. Alongside this was gained skills such as learning to cook in a slit trench, or knowing how to run with an old-fashioned fire hose, unrolling it as you go – all of this went on. We were taught first aid and home nursing by two delightful people: Sister Gibbs and the old Birmingham Quaker, Dr. Rutter. I remember he would talk about 'exercise tolerance tests' and to demonstrate his fitness in old age he used to plonk down a chair and step up and down on it thirty times, and then would count to see the pace of the pulse rate going back to normal. As for the adequacy of training, in the light of subsequent experience I think it

Route march: Green grow the rushes oh!

gave me enough confidence to do what I had to in hospitals and other places although, unlike some other members who went off to far-off, remote places and found themselves doing appendicectomies or giving anaesthetics, my first aid was rather humdrum. But I came out of training fitter; we also gained a sense of team spirit. This sounds very Establishment, but I think that was important.

It was important for me to have a unit identity and a home because I'm not someone who likes to step out of line. There are pacifists – and non-pacifists too, of course – for whom it is a kind of fulfilment not to conform – indeed bloodymindedness is almost an indulgence in some cases. I'm neither denigrating that stance nor praising my own, but there is a sense in which I rather like a kind of imaginative conformity; there I was very glad of the association of like-minded people supporting me. At the end of training we had to pass Red Cross first aid and our home nursing exams; then the camp commandant gave a report on our progress and for some of us, at a later stage, it was further training on a mechanics and driving course at Failand, Bristol, which was very useful.

Frank Edmead:

At the time the training seemed very relevant, but now when I look back on it, the first aid we did was pretty old-fashioned and nowadays the things we were taught to do with patients would be considered positively dangerous. When I re-read my wartime diaries, I am impressed with how much first aid and medical treatment we actually did during the war. It makes my hair stand on end the way we gave morphine injections, for instance. And the way we medically examined thousands of refugees which I certainly wouldn't be capable of today. But the training camp gave me confidence to do this. Above all, the training was enjoyable and I think this is the secret of good training: to get the trainees to enjoy it.

After this initial training, I went to the mechanics training camp at Failand, near Bristol. This was a very good course and I learned a lot in a very short time. After that I was sent to the Midland Assembly Depot – MAD! – and this was very different. They were waiting for the Second Front to open but in the meantime there wasn't much for us to do and they invented all sorts of unnecessary things. We had, for instance, to work on 'Serbian Barrels.' These were devices dating back to the Great War for delousing clothes. You had a boiler made from old oil drums which were placed on bricks – so we had to learn brick-laying too – the steam from the boiler was forced through a barrel containing the refugees' clothes until the lice had been killed. At that time we knew that Gerald Gardiner had gleaned from reports that these were out of date and we would be using DDT in our relief work in Europe. So it made us feel that our time was being wasted.

We also went on exercises taking two or three days to set up field hospitals. This seemed to me very artificial and a waste of time. I was a section leader in one and I was feeling so Bolshie at the time that I sabotaged it. There was a pervasive feeling there that we were regarded merely as training fodder – so different from the training camp where we were all so eager to learn. Even the FAU commandant and training officer behaved differently there. I remember we had a lecture from a well known sociologist in the FAU who was talking about how liberal ideology had more or less had its day and people now wanted authoritarianism, which he seemed to regard as a good thing. This seemed to be a symptom of some of the things I didn't like about the camp.

Robin Whitworth:

The training was not at all tough by army standards although the route marches were fairly tiring. Some people in Britain had very tough lives. Life in a public school was very tough. I didn't hunt myself, but people who hunted went out in all weathers and had a *very* tough time. And there is nothing quite so tiring as a night's dancing at the Four Hundred Club – bad taste, of course, but a lot of the better off people did go dancing at night. But you have to realise that a lot of those who joined the FAU did live extraordinarily comfortable lives – those who lived on little housing estates, who had devoted wives and went off by underground to their offices and came back to find their slippers put out – never a game of football, let alone a route march. But we all got on very well together. We'd run round the lake every morning and, yes, it's true, I *did* use an umbrella when it rained; the training officer, a splendid person, didn't seem to mind at all, so I thought 'Why not?'

Bishop Freddie Temple:

It was all so new, this camp life. Although I had played a lot of squash and tennis at Oxford, having to get up early in the dark and run up the hill and round the lake, and having to learn the first aid and all the others things, was quite demanding. I hadn't realised until I had joined them that there is a hierarchy amongst the Friends. I had always thought them equal. But the visit up to the Queen, as it were – Dame Elizabeth Cadbury – for tea, was very much a very royal visit. And when Paul, who was an incredibly energetic and wonderful character, appeared on the scene, everyone backed away as he was *very* much in control in the beginning.

Tom Haley:

Training camp: well, it was absolutely exciting – a totally new experience for me. Many of the people there were university men: bright-minded, energetic, committed Christians. People who really wanted to do their absolute best – very, very hard-working men. It was almost unnecessary to ask for volunteers because people jumped in when there was anything to do. It was a wonderful atmosphere: the friendliness, the keenness, the sheer joy of life. When you get young men of the same idea together, they form a terrific camaraderie. And this happened with us. And for me, coming from such a disruptive and hurtful home situation, it was something utterly new: I wasn't going to be trampled upon, I wasn't going to be pushed aside, I was going to be accepted as whatever I was, and I just loved it. Meeting people who spoke to each other with tolerance and understanding, not with bitterness, and not with any idea of just trying to beat the other person down – they were keen and intelligent, and at the same time good men. I met people who were doctors and who were students in different fields. I'd never met people with such natural assurance and belief in themselves, and who were completely unafraid to express themselves. The difference was tremendous. So really it was a great blossoming for me, and a new understanding of how one could live.

And the training was so good. I'll give you an example. Later when I was working in a London hospital, I was invited to attend an operation just to see blood, so to speak. I went along and stood at the back of the operating theatre. There were a number of students around the surgeons watching this operation. So this surgeon said to a student 'Do you know the signs and symptoms of a fracture?' and the chap mumbled away a bit. And the surgeon asked the same thing of all the students. And I was thinking: page seventeen, half-way down on the left-hand side. He saw me at the back and having tried everyone else without success, asked me the question. I said 'Yes, Sir, pain, loss of power, swelling, deformity, irregularity of the natural mobility and crepitus.' 'That's the way I like to be answered.' he said. So it was really funny: they'd forgotten more about medicine than I was ever likely to know! But it illustrates how well we applied ourselves to this training. We did our best and put something into it. So those six weeks – just six weeks – made a tremendous impact on me. Quite honestly, it was the most wonderful experience I was ever to have and it influenced the rest of my life.

Bill Brough:

I arrived by bus at my training camp on a cold, snowy day in January 1940. There I met a fine group of people – I've never met any like these before or since. The usual silly behaviour you get with any group of young people was remarkably scarce. We were a minority group so of course we needed the confirmation and the affirmation of each other. A lot had been at university and, apart from the doctor and the priest in my village in Northumberland, nobody had been to university or grammar school, so it was a new experience to be with such men. There was no class consciousness. One or two spoke in an affected kind of way, but very little of that – they were too good humoured and would have realised how ridiculous they sounded. I remember when we left Northfield and arrived at our digs in the London Hospital, somebody who'd been with me in the third camp was asked by a friend who had been in an earlier camp what kind of group we were. I remember him saying 'Well, we've got this son of an earl and a butcher.' I thought that fair enough, it was an accurate description, but I did think for a moment 'I wonder who the butcher is?'

The working class were certainly in a minority. I was unaware of anyone from my sort of background. I met Tom Haley later on and Tom and I seemed to be the people in the Unit known as 'the working class boys.' There were others, but Tom and I seemed to stand out: he was the cockney and I, the northern country boy. I remember very early on in Northfield, being on kitchen duty with this tall, pleasant young man who was an earl's son – he was the Honourable Oliver Beckett. I don't think he'd ever seen a potato before, and I think I was as strange to him as the potato. He'd never spoken to a butcher before; he'd never known anybody whose father was a miner. So I was as strange an animal to him as he was to me. He would have been the extreme end of the social continuum. Apart from potatoes, I had certain other advantages. I was one of the few drivers and there were many things I could do that the boys from universities had no experience of – I had some idea of how a shop was run, and by this time, because I had done some voluntary work in a local hospital, some idea of how a hospital was organised.

We had our small weekly allowance of 7/6d – enough to buy stamps, get a hair cut, put two bob in the collection money, perhaps take a bus somewhere. It wasn't a hardship, for me there was no difficulty. But I remember a conversation between two Unit men saying they were finding that they were spending £7 a week when they were in London – this was for shows, meals and concerts. They went on to say that they really needed £10 a week to do all this comfortably. These would have been unusual.

Sydney Carter:

Going into the FAU was rather like going into a kind of mobile monastery in a way. It was very important having a body like that for support at such a time. It was such an interesting body of people, I must say. Some were pretty well educated, some not. I was older than some and was made a section leader. I had to get my people here and there to do this, that and the other. I'm not sure that I was a very good section leader. I remember once when we were inspected that I hadn't inspected the pots and pans my group were responsible for very carefully. And somebody found a little speck. There was a Quakerly sort of reproof, and I thought 'Oh gosh!'

The local Quakers were very kind, there were plenty of them in Birmingham and they kindly asked us to nice meals and a hot bath now and then. That was good. We had lectures on medicine and nursing. I remember a doctor telling us about VD. His tone was hushed 'I must admit that in the last war I even had to treat some members of the Unit.' Silence. I thought 'Gosh!' Then somebody took a bite 'The only safe thing about VD is abstinence and purity...' Then I had a go 'I know it's a bit pompous of me to ask but isn't it in fact due to a germ or bacillus, or something like that? Could you not, in fact, get it from your own wife or husband?' This was considered. Everyone looked at me. He looked a bit puzzled too: 'What's this....?'

As we were finishing training, the bombs had started falling on Birmingham. I remember one night being in a cinema watching 'Gone With The Wind.' We had reached the part where Atlanta was being set on fire. Across the screen came 'Alert!' But we couldn't be bothered with that, we were right in the middle of this film. That was the night the Bullring was more or less finished off. Strange how you can be watching a film which holds you more than what's happening outside.

Tony Gibson:

Training? It wasn't too bad at all. I was always suspicious of what I thought of as the 'chocolate hegemony' and I continued, and have continued to be a bit dubious about how the people who were funding the thing remained in control. But I liked Michael Cadbury, the camp commandant, who was a very mellifluous chap. The camp was very well run. I would say my approach was conforming to the main thing in order to make it work, but also not entirely swallowing it whole. I think all the time, in most contexts I was in, I tended to be someone who would take a top dressing of Quakerism but was dissatisfied when it seemed to be too cautious or too – now what's the word? – too stubborn at confronting alternatives. There was an innate feeling that fundamentally things were not going to change. So my view of Friends was apt to be a bit arrogant. But I tended to congregate with people who liked to have a bit of a laugh and who didn't take things too seriously. There were one or two blokes who, when we got out of the camp to go and have a cup of tea, used to have a laugh and send up what was going on even though we were committed to doing the training.

Eric Turner:

I've often thought about training camp, in some ways it was a somewhat strange experience for me. On the one hand it was a great relief being with like-minded people, but I was living in a community of a kind I hadn't experienced before. Many of the men there were ex-public school, and in our camp we had a fairly strong element of Bootham and Leighton Park boys; there were also some grammar school boys and then some, like me, from elementary schools who had been at work since we were fourteen. So, although I felt a great relief at being there, those of us in our particular social group found it a little more difficult to know where we fitted in. There were times when we felt uncomfortable. One of the things I'd put my finger on now is that the chaps who had been to the public schools and Quaker schools had a degree of social confidence which the rest of us lacked. Of course many of us had worked, we'd had social lives, but we had never quite acquired the social confidence and intellectual certainty that the others had.

No one ever excluded us. If you felt excluded it was because you couldn't cope with the language and level of understanding they seemed to have. For instance, they had been brought up in the environment where ethical, political and religious matters were discussed at a level of sophistication, so in discussions you could feel out of it and not know what to say.

I remember feeling very intimidated at my interview in Gordon Square. I felt all the Unit people there very superior and many of them became very well known in later years as teachers, administrators and suchlike. I remember wondering at the time whether I could survive in that kind of society and after my interview, when they turned to me and said 'Well now Turner, we accept you into the FAU.' I might well have said 'No thank you.'

I later found that many of these senior men, behind the polish and confidence which seemed so intimidating to some of us, were in fact very kindly people who were able to see how the less confident needed to be nourished and helped. The great redeeming feature of the FAU was that it was essentially a very kindly community. Although some of them were awful snobs who hardly knew the life I had lived, most were people of great good nature and good will. Initially, I felt ashamed of my background, but I quickly came to see that this had conferred considerable advantages on me. The fact that I'd done quite a lot of practical first aid work in civil defence meant that I could do things some of the others couldn't and it gradually emerged that there were quite a few things I knew about that a lot of them didn't. So there was a balance: sometimes you felt deficient, that you couldn't cope, but always some balancing factor. As I gained confidence in the FAU, I came to realise that I was accepted for what I was. Although we were a very mixed group – the majority belonging to the middle classes with a few from upper classes and working classes – and were very different in our understanding of what our pacifism required of us, there was a unity within us which transcended our differences.

REFERENCES:
[1] Heather Cadbury recalls how the coffee became ersatz made with acorn, and how one of them hit a record of fifteen cups during one evening. Letter to Lyn Smith 31/1/97.
[2] From 'Chocolate Soldiers' song by Sydney Carter and Donald Swann, written for BBC radio programme of that title, July 1989.

CHAPTER 3

FAU Women: And The Dancing Had to Stop

'Women were welcomed cautiously into the Unit. Male chauvinism was there, yes – "Women!, what can they do?" It wasn't bitter or strong, but it was there all right. They came in initially in ones or twos but with no special organisation to help them. They were not given the same encouragement that men were given. They were on their own. They were "permitted" to serve. Put it that way.'

John Bailey

*B*Y OCTOBER 1940, with the London blitz raging, the need was clear: there were many jobs in the shelter and rest centre work the Unit was engaged in which men were not qualified to do. When the issue was raised in the Executive Committee and Council, there was a positive, albeit hesitant response – women would be permitted, but as full members of the FAU – well....

Tessa Cadbury (Rowntree), daughter of Arnold, was approached. She had just returned to Britain on the last Orient Express train from Istanbul to Paris via an Italy about to enter the war as Germany's ally. Tessa had gone to Turkey with the aim of finding a slot for FAU reconstruction work in the wake of an earthquake which had erupted on the Turkish/Russian border. She was an indomitable young woman who in the late 1930s had been active helping refugees escape from the Nazi threat in Vienna and Prague. If a willingness to face the 'arduous and dangerous' was the criterion for FAU membership, Tessa had certainly

47

proved her credentials. In the autumn of 1940 she was serving on the
Friends War Victims Relief Service Committee (FWVRS).

Tessa Cadbury:

Like the rest of my family, I had come to my pacifism by heredity and didn't really question it – you never took human life nor carried a gun. After Munich I did start to question it politically, but although I knew first-hand about Hitler's regime, it never caused me to think that war ever solved anything.

Then I was asked to form a women's section of the FAU. It was always put like that – as a 'women's section.' I had a letter out of the blue from Peter Hume. I had known him earlier in York and this letter was the first indication that the men had been thinking about it. By this time, in the autumn of 1940, the London blitz was on and his letter started 'For some time it has been abundantly clear our work in London in shelters, food and rest centres would be increased in value if we had a women's section in the Unit, or if there was a separate women's FAU with whom we could cooperate...'

It seemed quite obvious that women were ideally suited for shelter work – helping with the children, making sleeping conditions better, that sort of thing. So Peter Hume asked me to develop some ideas about getting suitable women and training them for shelter work as well as any other work which might crop up. I immediately got in touch with my old friend, Gwendy Knight, a qualified doctor, who agreed to come in with me, and from then on we worked very closely together. I had always assumed that we'd go ahead on the grounds that it would be a women's section of the existing FAU as I had no interest in forming another organisation; and when it was put to us later 'Wouldn't this be better?' Gwendy and I were both thoroughly shocked, neither of us ever dreamt of this.

I don't know what was behind the idea of a separate women's unit. Perhaps they thought they were competing with us being part of the same organisation. It was never verbalised, but sometimes we felt that they thought us very independent. And we *were*. Our set-up was very different from theirs – the thought of having officers! if we talked about that once, that was enough! We were never interested in having an organisational hierarchy in that way.

As things worked out, we were able to borrow from an uncle a family house, Barmoor, situated on the Yorkshire moors. We organised five, month-long camps and we recruited the women with the help of the FAU office and a letter in the Friend.

At that early stage, apart from shelters, we didn't really know what sort of work we'd be doing. The idea was to toughen them up and make them as adaptable as possible. The winter cooperated beautifully: it was very severe with deep snow, so we had a good physical setting to test us. Barmoor was a very rugged place, there was no central heating but we had fires and very primitive lighting and cooking facilities. In fact a real feeling of fellowship and friendship developed there.

The women were all in their twenties, with a few in their late twenties and some in their thirties. Some had experienced first aid or other medical training before they came. I would say that on the whole the women were more mature and experienced than most FAU men: most had some training or life experience after school. Some had held jobs; they felt that their jobs had lacked meaning in time of war and this is what led them to apply. More single women applied to the FAU than to the FRS which was looking more for long-term service and married couples. Women were always a minority in the FAU and only a few were Quakers – about a quarter in all.

Gwendy and I interviewed everybody. Often this would be on railway stations which was quite difficult as it meant travelling all over the place. I can't remember whether we asked them about pacifism, I think we assumed that's why they applied. I do, however, remember some of them mentioning that they wanted to do something which went along with their pacifist views. We were always so busy, no time to spare, so I don't think we ever sat down and had discussions about pacifism. The important thing was that we were all on the same wavelength. That was the idea of the interview. Several thought it wasn't for them and didn't join.

Although most stayed in the Unit after Barmoor, the women were in fact free to accept anything offered in the work line in any organisation. The men couldn't do that, they had to work within the Unit and this probably made for a more theoretical approach with them. I think the differences in conscripting men and women in wartime had a great deal to do with the different approaches we had.

As far as I remember, every time we asked the men at HQ for help, we would get it, but I don't think we asked for much when we were at Barmoor because Gwendy and I knew the set-up and the locality so well. It was all ad hoc, that's how we ran it. John and Edna Bailey came and stayed for a short time, and one or two FRS came and made a few suggestions, trying to be helpful.

Women were not invited onto the Executive Committee of the FAU. This didn't worry me. I'm not keen on committees so would have found it difficult. Gwendy, like me, was not interested in the structure, more so in the work and those doing the work. I can hear Gwendy saying 'Oh, that's just Friends' House, Gordon Square!' That's what a lot of men in the Unit couldn't understand: we were interested in the FAU and FRS, but weren't bothered about bureaucracy and the theory behind things – we were definitely more pragmatic. Give us the jobs – shelter work, rest centres, hostels and later foreign work – all those places that cried out for a woman's touch – do the job, then move on to where the need is.

Gwendy Knight:

When Tessa asked if I would help form a women's section of the FAU, I was delighted. At that time, having qualified as a doctor and worked for a time as a medical officer in the Quaker mental home, The Retreat, I was training in psychotherapy at the Tavistock Clinic. In 1941, with many of the staff going off into the services, things were very unsettled there, so it was a great pleasure meeting with Tessa again and having the chance to work with her. I loved the country and the thought of being at Barmoor again was very appealing.

I had vaguely heard about the FAU but I knew enough to know what its aims were and these certainly fitted with mine, being a birthright Quaker. My father, who was a teacher, had been given conditional exemption in the Great War, but his youngest brother and closest friend were both imprisoned. So I was aware of problems related to war from that time on. I went to all sorts of peace meetings from the 1920s onwards. When people nowadays say: 'We've been working so long and we haven't got very far,' I think: 'Oh, you little know, I've been going to peace meetings for sixty years!' But pacifism was taken for granted, just part of my background: the idea that every individual has a divine spark, that we are all equal in the eyes of God, and that no one has the right to take another life. My father always said: 'It doesn't matter whether pacifism succeeds or not, that's not our business. It might be a failure, but if it's right, that's what we've got to follow.'

When war started, one was aware that conscription for women might occur; there was the feeling that liberties were going to be very much reduced. There was also the fact that one couldn't share in the general enthusiasm for Churchill's exhortations – I always felt myself hanging back from that. Being a doctor I knew that I would be able to continue medicine somehow or other, but I wouldn't have agreed to being conscripted. I was given the chance of joining the Emergency Medical Service as an anaesthetist, but as this was under strict Government control, I had a conscientious objection to it. So when the offer of service with the FAU came, it was very welcome.

It was made clear from the start that we had to fit in with what the men said. At first they wouldn't accept anyone into the Unit unless they had been through a training camp, so we decided: well, training camps we'd have. Barmoor was very remote – the nearest station and supplies were in Kirbymoorside about five miles away, and we would walk there and back. We welcomed these basic conditions with open arms because we thought if they could cope there, they could cope in a good many places. There's nothing like living together for three or four weeks to find out people's strengths and weaknesses – you very quickly find those who volunteer to do things and those who wait. It was surprising how the girls rose to the occasion afterwards – they were put into some very difficult situations and managed extremely well. Later on the Unit did accept women who hadn't been to Barmoor, but I understand there was far more a group feeling among those who had attended our camps.

Just two or three of the men visited us. My impression is that they were far too busy with their own problems to think too much about us; if we were forced on their notice by asking them something, then they would do their best, but the Unit was full of men who were worried about what they were going to do: could they face just being orderlies in hospitals? What sort of opportunities were opening up? Could they get abroad? They were just full of personal problems so as long as we were managing on our own, that's all they bothered about.

As camps were finished the women were needed in hostel and shelter work during the blitz. They worked all night in very, very poor conditions. A lot of shelters were in very vulnerable places – under the old warehouses in the docks, or under railway arches. I think the girls were all extremely courageous, they were eager to do anything they could to help and they never complained. Being a doctor gave me a bit of authority and status, but I would say that women were just glad of opportunities that came along in the war, and accepted them.

I used to go round visiting them while collecting women for the next camp; I would also visit the house in Canonbury Place, London where about forty lived. It was all very shabby and grubby. Something I found very difficult about the Unit men was that they were so keen to be regarded as 'real men' and not get any favours, that they deliberately roughed it when they needn't have. Some of them, for instance, insisted on sleeping in blankets when there were sheets available – that kind of thing.

I always think it's much easier for a woman to be a CO than a man. Men have always got to prove themselves and, thank goodness, women don't. Any rate I feel it's much more a woman's nature to be far-sighted and think towards the future rather than be so worried about immediate status. There was always the fundamental difference between the men and the women: that women could easily find themselves useful work to do outside the unit, whereas the young men really depended on the Unit – for them it supplied the vital need.

By mid 1941, with all thoughts of having a distinct WFAU gone, women were admitted as full members of the Unit and pressed on with a full schedule of useful work. As well as the sterling work performed in shelters, hostels and rest centres, they also worked in Citizens Advice Bureaux (CAB) and as secretaries in Gordon Square. When the need arose they were recruited for relief work abroad. In all ninety-seven women joined the FAU and of these fifty-seven went overseas to serve in India, China, the Middle East, Italy, Yugoslavia, and N. W. Europe. Marjorie Asquith, after work on the home front, served in the Middle East and the Dodecanese.

Marjorie Asquith (Whittles):

My father was an old-fashioned trade unionist on the Left. He spent the First World War in the trenches and was mentioned in dispatches. But he hated the war. He saw men blown up next to him and hated the waste and squalor of it; he felt it terrible fighting backwards and forwards over the same little bit of ground. He was secretary of the Relief Fund of the British Legion and he would see people in our front room. He and my younger brother used to have tremendous discussions. My mother used to think they were rows and tried to stop them. I'd be listening to all this and it rubbed off on me. I got a scholarship to a school in a very conservative area of Redcar. Years later I found an essay I'd written at that school, it was very much against war. So I think I must have been a pacifist then but in an unformed sort of way.

It was while I was working on Defence Bonds in Harrogate that I met Dorothy Bishop. She was a pacifist who was planning to join the FAU. I decided to apply also because I felt the way she did – that killing and wounding people seemed terrible, also the loss of freedom, the way people are ordered to go and kill. I was absolutely certain then that I was doing the right thing. Now, facing the same situation, I am not so sure. But I would never have joined a unit involved in killing or bearing arms. It's a difficult one really because Hitler was so obviously terrible and had to be stopped and it was then too late to stop him diplomatically.

So I entered the FAU in 1941. I dealt with my tribunal myself. It never occurred to me that the FAU could be there and help. I think they were a bit taken aback by my going it alone. It was held in Liverpool and it was awful. I was terribly nervous and had to speak. I can only remember one thing: I said something about my conscience, and the panel said 'What directs your conscience?' and I answered 'What do you mean? My conscience directs me!' Terrible, isn't it? They gave me total exemption because I was already in the Unit. That wasn't fair in a way.

I went to Barmoor for training. This was a lovely big house on the Yorkshire moors run by Tessa Rowntree and Gwendy Knight. There were about twenty of us living there, all women, no men around then. They were some of the nicest people I've met in my life – it was all so classless and democratic. We took it in turns to work in different teams: cooking, cleaning, maintenance. We had talks and slide shows on basic hygiene and delivering babies – that sort of thing. We'd sit and talk in the evening. Tessa and Gwendy were a bit older than most of us and they organised it so that it was very easy-going. About half were Quakers, but we all went to Meeting. At first I found the silence difficult, I wanted to keep swallowing and coughing. We were paid about 7/6d a week pocket money. As we were kept and sheltered, this was fine; and we all lived the same.

Margaret Matheson (Briggs):

I was brought up as a Quaker, went to the local Meeting in Birmingham where I got to know Michael Cadbury. I have to admit that I had given no real thought to the question of pacifism: it is a very basic part of the Quaker ethos. I am just a pacifist.

When war broke out I had friends who were going into the army and friends who were conscientious objectors and my brother was a CO, so I knew people on both sides. I was lucky being in nursing; some nurses were directed but I was in the kind of job where I could choose to go where I liked. I had just started my midwifery training when war started. I went to Oxford where a lot of pregnant women were sent. I stayed there for two years and during that time the war impinged very little on my life. Apart from a bit of bombing in Cowley, Oxford was left completely alone. So my war at that time you could say was really unwarlike.

Then in 1942 I thought 'This is enough!' Bombs were falling on Birmingham where my parents were living, so I got a job as night sister in the Queen Elizabeth Hospital in Birmingham. I had been there one year and was due to get the ward I had been after when Michael Cadbury rang me and said 'We want you to go to China, how about it?' I went for an interview. They wanted to know what I had been doing and why I wanted to go; was I a pacifist, and did I agree with the FAU ethos. I was accepted and decided to go. So there I was in the FAU and off to China.

Pip Turner (Stringer):

I became a pacifist when I was fifteen after hearing a talk given at the Congregational Union annual conference. My father had served in World War I and talked a lot about the trenches when I was younger. On my seventeenth birthday I started a group of the Fellowship of Reconciliation in Brentwood and on my eighteenth birthday I joined the PPU. I was a socialist. I remember the thirties and the depression. Until I was six we lived in London and I can remember a man who had walked all the way from Wales looking for work; my mother invited him in and gave him a meal. I also remember the Jarrow march because some of the marchers stayed in Brentwood, where we were then living, for a night. I was also Christian and it seemed to be very unChristian to go killing people. You could say that I was ripe for pacifism at that time.

When war started I realised that I could eventually be conscripted. This didn't worry me. Several of the young men in the PPU had already registered as COs, so I knew of the provisions made. Any rate my job in the GPO was a reserved one. Then in the summer of 1943 a notice came round saying that a proportion of women would be released for nursing and other services including the armed services. I applied for release which was granted and went into the FAU, which I had heard about by then, on August bank holiday Monday, 1943. I had to go to an interview and was interviewed by Angela Sinclair-Loutit and somebody else whose name I can't recall. I didn't have to go to camp because after the first six camps they took women in singly. When I joined, I lived at Gordon Square for six weeks. I remember the door was opened to me by Sandy Parnis dressed up like a pirate – he had a red scarf tied around his head.

I would not have gone into the services, even though women weren't in the front line shooting people.[1] I was very keen to get into the FAU: it gave you a background where you were totally accepted and not the odd one out. It was so good working with a group of young people with whom you had so much in common and who were so interesting. All were committed to pacifism. All were Christian – we were asked that when we applied. I found it all very congenial. I always attended the Quaker Meetings held every Sunday and found them far more acceptable than any of the church services I had previously been to. There was no ritual, just a concern with what you were doing. The other thing that impressed me was that during the meetings of the Unit sections, things would sometimes get heated and it could be quite divisive. Then somebody would say 'Let's have a few minutes silence', after which things went much more smoothly – it gave time for everybody to think about what they were saying and to consider the other point of view. We usually came to good decisions after that. It was very democratic.

Angela Sinclair-Loutit (de Renzy Martin):

My parents used to change for dinner, and one of my earliest memories of my father is of him in his uniform which I thought very splendid and admirable. I was born in 1921 when the Great War was still being talked about a lot. My mother, who had been a VAD in the war, always spoke about it with a feeling of grief. My father had been in the war and I remember one day wondering if he ever stuck a bayonet in somebody, and being too afraid to ask. I also remember cutting a poem out of a children's newspaper about scarlet poppies of France – it was about the way the poppies managed to cover the death and destruction.

I don't know how old I was when it was my father's idea to re-visit Flanders. In some area they had reconstructed the trenches with sandbags and left the no-mans-land area with the trees all spiky and destroyed. There was a place called Hill 60 where there had been huge losses. We visited some war cemeteries, appalling in their numbers: straight rows of Portland stone white crosses. I remember the black iron crosses of the German graves, and it seemed like a grotesque chess game of black and white. And an Indian cemetery done in Indian style with stone-work in different patterns. It made the war very vivid, how these Indians had come from so far away to fight a European war.

Then later, in 1936, we motored through the Black Forest in Germany. I remember that before each village was a monument which looked like a land-mine or torpedo – these were to make the Germans war conscious – they seemed very menacing. We saw an archway in another town on which was written 'Juden nicht welkommen.' What did it mean? Then father arranged for my twin brother and me to join a group of Hitler Youth – I remember their patriotic songs and flag waving ceremony. All this added up to the impression that war was coming, rather like a thunder cloud gathering.

I was a student at Somerville College, Oxford, when war started. I had already found Oxford disappointing and with war starting, I wanted to get into it. But what to do? The main choices were between nursing and working on the land. I was told about a course run by Lady Louis Mountbatten in London. So I did this short course in first aid and home nursing. At the end of the course, Lady Louis said to me 'Well, you're very lucky, you're being sent to a military hospital.' I suppose she meant it would be nice to be surrounded by a lot of brave young soldiers. But I was sent to a hospital in Weston-super-Mare which was disorganised and unsatisfying.

I left this hospital after six months and returned to London wondering what to do next. Then I had a letter from a friend, Michael Watson, who said he'd found a wonderful organisation called the FAU. I went to the London students' hostel in Whitechapel and asked politely at the door if I could speak to Mr. Watson. The person at the door called up the stairs 'Mike!' which was lovely as people were normally so formal in those days. Michael wasn't there but this other chap was just about to set off to tour the shelters and took me with him. I asked if I could help in the shelters and they said 'Sorry, we haven't any women with us.' And I said 'But surely I could help, I've just done six months nursing and you're doing medical work.' So they told me that I could go back. The next evening I put on my nurses uniform and cap and went along to the FAU. They just wore ordinary clothes and were a bit scruffy. When I walked in they were having their evening meal and I had to walk up between the dining tables in my starchy apron. I felt terribly conspicuous, especially when someone said 'I don't think that apron will be very practical.' So I took that off and never put it on again.

Michael had mentioned that they were pacifists, that they disapproved of war. That removed an intense burden, to think there were others who felt as I did. I had this gut feeling that war was wrong. In the FAU there were all levels and brands of pacifism and gradually, talking to the others, I began to define my own position in relation to theirs. There were, for instance, those who refused to go on firewatching on the grounds that it would release somebody to go and fight. But anything that would save people from pain and destruction, I would do. As for wearing uniform when we went abroad, I remember thinking 'I couldn't care less what I wear. It is what I do that matters.' I didn't like those symbolic gestures. So really I was terribly relieved to find the FAU and would have been one of the first women in the Unit. I don't remember bothering to apply to join the FAU. As long as I could work with them, it never occurred to me to want to be a member. The men were much more conscious of belonging to something because they had been through the training camps. I don't think women's camps started for some time after I had started my shelter work. I can't remember ever being asked to go to a camp. Sometimes women say to me now 'What camp did you go to?' I have to say 'I never did.' Somehow it is part of my life pattern. I was always an outsider.

But I did have a tribunal and I remember putting a great deal of thought into what I wrote in my statement – this would have been about fifty/fifty Christian and humanitarian. I can't remember exactly where it was held – somewhere in London. I needed a witness and I was very impressed then by the tolerance of my father who was a retired and much-decorated Colonel in the army who came to witness that his daughter was sincere in her beliefs. I think he would have been appalled had his son been a CO, but since I wasn't behaving to his mind in a cowardly manner, and was making myself useful, I think he was quite proud of me. As I was already working with the FAU, I was directed to carry on.

I was pleased to have a tribunal, yes. It was rather like passing a driving test, being like all the others, to have the same status as the men. Had I been told to go into the forces, I would have refused and would have gone to prison if necessary. Tribunals were a subject of gossip: we all compared them. It was stressed that what they were after was sincerity of belief, not in fact what the beliefs were. How difficult it is to judge sincerity! I think tribunals were not keen on politically motivated pacifists, more inclined to tolerate religious bases. I also feel that it requires a lot of moral courage to be a pacifist, much more so if you're a man than if you're a woman – at least in that war. I do remember feeling embarrassed at times: my father had quite a large number of diplomatic acquaintances and most of their sons and daughters were serving in the forces. I was never accused of being a coward, but I do remember feeling embarrassed occasionally on his behalf.

Lilian Cadoux (Humble):

I know this sounds shocking, but I know others feel the same – I partly welcomed the war. It was going to bring excitement to our lives and I did have a romantic notion of everything to do with it because I thought: now I can do my bit. Florence Nightingale wasn't in it! I was on holiday in Eastbourne when war actually started. I had arranged to go sailing with a young man, so my initial reaction was 'Isn't that rotten. Now I shan't have my first sail.' The barbed wire went up immediately along the beaches and they were putting up the concrete blocks. Then came the blackout and more difficulties and the dancing had to stop.

I was never tempted to join the women's forces. Never. I knew if I joined up in any way it would be nursing. I wanted to join the VAD but there was a waiting list, so I joined the Civil Nursing Reserve and eventually went into full nursing training. It was whilst training in a hospital that my pacifism really emerged. I made friends with a girl called Olive Jarvis. One day she said to me 'Lilian, I have something to tell you, and when you know it you might not want to know me any longer.' I thought 'Oh dear, she's going to tell me she's pregnant.' But she said 'I'm a pacifist.' I said 'What are you worrying about, I think I am one myself.' For by this time I had read Vera Brittain and had thought a lot about the appalling waste in the Great War. Then I heard Vera Brittain speak in Edgeware and I hung on every word as if she was a high priestess.

Before long, Olive and I were of the age for call-up. We both knew about Friends and their work so we decided to leave the hospital and we presented ourselves to Friends Personnel Department – that is how I became accepted as an FRS member.

I was not called before a tribunal. A pity because I would have positively welcomed a chance to declare what I stood for. In fact I stayed up until two in the morning to write my statement: I was going to drag in the Treaty of Versailles and everything I knew – yes, I felt deprived of that opportunity to make my witness.

I worked in various hostels with the FRS in England and by and large had good relationships with the wardens and their wives, except for one thing – my frivolity. 'Oh Lilian, I *do* wish you wouldn't wear that lipstick' I remember one warden saying. And I am sure there was disapproval of my flighty attitude when I went out dancing – this would have been most unQuakerly. Well, I didn't particularly *want* to be Quakerly. I just wanted to work for a good pacifist organisation. So there was conflict there and in a way it's a pity that I didn't know about the FAU at that stage – it would have fitted me like a glove.

Towards the end of the war, I was getting more and more impatient as I so wanted to do relief work in Europe. With the FRS there had to be peace before we could go there in our Quaker grey, so I was very pleased when I was sent to Mount Waltham for relief training. At the end of the course I had to face a small panel of Friends where I was told that they were sorry but I was not considered suitable to be sent abroad because, not only had they received adverse reports by wardens of various hostels I had worked in, but it had been noted at Mount Waltham that I was out enjoying myself most evenings. I was far too taken aback to think of telling them that when I returned from my evenings out, I had typed up all my lecture notes and, as far as I knew, I was the only one to do this! It brought home the difference between me and the FRS, but

FAU Womens' Reunion, September 1985 at Barmoor, Yorkshire. Back Row, L to R: *Margaret Allen, Evelyn Connelly, Sue Carter, Jean Couper-Johnston.* Middle Row: *Vera Norgrove, Lilian Cadoux, Joan Hilling, Minnie Doherty, Hetty Budgen.* Front Row: *Dorothy Stapleton, Connie Bull, Freda Smith.*

all the same I was absolutely shattered. What was I going to do with my life?

By this time I had met Harold Cadoux on a training course, so I poured out all this utter, utter misery to him. He said 'What are you worrying about?' and said he didn't know why I was in the FRS in the first place, 'You can join the FAU.' So with a reference from Corder Catchpool, a friend of Harold's father, I was in the FAU in a very short time. I worked at Gordon Square for about six months until a place was found for me in a team in Germany and during that time got a good outline of the work the FAU were doing, working alongside some wonderful people.

FAU women were regarded as equal to men, completely. If a woman could drive, she would drive a heavy vehicle, just like a man. I hadn't been taught so I didn't, but I never had the slightest feeling that women were being relegated to the more traditional and boring jobs. In fact I was blissfully happy being in the FAU after the FRS. Quakers try so hard not to look disapproving, they look pained, and I had got fed up with people looking pained, and I honestly didn't mind a scrap about wearing khaki. I just wanted to get on with the job and the red crosses on my shoulder tabs were good enough for me. In Germany my attachment to the Unit developed even more; you had such a strong feeling of being part of this FAU family, and that's a feeling that has never left me.

Michael Rowntree:

I didn't come across women in the FAU until my time in Germany after the war. I don't think women went overseas in any strength until war had ended. With the civilian relief work in north/west Europe openings developed. By and large they were given the same work as men. But it would have been the job of the team leader to allocate jobs within the team and a note would have been taken of skills and attributes of different members, men and women. The general principle within the Unit was that anyone should be prepared and as far as possible able to take on any job within the sphere in which the team was working. Obviously women had some qualities that men hadn't and vice versa. I can see that in some cases they would be given different jobs than the men, but I don't think there would be any suggestion that they would be limited to being cooks or secretaries and suchlike. With civilian relief where you have large numbers of people in distressing circumstances there would be many situations where women would be judged more sympathetic to women refugees – this kind of thing. Basically the ethos of the Unit was to try to create situations where anybody – male or female – was in a position to do the same kinds of jobs.

REFERENCES:
(1) Women were not required to use lethal weapons, or take part in the use of such weapons, unless signifying in writing willingness to do so. See Braithwaite, C. *op. cit.* p.184.

CHAPTER 4

Hospital Work: 'Siberia', 'Super-heaven', and 'Jolly Good Hard-working Places'

'I found working in hospitals possibly the most interesting experience of my life, not even excluding China. The thing that staggered me was that I don't think I've ever been so tired in my life. I was at the peak of my fitness then but I was absolutely flaked out at the end of the day. We tried to be conscientious about learning for future use and we came away full of admiration for the nursing profession and the patients. I've never ceased to think that it's much the best education for anybody and what a pity that there wasn't conscription for certain services such as emptying bedpans and dustbins. To that extent I agree with Chairman Mao – that people who sit on chairs behind desks might reasonably be expected, now and then, to go off and do something dirty with their hands.'

David Morris

*T*HROUGHOUT THE WAR *hospital work became a major field of FAU activity providing a steady occupation of unquestionable usefulness both in gaining experience for work abroad and in helping to meet the acute shortage of staff. Numbers working in hospitals varied, rising and falling throughout the war according to competing claims on FAU personnel from the emergency services on the home front as well as demands from overseas.* (1) *In all, the Unit served in eighty-three hospitals in Britain: work in Gloucester, Bethnal Green and Arsley lasted for five years or more, others for shorter periods, some just to cover* *emergencies. Hospitals were classified into 'training' and 'working' hospitals, although the distinction was never a hard one. In the former, members were accepted for medical training in all departments while the latter consisted of the more menial work of orderlies, porters and manual tasks.*

In September 1941, a separate Hospital Office was set up at Gordon Square. Its first Executive Officer was Michael Cadbury – by then an old hand.

Michael Cadbury:

I started out in what we called the 'Siberia' of the Unit – Gloucester Hospital. This was said to be the worst place: if that didn't break you, nothing would. We worked in the City General Hospital which was an updated workhouse to which had been added ten huts as emergency wards. The patients in early 1941 were mainly civilian – old age and chronic patients and that made it tough. Portering was entirely done by the Unit. At this time – before the National Health Service started – there were three groups: the old poor law, the old voluntaries and the old civic hospitals; and those had to be blended together. The Unit was able to help in that coming together of those three, diverse, identities. We all learned a lot about administration. For me this was a wonderful new experience and a challenge because one saw people working in deadly dull conditions and we had a chance to *do* something. We were able, for instance, to develop occupational therapy: a lot of our men were skilled craftsmen and could help with this new concept of medical practice. We did a time-and-motion study, asking everyone to write down what they did all through the day – two minutes this, five minutes that. We made a good contribution there, there is no doubt of that!

We were up against quite a lot of hostility to start with, both from the City Council, and from within the hospital itself. One or two of the doctors refused to have us on their wards. One or two sisters made life hell for us 'shirkers.' But we expected that and got far less than one expected. Once they got the colour of our eyes, they were more understanding and knew that we weren't just shirkers, that we really wanted to help. That was the important thing that helped the Unit all the way through: we weren't running way from anything, we were trying to get *into* things.

My next hospital was Arsley, a different kettle of fish. It was a huge mental hospital in Bedfordshire, run by the Royal Free. It was a ladies' hospital run entirely by lady doctors, so to have male porters was quite something! We had a small team of about eight and we did the portering. It was a very isolated place and one of the things we did was to get these poor sisters and nurses into a gym team. Once they accepted that we were harmless, life became more interesting and fun.

After that it was Gordon Square in charge of the Hospital Office, looking after all the hospitals we were using for training. As more and more people came into the Unit, there was a great need for finding places for them because, at this stage, you couldn't get people out of the country. 'We'll do anything you want', we said. Usually we were taken as porters, but some hospitals, realising the calibre of the people sent, were willing to train them in theatre and other work. We were given extraordinary privileges. We were allowed to jump the queue and get into those jobs after a few months which was hard on regular nurses who had to grind away.

I touted around the LCC and Birmingham authorities and both were very cooperative. In London we had Mile End, Bethnal Green and Hackney hospitals and from these poverty-stricken areas we got our contacts with the shelters and the bombed areas. Some of the hospitals were in the front line – Chatham and Dover, for instance, were both very badly shelled; these were two very special sections. In Birmingham we got into three hospitals. We also went into Scotland: Bangour, the biggest hospital of all, was between Edinburgh and Glasgow and this is where they gave the best training of any we had – we were allowed on the theatre and able to learn a great deal. So much depended on the quality of the section leader: he had to win the confidence of the matron, doctors and staff and avoid the jealousy of nurses and sisters, for we were doing things they couldn't allow their own nurses to do.

A significant thing was that we were able to buck the very strict hierarchies existing in the hospital world then, because we were different: we were neither fish, fowl nor good red herring. We'd talk to doctors as their equals because many of us came from the same backgrounds. We'd tell a dictator of a matron that the way she treated her staff was terrible and would never be allowed in industry, that she'd never get the best out of them that way. She would be shocked. But sometimes one would take note – yes, we were able to get away with a lot because of our non-status status.

So Gloucester was 'Siberia', Bangour 'super-heaven', and the LCC and Birmingham were jolly good hard-working places. And all the stages in between these meant we learned an awful lot which paid dividends later on. Hospital service was an essential part of training: it was the only qualification we had to offer. We didn't come in as sergeants, sergeant-majors and officers. We came in as chaps who'd been through first aid, ambulance, and hospital training and it was that training which enabled us to do work all over the world.

Arising from its contact with many short-staffed hospitals, the Civilian Service Corps (CSC) was started from FAU headquarters. This was at a time when there was a long waiting list of FAU applicants awaiting training camp places alongside an increasing demand for medical orderlies. The FAU set up the CSC to recruit COs for such jobs, not as members of the FAU, but as paid employees:

Arthur Hinton:

I had applied to the FAU but was told that owing to its limited resources and long waiting list of applicants, there was no chance of my joining it for at least a year, but that it received requests from hospitals and other institutions for medical orderlies which it could not fill. So, after an interview at Gordon Square, I was offered a post as hospital orderly at the General Hospital, Ramsgate. I spent the next sixteen months at Ramsgate – one of a group of four COs who worked in the hospital and lived on the top floor of a house next to the hospital. This was luxurious living, two to a room, a bathroom and proper toilet, and the pay, after deduction for board and lodging and insurance, amounted to over £2 per week. I had never been so well off in my life and would not be again for several years. It was useful work but I hankered after something more active and re-applied to the FAU. I was called for an interview in May 1942 and was accepted for a training camp in July. I left Ramsgate, not without regrets for I had made several friends there and had gained much from the experience of working in a hospital.

David Rowlands:

I went down to the City General at Gloucester in the first party. On arrival we found six men in brown, rather greasy overalls and they were called 'Bone's boys'. They were COs and had been organised there by the Rev. Walter Bone, a Unitarian minister.[2] We realised that we were really going to be up against it in Gloucester because the matron hated COs and it was very clear from the start that she did, and most of the other people in the hospital seemed to be against us, so everything was done to humiliate us. We weren't allowed to go into the hospital at all, we were considered a lower form of life. My job was to collect and deliver the pig swill and to take the foul linen from the chronic wards. I had to drag this very soiled linen down to the laundry. Nothing like chutes, it had to be manhandled all the time. Another thing we had to do was to meet the tramps because they were allowed to doss for one night provided they did a job before they left in the morning. One of my jobs was to try to organise the tramps and get them to help push the heavy handcart, but they would just have a hand lightly applied to the handle of the cart while I had all the weight to push. I remember once being in the town with a load of pig swill on the handcart and a bearded tramp alongside and stopping at the traffic lights; who should be there, waiting in his large limousine, but a business friend of my father's. I hid my face in my chest lest he should see me.

The conditions of this workhouse hospital, where the chronics were housed, were truly Dickensian. I remember women, with pig netting over the top of the beds, clawing at the netting. This to me was horrific; and the fact that we were all depressed because of our unpopularity made it all very difficult. But we took it, we didn't complain and did everything that was asked of us, and people gradually began to come round. Bone's boys joined the FAU and we had quite a section there and reinforcements were brought down and the situation gradually improved. Over the months we got onto

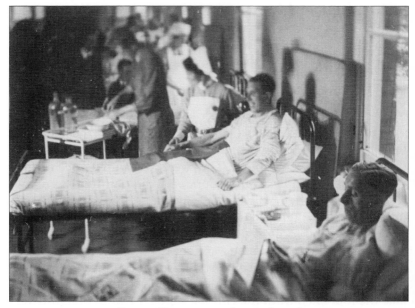

Sent to Gloucester – a hospital ward.

the wards and before I left we even had the admiration of the matron, which I would never have thought possible. I think that this was one of the greater challenges of the war because later on we were valued, but here, at the start, we certainly weren't and it was very depressing.

Ted Dunn:

Gloucester hospital? Yes, it had the reputation of 'being sent to Gloucester.' I was sent immediately after training from the 9th camp. There were about forty of us there – the largest section in the FAU. Our job was to do all the manual work from the basement to the wards. Most of my time was spent in one of the male chronic wards – they were incontinent and senile. Except for one sister, we staffed it. I remember one very cold night when about seven or eight died. I had to lay them out. I became quite blasé about it. I remember one nurse came up to me and asked me to stop with patients when they were dying. I said 'What for?' She was quite shocked that patients had died without anybody being with them. Later I saw her point, but at the time it never occurred to me.

This training gave us a knowledge of hospital work in general and built on the first aid we had done in Manor farm. The real training began when I was asked if I wanted to go to Ethiopia. Then, I went up to the Middlesex Hospital in London where a whole ward was taken over by the forty of us due for Ethiopia. We were sent out to various London hospitals for specialised training. One was the School of Tropical Medicine. I also went to the London Hospital's outpatients' department – really to keep my eyes open and learn. When we arrived in Ethiopia, we were given further training in the Menelik Hospital in Addis Ababa. All this added up to a wonderful experience for what I had to do later in Ethiopia.

Freddie Temple:

Once, when I was with the group at the Weymouth hospital, there was a pause in the ward and whoever it was on duty said 'Let's have some sausages and eggs.' So we cooked ourselves these and to our astonishment not only the sister, but the matron appeared and said 'Do orderlies cook themselves sausages and eggs in the middle of the night?' It made me realise it is always unwise to ask a rhetorical question. For one just replied 'It appears so matron, it appears so.'

I think we had a different position within hospital hierarchies: we did stand up to the matrons and others in authority more. This was due to our individualistic approach as well as the fact that we weren't, in the end, under their authority. It continued right through. I remember in the Tobruk hospital when working on nights; early in the morning we had to go around washing the patients. Water was always short and there were some black Cameroons and some white South Africans in the ward. I remember coming up to wash the white South African, and him saying 'not unless you've changed the water after that nigger!' So I just picked up the bowl and went on to the next and he didn't get washed that morning. It never happened again.

Paul Townsend:

After my initial training, I was told to go to the medical emergency hospital in Orpington. When I arrived there I was told to report to the sister on ward three – the genito-urinary ward. She was a real dragon. Donald Swann was in the the ward next door. We both wore a kind of ironmonger's coat with 'FAU' embroidered in red on the pocket. As Donald walked in on his first day, one of the patients looked up and read his front pocket 'FAU! What's FAU? Fuck All Use?' That was our little introduction.[3]

I worked very hard there. My major task in that ward was washing out people's bladders with silver nitrate solution; also doing bedpans and bed-making, sterilising equipment and suchlike. I was on very happy terms with the nursing staff – I never experienced unpleasantness or prejudice. After all we were very willing workers and people were in need of help.

Some of my duties stick in my memory: we had to bath a number of old chronic men every week. I had to bath about eight old gents, getting them into the bath, bathing them, and hauling them out, then dressing and returning them. I must say that brought me face to face at that stage in my life with things I'd never faced before.

There was also a great deal of joking and laughing. One joke – rather a bit of black humour – relates to one of these old chronics we had to bath. It was quite difficult getting them into the bath. I'm not terribly robust and I had to use the back of the bath as an inclined plane, rather like launching a ship. Well, this old gent had the most enormous scrotal rupture, and although normally I would have hoped to behave in a more tactful way, I was shocked and looked at it in a way that he noticed. 'Boy, you're noticing that. Do you know how I got it?' 'No Dad, I don't know how you got it' (we called these old men 'Dad'). He said 'I was entertaining of a thousand people with my leg round the back of me neck.' So that was that!

Hugo (Hugh) Powell:

Just before I went abroad, working with the Hadfield Spears Unit, they called me up to London during the blitz to work in the East End hospitals. I was working on the TB ward. It was very extraordinary, very Kafkaesque. Most of the patients were too poor to be treated properly elsewhere in proper sanatoria. They were simply dying there, with enormous mugs used as spitoons beside them. We emptied these regularly and they died regularly. That was one's job: looking after helpless old men with no families. This was a total change from my Art School world but I adapted to it very well and had all sorts of new experiences – in the operating theatre, for instance, although in a very menial role.

Very early on I found that I seemed to be good at coping with damaged people. I'm not saying that I was technically good at it, but I seemed to have a natural rapport with the patients and an ability to say the right things and to give comfort. I could also move wounded people and make them reasonably comfortable. Although I had to face some demanding situations abroad when working with the Hadfield Spears Unit, and the battle casualties were very different, this early experience proved very useful and gave some idea of what we would be up against.

Pip Turner:

I had joined the Red Cross in Harrogate before joining the Unit and had done about fifty hours in the local hospital; so I had some nursing experience before going into the Unit. But once in the FAU, I did six weeks at the Hackney Hospital, working in outpatients. From there I went to an Emergency Medical Service, EMS, hospital at Lichfield and worked in a pre-fab in the grounds of a large hospital. I was the 'dirty nurse' in the operating theatre – the one that removed and carried out the parts that had been extracted and washed the gloves and cleaned up. I was known to be a CO, but we were all doing the same job and nobody minded. I think some of the men might have had an aggressive response from some of the nurses. I think that the issue of being considered a coward applied to men rather than women. People always talked to each other more during the war, and if I was travelling on a train, say, and said that I was a nurse in a London hospital, people respected that. Whereas a man would have got a different response: why wasn't he at the front? They regarded women as brave simply to be in the London area nursing, whereas the men would be regarded as cowards because they *were* nursing.

Lewisham Hospital: after the flying bomb.

Stephen Verney:

The hospital work I did in England before joining the Hadfield Spears Unit varied from carrying corpses down to the mortuary to shaving the pubic hairs of men about to have operations – this scared them considerably as it was done with an open, cut-throat razor. Of course later on in the Hadfield Spears Unit, when dealing with war casualties in Syria and Tobruk, I was doing much more. I can remember giving an enema to a French Captain, who looked over his shoulder with some alarm at this rather inexperienced-looking Englishman, saying 'Doucement, mon brave, doucement.' (Gently, my good chap, gently).

I remember one terrible moment when I was giving an anaesthetic with chloroform on an open mask, which would strike horror into the heart of anybody today. We started with chloroform and went on to ether. I was told that after a bit the man would stop coughing and that would be a sign to me that he'd gone under.

Well, he went on coughing and I went on pouring the stuff onto his mask. Suddenly the surgeon leapt up and said 'His blood's gone black!' We whipped the mask off and the patient was purple in the face and spluttering at the mouth and gasping between life and death. The doctor, who didn't usually pray, cried 'Jesus Christ, save us now!' and started pummelling his lungs and giving an injection into his heart, trying to get him breathing again. As a last resort he got a blunt instrument and pushed it up his arse. The man went 'Oooh!' and started to breathe again. The next morning he was perfectly alright and never knew the hazards he'd been through under my unskilled hands.

Alan Taylor:

It was whilst working at the Lewisham Hospital that a flying bomb fell right onto the administrative block right between two wards and demolished the three floors there. In fact casualties were light but all patients were evacuated from the whole block of six wards. Most seriously, in the middle of the part damaged and now on fire was the dispensary in which we had a whole stock of oxygen, carbon dioxide and nitrous oxide cylinders. These were now dangerously exposed and liable to go off like shells if overheated. Three of us cleared them from the fire. We got recognition for this with a British Empire Medal. They didn't want to offer this award only to have me turn it down, so they wrote first asking whether I, as a CO, would accept it. I could see there were arguments on both sides: one shouldn't accept awards from a government one didn't agree with; on the other hand, I did feel a bit of natural pride. And it was a little demonstration that COs and cowards are not synonymous.

Looking back, I think the FAU hospital experience gave a wide experience of nursing and outpatient treatment as well as pharmacy work. It stood me in very good stead in my later medical training and then, as a doctor, I appreciated more what nurses and other ancillary staff had to do. In fact it was my FAU hospital experience which had inspired me – as it did many others – to become a doctor. And it gave me a better appreciation of the patients' attitudes too. The profession can be very hierarchical and it is all too easy to be the doctor and order what's best for the patient without realising some of the thoughts going on in the patients' minds.

At one time during the war the Medical Research Council appealed for volunteers for the guinea pig scheme. Six of us went to the National Hospital for Nervous Diseases in Queens Square. The project was under Professor Carmichael who was working on acclimatisation and heatstroke. There was also another project under Dr. Harry Platt, a nutritionist.

We had a 'tropical room' erected in one of the big wards and we lived in this for three days at a time when various experiments were done: there was one on our blood volume – we were injected with a dye and they assessed the volume of our blood. We had an operating table on which we lay for long periods until we were totally relaxed, and then we were tipped up and the pooling of the blood made all except one of us faint. We wore a big metal boot which measured the increased flow of fluid to the leg. We were also at times given extra plasma to try and vary our blood volume during experiments.

We also did work on a treadmill; and another was carrying heavy weights up and down stairs with big bags attached so that gas analysis could be done and our oxygen consumption measured. There was an experiment in which we were immersed in sea water to check effects of the salt and of the cold. This was the time when the development of wet suits was starting.We also did some work on sleeplessness: after doing agility and coordination tests until we were trained to a peak, we were kept awake for seventy-two hours. The interesting thing was that despite not even nodding off at all during that period, our agility and coordination improved over the whole period.

On the nutrition front: we lived for weeks on a controlled diet of salt-free, dried food to which vitamin B was added.

Nothing was ever explained to us in detail – a pity really, as we'd have liked to have been put in the picture. As for discomfort: living in that tropical room and being tilted up until you fainted was the most uncomfortable, but I wouldn't call it suffering. I remember though, whilst working in the Hammersmith Hospital I was rather shanghaied into having one of the early cardiac catheters inserted into my heart. I remember a great furore about this because the doctor who was responsible for the Unit people there found out about it and was very incensed.

Doug Turner:

There were quite a few projects in which COs cooperated with the medical authorities. I know some of our members helped with medical research on malaria and typhus with Dr. Kenneth Mellanby. Some of us were guinea pigs. There was a project involving starvation where the guinea pigs went into residential establishments where they were put onto very severe diets. There was another one concerned with scabies and other diseases then occurring. I took part in one concerning the yellow fever vaccine. Apparently the American authorities were concerned because the vaccine was causing deaths among their forces. I was injected with the vaccine and then had weekly check-ups under control conditions and I had a letter of appreciation when it was finished. I think COs volunteered because we wanted to express our pacifism creatively and we could do this by contributing towards the health of *all* people. After all yellow fever is not just a disease affecting soldiers – it has a civil bearing as well.

Angela Sinclair-Loutit:

While I was working at the Archway Hospital, some of us volunteered as human guinea pigs. One experiment was to do with the effects of living on lifeboat biscuits. We were given as many as we wanted. We could heat them up with hot water or eat them dry, but we could not eat anything else. I lived on them for about a week. I did get quite hungry and very fed up with the biscuits which are something like digestives – neither sweet nor salt. Then I took part in a malaria experiment. For this we had to go twice a week to laboratories at Reading where we were bitten by malaria-carrying mosquitoes. We were given a glass jar covered with a piece of gauze with about twenty mosquitoes flying around inside. We were told to take off our stockings and hold the jar to an area where its mouth covered the flesh of the thigh. These mosquitoes, by then starved and very hungry, bit through the gauze. You could see them swell up with blood. This was done for about fifteen or twenty minutes until enough of them had a bite. Then some of us were given the proper treatment tablets and some given controls. Some of the guinea pigs got malaria but I never did. I didn't care, I was prepared to get malaria. I was only too delighted to do what a lot of other people didn't dare do.

COs were anxious to do that sort of work for the same reasons as mine. At the Archway Hospital there was a certain amount of resentment against me because other trainees weren't allowed to do midwifery until state registration, and they didn't see why we in the FAU should be allowed to. There was also one old char there who somehow discovered that I was a CO and she did her best to make life hell for me. She went around the patients muttering about me. I felt so miserable at times because of this old woman that I dreaded going to work in the morning. Then one day a News Chronicle journalist came and asked to see the nurses-cum-guinea pigs. It was a nice sunny morning and Susie Carter and I went outside and had our pictures taken on the lawn. The next day there we were on the front page of the News Chronicle with the story about the nurses who undergo nasty experiments. When the patients saw it they said 'Is this you nurse?' and when I said 'yes' they were very impressed. I was completely thrilled inside because I never heard one more word from that char.

One of the main forms of FAU activity in the First World War had been service on ambulance trains. There was very limited opportunity for such work in the Second World War: in 1944, just after the Normandy invasion, a section was sent to Godalming to serve on an ambulance train with casualties from across the Channel. Earlier, in the crisis winter of 1940/41, a team of eight men waited with their ambulance train for orders.

Stephen Peet:

The purpose of the trains was to evacuate hospitals from one part of England to another; especially all east coast hospitals in order to make space for casualties if the invasion took place. Our train had been carrying fish and our job was to scrub it out and re-paint it; then racks were built both sides to hold the stretchers. In September 1940, when the invasion was expected, we were suddenly sent to a hospital near Chelmsford. We got the patients out of the ward on stretchers and into the train, and off we went across the country. It was all very sudden and hadn't been organised with food and drink. I remember we had some emergency rations and at 6am the train came to a halt near a bridge and the hospital doctor commandeered food from a nearby village. Thankfully, none of the patients were seriously ill and our main task was trying to keep them warm and fed and dealing with bed pans and suchlike. We went right across England and unloaded the hospital in Bradford. When we arrived in our filthy overalls, the mayor was there to greet us and we were given a sort of banquet meal in a posh hotel.

After this the train moved to a siding in Newmarket station and just sat awaiting orders. We made ourselves useful to the billeting officers for London evacuees, going around the various houses and estates looking for possible places for the bombed out Londoners. The ignorance of some of the people in the big houses was really incredible. I remember one woman who had had about twelve or fourteen servants. 'Your chauffeur's cottage above the garage, has it got a lavatory?' 'I expect so.' 'Has it got a bathroom?' 'I don't know.'

I wrote a letter to *The Times* suggesting that these trains should be turned into mobile rest centres 'instead of herding weary home-less into large and vulnerable halls' I wrote ' to put them into these trains with their salved belongings and move them before the next night to pre-selected evacuation areas where billets might be available. Then the train at its destination can be used as sleeping quarters and HQ until everyone is settled in.' There you are, letter in *The Times*, nothing done about it, but I did my best. Strange: 'the "salved" belongings!' October 1940, exactly fifty years ago. Very strange to see yourself using a word you don't even know!

REFERENCES:

(1) In August 1940, 230 members were working in hospitals. The number remained at about 200 until mid 1944 when, with overseas service a priority, they fell by June 1945 to 60.

(2)   Walter Bone was on the Methodist lay preaching circuit when he heard
of Quakers and become one. During the First World War, he served
at the front with the FAU. When there seemed no possibility of working
full time for the Society of Friends he trained to be a minister in the
Unitarian Church. Gloucester and Nailsworth Monthly Meeting
wouldn't accept his transfer certificate and he remained a member of
Cape Town meeting until his death in 1944. At that time he was
running hostels for the troops in Alexandria, Egypt. A life-long
objector to vaccination, he died of smallpox; an outspoken pacifist,
he had a full military funeral.

(3)   Another version, FAU – 'Futile And Useless' was coined by the
Registrar at Broadgreen Hospital Liverpool, according to FAU
member Alfred White. At Gloucester, a member gave the flippant
response 'Free and unattached' when asked by a nurse (Brian Bone).

CHAPTER 5

The Blitz: All Together Now

'I was working in the docks area in the middle of the blitz. It was hectic at that time – the ambulances coming in and out, driving through all the mayhem. I was so impressed with the East Enders and their support for each other – it was very striking indeed. Outside too, one noticed travelling around a completely different atmosphere. For a little while we all became completely un-English.'

Bernard Fisher

WHEN THE FAU was re-formed in 1939, the expectation was that its work would be mainly in the ambulance field, and in France. As time went on, keen and trained men were being turned out of Northfield aching for worthwhile work. But in the 'phoney war' period, apart from an opportunity opening up with the Finnish 'winter war', * *there was still no signs of need in France or elsewhere. What was to be done with the trained and keen young men? It was decided that the Unit must be held together at all costs and that members should be occupied in a useful and creative way, for sooner or later the call would surely come. Paul Cadbury with his business and government connections was very important at this stage, and there is no doubt that a lot of Cadbury and Rowntree money went into keeping the Unit together and getting it moving. The scheme for further training and work in hospitals helped enormously – indeed, hospitals, as we have seen, were the great standby, especially in this early period. Also, in off-duty hours, valuable social*

---

* See Chapter 6.

work was undertaken by Unit members. Professional teachers, for instance, soon found work with the free-range children who had missed evacuation and whose schools were now closed. Others helped in boys' clubs and the demand was such that a few members left hospital duty for full time social work.

All this helped to fill the vacuum created by the phoney war. But by the spring of 1940, many were getting restless and morale was reported to be at an all time low. Feedback from the Finnish group of their adventures and experiences only served to heighten frustration in those aching for action. A report to the FAU Council at this time reads: 'There is a very natural spirit of frustration and dissatisfaction amongst those members who are trained and for whom no opportunities of work have opened up.'

This is when John Bailey and Freddie Temple – 'the two bishops' as they were known – were given the job of going around the different sections with the brief of assessing the mood and morale of the men.

Freddie Temple:

This was a very interesting job. We met lots of people in hospitals or wherever they were. We found a lot of unease and restlessness during the phoney war period because they had all joined up with the great purpose of doing things and they were trained up and ready to go. So there were lots of grumbles about inactivity, also it seemed to me that the spiritual side was lacking. I don't think Paul Cadbury really understood this. He had dealt with it rather as he would have done if the work side of Cadburys had been discontented. You know, 'how do we keep them quiet?' So there were grumbles about democracy and about the running of the Unit – the old problem of the centre being out of touch with the grassroots. But, yes, when it came to it, the centre *did* listen when we reported back: we were always given a good hearing.

John Bailey:

We found that what the sections wanted, above all, was autonomy: to be able to make their own decisions. And the Executive Council worked out a scheme whereby they were granted autonomy in all but top-level decisions. In that way we evolved our democratic ethos which developed apace as the war went on. But at this stage of the phoney war, we found that very few of the men felt completely happy with their positions. But then, on 7 September 1940, the London blitz! And there was the FAU, bang in the middle of the East End, right in the thick of it.

The Unit reaction was swift: it was quickly agreed that the FAU should embark on relief work. By the end of the first week twelve men were at work in Rest Centres, and by the end of the year, two-hundred members were engaged in air raid relief work. Early on, the practice of carrying out detailed surveys, based on first hand information, was started, the aim being to encourage official action. This continued throughout Unit relief work at home and abroad. Working in close cooperation with the LCC, the FAU continued its work in the London hospitals – but now dealing with blitz casualties and evacuating patients and some hospitals. The Unit also provided teams to work in shelters: improving conditions, serving food, drink, first aid and providing entertainments.

The setting up and manning of Rest Centres for bombed out Londoners became a major task: by the end of 1940 the Unit had provided staff for ten Rest Centres, working on alternate twenty-four hour shifts. These were spread throughout London – in the East End, Stoke Newington, Westminster, Paddington, Battersea and Deptford; and in the provinces, when the raids spread out from London. One of the Unit's main jobs was preparing the centres. This meant squads of carpenters, painters and cleaners arriving to clean out whatever building had been found; then planning the accommodation, arranging the structure and getting whatever furniture, beds and blankets into place ready for the bombed-out Londoners. The demand was very heavy in the autumn and early winter of 1940/41 when the raids were at their peak, and there were still eight in working order at the end of 1941. The Unit also played its part in fire-watching, providing mobile canteens and running communal homes for evacuees in relatively safe areas of the city. When the raids first started, the Unit found that it had great freedom of action, but as the London authorities began to organise and assert themselves, this was gradually attenuated.

Tom Barnsley:

My move to London coincided with the first bombs dropped on the city. I was actually going towards the Mile End Hospital when the first bomb fell between Hackney and Bethnal Green. After that it was all hell let loose and it lasted for the next six to nine months. We saw terrible casualties in the East End hospitals – that was a real initiation into death and destruction. At that time there would have been a couple of hundred of us in London. I think the FAU must take a lot of credit for the influence it had on the LCC in organising the air raid shelters. Many were situated in the tubes where locals would flock down at night. Also we played a big part in setting up and running the Rest Centres which were created in converted schools and parish halls. Relief was totally unknown in the First World War and therefore had not been planned for in any way. So that was both a very useful further training and a very positive feeling that 'Right. This is now the civilian population.' And strangely, I felt that it was the involvement of the civilian population which tempered and in some ways changed the view of the average civilian towards the pacifist. They began to recognise that it wasn't a cowardly conchie, but someone quite different who was dashing about the streets: helping, collecting, feeding, comforting, binding wounds, driving, digging in the rubble to bring people out. These people refused to fight. OK. But what they were doing proved that they weren't dodging the danger, that they weren't cowards. From then on, I certainly got the feeling, whether it was working with the military direct as we did later, or with the civil authorities, that we were looked up to and respected as people who had unusual personal views but were getting on with the job to sort out the mess of war.

Angela Sinclair-Loutit:

I was allocated to a group of three people who visited the shelters in parts of Stepney. We carried little Red Cross bags with cough mixtures, aspirin and sticking plaster in it. I don't know how much we really helped those people. Really we were reassuring nervous people, and those who had left their homes bringing their little children to safety. The FAU ran a canteen bringing cups of tea and

'I can see the spirit of an unquenchable people.'
(Winston Churchill 12/4/41)

Tin hats at the ready: all together now!

sandwiches. I remember talking to people but must have been a dead loss at first because I couldn't understand their cockney accents and often didn't know what they were talking about.

We had a base which was in a condemned school – a very bleak place. And we'd go there after the all-clear went and we had finished our shelter rounds. It was then that I started smoking because of the great camaraderie between people; it seemed vital to have a packet in my pocket so that I could offer them around. Some of the conditions in the shelters were awful: no sanitation, often no heating provided so people got charcoal braziers and the smell of sulphur fumes was frightful – so cigarettes were a protection against these. The air raid wardens were very friendly; they looked on us as rather weird people coming from quite outside their world. Stepney was a world of its own, and the FAU certainly were not Stepney people.

Cable Street ran right through the area I worked in. On the north side were the Jews who had shops along the Commercial Road, and on the south side were the Irish who had originally dug the dock. They divided like oil and water. They were entirely different and this was reflected in the way they kept their shelters.

I remember the Jewish shelter which was beautifully whitewashed, well equipped, with little fold-up cafe tables, a very properly run canteen where people paid tuppence for a cup of tea – very well organised, very clean. But I remember going into that shelter (which wasn't on my beat) at the moment the sirens had gone, and a huge groan went up and the people were really scared. I don't remember anything like it in the Irish shelter, they were much more jolly, but the organisation and cleanliness nothing like the Jewish shelter.

One very vivid memory I have of the blitz: this was in Wapping. I think it was Metropolitan Wharf, one of the big ones along Wapping High Street. One night there had been a bad raid and there were more than a thousand people in the shelter. Suddenly there was a little stream of water coming into the shelter. We went to look. It was like a plumbing leak in a house. Somebody said that a bomb must have exploded in the river and somehow pierced the wall. It was not a great gaping hole, but it was coming steadily into the shelter and there seemed no way of stopping it.

The FAU workers had responsibility for this shelter and it fell to me to decide, as the water rose up the wall, whether to get the people out or not. I mean they could all be drowned like rats. But the bombs were still falling outside, so it was the devil and the deep blue sea – what to do? It wasn't too long before morning and we knew the planes would go if we held on. So we waited and the water did in fact come up to the table top level. We were all climbing on tables to keep dry. People behaved very well, there was no panic, but it was very frightening.

Then there was another huge raid in March 1941 on another wharf. It was the raid where the fires burnt the longest afterwards, for about four or five days. Quite early in the night somebody brought in a fireman who had fallen off a ladder and injured himself and he was obviously in pain. We all decided that he should go to hospital but that he'd have to wait for the all-clear. But this man said 'No, I don't want to go to hospital, my wife will think I've disappeared in the raid.' There was a phone number and I promised that I would get a message to his wife and ran out of the shelter to do this. As I ran down the street where the phone box was, it was a most extraordinary sight: people forget that unless there was a moon, it was really dark with blackout. But the street was gleaming like when snow has fallen, and it was soaking wet – this was foam from beer which was flowing down the street. And it was all lit with a lovely pink glare from a house on fire with flames shooting up above three storeys, which I passed. It was very useful for me because those flames lit up the phone box so well that I could see perfectly easily to dial. Another miracle was that the phone worked and I was able to get a message through to his wife. I won't forget that night – 360 points of the compass, lights everywhere from the fires.

Stephen Peet:

Two of us had film projectors and when we were on day duty at London Hospital we borrowed Charlie Chaplin and other films and went around the shelters where the FAU were working and gave film shows. It was then suggested that I should make a film about the FAU. I had a camera and the projector and did it over the first few months of 1941. I went all over the country filming little sequences of what the FAU were doing. One of the places I filmed was in what was called a 'model air raid shelter' in the city of London. This was a show place to show just what could be done to help people in permanent residence in an air raid shelter. In general, we were doing things to keep morale up: we helped organise concerts, we had dances and games and posters on the walls, and a first aid room. And by chance, the FAU man on duty was Patrick Barr, later to become a well-known film and theatre actor – his one unpaid part![1]

Then one night I was on duty there myself. This was during the second biggest raid of the war, in May 1941, when all the buildings around St. Paul's were on fire. We had to evacuate all the shelterers because the wardens came and said that the whole building above us was burning. So we went to another shelter down the street and during that night moved three times. At one of these shelters, the warden came down and said to me 'Come with me, it's fantastic!' And, very stupidly really, I went up on the roof of the building and saw what looked like some of those famous wartime photographs: firestorms around St. Paul's. All around the city, fires were burning, and there was St. Paul's in the middle of all the flames and smoke, and with planes still flying over. It was an unforgettable scene. Walking back from there to the students' hostel, first through the city of London and then out to the East End, through all that devastation and broken glass and burning buildings – it was unbelievable and awful.

We were one of many groups working in the shelters. People were brought together by common difficulties during these raids, the spirit was wonderful. I remember vividly the conversation of two old women in Stepney. Posters had gone up saying 'Bomb Berlin!' I don't know who put them up, maybe it was just graffiti, but I was most moved hearing one of these old women saying 'Y'know, I don't hold with this bombing of Berlin business; it's bad enough being bombed here, but to think of it happening to other people is awful...' I thought this quite extraordinary.

Then I worked in what we called an evacuation centre. This was a huge house in High Barnet, and it was set up as an experiment for bombed out families from East or West Ham. We ran that – about four or five of us. There were eighty-five people in that one house. Usually a family or two families in the big rooms and everybody ate communally. The idea was to get people out and away and the breadwinners were still able to travel to work but live as a family. Running it was a very demanding job: who lives in which room? Who looks after the chickens in the garden? Organising the sittings for meals. I don't know how successful it was as an experiment. Somehow I don't think it could have been, otherwise other large houses would have been commandeered in London for the same task. But we tried.

Brenda Bailey (Friedrich):

My job was to look after the children in the air raid shelters. Most of the children were evacuated but some didn't like where they were sent and came back, and some families didn't want their children away in strange places. So generally an FAU man and woman would go to all the air raid shelters. I was usually in Wapping. There were about nine shelters in the warehouses – all the different warehouses had their own distinctive smells – I vividly remember one in a spice warehouse. We had first aid kits and doled out aspirins and band aid and we had an ambulance service and a doctor we could call on. We were really there to encourage the social life that was developing in shelters and to provide activities for the children, so they weren't too much of a nuisance to the adults; and we'd sort out any problems occurring between different families.

Halfway along the shelter round was a floating wharf of the Port of London Authority, and we generally used to go down there for a short breather. It was lovely to get down to the water level and to talk to the lighter man, and watch the searchlights overhead criss-cross the black sky in the most amazing way. Occasionally, you would see a plane being brought down; sometimes, during dog-fights between British and German planes, you'd see pilots falling down in parachutes. There was an eerie feeling about Wapping High Street in the moonlight: the stark moonlight against one side of the warehouse and the deep, deep shadows on the other side – I could almost paint it. Very often at the end of my shelter round we would stop off at the Prospect of Whitby, which was the first time I had ever been to a pub or seen anyone drink alcohol. But a lovely fraternity developed between all the people in that area and for years after I would go down there and somebody in the street would say 'Hi Brenda!' It was a very warm feeling.

It was while I was working in that area that I heard about my father, Leonhard Friedrich, being interned in Buchenwald. I was walking along Hackney High Street and had just opened the Red Cross letter. I cried all the way. My FAU colleagues were very understanding, but everybody had hard stories in those days, so it was nothing exceptional really. At least I knew that my parents were alive in Germany, and many Jewish children I knew had left their parents behind and didn't know what had happened to them

Tom Haley:

As a result of the terrific bombing, many people were rendered homeless. The FAU decided that it would be a good idea to open up certain buildings as Rest Centres for the homeless. They took over Mansford Street School in Bethnal Green, which was about 200 yards from where I was born and lived my young life. I was in the team that first opened this rest centre and when the raids started, the survivors would be directed to us and we'd receive them and hand them blankets and bed them down wherever we could. At that time we didn't have any beds, but we had a supply of stretchers which were made with a kind of strong wire in about an inch mesh between the handles which people sometimes used as beds in their extremity. We also had arrangements with places like Lyons to supply food.

People would come in shocked and distressed because they'd lost members of their family or their neighbours, and their places had been bombed down around their ears – this would be in an area, remember, where there were hundreds and hundreds of houses cheek by jowl. After a few days with us, doing our best for them, they would get to contact their own relatives and make arrangements to get out of this temporary place; or the authorities would find somewhere for them. If they had to stay longer, then they'd come to us and say 'Right, can we help you to cater for those coming in?' So they came round and found their strength again – resilience is the word.

Then the authorities hit on the idea to put their own team in to staff the place, so we became redundant. So off we went to another school in Bow, also in the East End, and we did the same thing there: opened up the place, got the routine going and then, again, the authorities stepped in and put their own staff in. So that was very, very useful work.

This was a very busy and satisfying time: we all worked very hard and very long hours. But it was the sheer amount of death and destruction that one could see as a result of the air raids, that made me convinced that here was proof that I was never going to be a part of causing this kind of mayhem, because what was happening to us was obviously happening to the Germans. Even more strongly than ever, I was sure and determined that I would never be a part of this. At the same time I was very grateful for the opportunity to be able to help relieve the dreadful suffering that was going on. After all, if my tribunal had said 'We believe this man is a traitor to England, and should be shot' then I would have been shot and there would have been no chance of doing good in some form of another.

This was worthwhile service, but I wanted more. What I really wanted was to get where the action was. Although I felt that I ought to do as much as I could to alleviate suffering, I also felt that there was no way in which, as a CO, I should be free of the difficult situation which the armed forces were in when they had to actually go and face the enemy. Although I wouldn't be armed like them, at least I wouldn't feel that I was hiding in the background or doing something in a safe place. I wanted to prove that I could go where it mattered, and wasn't afraid – I was afraid really, but I was prepared to go in wherever I was sent and hoped that would be in a war atmosphere. The most difficult thing to get across to the people who didn't understand my position was the issue of cowardice. Therefore it seemed to me necessary to prove that cowardice had nothing to do with it. So when a notice went up saying that the FAU was considering sending an expedition to China to work with the Chinese Army, my name was the first on it.

REFERENCES:

[1] There were several 'model shelters' run by by the FAU, which were designed as experiments to show how shelters could be well run. The one under Lloyd's in the city of London attracted a lot of media attention and several of its innovations were introduced in other shelters. Another, in Derbyshire Street, was chosen as one of the shelters to be visited by the King and Queen on their East End tour during the summer of 1941. Stephen Peet continued filming after the war. He won critical acclaim with the BBC documentary series 'Yesterday's Witness', which he devised and produced.

PART TWO

GO ANYWHERE, DO ANYTHING

CHAPTER 6

Finland and Norway: We Became Veterans

'The crises brought about by the blitz helped a great deal to provide worthwhile service. But, although this did occupy a considerable portion of our manpower, it didn't satisfy the whole group many of whom thought "this is all very well working with civilian operations, but we were recruited to help those also involved with the fighting. Where is the fighting?"'

Michael Cadbury

THROUGHOUT THE WAR, many Unit members were content to remain on the home front, preferring to keep aloof from the military and providing useful relief and humanitarian services as the need arose. Others were keen to serve overseas and, although accepting that this could only happen under broad military control, insisted on a civilian setting. But there was also a sizeable group which, like Tom Haley, had a strong urge to be in the thick of fighting. They had joined the FAU hoping for and anticipating 'the arduous and the dangerous', to 'go anywhere and do anything' as their slogan – GADA – explained, and for many this meant accepting attachment to military units and working under direct military discipline. If the Unit's purpose was the relief of suffering caused by conflict, then surely proximity to the battlefield was essential. Reasons were often more complex: mixed with the straightforward urge to share the suffering of battle was the need to face danger and risks in order to end the feeling of segregation from society which their CO status imposed. Linked with this, was the anxiety not to be labelled a coward: members felt the need to justify themselves, not only in their own eyes, but in the eyes of family, friends and society.

One might well ask: since these active young pacifists were so keen to work with the army, why didn't they join a Non-Combatant or Medical Corps as other pacifists in uniform had done? Why go to all the trouble, as Roy Ridgway had, to register as a CO, appear before an unsympathetic tribunal, and then have his appeal turned down, with a sentence of three months hard labour, only to enter the FAU and work there in the Hadfield Spears Hospital Unit with tough, forward fighting Free French units in Italy and France? But as Ridgway explained: 'I wanted to make the choice myself. My conscience made me volunteer for the FAU.' For him and other like-minded men, to join the army even as a non-combatant would have meant violating their deeply held convictions.

During the phoney war period, the FAU Executive Committee was working hard and using every possible connection to find openings for the Unit. Disappointments abounded as one hopeful scheme after another fell through. Then, on 1 December 1939, the 'winter war' between Russia and Finland started and it was during this war that the Unit actually gained its first experience of working alongside fighting troops overseas.

FINLAND

On 12 December the FAU volunteered to send, under the aegis of the British Red Cross Society, a contingent of twenty ambulances, together with kitchen cars, a repair car and manned by nearly sixty FAU men. Surmounting enormous obstacles of bureaucracy, organisation and funding, Alan Dickinson and Michael Mounsey made history as the first Unit members in the Second World War to leave the country. To their great satisfaction and relief they were welcomed in Finland with the news that they could work at the front under Finnish army direction.

On 18 January, the first half of what became known as the 'Finnish Convoy' set off from Newcastle on the SS Iris, leaving their vehicles to be shipped later. They met up with Dickinson and Mounsey in Bergen, and after a frustrating delay of three weeks waiting for their ambulances, a small section of the first party, led by Richard Early, set off through Norway, Sweden into Leppasyrja, their destination in Finland. The remainder of the first party, under Oswald Dick, followed on, joining the

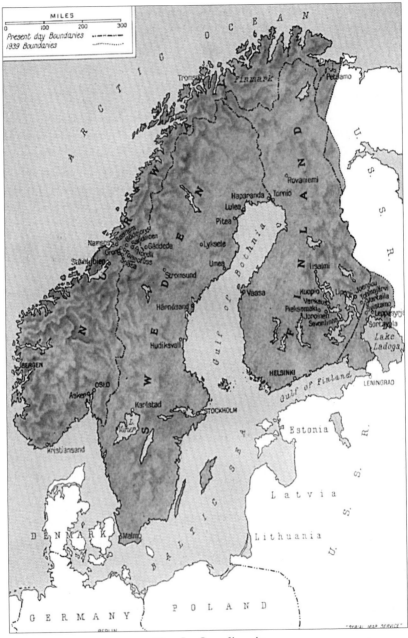

Map I – Scandinavia.

advance party at Leppasyrja on 2 March 1940. The party then divided into three groups for work on the Lagoda front. Richard Early with fourteen members worked in the HQ area and were kept busy ferrying wounded to the Casualty Clearing Stations and first aid posts, often coming under attack themselves. The second group under Ralph Smith, were based in the Soanlahti area, and had rather less to do. The third group, under Alan Dickinson, moved to a base further north and, of the three groups, had the busiest time, coping with lots of casualties.

Just as the Unit was getting into its work and feeling that it was at last giving the service for which it had been trained, peace broke out. But this was a peace without rejoicing, because the area in which the Unit was working, the Karelian isthmus, was now ceded to Russia under the terms of the peace. For a further five weeks the FAU, first based at Joensuu, and then at Liperi, and still responsible to the Finnish army, remained to help transport civilians and wounded soldiers from the area. On 25 March the second party, under Brandon Cadbury, arrived in Finland to join in the task of evacuation of civilians into recognised Finnish territory.

Michael Rowntree:

As we crossed from Newcastle to Bergen, we got our first real taste of the more tragic side of war when the ship picked up some survivors from a Danish ship that had been torpedoed. Arriving in Bergen, I was greatly impressed, having got used to our blackout, seeing all the lights blazing. We then caught a train to Oslo where we waited until our ambulances arrived; these had been transported on a separate ship which had been frozen into the ice off Kristiansand. During this time we were taught to ski by Norwegian students from the university who were passionately pro-Finn and anxious to help. This came in very handy in Finland as we used skis to get around in the woods. Well, eventually our ambulances turned up and off we went to Stockholm where I celebrated my twenty-first birthday by drinking milk in a Salvation Army hostel. We then drove further north through Tornio and down into Finland to Savonlinna where we were dispersed into various groups and sent out to work with the Finnish Army. I was in a small group, living in a dugout in the snow, in the forest about three kilometres from the Russian lines.

Our work was transporting Finnish casualties back to the base in Savonlinna. Driving back on one occasion, we had our first experience of being bombed by a Russian plane. There weren't many casualties on the front where I was stationed – I probably didn't see more than twenty or thirty during my time there. That winter of '39/40 was intensely cold; our dugout was freezing, we had a wood-burning stove in it which was a bit of a fire hazard but at least it kept the dugout warm. This only lasted for about two or three weeks because peace was declared after that.

We were in the Karelia area which the Russians annexed at the end of the war. Most of the Finns chose to leave their homes and move back into the mainland rather than take their chances with the Russians, so we stayed on for another month or so transporting refugees and their possessions in our ambulances. We also carried a number of Russians prisoners too. I remember one injured prisoner whom I was able to converse with because of my bit of German. He was actually a Sudeten German who had been attracted by Russian propaganda before the war and was now in the Red Army. Oddly enough, he had a married sister living in Birmingham!

Looking back on the Finnish expedition, this must have cost a lot of money at home: we raised twenty-odd ambulances and we were kept and resourced, and really our contribution was very slight. Having said that, I think we did greatly by the Finns because they tended to think theirs was a forgotten war and they really seemed to appreciate the fact that Britain had sent an ambulance unit. I doubt that many of them distinguished between us as a pacifist unit and a British government operation – it was just that *Britain* had come to their help. So, although the help we gave was slight, it was worthwhile. Certainly from our point of view it boosted our morale because at the time we felt that we were doing something useful. Also we enjoyed it: we were young, it was unusual and exciting and not too horrendous and painful. There were one or two sad sights: the casualties, and one or two kids who had been blown up on mines – that was upsetting. But the interest of the job generated enough euphoria to go along with the boredom – yes, we were learning that anything to do with war is seventy per cent boredom because most of the time is spent in kicking heels, doing nothing.

Michael Harris:

When the Finnish war broke out, the fighting was very intense and the British were dithering about wondering whether to go in and help the Finns against Russia. I believe at one time there was an expeditionary force planned. So the Government were quite keen for us to go; in fact the country was very pro-Finnish because the great Russian bear was playing up and trying to occupy a small country. We went into further training which involved a lot of driving with heavy trucks. Our ambulances were painted white as camouflage for the snow. We were fitted out with sheepskin coats and fur hats – it was all very primitive and rather, I imagine, like going to the Russian front in the First War.

Fairly soon after my group arrived peace came and one of the conditions was that the Karelian Isthmus would be turned over to Russia. Later, of course, Finland joined in on the side of Germany and was fighting again against Russia, but at that time the poor Finns still counted as allies and we now turned to helping the evacuation of the people. That was very sad because you went to a farm and had to take the families out and they could only take what they could carry. So some of these very lovely villages with wooden houses were completely evacuated. One thing I remember which made me grow up quicker than I would have done otherwise happened when we were driving an ambulance full of people on one of their very treacherous, icy roads. Suddenly there was hammering on the roof and cries of 'stop! stop!' One of our women passengers had gone into labour and I had the job of delivering twins. I can't remember whether I knew the facts of life, but certainly I didn't know much about the more sordid side of giving birth. I had a book. It was very messy but I did what I was supposed to do. The poor lady couldn't speak a word of English, nor me a word of Finnish. But she was tough and the twins were fine, and when we arrived at the transit camp, she clambered down with the babes in her arms. Everybody teased me very much afterwards.

Ronald Joynes:

I went out with the second party. When we arrived in Oslo, we caused a bit of a sensation as we were wearing British Red Cross khaki with jackets from the First World War which were buttoned to the neck. We drove to Stockholm in very bad conditions as that winter was very severe and arrived just before the war in Finland ended. I vividly remember having a cup of coffee in a large restaurant in Stockholm with a few friends where an orchestra was playing. Suddenly it started to play Sibelius's 'Finlandia' and do you know, everyone in that restaurant stood up in respect for the Finns. I was deeply moved – it still moves me to think of it...

Although the war was ending, we knew we weren't going to have an easy time. When we got to Finland, we found we had to paint over the red crosses on the tops of our ambulances because we were machine-gunned by the 'Molotovs' – the Russians planes. We were told, very seriously, that Russian pilots in briefings were given maps with red crosses on would-be targets; therefore if they saw a red cross anywhere, they would bomb it. This was told us by a responsible Finnish officer.

We found that the Finnish army lived in far more spartan conditions than our own army: rations were sparse and we soon learnt the art of survival. Two hot meals were served: one was a very thick porridge and the other a very thick stew. Some had porridge in the morning and stew in the evening and the others the other way around. So we would dodge around and sometimes get a couple of helpings of that stew. They were very keen on saunas – as essential to Finns as air conditioning was said to be to the Americans later in the war – these saunas were erected right up to the front. Finns were very tough fighters with tremendous ability on skis, and they would creep up to the Russians in the darkness in their white camouflage ski suits, and knife them. It was a very bloody war – the slaughter was very bad on both sides.

The Finns were very stoical about accepting evacuation from their homes when the war ended. They took their cattle when they could. It was all done very efficiently. We had to be on our guard with infectious illnesses because families, understandably, were desperate to keep together and dreaded having a member taken off

Ambulances in a wood in Finland.

to a hospital. We'd take twelve or more in an ambulance and in all transported great numbers.[1] Humour – ours and theirs – got us through. We were helped by their 'Lottas' which is a woman's organisation similar to our First Aid Nursing Yeomanry (FANYS). They were magnificent – very helpful, very cheerful – and wore grey uniforms. We enjoyed it: we were doing something useful *and* getting two stews a day – with a bit of wangling!

When we established ourselves in Joensuu after the war ended, we lived in tents which had been dug down through the snow. The pole of the tent was formed by the chimney of a stove which we fed with birch wood. The object was to keep the stove going for twenty-four hours a day which meant we had a rota during the night to stoke it up.

The roads were really atrocious. Most had deep ditches into which snow would be ploughed when it was falling. This meant it was impossible to tell where the road ended and the ditch started. We soon became expert in de-ditching; we all carried block and tackle which we learned to use very expertly. At first, when anybody ditched, there would be a crowd of willing helpers, but gradually only those immediately concerned were left. This was due to the cold outside. The petrol tanks and engines were very exposed and the only way of unfreezing was to get down on the road, unscrew the top and blow down it. Also our chains were suitable only for England and they would often break at the worst possible moment. Repairing them and putting on extra links wasn't easy, especially when, unlike today, you didn't have a supply of hot soup and drinks. I'm making it sound like a North Pole expedition, but those were the problems, we were *very* far north.

We had one or two crises when it was suggested that we might carry troops. We had big discussions about this, and it meant negotiation with the Finnish Army to make it plain that we would carry wounded and injured troops but not transports. It was a difficult decision because, although they weren't wounded or sick, they were often fatigued to the point of being sick and desperate for help. It was a very difficult decision to turn them down. Now and again one would take a soldier on the running board. Fortunately, the officers with whom negotiations had to be made, were always understanding.

All this time we listened avidly to news of England. Then came the news that the Germans had invaded Norway. We felt that our work for the Finns was nearly completed as they could easily do the transporting work themselves at that stage – Norway was where we should be. An offer was made through London to the War Office, and we were accepted. We then had to organise ourselves out of Finland into Norway.

We found the going even more difficult because the thaw had started and many of the roads which were passable when frozen became impassable. The frozen lakes were particularly treacherous. We were provided with long tree trunks which were passed through the cab through the windows so that if the ambulance did go through the ice, there would be a slight interval during which the poles would catch on the ice and the driver would have time to get out, grabbed by the squad of men waiting at the sides. There were a few hairy moments but we all got through to the Namsos area of Norway.

NORWAY

Michael Rowntree:

We crossed into Norway on 1 May 1940 – being a bird nut, I remember hearing the first chiffchaff as we crossed over. That wasn't all as we had our first experience of active hostilities in our own Anglo/German war by being machine-gunned by a couple of German planes on our way across. We had re-painted our red crosses on the vehicles by then and hadn't expected that ambulances with red crosses painted on the roofs would be attacked. Then we arrived in Namsos and were split into different groups: some to work with the British, others with the French and some with Norwegians. In fact our contribution to the Norwegian campaign was even shorter than our contribution to the Finnish war because again the thing folded up around us within four or five days of our arrival when the British decided to withdraw. We got the message one night to say that if we wanted to evacuate with the British forces, we had to be on the quay at Namsos at 4am. Being based in Godejord, some distance from Namsos, we realised this might not be possible, but we drove off through the night and arrived just after 4am to find that the last boat had left considerably earlier. It was fortunate that we did miss it because that boat was sunk with a good many casualties.

Ronald Joynes:

We had to be very careful not to say anything about the evacuation because the Norwegians were worried about this happening. In fact relations with the Norwegians weren't very good. When it was time for the British to go, all the officials in Namsos were locked in the church so they couldn't get out and spread the news that the British were going. The Norwegian campaign was a complete shambles: everything that could go wrong, did go wrong. We heard all sorts of stories: anti-aircraft guns transported on one ship, ammunition on another; officers who thought they'd be doing a bit of fishing taking more fishing rods than anything else; aeroplanes lined up on frozen lakes, easy targets for German planes. There is no doubt that the Germans had control of the air.

With the last evacuation ship gone, a completely new chain of circumstances started up. About turn: we grabbed a large drum of fuel and back we went towards Sweden leaving a completely destroyed Namsos – just the church and hospital left standing, everything else a huge pile of rubble. The first time I'd ever seen such a sight. Not an inhabitant in sight, all gone into the hills around. Before we could turn off into Sweden, we had to go south for a while and the Germans were coming up from the south, so every time we rounded a corner we expected to run into a German convoy coming the other way. But we made the crossroads and got back into Sweden, to the village of Yededa where we were warmly welcomed, given baths, fed and interned for a day. We were then put on a train to Stockholm where we donated our ambulances to the Swedish Red Cross apart from one which had been appropriated by a Norwegian farmer who painted out our insignia and used it as a farm vehicle for many years after. In Stockholm we stayed in the Salvation Army hotel – very wholesome, very friendly. Then we shopped around for civilian clothes. We all went to a big department store where we were given a free hand to buy a suit and shirts of certain value. Out of twenty-five, fifteen of us chose the same suit, a grey pin stripe. As Mike Rowntree said 'we emerged looking like the second row in a male chorus line of a musical comedy.' We then settled down waiting to get to Narvik. Narvik fell, and France fell, and we realised gradually that we'd be in Sweden longer than we thought.

Thirty-one men were now stuck in Sweden; the other twenty-five managed to get back to England with the evacuating troops. Michael Harris was among them:

Michael Harris:

We did a certain amount of evacuation of the wounded, but not really very much because the retreat was so very rapid back to Namsos which was the evacuation port. We got there one day and it was entirely in flames, very badly bombed. We had to drive all our ambulances onto one big heap and disable them. All our equipment was left behind as we were allowed to take just one kitbag with us. That splendid old General Carton de Wiart was in charge

– he was famous because he had one eye, one arm and one lung. There were a few ships still in the harbour. Mountbatten was there on the *HMS Kelly*. We were put on a troop transport, jammed full, one of the last ships out of north Norway. We sailed out in convoy and were very badly bombed. We were in the bottom holds and could hear bombs falling. It took three or four days to Scapa Flow where we were transferred to another boat bound for Glasgow. One was really the worse for wear because the sanitary arrangements had given out and the food had given out, and the British troops were very Bolshie – they felt the whole thing had been grossly mishandled. The air cover had been non-existent, they hadn't really fought and had just been pushed around and the British Tommy doesn't like being pushed around! We were held up in the Clyde because there was going to be a reception party to meet the returning 'heroes' from Norway – that really got the soldiers down. Finally, when we got to Glasgow, everybody was lined up in an enormous customs warehouse and I think it was General Ironside who came to address the troops. Well, they all began to hum and if you imagine 5,000 humming men, you can understand why he couldn't make himself heard. They were very upset.

Although the Finnish Convoy had only done six weeks' solid work, valuable lessons had been learned, especially the need for more systematic training. Members had also come up against some of the difficulties which were to dog them throughout the war: the question of what to carry in their ambulances – should they, could they, carry uninjured troops? There was the problem too of trying to explain, often in broken language, why they could not carry weapons and ammunition to people who were actually enduring enemy occupation and whose culture had no concept of, nor tolerance for, pacifism. But although the Finnish experience was short, and a whole group en route had missed the opportunity of actually serving at the front, there was a sense of satisfaction and a confidence that lives were saved and people helped. Was this not traditional Friends' work? Here, then, were the pioneers who gave those at home itching for service both hope and inspiration; the Unit's reputation was being built up, it had proved it could operate under army control. Its work with refugees which was to last throughout the war had started.

Newspaper articles were written, outlining and paying tribute to FAU service in both Finland and Norway. [2] *The Finnish Minister, His Excellency de Gripenberg, stated on his return from Finland in early 1940:*

Everyone in Finland was loud in their praises of the Friends Ambulance Unit. They have achieved great praise from all responsible military authorities for whom they work and it was the universal comment that no work was too much for them and no battle too fierce for them to help the wounded. They have achieved a unique reputation in Finland for their work. [3]

In an albeit modest way the Unit had made its mark, and was confident of being considered for similar tasks again.

Derryck Hill:

There's no doubt, this was the initiation of the FAU abroad in World War Two. There was a tremendous kudos in being there. You didn't have to say 'I was in Finland', it was known and recognised. There is no doubt about it, we became very practical and airy-fairy ideas went out of the door during that period – it was a tremendous shake-down. I think we moved the refugees with considerable sympathy and had a lot of empathy for their feelings. Over and above that we came to terms with the day to day organisation. We developed as little sections and I think that's true of the Unit throughout the war: we might, at times, have belonged to a bigger group, but the story of the Unit as such is really of small units of probably half a dozen people. During the evacuations we usually only moved two or three ambulances at a time, driving in pairs because of safety. We suffered all manner of incidents, sometimes a survival existence. It taught us a great deal about dependence on one another. Brief as the Finnish convoy was, we became veterans: most of us had been under fire and until this happened, you never knew how you would react. And during the evacuation from Norway, one felt very close to the troops. They had been in a hopeless situation: they were not trained for that war and were not equipped to hold Norway. I remember on the ship coming back from Namsos, it was crammed and we were all jumbled up, pacifists and fighters. All tired – very, very tired, all wanting a quiet corner to sleep in. It was either that or watching the show going on: a fantastic sight, terrific barrages. The irony of the situation struck me more than once. How can they possibly miss us? It was them and us alright in that situation. Neutrality is alright person to person, like in later situations when we treated Germany casualties with the same consideration as our own. But when you're being shot at or shelled, then it was very much them and us.

For the twenty-five men who returned from Norway to England, it meant settling down to the more humdrum work on the home front – hospitals, and then with the blitz, shelter and rest centre work. For some, this experience was not without irony. Michael Harris, for instance, recently returned from the Finnish/Norwegian campaigns, was first sent to a section of Gloucester Hospital which had been turned into military wards. Dealing with wounded British Expeditionary Force (BEF) soldiers, themselves evacuated from France, he was 'given a bit of flak. But I could understand it, they were badly wounded and there were a lot of deaths.' For the thirty-one stranded in Sweden life began to take some bizarre, even comic turns. Unsuccessful attempts were made to evacuate all British personnel via Petsamo. Eventually John Gillespie, who managed to obtain an Irish passport, got away leaving thirty frustrated men behind trying to find a way home.

Michael Rowntree:

We were, of course, very anxious to get back to Britain: it was the summer of Dunkirk and we were all very worried. We tried all sorts of schemes: at one stage even with Swedish fishermen who were prepared to run the German blockade to get us through. We also tried to get back through Russia; but the Russians knew that we had been in Finland helping the Finns and somehow knew we had carried wounded Russian prisoners in our ambulances, even accusing us of torturing them. So that was off. I did a bit of English teaching and, with all the arrogance and rashness of an Oxford undergraduate, taught in a summer school run by the British Council for Swedes who, in happier times, would have gone to England to learn.

Then eventually, in August 1940, an exchange was arranged between the British and German governments. There were about

250 British troops interned in Sweden from Norway, and about ninety German airmen who had been shot down by the Swedes while flying over Swedish territory. An exchange between these two groups was arranged. That seemed to be the common currency: ninety German airmen worth 250 British troops.

The British Government chartered an old tub which was sailing from Petsamo in the north of Finland to Iceland, and six places on this boat were offered to those of us left in Sweden. We drew lots and I was one of the lucky ones. So off to Iceland where we spent ten days; we then took another ship, arriving back in Britain, on 26 September 1940 – just in time for the blitz.

Ronald Joynes:

Most of us wondered if we'd get back to the England we knew. You see, whereas everyone in England knew about Dunkirk and that things were going on almost normally, Stockholm was full of German propaganda. There was a propaganda shop in the main street and when France fell, the window was filled with a huge map of France with Paris covered with a swastika flag. The following week that was replaced with a huge map of Great Britain with a swastika flag covering London. The cinemas were filled with German news trumpeting their successes. We saw films of Holland being bombed, France falling, Paris occupied by the Germans. Most worrying, preparations for the invasion of England with barges being prepared all along the French coast. We had no means of knowing this wouldn't happen and expected we would return to an occupied country.

I spent my time with an ear to the ground trying to find ways to get back. After John Gillespie got away and then the other five under an exchange agreement with the Germans, I spent a lot of time at the British Embassy where I met several characters and I got involved with some pretty bizarre schemes to get us all home. One of these was a Swede who had been very friendly with Field Marshal Goering's first wife, who was Swedish. I met this man who told me that he was actually in touch with Goering and that if we could get him to England, he felt sure he could set in motion negotiations for a peace. Evidently he knew Duff Cooper and felt he would be taken seriously and then arrangements could be set up for a meeting between Goering and his British counterparts to end the war.

This was extremely attractive to me – naive perhaps, but attractive. At that time there were lots of Germans in Stockholm and, supposedly, spies under every bed. So I proceeded to make arrangements in a Le Carré sort of way. But before I got very far, I was told by Oswald Dick, who was then our CO, to lay off.[4] He had been summoned to the British Consul who told him that they had information that one of our number was engaging in activities which were of an espionage nature and it must be stopped at once. So I had to call the whole thing off and never did discover whether I might have brought the war to an end. But it was a nice little episode.

About this time our relations with the Russians improved enormously. Previously I had dealt with the very hostile Madame Kollantai, a well known Bolshevik – large, drab, a very unfriendly lady with unkempt hair. But by this time, Sir Stafford Cripps had become our Ambassador to Moscow, and we were told that if we applied for visas, they would be granted. We rapidly re-assembled everybody in Stockholm and began the chase round the embassies to get visas; we needed: Russian, Turkish, French – in order to get into Syria – and Egyptian. Eventually these were obtained and we booked our passages, believe it or not, through Thomas Cook, and we were given an itinerary much as we would be given today, and left Stockholm in two parties. I was in the second, following up the rear, paying the bills as I was now quartermaster. We stopped at Riga, but weren't allowed off the planes, thence to Moscow airport where we noticed long lines of ancient aircraft which looked as if they had been there for years. We then went through very strict customs and were taken to a dingy hotel, the Savoy.

We were warmly welcomed by our Embassy as the first British visitors to Moscow since the war. We were taken out to the Metropole Hotel. We had very little money so I could only afford to buy bread, cheese and vodka for the men, not the sumptuous meals going on around us. That night we were shown around Moscow by guides. I was busy getting currency and passports stamped but I saw quite a bit of Moscow and went to the Bolshoi ballet with the others for part of the show. We were given a very nice English tea in the British Embassy by Sir Stafford, his wife and one of their daughters, which we all thoroughly enjoyed. Cripps told us a lot about what was happening at home and it was an altogether delightful occasion. After a few days we were conducted to the station for our journey to Odessa. We travelled down through Kiev, leaving a very drab Moscow for a brighter, warmer country where the people weren't all dressed in shawls and grey uniforms.

In Odessa we were taken to the magnificent opera house where we saw a performance of Tchaikovsky's Queen of Spades. We then travelled by boat to Bulgaria, then Istanbul where – having visited many of the tourist attractions such as Santa Sophia and the Blue Mosque – we took a boat across the Bosporus into Syria where we took the Taurus Express to Aleppo. Here we were taken to a small, full hotel. The proprietor was very pro-English because he turned out every guest. These poor bleary-eyed souls paraded past us in their bed clothes carrying their shoes and things, and we were put into their warm beds. Most of our men got into their beds fully dressed. At the end of the allocations, just Tom Burns and myself were left. The proprietor indicated that we'd have to share the last single bed. A great show was made by Tom who made it quite clear that the last person he'd share a bed with was me!

It was then off to Tripoli by train and then cars down into what was then called Palestine where we were ushered through the frontier by British soldiers – the first English we'd heard for some time, and every other word just four letters! Next stop Haifa, then down into Egypt, across the canal into Cairo. There, we were greeted with surprise by the British Red Cross who had been cabled that 'twenty-five friendly Swedes' were coming. Instead they got twenty-five Englishmen – some of us Friends! That was in October 1940. We were back in the war.

REFERENCES:

[1] Within a twelve day period, 35,000 miles were covered and 2,500 evacuees moved on roads which, with the melting snow, resembled mud baths. Davies, A. Tegla, 1947, *op. cit.* p.22.

[2] *Sunday Times,* 5/5/1940, for example.

(3) Finnish Convoy members were awarded the Winter War Remembrance Medal with ribbon 1939/40 in recognition of their service in Finland. Because of the Finns' alliance with Germany later in the war, the medal was not released until some twenty years post-war.

(4) It was in Sweden that 'a palace revolution' occurred during which Richard Early and Alan Dickinson resigned, with their respective positions being taken over by Oswald Dick and Michael Mounsey, with Ronald Joynes as Quartermaster. On many occasions in the future, similar changes of officers took place – all part of the development of Unit democracy.

CHAPTER 7

Egypt and Greece: Another Evacuation

'It was whilst working in the 8th General Hospital that we saw
examples of man's inhumanity to man because some of the
Egyptian orderlies were dreadfully uncaring to the poor Libyans
who, after all, were Arabs like them. And I saw one of the best
left hooks ever delivered by one of our number – a Quaker from
Bristol – to an Egyptian orderly who had roughly picked up a
wounded Libyan by his broken arm.'

Ronald Joynes

*ARRIVING IN CAIRO on 21 October 1940, the twenty-five
veterans of the Finnish Convoy, still wearing their World War I
jackets and odds and ends of Finnish equipment, created quite a stir.
They had, after all, been in some pretty unusual places and had experienced, albeit briefly, two war zones; it was no wonder that Richard
Dimbleby was keen to interview Oswald Dick for a BBC broadcast.
After a spell of sightseeing, they were sent to Alexandria in ambulances
donated by the Australian Red Cross where they took up duty as part of
the Ambulance Car Company for the 8th and 2/5th General Hospitals,
sharing quarters with the other ranks of the 8th General Hospital. This
was the FAU's very first contact with the British Army which was somewhat mystified by this group where, among other peculiarities, officers
and men acted on terms of complete equality, calling each other by their
first names. They were very well received by the 8th General Hospital
where, as Ronald Joynes explained, 'although we were wearing these
Great War tunics, and were soldiers outwardly, we were always known*

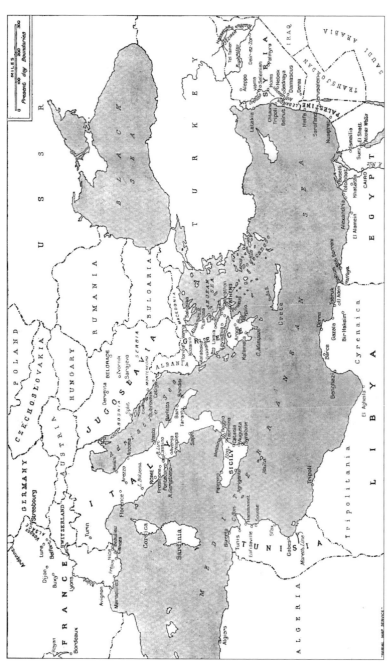

Map II – The Mediterranean Area.

– affectionately, I think – as the "twenty-five conchies". I was able to quote this later on to some of our Quaker critics in England.'

Before settling into their accommodation at the 8th General Hospital, they had discovered Dalys, a large, clean and comfortable pension *situated on the sea front. All Unit members who spent time in Alexandria vouch for the wonderful care and friendship shown them by the kindly French/Syrian proprietor, Madame Haddad who adopted the FAU as her own. When they left to take up accommodation in the 8th Hospital, she made her* pension *into a 'kind of NAAFI' for the Unit. It was a haven where they could find comfort, a cheap, good meal, listen to the wireless and music, play ping-pong and always receive a very warm welcome. As many Unit men have said 'Madame Haddad really became a mother to us.'*

The war situation when they arrived meant that work was very scarce: a month before their arrival, the Italian forces had crossed the Egyptian frontier and penetrated as far as Sidi Barrani where they stayed for nearly three months. A short time after their arrival, Italy invaded Greece. Meanwhile Egypt was filling up with troops. But for the FAU at this time, it was the case of just the occasional ambulance run, and little more. They worked hard and willingly within the hospital as orderlies and doing other menial tasks; and they tried hard to adapt to British Army methods without compromising their pacifist position. The army, however, took little notice of them. All this inactivity led to a slump in morale, which was relieved in part by a determination to return to a training regime of PT, first aid, stretcher drill, and driving their new vehicles. Thus a sense of community returned as they lived and trained together once more, and Dalys was always there!

A change in tempo came with General Wavell's push in December which drove the Italians out of Egypt and Cyrenaica; trainloads of wounded British and Italians needed transport from Victoria Station to the two hospitals. Soon the section found its hands full again, and seeing the suffering of the wounded they transported, and their exhausted, lousy, state, the section began to pull itself together as an enthusiastic, efficient unit once more. But as the British advanced into Libya, casualties were evacuated by hospital ships from Sollum and Tobruk; this meant that call-outs, although heavier in respect to numbers of casualties, became less frequent. Boredom was setting in once more when the challenge came from Greece.

When the Italians invaded Greece, on 28 October 1940, the possibilities of FAU work there had been discussed, but although the section's work in Alexandria was spasmodic and undemanding, the danger of air raids on Alexandria meant that the authorities were reluctant to release them. However, the Unit had consistently pressed the Red Cross to let them take the ambulances which had been promised the Greeks, and at last, in late February 1941 the go-ahead was given. Preparations were made and in a howling March gale, the section – now depleted to twenty men – drove to docks where ten ambulances, a utility truck and equipment were waiting, and boarded the Dumana, *sailing for Piraeus on 21 March 1941:*

Martin Lidbetter:

At the stern there was a small gun which most ships carried in case of attack by submarine or aircraft, and we were asked to man this in case of need as we had no other work to do on board. We refused to do this, and our pacifist reasons were understood and accepted.

The convoy was attacked several times by low flying Italian aircraft, and as darkness fell we were approaching the island of Crete where we had to moor for the night as no navigation lights of lighthouses were operating, so we put in to the harbour at Suda Bay, Crete, where in fact we remained for five days while the nearby naval battle of Cape Matapan between the Royal Navy and the Italian fleet was being fought. We were moored close to the cruiser *York* which, before dawn one morning while we were still sleeping, was torpedoed and sunk by Italian mini-submarines.[1]

Ronald Joynes:

We eventually arrived in Piraeus on 31 March 1941 and were immediately assigned to the Greek Army which was operating in the north, near the Albanian border. En route, we received the news that the Germans had declared war on Greece and were invading. We were given two sixteen-year-old boy scouts as interpreters, and brave lads they were too. We sent them back after a while, fearing for their safety, and made our way along precarious mountain roads to the north, where we saw men who would do anything to defend their homeland – the Greeks put up an *enormous* resistance.

We went straight through the lines – British and Greek – until we arrived to find that the hospital we were supposed to evacuate had already been evacuated. We were then confronted again with the problem of transporting armed troops. With the Germans entering the fray, the Greeks were retreating and we were retreating with them. They had no transport and they were in the same sort of condition as our Dunkirk survivors had been: footsore, weary and hungry. We were exercised as to what to do. I think we did the right thing in giving lifts to those at the end of their tether – only on the running boards. One or two members felt very keenly about this, but it never really divided us. The worst thing of all was to see the situation of the civilians: they were very short of food and there were no rest centres or any help. We had to harden our hearts. When we stopped for a feed we would be surrounded by villagers. It was my job to husband the rations – I don't say that the odd tin of bully

Suffer the little children .... Greece 1941.

beef didn't find its way into the crowd, but it was an early introduction to the problems of refugee work. The big problem was to
keep oneself well and fed while all around people were hungry.

Our journey back to Athens was under air attack most of the
way and the ambulance I was in was hit by a small bomb. I was
with Freddie Woods and we had secreted a bottle of gin – good
Quakerly beverage – in our ambulance and our first thought was
for that! The vehicle was put out of action and was towed into
Athens in the dark of the mountain road. A small group of us stayed
in Athens for a week, transporting the wounded around the Athens
area which was being badly attacked by then; the remainder transferred to the Australian Army in the north.

We realised that we would soon be evacuating again. It was then
that I began to realise how dependent I was on the armed forces.
I had got away from Namsos with the help of the British holding
up the Germans; here I was doing it again in Greece. I suppose my
principles began to change around this time. The dreadful waste
of it all affected me deeply. What were we achieving? The Greeks
were going to be left holding the baby just as the Norwegians had
been.

We left Athens by train, driven by a terrified engine driver who,
every time he heard a Stuka, leapt out into the bushes. In the end
he was persuaded to stay put by an RAMC officer with a large
revolver who drove alongside him in the cab. We got as far as we
could by rail and then changed to lorries until we reached Navplion
to the south. We hid in olive groves by day, trying to escape the
dreaded Stukas and were told to march down to the beach at night
in an orderly fashion and line up into the sea where landing crafts
would take us to a destroyer. I had a problem because I had my
accounts books tied round my middle. I was also wearing a pair of
high riding boots I'd had made in Egypt and was determined not
to lose any of this. We brought up the rear, at the Commanding
Officer's request: he thought that this would encourage the rest as
we would show no fear – little did he know!

When the time came the entire column closed ranks and
marched out into the sea, but only one craft came in and the front
ranks of the RAMC chaps were just getting up onto the ramps,

when up it went, and the craft backed out to the sea full up. Then you really saw the British Army at its best because the entire company called out to its commanding officer just what they thought of him leaving them on the beach. So we all waited in the sea for another one. This time I just made it because again I was at the back, and I am indebted to one of my colleagues who, as I was disappearing beneath the water, hauled me up into the back of the landing craft – by that time I wasn't feeling too good as I had a mild attack of dysentery. We were then taken down the coast in the dark, off-loaded into a little bay and told to hide in the olive groves and caves until the next night. I remember so vividly lying in a cleft of rock covered with branches, and then being conscious of a shadow. This was of a young priest standing over me. Without saying a word, he gave me a hardboiled egg, a ship's biscuit and a glass of retsina, and silently left me. I've never eaten a hardboiled egg without that scene coming back.

We carried on in that fashion, boarding ships at night and hiding by day, for three days. Happily we ended up at a beach where the rearguard was being evacuated. There we waited with a large group of New Zealanders and Australians and it was really chaotic, nobody in charge, and at one time there was a really ugly scene when a ship's barge came ashore and Australian officers drew revolvers forcing the troops back on shore away from the barge. It was frightening just to be in the area. But this was *it!* We were eventually rowed out to a destroyer, the *Isis*, where we were given hot cocoa which tasted just like nectar. I remember lying on a gallery of 3.7 shells without a single thought except to rest. The following day we were taken to Crete and given cocoa and soup – see what a big part food plays! – then back to Suez and Alex.

What of Oswald Dick's party? This had joined up with the Australians as planned. With the German control of the air, army trans-ports were bombed without respite and up and down the roads of Greece the FAU ambulances carried the sick and wounded, weaving in and out of transports, dodging craters, often stopping to pick up survivors of the bombing raids. But when it became obvious, on 23 April, that the Germans were only a few miles off, the section was ordered to evacuate, first to Athens and then straight on southwards to the Kalamata area which was reached on the night of 25 April. During the night, the section joined a long column of troops waiting to board a ship that lay nearby, but after a while it drew away which meant a retreat into the olive groves to find shelter from the intense and continuous Stuka attacks which came with daylight. The following night, another attempt was made but no luck again, nor any hope for the exhausted and dejected group that they could now escape by sea.

Then came the news that the nearby Town Hall was filled with badly wounded casualties with only a few poorly equipped Greek doctors and nurses to cope. Once more the section set to, desperately trying to create some order out of the chaos – cleaning up, dressing wounds, nursing and feeding the patients. That evening the Germans arrived. The section carried on with its work, but now they were prisoners of war. [2]

REFERENCES:

[1] Lidbetter, H. Martin, *Friends Ambulance Unit 1939-1943; Experiences in Finland, Norway, Sweden, Egypt, Greece and Germany,* p.73.

[2] Sir John Crofton, then a doctor in the RAMC, has paid tribute to the FAU for 'the superb work they did under the very grim circumstances of the retreat'. He managed to escape, but his friend Archie Cochran told him what a tower of strength the FAU were in the grim POW conditions in Greece (letter to Pat Rawlence, 1998). See Chapter 15.

CHAPTER 8

The Western Desert: Thank God for El Alamein

'If you look at the FAU as a whole in the desert, it was quite an interesting situation. There was the Greek unit, attached to the 15th Casualty Clearing Station (CCS);the Robin unit, attached to 14th CCS; the Mobile Hospital which had an FAU unit attached to it; there were the Field Transfusion units which had FAU people attached to them – they used to roam around attached to the various CCSs. In additions to these, you had the Hadfield Spears Unit (HSU) floating around as well. There was quite a lot of inter-visitation: often we'd pull up next to the 14th CCS as they were moving into position; or you'd get the HSU passing by, or the blood wallahs coming in. Altogether it was an interesting bush telegraph whereby you could find out what was happening in the Unit as a whole.'

Derryck Hill

*A*T THE START *of May 1941, the seven Unit evacuees from Greece were joined in Egypt by six men sent from London. After a short interval the Hadfield Spears Unit (HSU) – an FAU section working with the Hadfield Spears Hospital in Syria – put in a request for reinforcements which meant five of the newly arrived group setting off for Syria leaving only Albert Hey behind.*

Meanwhile, the Unit – its reputation enhanced after Greece – had been offered a chance by the Medical Directorate of working in the Blood Transfusion and Resuscitation Department in the 64th General Hospital (the old, renamed 2/5th) and five men departed to train there. Gradually,

116

*with experience, their responsibilities grew, while the output of blood
increased considerably. In June 1941, Major (later Colonel) Buttle, chief
of Blood Transfusion work in the Middle East, asked for more men to
train in the 15th (Scottish) General Hospital in Cairo. The FAU also
played an important role in the blood-transfusion units (BTUs), working,
for example, with the BTU that was responsible for supplying all the 8th
Army's area with blood.*

*At this time the section was told of a donation of ambulances about
to arrive from America in the summer of 1941. Who was going to man
them? A request was duly sent to London for the first large group of reinforcements to the Middle East. Thirty-six men were selected, under the
command of Peter Gibson with John Bailey as his second in command:
six were earmarked for blood work, the rest as drivers. They left England
on the crowded troopship* Cameronian *in July 1941 with another FAU
section bound for the Hadfield Spears Hospital in Syria. Troopships often
provided the first opportunity for the Unit to meet their service counterparts and the challenge thus began of finding how they, as pacifists, could
serve alongside army personnel without feeling aloof and uncomfortable,
or feeling that they were violating their integrity of conscience.*

Derryck Hill:

This was to be my second experience of a troopship but the
scramble out of Norway was really something quite different from
this. Pacifists on a crowded troop transport is in itself quite an experience. We slept in hammocks on the mess deck and mixed freely
with the troops. These were mixed groups of: Royal Fusiliers, Welsh
Fusiliers, RAMC and various other units. We went out in a very
big convoy which took a circuitous route to avoid U-boats. Many
concerts were held on the *Cameronian* and the FAU made a big
contribution, both in performing and in writing a lot of the material. Several of our section were Cambridge people, so it was right
up their street. We also took part in the tug-of-war and got through
to the semi-final having knocked out the Inniskillen Dragoon
Guards and Welsh Fusiliers – I think we went through about eight
groups before we were defeated. It was really a matter of brain over
brawn as our strategy was lying on the ropes and tiring our oppo-
nents out. We used to be called 'bloody conchies' at times; there's

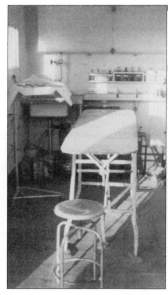

Bottoms up – repairs in the desert.   *'Greek Unit' operating
theatre.*

no doubt there was a mild antagonism here and there, but really I
was surprised there wasn't more. Winning the tug-of-war did much
to improve our image, also our contribution to the ship's concerts
helped.

*The party, keen and eager for service, landed at Suez on 18
September where the new ambulances awaited them.*

*At that time in the Middle East, two Mobile Surgical Units (MSU)
were in existence: one given by the Robin Shipping Line and the other
by the Greek Red Cross. These were set up as the answer to fast-moving
tank warfare – if tanks moved fast and wide so, it was argued, should
medical assistance. It was hoped that by having Mobile Hospitals and
CCSs well behind the lines, the immediate work near the front could be
done by the newly-formed MSUs which were fitted out with theatres, X-
rays, sterilising plants and whatever was deemed to make them fully effective. The Robin line and the Greek Red Cross Unit were attached to the
14th CCS and 15th CCS respectively.*

Number 1 Mobile Hospital had also been set up – this was a complete mobile tented hospital. Eventually it consisted of thirty-four vehicles which included a sterilising van, X-ray lorry, electric power plants, steam generator and a diesel kitchen car. Originally, it held one hundred beds, but often, in times of emergency, its capacity was more than doubled.

For the newly arrived section, the end of September and beginning of October 1941 was spent training. From late October and early November, the sections began moving off into the desert, having joined their respective units.

For the campaigns of 1941-42 the Unit had four groups with the British Army: six joined Number 1 Mobile Hospital. Sam Marriage was in charge and this became known as 'Sambo's Circus.' 'Headley's Light Horse' consisted of nine men under Henry Headley, and this undertook the driving for the Greek Red Cross Unit – part of the light section of the 15th CCS. Eight joined the 14th CCS in two groups: four men under Vivian Ramsbottom to join the light section of Robin Line vehicles, and four under John Bailey to remain with the heavy section farther behind the lines. Other members were allocated to various sectors of the BTUs.

This, then, was the situation in November 1941, just after General Auchinlech's push to El Alghelia. Then came the German counter-offensive with Rommel's drive and breakthrough at Gazala and then on to El Alamein. Later came the Allied counter-offensive with the second battle of El Alamein, the push forward, the Axis retreat and eventual surrender in May 1943.

During the campaigns, the section had been joined in the Western Desert by Unit members attached to the First Free French Division. Except for the actual fighting, the FAU shared fully the life of Allied troops in the desert campaigns: the boredom, the spasmodic excitement and fear; the sweltering heat, sandstorms, flies and lack of water: the advances and victories, the routs and chaotic retreats; with place names such as El Alghelia, Sidi Barrani, Bir Hacheim, Tobruk, Mareth and Akerit as evocative to FAU members today as to army veterans.

Derryck Hill:

I was in the section known as 'Headley's Light Horse.' Our team consisted of a surgeon, who was a Major; an anaesthetist who

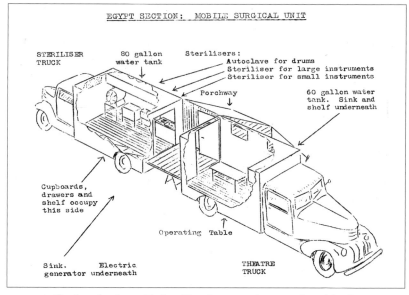

EGYPT SECTION: MOBILE SURGICAL UNIT

STERILISER   80 gallon   Sterilisers:
TRUCK   water tank   Autoclave for drums
                                      Steriliser for large instruments
                                      Steriliser for small instruments
                              Porchway   60 gallon water
                                                    tank. Sink and
                                                    shelf underneath

Cupboards,
drawers and
shelf occupy
this side

                        Operating Table

Sink.   Electric   THEATRE
generator underneath   TRUCK

*Back to back or side by side, the operations continued in the
mobile theatres.*

was a Captain; a medical officer – also a Captain, an RAMC Staff
Sergeant who served in the operating theatre, and an RAMC
Corporal who assisted the anaesthetist. The rest of the team was
us – six FAU, with Henry Headley, our 'Corporal', in charge. We
were part of the 15th CCS. The unit we were attached to was a
close Territorial Unit, Geordies, from Newcastle, under
Lieutenant-Colonel Waite, who was a very friendly sort. We had
quite a spell doing experimental training runs into the desert. The
important thing was going to be the speed of setting up the unit.
We had a huge 150 pound tent which we got very good at putting
up quickly. A vital part consisted of a sterilising ambulance and
another ambulance which contained the operating theatre. We
reversed these back to back and the flap of the sterilising truck
dropped onto the operating theatre which formed a way of moving
from one to the other. Initially, there was no cover for that area,
but we constructed a wooden frame to provide a porch entrance
with a canvas flap which fitted right over the top joint of the two

vehicles. Later on there was further refinement when the ordinance people fitted a proper tubular frame – a sort of annexe – which enabled us to hold patients awaiting operations. Our basic job, as well as setting up, was driving the two supply wagons and the water tank; but once we were forward and operative, then we'd turn a hand to anything that needed doing.

Eventually, we moved forward with the 15th CCS, up the desert road towards Mersa Matruh. At some point along the road we broke off into the desert. This was the time of Auchinlech's push. Our MSU left the CCS between the main road and the wire which ran from north to south across the desert, and went ahead. We went beyond Fort Madeleine and set up the MSU, receiving our first casualties from a tank battle south of the Tobruk area.

We would operate at very short notice. I reckon we could stop and be operative in five minutes. If a flap was on we could break and run within two minutes. When we used the 150 pound tent, that did slow us and eventually we did away with it, especially when we got the annexe linking the sterilising and operating ambulances, where patients could wait on the spot. We were very often in the vicinity of the CCS – it depended how extended the battle lines were. If a push was on and going well then the lines of communication were extended and you could be leaving the CCS and Mobile Hospital way behind. The practice that developed in the MSU was giving first aid, surgical aid and treating burns, making the men as comfortable as we could. If they were badly wounded, the technique was to clean out the wound, stuff it with sulphonamides, bind it or lightly stitch it, and send the patient back as quickly as possible to the CCS further behind the lines or the Mobile Hospital. In the later campaigns where there were railway connections, we could sometimes evacuate direct to the railway lines and get patients up to Cairo or Alexandria for treatment.

So we would move up, quickly set up shop, operate right into early morning and move again at daylight. We were very much a unit that moved at the drop of a hat. There were times when we had long leaps forward – for instance, when Auchinlech got as far as El Alghelia, we had to do some long runs to catch up with him. If there was a sustained action going on it could be very exhausting. Often flaps developed at night. It was not unknown to be operating to 2am and then get the order at 5am to move. We cooperated with the Light Field Ambulances who would pass on patients needing surgical treatment. There must have been some system of keeping in touch but I wasn't involved with that.

If a flap was on and everyone was chasing back, quite often we'd have a patient on the operating table and we'd stay put and finish before getting away. More than once we waited in terribly quiet circumstances, feeling all alone – everyone had gone back. I remember the time when we were operating in the middle of a huge flap. We were all biting our fingernails, watching everything go by in considerable disorder, and when you see tanks dash by you think 'What's next?' We had this abdominal case on the operating table and I remember a signals officer dashing out of a Bedford truck yelling 'Jerry's just two miles up the road. Best of luck!' We got the patient off the table not long after, broke and cleared, and as we cleared so the Germans started shelling our vehicles. We were often bombed: Jerry recognised the Red Cross, true, but he seemed very accurate in missing us! More than once we'd use a diversionary system: rather than go due south, we'd go due south, turn east, then turn back north. We were never on roads in the desert: we went up in September and didn't see a macadam road until twelve months later. Driving could be very tricky, especially down escarpments – and often we'd be driving at night. Dangerous? Not more than what our people were facing in the East End of London.

My job with the MSU was that of mechanic. We had a small generator which consistently played up and my time was often spent fiddling around with it trying to get it going, or keep it going. I also did maintenance on the vehicles used for stretcher bearing. Occasionally, we all had to give a pint of blood when things became desperate. My involvement with the theatre and steriliser was fairly limited although I was called in on occasions to help.

One of the first things I did was to hold a leg and to realise that it wasn't connected to a body – a bit shattering. Whilst fighting was on, when we'd get the wounded, 95% were serious cases, lots of abdominal wounds and burns. If a tank was hit and set on fire, it wasn't easy getting people out, and often they would have bad burns on arms, faces and chests. I was always very impressed with the burns cases. Some must have been suffering excruciating agonies, yet they were always so cheerful and would joke about things. I think the fact that we were up so near the front was very important for morale – and some were very surprised at the sophisticated nature of the treatments we gave. When I think back, it was very much a developing pattern of medical care in the desert and I believe a lot of the treatments arose out of the Spanish War experience.

During the time of Auchinlech's push we were kept very active, but then we'd have months of doing very little – just the odd casualty from bombing or mines. But when things were quiet we'd get medical cases. We had some really terrible cases of constipation for which the desert diet was responsible. Essentially, this was bully beef, biscuits, tinned potatoes, tea, sugar and tinned milk – very little fruit and no fresh vegetables although vitamin pills were issued.

The desert was a vast place and things were very fluid. It was rare not to see vehicles somewhere. Early on there was a problem with leaking petrol cans which limited Auchinlech's push as several units ran out of petrol. This was resolved later by using German Jerry Cans. The 7th Armoured Division used to cut discs out of the old cans and paint signs which they placed every mile or so – 'Trafalgar Square', 'Marble Arch' – that sort of thing. These became very real points in the desert and provided a little bit of home too. Even so, it was easy to get lost. On one macabre occasion when we were south of Tobruk, we had lost our staff car and were left on our own. We had gone so far and had stopped the lorry trying to work out where we were. Suddenly, one of our men appeared, ashen faced, whispering 'I think we've run over somebody.' We couldn't believe it, but went back and sure enough there was a body wrapped in a blanket. We were on the edge of El Adem cemetery and the wind had blown the sand off a very shallow grave. It was eerie and very unpleasant to have run over this corpse.

We had very good relations with the Geordie soldiers we worked with in our MSU and the 15th CCS. The Staff Sergeant, who was the theatre assistant in 15th CCS, was an Indian Army regular – as foul-mouthed as they come. I remember one day somebody saying something nasty about us and him dressing them down in the ripest language he knew.

David Rowlands:

Our Hadfield Spears Hospital had moved into the Western Desert from Syria in early 1942. We worked for a time near the Halfaya Pass and then moved up to Tobruk where we divided – the main section working in wards of the British General Hospital and British Hospital. In May, when things hotted up and the retreat was on, the section moved to Sollum where the main hospital was set up. From there a poste avancé – a Forward Theatre unit – was sent out. I was part of this as mechanic-cum-steriliser and general factotum. We first set up at a place called Mekili where it was known that the Germans were on the move. But no one knew where they were and there was a great feeling of apprehension as we had no idea of when we'd be surrounded or what would happen next. I remember so clearly, one evening a rum ration was issued – this was done only under exceptional circumstances when there was great stress and fear. We all brought our enamel mugs and queued up for our tots. There were movements during that night, we could hear gunfire. No one knew what was happening and we didn't get any casualties in.

We then moved off to another site – a piece of sand called El Azragh on the map. We dug in there and had an operating theatre dug into the sand. One day we were eating our meal when we saw a single plane appear high up, and we saw bombs actually leaving the plane. There was just time to scatter into the slit trenches we had dug. I had one which I could just about squeeze into. Nik Alderson, the leader of our section, was in the neighbouring trench. We heard a tremendous crunching as this stick of bombs landed, and there were flames and smoke. This gradually dissolved away, and when we looked around we found that Nik was no longer in his trench and the parts of his body, some of which were recognisable, were strewn around. We collected the pieces into a rubber sheet and carried it into one of the tents. What is one more death in a war where we had seen so many killed! But when it was someone as near to us as Nik had been, then we were all very deeply affected.

It must have been within fifteen minutes of this happening that Mike Rowntree appeared. He said that if he hadn't stopped to bird watch on his way up, then he would have been with us and most probably in with Nik, as they were very close friends. But we had to carry on and within ten days or so we moved to Bir Hacheim – nothing there but sand and an old fort. We dug in there. We had a good team of French medics and orderlies, and some excellent lorries that were designed to join together side to side. We couldn't actually sink them into the ground but the engines and bonnets were sunk into a trench which was dug out of a slope, so it was possible to have a relatively safe place for other than a direct hit. A lot of very serious surgery was done in those lorries, at Bir Hacheim.

We frequently had what we called 'Stuka parades.' They always came out of the sun, always out of the sun, and screamed down on the camp. It would have been in contravention of the Geneva Convention to have a Red Cross protecting the artillery, so we were open to bombing. As we were there for quite a long time, we made ourselves very comfortable. We had pneumatic drills and our African orderlies – very big, strong chaps – dug out what was the equivalent of a room underground, and we found a lorry Chassis which we stripped down, putting it across the top of this cube with barbed wire stakes to the side and then sandbags on top of that, and sand atop of that, so that we were invisible. My friend David Smewing and I shared one which we called 'The Davids'. We were cool down there in the heat of the sun and, except for a direct hit, we could sleep calmly. We pulled out on 23 May. We went through quite a lot there, but the real siege started after I left when the group staying behind with Captain Thiboux received the full force of the Germany Army. These were the heroes of Bir Hacheim: they held out and by holding out enabled military actions to take place to the north – a great contribution to the Allied effort. In the Free French annals, Bir Hacheim was the great feat of the war.

Hugo Powell:

After the retreat of June 1942, the next big push was El Alamein. I was with a poste avancé on the coast for a long time and was aware of a massive build up for a battle at some point: new troops pouring into the delta and moving up into the desert. Right at the time when the battle was due to start, we were moved south to the edge of the Kantara depression, a sort of salty quagmire which protected the flank. Then just before the battle started we moved up through this huge belt of artillery, almost wheel to wheel from the Kantara depression to the coast. We went through at sunset and then moved forward in the dark and stopped and set up our little encampment in the dark. Then about 11 o'clock that night of 23rd October, suddenly all hell was let loose and behind us we saw this great arc of artillery firing away – a terrific din. An awesome, crashing noise with shells zooming overhead. I always remember it because it was so like war. Just at the time that we thought we were going to get busy, we were told 'You get your heads down and get some sleep because we're not going to be needed until the morning.' So with this tremendous din going on, we covered our ears and slept for a couple of hours.

It was still going on in the morning, but immediately we pulled up and went forward. After that I can remember very little except scurrying in and out, going through minefields, backwards and forwards, taking patients until, suddenly, it was all over and streams of prisoners were coming through.

El Alamein is all muddled up now in my mind. There are little vignettes. You'd have moments of wondering where on earth you were. Imagine being in a small surgical tent, with the surgeon getting on with an operation and I would be preparing people. Then suddenly you'd realise that the infantry were coming up from behind us, spreading out around our little tent with fixed bayonets, and you realised how close to things you were. We went for days without sleep. I think it's one of the curious ways that one endures the alarms, fears and excitement – one is half drugged with the fatigue of the thing. You get a curious nightmarish kind of feeling, particularly when you get to the third or fourth day with almost nothing in the way of sleep. One is hardly sane – it's a curious, drugged situation. That's the best way of describing it.

Minefields were usually marked, but you couldn't always rely on them being cleared when they should have been. Once I was given the job to guide the hospital trucks up a track through a minefield to the hospital. I had done this several times, and on the fourth time, the truck behind me blew up on the track that I had been guiding him through. Mines were pretty alarming, especially at El Alamein, where both sides had lost track of them – they had been over the ground several times and really didn't know where all the mines were. In fact, the farther we advanced, so we put sandbags on the floors of the trucks because we were so frequently going over things that exploded. And the dust! Dust stirred by the battle and dust storms. You changed dressings as seldom as possible. My chief work in the poste advance was giving lots of plasma, keeping the men warm, giving morphine and various pre-operative drugs.

I have to say that at El Alamein, the system didn't work particularly well because the battle was so fast moving. We seemed to spend ages scurrying in and out of minefields, digging holes to put the tents in – very difficult with loose sand – then building up with sandbags, then getting the tent up and ready for patients. Then the order would come 'Move!' and because we had to carry as little as possible, each time we had to empty the sandbags – it was a very, very energetic time. We were active throughout the battle, no time for sitting around. I was very conscious that I had chosen to do this. I was a pacifist, and had found the best way of expressing my belief that one ought to relieve suffering. And one took pleasure in caring for wounded Germans as much as 'our side.' But you couldn't help feeling very attached to the soldiers you were serving, they were the people you knew.

I thanked God for the outcome of El Alamein. It made the end of the war closer. It was interesting to see all the prisoners coming in, mostly Italians who were, quite openly, jubilant. Some playing guitars. You could pick out the Germans, uniforms or not, they stalked along not looking at all pleased with life.

I saw several of the Generals at one time or another. I remember meeting Wavell, earlier in Syria. This was during the fighting. He'd come to look at the front or something at a time when we were absolutely overburdened with casualties, some very badly wounded. We were based in a Nunnery and we took those we could not save into a shady courtyard to die quietly while we were coping with those we could save. I was taking a stretcher party through a door and there was an English officer standing with his back to me, scratching his navel and deep in thought. I called 'Gangway please!' He didn't take any notice, so I said again 'Gangway please, wounded! Don't you know the rules?' He got out of the way. Later there was a parade and General Wavell was in it, and I recognised him.

General de Gaulle used to come around occasionally. He was rather like one of those effigies that they take round Italian villages – absolutely rigid in the back of trucks. One of the nicest Generals was the one at Bir Hacheim. He was an Alsatian and would come into our poste avancé after a battle to see how we were getting on. He'd sit down informally and talk to the wounded. The effect on morale was quite terrific. One became very aware how leadership of that kind mattered

One night during El Alamein, I was left with a group of Foreign Legion, three Sergeants and a number of other badly wounded men. In the middle of the night, I had trouble with a man in considerable pain. One of the Sergeants told me that I was not to give him any more morphine, whatever the circumstances, but to fob him off with other drugs to kill the pain. I steadily refused to give him morphine injections despite his pleas. He happened to be a Prussian and his friend on the next stretcher was Swiss. In the middle of the night, the Swiss suddenly produced a pistol and pointed it at me saying 'You will give my friend morphine. Now!' I refused of course and explained why not. He took the safety catch off and waved the pistol about, but eventually put it away saying that I would pay for it in the morning. In the morning the Sergeants told me 'You were lucky, he's killed four people so far.'

The surgeon came round the next morning and I moved away so that the Swiss could talk to him. When he left, the Swiss called me over and said 'I hear you were absolutely right.' Then he solemnly gave me his signed photograph and said ' I understand that you belong to some curious sect that won't allow you to kill people. If you ever want anybody killed, just come to me!' This was the sort of very useful education for somebody brought up in my idealist background. I think he genuinely would have killed somebody for me if I'd asked him.

After El Alamein, we had a bit of a rest and re-training: we'd had a pretty good mauling both at El Alamein, and before that at Bir Hacheim. We then went on right across Africa and were involved with fighting along the Mareth Line into Tunisia in 1943.

CHAPTER 9

The Hadfield Spears Unit:
The Arduous, Dangerous and Bizarre

'The Hadfield Spears Unit had a delightful surreal quality. It was perhaps one of the most extraordinary units that existed anywhere in the war. To have such marvellous cooperation between perhaps the most chauvinistic collection of Frenchmen imaginable and pacifists, many of them Quakers, was truly astonishing – let alone the bizarre mix of people making up the hospital....'

Hugo Powell

*M*ENTION HAS ALREADY *been made of the work done by members of the FAU section attached to the Hadfield Spears Hospital in the Western Desert. But the Hadfield Spears Unit – the HSU – had, in fact, been operative before this during the internecine fighting between the Free French and the Vichy French in Syria.*

The Hospital had been set up by Mrs. (later Lady) Spears, alias the novelist Mary Borden, in cooperation with Lady Hadfield, in the autumn of 1940. Mrs. Spears was the wife of General Spears, a Conservative MP, who had been responsible for getting de Gaulle out of France and into England in 1940. The Hospital was attached to the First Free French Division, which consisted of those who had rallied to de Gaulle in 1940. It was a mobile hospital which started with eighty beds. The surgeons, doctors, pharmacists and administrators were officers of the French Army. There were also French NCOs and other ranks who worked on administration and the kitchen and forty-five Senegalese who did unskilled work. The eight nursing sisters were English and were responsible for the

129

theatre, the wards and reception. There were also six women drivers of the Motor Transport Corps (MTC) who drove the six staff cars.

The FAU had been asked to provide a section of fifteen men to drive and maintain the Hospital's trucks. As the Hospital was almost without trained medical orderlies, the Unit also made a contribution here. In fact, the FAU was delighted to be presented with such a wonderful opportunity for satisfying work in that frustrating year of 1940. In time, as the Hospital expanded, so did the FAU, reaching the figure of thirty-eight. As well as their original roles, they went on to provide the Hospital's quartermaster and electrician, took on the laundry, were responsible for the mortuary and many other odd jobs that occurred in a mobile hospital. They also had the task of loading and unloading the trucks and setting up the tented Hospital and camp when they arrived at a new site. Nik Alderson was the HSU's first section leader. When he was killed in 1942, he was replaced by Michael Rowntree.

On 23 March 1941, the Hospital embarked on the Otranto *expecting to join French troops operating in Eritrea and the Sudan. Instead they found themselves in Palestine where they were joined by the Commanding Officer of the Hospital, Colonel Fruchaud, and a French detachment which had come up from Eritrea. It was then off in convoy across Transjordan into Syria, crossing the border at Deraa, arriving in the midst of the bitter French internecine war. Soon they were joined by the party of five reinforcements that had been sent up from Cairo.*

David Rowlands:

Deraa was a place of great significance so far as the Free French were concerned. At this time French were fighting French and I think probably, in my experience, this was the most bloody time of the whole war. Although everything in the Western Desert was on a larger scale overall, at Deraa we were overwhelmed with Free French casualties. I remember we were set up in this God-forsaken place, thick with flies. A lot of us had dysentery, and the casualties were pouring in faster than we could cope with. I always remember Captain Jiberet and his calmness when you had stretchers as far as you could see outside the reception tent – people with shattered legs, with facial and throat injuries. There were horrible sights. I felt at this time it was just more than one could stand – day and night it went on and on; and yet somehow we kept going.

I remember we ran out of orange boxes from which a Breton made hasty crosses for burying the dead. I remember the exhaustion of Captain Asquins, one of the medical officers, he had dysentery and could hardly keep going. But Jiberet was the tower of strength, and right through the war he was the same. I don't ever remember him being ill or losing his temper. He was remarkable.

The civil war aspect was very disturbing. There was a time when we had two brothers from the Foreign Legion in, and they were fighting on opposite sides. This was very upsetting. There was a big petrol depot at Deraa which was hit by a bomb right alongside of us. The whole thing went up and it was lucky that we didn't lose patients as a result of it. Then on 22 June 1941, we had news of the fall of Damascus to the Allies. This was a tremendous boost, and on the 25 June we packed up and drove from Deraa with its horrible flies, its filth and stench of bodies and death, to Damascus which was virtually untouched. There was an oasis with running water – unbelievable. We were installed in the Italian hospital there: perfectly clean, well equipped with Italian surgical instruments and everything on hand; it was wonderful. It was run by nuns. We were also very busy there, but working in good conditions.

Hugo Powell:

We had been told before going into Syria that the Vichy French would rush to welcome us, except for a few skirmishes here and there. The reality was *very* different. I remember early on, the Free French went forward to parley with the Vichy and they were just shot off the road, and a nasty battle developed which gave us our first experience of battle casualties. This in itself was fascinating for a pacifist because one would be working in a tent in which you had black tirailleurs from both sides being treated together. And you realised how awful it was because there were people from the same villages, even the same families, fighting each other. I can remember furious arguments between Vichy officers and our French surgeons, despite their very serious wounds. It was a real eye-opener for me and made me realise early on the fanatically patriotic people we were serving. I remember one officer dashing into the hospital saying 'Look, I'm fighting in tank battle out there. I've been wounded in the side. For goodness sake do something quick. I don't want to see the doctor, I just want to get back into the fight.' He showed me a gaping hole in his side. 'Look you're not going back into that', I told him 'you'll just drop dead in that tank.' That sort of thing happened all the time, on all our battle fronts.

A most curious thing happened to me while I was there. I'll never forget it, because it is one of those little ironies which I appreciate so much. As a teenage boy, in my school holidays, I had been in the Welsh valleys where unemployment was very high, helping the miners level the slag heaps. I had kept in touch with some miners, and the head of the miners' community in which I had worked wrote me a letter which was full of pleasure and excitement saying 'Employment is splendid in the valleys, we are making steel again.' At the time I received this, I was sitting in a shell hole, with shrapnel all over the place. I thought 'It's a pity his employment has to come from this', because I'd seen a lot of people killed and wounded that day.

It was chiefly in Syria that one got an impression of a very disturbed state of Anglo/French relations. General de Gaulle was determined to attain maximum control of Syria, while the British had their own ideas on what should be done: the war wasn't going well in Libya at this time, and there were considerations of where troops should be placed. There was also the problem of what should be done with the Vichy prisoners, once the war ended. Not a happy time for the liaison people. The French always seemed to trust us – les Quakers, although they were suspicious of everyone else. The Spears Mission was there in Syria. This had nothing to do with the Hospital, but of course General Spears was running it as chief liaison officer between Britain and the Free French, so there was a deal of coming and going. We got a picture of what was going on because Lady Spears would come and speak to us as a group occasionally, and she was often quite indiscreet about the various arguments going on in this extraordinarily difficult political liaison.

Hostilities ceased on 13 July. Just prior to this, the section had suffered its first casualty when James Tonks was killed in a driving accident. He was buried, alongside the French Captain who had been travelling with him, in the military cemetery at Damascus. Later, a memorial stone was set up in the Friends' burial ground at Brummana, in Lebanon; this was carved by Hugo Powell, a sculptor.

With the cessation of hostilities, there was little work, apart from medical cases and accidents. In August 1941, the Hospital moved from Damascus down to Beirut on the coast, eventually moving into the pleasant premises of St. Charles Hospital, which had previously been run by German nuns. The section was now reinforced by another eighteen men who had sailed on the Cameronian. *Beirut offered the HSU an interesting and satisfying social life: there was the large and friendly American colony centred round the American University; also a very welcoming group of Friends which meant regular meetings for worship as well as the warmth of their hospitality.*

In the meantime, Nik Alderson had been actively looking for other work to occupy the HSU. The hostilities had produced a serious shortage of wheat in Syria and Lebanon. The Spears Mission had organised a wheat distribution scheme for which the FAU undertook the driving. But there was another very obvious need which had been noted: the very scanty medical services for the Arabs of the Damascus oasis and for the Bedouin of the surrounding desert, which had existed before the war, had all but disappeared and diseases were rife. Surely this was work for the HSU? This is when Nik Alderson, with the help of Lady Spears, the Area Commanders, the Syrian health authorities and village headmen, set up a series of mobile clinics which used the Hospital transport and was provided with drugs from various sources.

For the main Hospital, the respite in Beirut was not long lasting. With the fighting in Syria done, the Free French troops were moving off to take part in the Western Desert campaigns. On new year's eve, 1941, the Hospital left for its work in the desert campaigns, leaving behind two vehicles and two members to continue the clinic work. ★

We take up the HSU story at the end of the desert campaign in North Africa in May 1943. It was then based at Zuara in Tripolitania, where

★ See Chapter 12.

members enjoyed a well-deserved period of quiet, rest and, for some, leave and travel.

It was at this time that General Leclerc's column had arrived in Tripolitania after a dramatic dash from Chad to take the Italian armies in Tripoli on the flank. It was in the throes of being formed into a Division Blindée – the 2nd Armoured Division of the Free French. To staff its rudimentary medical services, thirty FAU men were requested. Three were detached from the HSU, under Hamilton Mills; they were soon joined by a larger party from England and a smaller group of FAU men in Egypt (see chapter 10).

For the HSU itself, there was another move – this time to Hammamet in Tunisia where Christmas 1943 was celebrated with a series of bois-terous 'Spears parties' with each section of the Hospital performing skits on the others. By now this odd mix of nationalities and social classes was developing into a cohesive working and social unit although there were a few problems with the women drivers:

Freddie Temple:

There was this bunch of of extraordinary – now they seem very old-fashioned – women drivers of the *very* cut-glass, upper class voices who thought themselves *right* above everyone else. A few years ago a very misleading TV programme about the HSU – 'Silk Stockings and Tin Hats' – concentrated wholly on these drivers who made out that it was all a great lark: 'no more caviar and cham-pagne, just bully beef, like the boys.' They called the really mar-vellous group of English nurses 'the nannies' in a very derogatory way, although these were hard-working, highly qualified, nursing sisters. Then, oh dear, shame, there was us – the FAU – whom the drivers called 'dogs bodies' and treated us likewise.

David Rowlands:

These drivers, with backgrounds totally different from many of ours, looked down on us – some more than others as they did seem to have slightly more tolerance for Quakers than for those of our group who weren't Friends. The first thing we had to do before erecting the tents was to fix the latrines. This was often late at night

Lady Spears with Col. Vernier. Silk stockings, tin hats and peep-toed shoes as well!

when we hadn't eaten anything all day. They did nothing to help, we were expected to do it for them and put up their tents too; and we did resent this. With the nurses, it was very different, they were professionals, not debs or society ladies. They warmed to us and we to them all along. As for the jobs these drivers did, I would say that very often they weren't necessary. I often wondered about their function. They were occasionally requisitioned to drive a French officer from one place or another, but they tended to go off to places where there would be an officer's mess and a lot of social activity and of course they were much admired and many of the army officers – who *didn't* have to put up their tents – wanted to take them out and give them a good time. Although they were supposed to be trained in maintaining their vehicles and should have been able to change wheels and mend punctures, we tended to do most of this too. No, the drivers, I feel, were not a vital part of the HSU set-up. Lady Spears, of course, was.

Michael Rowntree:

We regarded Lady Spears with a mixture of exasperation and affection. She wasn't the easiest of characters to deal with and although she approved of us as a unit, she certainly did *not* agree with our pacifist views. She would tell us quite frankly, not exactly that we were dodging the column, but that we were shirking our responsibilities as individuals. She couldn't, or wouldn't, understand the religious bases of our pacifism at all. I don't think she insulted us, she would just say what she thought without worrying about the effect it had on others. I think there was a class element quite apart from the pacifist issue. Her favourites were her 'gels' – the MTC drivers who, in the main, shared her view of us – that we were cowardly and using our views to get out of the dangerous jobs of the services.

She was not an easy character, she was arrogant and certainly liked getting her own way, and usually did. She was keen on playing bridge and would draft suitable FAU members in to make a four

Nick Alderson, leader of the section, killed in Libya on 14th February 1942 by a bomb, stands second from the left.

whenever she couldn't get more suitable partners. She was eccentric to look at – I don't think it would be too cruel to say that she was quite ugly. She was very forceful and able and certainly the Hospital could not have existed without the direction she gave it in the early days.

Jim Cottrell:

There was the time when Lady Spears appeared – it must have seemed out of the blue – into the hospital in Tobruk calling 'I've arrived with my gels. Where shall we go?' 'You go back Madam!' said the appalled medical officer. 'Certainly not!' she replied, so we stayed in the Tobruk area in a hospital beside the sea. Lady Spears was always a wee bit odd to look at – even in those days to a twenty-five year old she couldn't be regarded as a smart lady. Her clothing was odd in the extreme. Her colour schemes were extraordinary – sometimes all white with World War I medals across her bust. Other times, red all over the place: her mouth, her shoes – everything red. But she was never anything other than perfectly friendly and straightforward to us.

Michael Rowntree:

Humour was a large part of off-duty life in the HSU. We developed Franglais called 'Spears' – French laced with English. Some of us were better linguists than others, this applied to the French too. But this rather matey language of our own developed apace, and some of our regular slang had rather embarrassing results in polite society. Some of us who moved into France later had to watch our step or else we'd come out with phrases of rather a salty nature in inappropriate situations. We also had a wonderful range of Anglo/French songs which have been sung at reunions ever since. The tradition is to add one new verse at each reunion relating what happened at the previous reunion. As well as songs we composed limericks. I remember one night in the desert where we all set to, writing limericks about each other and about the French, and what we were going to do after the war. One of our number, who was a very accomplished writer of light verse, wrote a wonderful sketch about an imaginary reunion in twenty years time and the positions

Tobruk 1943 – Bung it in Jesus!

we'd all occupy when we came to the reunion. It was quite interesting looking at this at some of the reunions and checking where
he'd been right and where wrong. In several cases it was startlingly
accurate and in others wildly false. But there's no doubt there was
a lot of light-hearted banter and a lot of accomplished wit in some
of the social gatherings we had.

I recall the good games of football we played. One was against
the Foreign Legion – this side, of course, being made up of a range
of nationalities. There was a great bearded Spaniard called Jesus
de Mendoza. I remember some of the semi-blasphemous shouts
from the touch line: 'Bung it in Jesus!'

As for our pacifism – most of the French hadn't a clue as to
what it was all about. They knew we were conscientious objectors,
but they couldn't either rationally or emotionally appreciate our
position – our well-springs. Colonel Vernier was the one exception.
We were incredibly fortunate in having him in that his brother, a
pastor, was a pacifist – one of the very few French pacifists. So

Vernier was at least able to understand and to some extent sympathise with the stand that we took. The same could not be said for Colonel Fruchaud, our first colonel, a brilliant surgeon who had worked in the Spanish Civil War. He had no time for us and was transferred to another unit because he just couldn't understand or tolerate working in such as unusual set up as the Hadfield Spears Hospital Unit. But Vernier could and did, and became a great friend. He was a very unusual, unorthodox character with a great sense of humour. Without him the Hospital would have been a very different set-up, and he was able to get over the kind of tensions that inevitably arose in such a mixed group – it was thanks to him that our cohesiveness was developed and maintained.

By the spring of 1944, the respite was over, and once more the Hospital moved off into a war zone. The First Division received orders to join the Corps Expéditionnaire which had been operating in Italy throughout the winter. On 4 May 1944 the Division and Hospital sailed round the hump of Vesuvius into the bay of Naples and onto the soil of Europe – for many, it was the first time for three years. For the French, it was a big moment, an important stage on their long way home.

Hugo Powell:

We went over in Liberty Ships. The journey was very alarming because we were all bunged in the hold at night and a guard put over the hatch because they were afraid of people smoking and giving away our position to submarines. The ship would be going along and suddenly the engine would stop and the ship would start to creak and you realised that a sub was around and then you started wondering what would happen if this crammed ship were hit. Unfortunately, I had conversations with crew members and was told that nobody ever escaped if you were hit. It had its comic atmosphere too, watching all these different nationalities amusing themselves. I remember the Vietnamese had a pig with them, others had rabbits; it was quite a menagerie. I'm sure a British ship would not have permitted it. It was wonderful seeing the Vietnamese battalion going off on the gangway at Naples, and the last man in the column, whose rifle was being carried by the man in front, clutching the squealing pig.

Naples was in a really dreadful state. Neopolitans were supposed to be unloading our ship, but they were starving and weak and could hardly do the job. As we unloaded our stuff, we discovered under the floorboards of this Liberty Ship a mass of tinned provisions which we understood was for the starving of Europe. We asked about this, and were told not to touch it. I'm afraid this was one of the times when one ceased to be honest. We used to pinch it in large quantities and smuggle it out into the town to feed some of these poor Neapolitans.

Roy Ridgway:

We very soon went into action. This was in May, just before the battle of Cassino and our first site was San Clemente. I remember the convoy moving very slowly towards the front line and Michael Rowntree holding it up while he got his binoculars out to look at some rare birds he'd spotted. There was a certain corner we had to turn quickly because German guns were trained on it. Monte Cassino was not far off.

On May 11 – the eve of the battle of Cassino – we spent the whole night putting up the huge hospital tent wards and preparing for the casualties. I remember we were all sitting on the side of the hill, and suddenly the artillery started firing. It was tremendous, a bigger barrage even than El Alamein. We dug fox-holes. There was tremendous tension. Then, in a moment of silence in the darkness, I heard this typical English voice say 'I can't help feeling that Jerry's going to reply to our little follies.' This was Freddie Temple's understatement; and it really eased our tension. Soon guns were firing from both sides, there were flares in the valley, all hell was let loose and the whole of the mountain opposite seemed to be on fire. And, strangely, in the middle of it all the nightingales were still singing. Amazing. We were set up right in front of our heavy artillery and shells came right over the hospital.

The next morning the casualties were brought in – hundreds of them, filling the wards and some on stretchers outside. People were going around with tea and looking after them in various ways.

I remember the French were very anti-Italian at that time because of the 'stab in the back', and when Italian civilians caught in the cross-fire were brought in for attention, they were dealt with last of all. In resuscitation I worked all day and night. We had some terrible cases: I remember one very young lad with shrapnel in the spine saying 'Will I get over this?' 'Yes, of course you will.' I assured him. He died during the operation. Another case was a man with his brains hanging out. I said to the doctor 'What shall I do with him?' and the doctor replied 'Oh just leave him there until he gets better.' People turned the most horrific things into jokes – it was a kind of defence. Some of the patients were incredibly brave. I recall a man with both his feet crushed and when I asked him how he was he said 'Well, I couldn't run a mile now!' That sort of thing. It went on and on and was ghastly and we were all terribly tired and as scared as anybody else. After a few days, the Germans retreated and the Colonel, who was treating the Hospital like a cavalry unit said 'Ah advance!' He seemed to be enjoying the war immensely – he was like a schoolboy and would delight in watching bridges being blown up.

In the middle of one night we packed the Hospital up and moved forward along this dirt-track of a road with mines on either side and the smell of dead horses and corpses, and drove forward in the darkness. We arrived in a field some miles further north into the Liri Valley, to the village of San Giorgio where the French were attacking a sector of the Adolf Hitler line. We were hard at it for about two weeks there. The Colonel had put our hospital right in front of the French Army HQ and it was camouflaging the guns behind as well as the Army Command Post, which was very naughty of him. Some of us complained about this because he was protecting the French Army with the Red Cross, which isn't done. We were right by the battle at this point. We could see the Monastery on Monte Cassino being dive-bombed by the Americans, this was the dominant position that had to be taken. This was the 'Battle of Cassino.' We weren't aware of this at the time. We only knew that there was a lot of slaughter and that we were breaking through the Germans lines. I was working again in resuscitation and I remember the shells were coming closer and Michael Rowntree shouting 'Getting closer. Don't you wish you were back in the clinics?' Then

I remember being in the resuscitation ward with Doctor Jiberet who was putting a needle into a vein for a blood transfusion when a huge chunk of shrapnel fell at our feet. He didn't flinch but just went on doing this very delicate task. A few more inches would have finished us both.

Although we got so tired, it was better working than being off-duty. I remember lying in a ditch with a couple of our men, wondering which way to lie: if one side then shrapnel there; if stomach down then a wound in the spine; if lying on the back, then the stomach would get it – and you knew all the implications of such wounds. On duty you had a job to do and so forgot about personal safety.

The refugees were streaming away from the front lines, clutching their belongings. Bridges were blown up, towns and villages destroyed – just like the pictures of the First World War. We had some German prisoners, some very scared: they thought they were going to be castrated and other terrible things would happen to them. We treated all our patients the same – French, German, Arabs, Russians. I knew enough of each language to say 'Hello'; and I remember seeing them all together in this one ward – all brothers together in misery, all this common humanity caught up in war. The different personalities: the stoical German, uncomplaining; the jokey Englishman; the Frenchman – Oh-la-la!

We were really integrated into the army at that stage. Debates about pacifism were no longer relevant. We liked to see the Germans driven away – this is just human. It had been the same in the London blitz: we liked to see our fighters go up, driving the Luftwaffe away. It was something we spoke of: it was very difficult reconciling our feelings of partisanship with our pacifism. Yet I think we kept alive this feeling that the enemy is not an evil person, that he was someone like ourselves, with the same feelings, and that survival was the same for us all. It wasn't me, an Englishman, against the Germans. It was surviving with the rest of them. Patriotism didn't enter into it. Winning the war didn't enter into it. Survival was the thing and the sooner the war was over, the better.

This is where I wanted to be. I'm very glad I was there to see what the reality of war was. I had talked about the horror of war and here I was in the midst of it, seeing human beings doing the most horrible things to each other, yet fundamentally, having the same needs and feelings. And because of some politicians, or a madman like Hitler, they were drawn into this terrible conflict. I felt 'I have been there, and seen the hell of war and the bravery and the courage and the way "enemies" can get together. There is no enemy really. I am still a pacifist.'

After this we drove our trucks to Rome and were the first British to arrive there. The French requisitioned Count Ciano's house. We stayed there and we pinched his wine from his cellar – I remember the Quakers objected to this! The people came out to greet us. We had an audience with the Pope – how funny, Quakers having an audience with the Pope! We waited in the Sistine Chapel for him; he kept us waiting a long time. We were told that we had to kiss his ring. I wasn't going to do that. In the end I went off to a teashop. Some of the others spoke with him, Freddie Temple was one.

We stayed in Rome for a while and loved it. Then we went up further north to Lake Bolsena, where we were within a mile or so of the Germans. I remember listening to the radio and worrying about my family in London with the flying bombs. Also, being horrified by hearing our position described exactly over the air. The Germans did some terrible things, like leaving booby traps attached to dead bodies, so anyone removing them would be blown up. Ghastly things done. Then the Division was withdrawn to a transit camp in outside Naples for reorganisation and re-equipment. The Normandy landings had taken place and we were to land in France to form a pincer movement.

CHAPTER 10

With the Fighting French: Joy and Pain of Liberation

CITATION
Rowlands, David – of the British Army – Hadfield Spears
Hospital, 1st DMI

'English nurse of Hadfield Spears Hospital since its beginnings in October 1940. Very good operating theatre nurse. Particularly distinguished himself by his sangfroid during the bombardment of the Hospital during the days of 22 and 23 May 1944 at San Giorgio de Liri in Italy. Has equally demonstrated his qualities on 15 August 1944 in the course of the landing of the 1st African Commando Unit at le Canadel, being trapped in debris by bombardment in the station where he had established his aid post and, extricating himself from the ruins with some injuries, set to work at once in a neighbouring house.'

This citation carries the award of the Croix de Guerre
with Vermeil Star.
Coste-Floret, 12 June 1947.

IT WAS DURING a night in mid-August that a small group of the Hadfield Spears Hospital slipped secretly out of their Italian camp. It had left to take part in a 'Surgical Commando' accompanying an advance party which landed on the Riviera coast of France on D Day minus 1. The group was led by Col. Vernier and consisted of a driver, a nursing sister, two Frenchmen and one FAU member, David Rowlands.

144

David Rowlands:

I was approached by the Colonel and told of the plan about three weeks before we actually departed. It had to remain absolutely secret. We started making preparations: Pierre Merjier, the chief pharmacist of the Hospital, and I were given the job of making up a dozen big baskets of all the materials that would be needed for emergency operations immediately on landing. Each had to be self-sufficient so that if some were knocked out we wouldn't be missing a vital piece of equipment. I've often wondered, out of all the FAU, why me? It could be that my French was better than the others due to having been to school in France. Also, having done a mechanics course, this was useful with medical equipment. I had also switched over from the mechanical to the medical side whilst working in Tunisia, so I had experience of working in the theatre with the Colonel and seemed to have a special rapport with him. Whatever the reason, I did feel very privileged that he had asked me. In the middle of the night in early August, I heard the Colonel's voice at the entrance of my tent saying 'Are you alone?' He then told me that we shortly had to leave. Michael Rowntree had woken up by sounds of us moving about and Vernier was worried that he might make trouble and tell me that I shouldn't go. But I had disobeyed the Colonel and had told Mike. I felt it my duty to do this and I trusted him. So the whole outfit was Colonel Vernier, Captain Jiberet, the anaesthetist, Sub-Lieutenant Merjier, the pharmacist, and the adjutant, Noceto, who was a VD specialist. Joan Pryke was the nursing sister and one of the drivers, Rachel Howell-Evans also came – I think Colonel Vernier had great faith in Joan Pryke and probably felt that it wasn't wise to have just one woman on the team.

We spent two days off the coast south of Paestrum practising landing and disembarking. We were then taken aboard one of three troopships and sailed at 11am of the morning of 11 August. Various ships joined us off Acropoli including an escort. On 12 August we observed the north-east tip of Sardinia and Corsica in the mist ahead, then it was on and into Propriano. The beach was steep which meant the ships could anchor close to the shore; it was a snug, sheltered haven, ideal for final preparations before the actual invasion in France. The main body of the troops were about a

kilometre inland, but our little group were bivouacked in a vine-
yard only ten yards from the beach. We were sternly warned by the
Colonel about talking to goatherds and shepherds, saying that there
would be drastic consequences if we spoke to anyone on Corsica,
so we kept well away.

In the evening there was a general assembly on the beach and
final orders were given by the Colonel in charge of the landing operation. First of all he had a silence in memory of those who had
fallen in the early days, and then we had a special last supper on
the beach including freshly baked white bread from the ship. We
then had a final bathe in the crystal clear waters before getting back
on to the ship. I remember being very moved waiting there with
the ship silhouetted against the night sky.

On 14 August we embarked from that beach in our landing
craft and were swung on board the *Prince David*. It was a most
impressive sight seeing the convoy at full speed in perfect weather
– blue sky, calm sea and heading goodness knows where. There

Southern France – Landing beach.

The French invented the words 'Off-road' vehicle.

was a lot of tension as the last light of day dwindled. We then went below and were given a square meal and the crew was put onto action stations with all ventilators shut off to prevent any noise – this meant unbearable heat on the ship. Suddenly there was a lot of activity and the first wave asked to stand by. The lines of rubber dinghies went off and we had a very moving message from the Captain of the ship, wishing us all good luck. Our turn came at 11.30pm when we were lowered into an inky black night. We gradually got used to the darkness and chugged along in the landing craft. I remember hearing the Lieutenant in charge giving the distance at a point where we could actually smell the pines. This was a great thrill to the French who knew they were actually approaching their own country at last. We eventually crunched onto the sand and the Colonel, Jiberet and the two women went inland leaving Merjier and I on the shore to guard the paniers that we had brought up. But at this point there was sudden panic when it was discovered that we were on the wrong beach. Merjier got into the landing craft and went off. I was left on the beach with Noceto. At this stage there was a lot of mortar fire so Noceto and I went up into the cover of the woods, waiting.

As the day dawned, we could gradually see our surroundings and we went further inland. At about 5am we approached a house, announced who were were and got a tremendous embrace from the couple in the house. The man was a local doctor: we were in the right place! It was soon after this that an Allied bombardment started strafing the beach, and then bombing. The navy were bombarding Cap Negre. which was nearby and we were clear of that, but not of American aircraft. There was considerable panic amongst civilians; the doctor and some of them took refuge in the nearby railway tunnel with some of the wounded. Noceto and I went into a building in the station itself and assembled some of our material. We didn't have a surgeon with us but we did what we could. But shortly a bomb demolished the railway station and we were all half buried in masonry and splintered wood. There were numerous casualties at this point: I remember a soldier with his foot blown off and several civilian casualties. About 10.30am aerial activity ceased and we found a handcart on which to transport the surgical equipment. In this we were helped by some Armenians and Poles in German uniform who had been taken prisoner; they also acted as stretcher bearers. We then went into a house which was turned into a dressing station. By now we were very anxious for the fate of the colonel and the others.

We found later that they had gone straight inland and had walked for some miles. Merjier had contacted them and it was a great relief when the whole team met up. The Colonel immediately examined patients and operations were soon in progress. These had to be done mostly on the ground on stretchers, and we had problems with ants crawling over sterile areas, but we did our utmost for the patients in the most difficult circumstances; I remember the Colonel operating on a perforated ulcer by the light of candle and a very small headlamp. We had the good fortune of finding a German NCO amongst the prisoners who was a medical orderly and his services were invaluable. We then found a bigger house with better space and hygiene. At this stage the civilian population had found an ancient vehicle which we used to evacuate post-op patients. The Allied advance was very swift as there had been far less resistance than had been expected, and we all moved in our ancient lorry to Le Lavandou where we set up in a seaside hotel. The civilians were wonderful: they brought sheets, blankets and did everything they could to help us.

Although the advance had been tremendously swift, there had been great resistance at Toulon which meant the hospital had been overloaded. The less severely wounded were sent back to us and it was at this time that we were working day and night almost falling asleep on our feet – the Colonel operating and Jiberet giving anaesthetics. We were then attached to the Medical Battalion for the advance up the Rhône valley. There were still pockets of resistance, but it was an incredible experience to be on the move at last. We passed through Toulon with the shattered dock area and, once more, the sickly smell of death, then on to a desolate and empty Marseille. Next we went to Aix-en-Provence and here the contrast was staggering: it seemed totally unaffected by the war. The pavement cafés were in full swing with waiters wearing little waistcoats handing out drinks. We went into a nice little bistro where we were served – sunshine and wine flowing well. We were among the very first to cross the Rhône. All the bridges had been blown and our vehicles – jeeps by then – were transported in pairs, lashed to planks on pontoons driven by three lusty outboard motors which went in fits and starts but got us across. All the while melons and other welcoming gifts being thrown to us as we passed by. We reached Lyon just as the Germans were pulling out, mainly on bicycles. No triumphant entry because firing was still going on. In fact shooting continued sporadically for several days; but gradually this died down and on the 8 September at Frenchfield we were united with the main Hospital. I was received with open arms by my FAU friends, but there were words between the Free French about what had happened.

Looking back on this episode I can understand their resentment. I do think that the Colonel had behaved irresponsibly in leaving the Hospital in the way he had. After all, he was in charge of the whole Hospital and he left with a note simply saying that he had gone. Commandant Coupigny, another surgeon, so I heard later, was absolutely furious when he woke up and read the note. As for risks, I recognised these at the time and gave Gordon Pearson a note which included a will before we left. I felt it quite on the cards that we might not survive. But compared with what some people had to face, it wasn't that risky. Also, despite the heavy casualties at times, I always felt in control. We worked flat out for seventy-two hours at a time but it was never like Deraa where we had felt totally overwhelmed – that was more than a human being could cope with. It was lucky that the Germans hadn't got crack troops down in the south, otherwise the resistance would have been much greater.

The main Hospital had moved off from Naples on 29 August and landed at Fréjus, west of Cannes. No news had been received of the Colonel and his 'Surgical Commando' and the difficulty was to find them. Eventually, as has been explained, they met up at Lyon.

Roy Ridgway:

We didn't know what to expect as we approached Fréjus. I was asked to stay behind on one of the ships while the landing took place to look after the vehicles. I stayed there all night, expecting to be bombed. But the Germans had fled. There was no resistance at all for the landing on the south of France. Very few people know about this landing. The Fréjus beach landing was mainly a Free French affair. The feeling on board approaching the beach was terrific. The French were full of pride and joy that they were returning to the land they had fled when defeated. I remember one man who had been away for a long time. He was very drunk and when he arrived he got into his jeep, ran into a tree, and was killed – just after landing on his native soil, after all those years.

It was terrific, terrific! We drove up the Rhône valley – I was in my little truck – and we were fêted and greeted everywhere by shouting, joyful people throwing grapes at us. Everybody cheering and handing out bottles of wine. I'd been drinking rather a lot and was driving somewhat erratically. The gendarme put up his hand. I thought he was going to stop me from driving, but instead he took out a bottle of wine from under his cloak. We were the first in when Lille was liberated. I remember the dancing in the streets. I felt very French. Everybody loved us.

It wasn't all joy though. The French were anxious to prove that they had not been collaborators and some very nasty things happened. I remember moving into a hospital in Lyon where our Frenchmen were taken into the mortuary by people who told them 'These are the Germans we've killed. We got them as they were retreating.' Women who had been friendly to the Germans were publicly humiliated and had their heads shaved before jeering crowds.

The front moved incredibly fast as there was hardly any resistance. We arrived in towns the Germans had left the day before; we found uniforms and playing cards discarded in their haste to get away. Our lines of communications were very stretched and often we had to go back for water and other resources. All the way up English civilians appeared from nowhere; they'd been caught in the south of France when the war started. Then the Germans made a stand at the Belfort Gap. We requisitioned a château for our Hospital and got out of tents into a building and started to treat the casualties which, once more, were coming in. Then we were called to a place called Le Hohwald, near Strasbourg where battles were raging. The object was the defence of Strasbourg as the Germans were advancing on it. It was all part of the Battle of the Bulge. We set up the Hospital there and treated a lot of casualties. Then came the message from General Leclerc, of the 2nd Division: 'Bravo! Strasbourg is saved.'

At this stage we were all becoming very depressed because the war was coming to an end and people wanted to go home. I remember Lady Spears coming and giving us a pep talk. There was a great argument about Quakers having lost their ideals. We were all disillusioned and conscious that we weren't the young men we had been at the start of the war, wanting to show the world how it should behave. We realised that we had become involved in it as much as anybody else. There was a general lacklustre feeling of burden which the military felt too. The battle had been won – there were long periods of doing nothing and we wanted to get home to get on with the work of peace. People went home on leave and came back; some had been overseas for four years or more. We had been invaded by French personnel by that time – people who had been in the Maquis – and the English were not needed so much. We were almost redundant. It was war weariness as much as anything. But at that point, just when it seemed the war was coming to an end, things changed and we were sent to another front on the Riviera, near the Italian alps.

Michael Rowntree:

The last months of the war seemed to us a particularly tragic time. As May approached, it seemed obvious to everyone concerned that the war would end within a matter of days, but for political reasons, the French found it necessary to attack a very strong position in the mountains in order to try to get into Italian territory to hold as a bargaining counter when peace came. The tragedy was that they had as many casualties in that last week of the war as in any of the major battles they had fought during the war. It was heartbreaking to be in conditions of considerable luxury in a Riviera hotel and to have all these casualties pouring in when we all knew that the war was going to end within a week. We all found this very hard to take: a terrible example of how political expediency can impact on the lives and deaths of men.

At one stage, earlier in the fighting, the Hospital had been based near Royan, north of Bordeaux, where the Division had been dealing with a pocket of resistance. When it was moved to serve the defenders of Strasbourg, a small surgical team was left behind:

David Rowlands:

We did have a really extraordinary experience with the German forces. The hospital had been called away leaving a small poste avancé to look after the remaining patients. During this time there was a massive Allied bombardment on Royan on the Atlantic coast. There were pockets of German resistance there, as well as La Rochelle and other places along the Atlantic where the Germans were supplied by Spain long after the liberation of France. And these Germans were quite comfortable in these pockets, and the aim was to flush them out, which the bombardment attempted to do. But this time the civilian area was hit.

On 9 January 1945 a German car with a white flag arrived where we were staying. It was made clear by the German officer that they were overwhelmed by the weight of the attack on the civilian population and had no means of evacuating the wounded and at any rate wanted medical and surgical help. A two day truce was agreed and the plan was that we would be escorted through the minefields by the Germans, to reach the patients. It was quite extraordinary: we each had an armed German on our running boards, headed by the senior officers. A lot of civilians had been killed, but there were many wounded we were able to help. The main thing was to arrange to evacuate the patients, which we did successfully. It was a short visit, but we were well looked after in the school we were given to work in. I remember vividly a young woman coming up to me saying that the English had killed her husband. She said she was sure it was the English and she produced some papers taken from the pilot's pockets – he had been shot down – as evidence. She was very bitter. I didn't know what to say to her. When we left, people came and held onto the backs of our lorries, but the Germans beat them off and they had to stay. We were given safe conduct and escorted back through the minefields to the frontier. It was an extraordinary experience: whereas we had seen in the Western Desert bedraggled, dejected, miserable, thin and wasted German prisoners, here were these arrogant, proud and fat Germans, obviously feeling their military might was still intact. But they were absolutely correct with us according to the Geneva Convention. I felt no hatred for them, but I did have the feeling that they were "the enemy." Yes.

Roy Ridgway:

We were in the south of France when the war ended in May. There was a terrific celebration: fireworks and people throwing hand grenades into the sea and shooting guns in the air. They dragged all the furniture of a collaborator out of his house and made a huge bonfire of it. I remember driving in a jeep over the Italian border with the Colonel. We had swopped hats and I was saluted everywhere. Everything was quiet in Italy – the Italians were not celebrating, of course. I wrote in my diary that my mood could be best expressed by W.H. Auden's: 'The stars are not wanted now. Put out every one. Pack up the moon, and dismantle the sun. Pour away the ocean and sweep up the wood. For nothing now can come to any good.'

Hugo Powell:

The 1st Free French Division was very special. But in a way it had a touch of tragedy about it. They had been away for so long. I think it was almost a mystical feeling for them getting off the boat and onto that beach. The Resistance had been very active, and they weren't always received with the open arms they expected. Then de Gaulle, for obvious political reasons, wanted to amalgamate young resistance people into the Division, and not all of them were willing to be bossed about by these soldiers who, although they had been fighting, had been out of things at home. Most of this was coped with quite well, but there were terrible tensions underneath. We were always well received, always magnificently looked after in our billets, but some viewed us with misgivings. Every time we entered a liberated town some very unpleasant things were going on. There was a tremendous amount of cruelty and injustice and lots of old scores being paid off. This caused friction between us and the Free French because we protested from time to time about various abuses; really we were grateful that we didn't have to go into Germany with them as our friends from the 2nd Division did.

Michael Rowntree:

Our end with the Hadfield Spears Hospital was unfortunately clouded by political factors. There was tension existing at that time between the British and General de Gaulle who, by the end of the war, was back in France. De Gaulle had always suffered from a complex that he had to depend on British support throughout the war and was anxious to sever any links and establish himself as an independent force as quickly as possible. To celebrate victory, on June 18, there was to be a big parade down the Champs Elysées. We were invited to take part and we drove our lorries and staff cars as part of the defile down the Champs Elysées and into the Place de la Concorde where General de Gaulle and others were taking the salute as the French forces drove past. We swept past him with our British flag, and at that moment a group of our former patients, shouted 'Vive Spears!' At that time relations between de Gaulle and General Spears, representing the British, were extremely tense and this cheer is alleged to have so angered de Gaulle that he ordered that the British contingent of the Hadfield Spears Hospital should be sent home from France immediately.

Our French colleagues were extremely annoyed and resentful of this, they were angered by the fact that we had, in effect, been kicked out of France having worked with them for four years. The irony of it was that when we finally came to leave from Le Trilport, our base near Paris, to drive to Dieppe, we were seen off and played out by the full band of the Foreign Legion. The additional irony – and this shows the slight difference in formality between the French and the FAU – was that the band turned up unexpectedly at 7am; most of us were still in bed and certainly not in fit state to be played out to Dieppe. So we hurriedly assembled the vehicles and drove them out away from our encampment with great panache, then drove them around a corner and waited until the band of the Foreign Legion had dispersed. We then went back and had our breakfast.

Finally, at Dieppe, the Colonel and several of his officers and nurses turned up at the quayside where we all joined together, to the astonishment of the troops on board, in lustily singing the songs that had seen us through the war years.

It is sad that the demise of the HSU should have been soured in this way by de Gaulle. There is no doubt, we were a peculiar mix of people which, on the face of it, had very little chance of working. But surprisingly it worked very well as a cohesive and effective unit throughout the war and this move of de Gaulle's didn't in any way affect the close relationships between the British and French members of the Hospital which have been continued through regular reunions since the war, alternating in Britain and France.

SUR LA DISSOLUTION DE 'SPEARS'
TRILPORT, June 1945

1. Le jour de départ n'est pas loin   (Bis)
   Et chacun ira dans son coin   (Bis)
   Ils sont ensembles, Kit & Jacko, Smew et Oscar,
      le père Boillot
                   Depuis Syrie   (Bis)
                   Deraa, Damas y compris.   (Bis)

2. Ensablés avec le Khamsin
   Des mois passés a Bir Hacheim:
   Fruchard, Aurès, La Buterne, Abouchard et les citernes
       Ça tient, ça tient
         Et à Sollum tout le monde revient.

3. A Sollum on a rencontré
   Le médecin commandant Vernier
   Avec Thibaux, Schick et Merjier, Jiberry, Petit, Yanzi et
       Toute l'équipe
         Filait au Caire au dernier type.

4. L'avance vers Tunis était fou,
   Et puis Afrique étant à nous
   On s'installa à Zuara – une sorte de Riviera
       Kuacou, Kuacou
         Est sorti pour – – – se balader.

5. Pendant les jours en Tunisie
   Sous vent et de la boue et pluie,
   Hadj et Maheut, Joan et Olly, Noceto, Daniel et Solly
       Voyaient, voyaient
         L'arrivée de Jacques Duprey.

6. En Europe enfin débarqués
   Bougrement on a boulonneé
   San Clemente, Frosinone, Rome et Montefiascone
       Ça pu, ça pu,
         Du cheval mort sur la rue.

7. En août on se trouvait en France
   Passant par Vals les Bains – quelle chance
   Roger Whiteley il se marrait, et Coupigny se bagarrait;
       On sait, on sait,
         Que Speeeeers est arrivé.

8. Pendant toutes les campagnes depuis
   Spears a travaillé jour et nuit:
   La cuisine, les dentistes, brancardiers et garagistes
       Les Miss, les Miss
         Et *même* les conductrices.

ENVOI

C'est vrai Spears n'est pas donc foutu,
L'esprit vive toujours entre nous
Grâce à Vernier, sa famille, tous nous autres sont réunis.
    Quelle chance, quelle chance
    Vive les Verniers, vive la France!

Although it was the HSU which participated in the post-war Victory Parade in Paris which so infuriated General de Gaulle, it was another FAU group which was hailed by a French underground newspaper as the first British people to enter *Paris on its liberation. These were the men who served with the Medical Battalion of the 2nd Division, under General Leclerc. This Divison Blindée, as we have seen, had been formed in Tripolitania in the spring of 1943. It was equipped and organised on American lines and, unlike the voluntary nature of the Hadfield Spears Unit, FAU members had to fit into a medical service of American Army pattern which meant they became one of the two FAU units integrated most fully with the armies, operating right up at the front (and sometimes beyond) alongside their military comrades.* [1] *Three men, led by Hamilton Mills, had been detached from the HSU for duty with the 2nd Division; they were joined in Rabat, north of Casablanca, by a larger party of thirty men from Britain and a small group of FAU men in Egypt; Hamilton Mills was in command and Bill Spray, newly arrived from Britain, the second in command.*

Derryck Hill:

    In the spring of 1943, I was back in Daly's again having had a bit of leave, when I heard that with five others, I had been designated to join an FAU unit, similar to the HSU, which was to be attached to the newly formed Free French 2nd Division being assembled in Tripoli. The six of us were the basis of a unit to be joined by a large group coming from England to complete it – I was the sole survivor of the original Middle East section. The French, under General Leclerc, had come up from Chad. Their transport was in a terrible state, totally decrepit but this, we learnt, was going to be re-equipped by the Americans who were based at

Casablanca. So to Rabat, near Casablanca we went. There we were based on the race course. It was a superb summer. I can still see and smell the spring flowers – lovely blue narcissi, about two inches high, blooming everywhere and there were nightingales singing in the wood across the track – bliss! I remember the first supplies we drew from the Americans. I couldn't believe it! Imagine, after the lack of comforts of any kind, to suddenly be issued with whole cartons of cigarettes and to be given not one, but two chickens in a case, and a five pound tin of bacon. Fantastic! We were then allowed to draw the American PX (our NAAFI) – unbelievable! We also ran into American Quakers there who were working with the American Relief Service. They had a lovely flat which we were invited to. We also had opportunity for meetings for worship which had been difficult to hold on the open plain.

We were given a very warm welcome by the French and had very good relations with them although they drove us round the bend at times. We eventually got our ambulances and started training for our function which was the motor ambulance convoy (Ramassage), of the third company, part of the 13th Medical Battalion, providing medical services for the 2nd Division. I'd say that we were a very happy unit. The French were absolutely elated because they were now well equipped and ready to fight for France. The Americans went over the moon to equip them well. But it was strange: the French were very proud of their new equipment but resented very much their dependence on Americans for this.

In May 1944, after our training in Rabat, we heard that we were going back to Britain for the Second Front. So it was further training in Cottingham, near Hull. We heard about D Day as we went across north Scotland and went into the Humber. At that stage I left. I'd had my share after three years. The section saw a lot of action being with an armoured division and the man who took over my position got killed. Later, I was sorry that I didn't go with them. My friend, Bill Spray, did.

Bill Spray:

Humphrey Waterfield and I were chosen to go to England from Rabat as part of an advance party to prepare the way. I remember

Humphrey, who was an artist and scholar, teaching himself Greek on the ship, reading Plato in the original to the astonishment of everybody, including me. When we arrived in Scotland, the Chief Petty Officer took me to one side and said 'Sir, I want you to know it's been a great privilege to have you two gentlemen on our ship. We know you are more than you seem.'

There were slight difficulties at Cottingham when the French arrived. It became quite tricky with the local female population. It was horrifying to come back to one's country, finding schoolgirls lining up outside the camp as prostitutes and trying to explain to the French that not all English girls were like this. Also, when you went into a pub, it was obvious that you were different from anyone else the locals had met – obviously not French nor like the other English soldiers they'd met. Therefore, explaining that we were COs could cause the atmosphere to freeze a bit. But it wasn't really serious, and then pretty soon, on July 20, we set off for France.

The French would describe their return in quite a different way from us. I mean we were excited beyond words being COs in a total war, doing at last what we had wanted to do. But the Frenchmen were immensely moved; overcome when, at last, treading the soil of their homeland we landed at Ste. Mère-Eglise on the Normandy coast. It was a bit chaotic at first with people getting lost in the dark and mixed up. We were part of the US Third Army. The American control grated a bit, but France it was! General Leclerc was there. He always wore British battle dress – partly out of affection for the British whom he admired, partly to distinguish himself from the Americans. Soon I was told to go to Cherbourg to establish a French base hospital with a French doctor. It was an interesting experience in Franco/American liaison. The Americans were not always sensitive and their language ability was even worse than the English. The French were prickly: after all it was *their* country and what use was all this new-fangled, complicated medical equipment anyhow? I remember a really marvellous American blood transfusion system which the French just couldn't understand. They virtually cast it aside and went back to the jug and needle. You see they had been brought up in the colonial medical service and their techniques were not at all modern.

Almost before we had taken breath, we were in the Normandy campaign. The trouble with being involved in these things is that you never know what you're doing. What I gathered later was that initially we were driving north to link up with the British who were pushing down to close the Falaise Gap. We set off on 7 August and 10 August was our first day of action. This was made memorable by Tom Newby. His was the third ambulance I had dispatched to pick up wounded. He came back and was so excited, he could scarcely stay inside his ambulance. His speech wasn't always the clearest at the best of times. He jumped out and gabbled 'Ibincatu.' I said 'Tom, do tell me but clearly.' Eventually, he said 'I've been captured.' 'Tom' I said 'Take a deep breath, let's hear what happened.'

What happened was that he had gone in search of wounded with the ambulances and had got separated. The map references had been out but the other two found their way back safely. Tom was left alone and went towards a group of people in the distance, and to his astonishment they turned out to be Germans. So he very sensibly showed his red cross, gave them cigarettes and passed the time of day with them and then said 'Well, now it's time I must be getting back.' He turned the ambulance around and drove back. What with one thing and another, the Quakers were the heroes of that day because we evacuated wounded from a dangerous situation. I was supposed not to be going out, but I got fed up with being left out and, although allegedly in charge, became one of the ambulance drivers or assistants, whatever was needed.

My first excitement came when we moved to Alençon. We moved into a dreadful shambles. The first company was in the process of leaving and seemed far more interested in that than in their patients. We got the worst of the patients into our ambulances and began the evacuation to Le Mans. Derek (Sayers) drove – and became more and more incensed with the stupidity of the French in convoy – whilst I did my best with the drip transfusion case at the back. It was obviously a case of touch and go, and in that hot afternoon Derek and I sweated pints at every unnecessary stop. This was the first time that a man's life rested on our care and speed in arrival. It's a sobering situation but amazingly inspiring, under the stimulus of necessity. I remember I even thought of using the drip rubber tubing as a connection between the water bottle and mouth. Hitherto we'd had to stop each time the patient asked for a drink. Fortunately we reached the hospital in time and within three minutes he was having expert attention. On the way back I had my first experience of heavy bombardment. We were driving along and suddenly the Americans shouted 'Get all those lights out and jump into the ditch!' We got down just when everything around us started to break up.

In the battle areas we worked through finding our wounded, there were always obstacles to get round. We were several times in front of front lines. On one occasion, Derek and I drove out of a village to see a German column just ahead of us. Also, the whole point of being attached to a tank column was being up where they were. The French never worried about the fact that our lorries were not as well protected as their tanks. There were at least two occasions when we were side by side with tanks, evacuating the wounded, when there were supposed to be armoured half tracks, instead of us, which would have withstood a certain amount of shelling. I remember the tank commanders being astonished that we had been allowed up there, and me saying 'We are obeying orders.' I remember once being terribly frightened by this. But they were always very grateful. A village could be ours during the day, and evacuated by night and re-occupied by the Germans. If you had evacuated somebody and were returning, it was quite easy to take people into what had become enemy territory. I remember once having a very difficult journey because we didn't know exactly where the Germans were. I went back onto a road by which we had advanced earlier in the day. There wasn't another vehicle on the road and Arnold, my driver, and I knew the danger of snipers and the forest on either side would have given cover for a large number of troops. We passed burning tanks from which anything might appear. Our worst moment was on perceiving ourselves covered by a very business-like rifle barrel sticking out of the window of a derelict house. Fear did the usual trick of half swallowing and then regurgitating the heart into a new tense strain of excitement as we crawled slowly past. Then the rifle turned itself into a harmless stick, and we laughed hollowly.

We were immensely grateful for the red cross; we were never bombed or attacked directly. The nearest one came to this was being bombed by our own artillery. Also in bombing raids the bombs nearly always came nearer to us than to the enemy they were supposed to be hitting. We were all a good deal wiser after those three or four days of fighting to close the Falaise Gap.

The FAU group stood up to battle extraordinarily well. We were all pleased that we'd had our first experience of being thoroughly frightened, and that we had done our job and survived. Also, we had survived with a certain amount of credit to our ingenuity and ability to improvise – these were the things you depended upon. Part of the uncertainty of the situation was the excitement of the French. For instance, there was this lovely, excitable French doctor who never stopped to think but would go beetling off – time and time again he ended up in front of the tanks. I would say that, on the whole, we ambulance drivers knew quite a bit about the dispositions of enemies and friends. We were going backwards and forwards far more than the tanks were. All the training we'd had came to our aid. I guess we saved quite a few.

We always insisted on treating German wounded equally... There were two kinds of Germans. The kind that was sullenly and committedly Nazi and to whom one's ministrations didn't get through at all. They wouldn't have been at all surprised if we had killed them there and then. Others were just human beings. I remember giving one youngster a cup of tea and he was so surprised to have this and a cigarette given him, that he produced from his pocket a letter and photograph from home, breaking down into tears. But we never really knew what happened to them as they went down the line. The internal French Maquis, no doubt for very good reasons, were far more venomous than those in the military machine. Well, the Falaise Gap was closed and then the buzz went around that it was Paris. Paris! This was terrific.

I don't think I'd ever attached any particular meaning to the word 'liberation' until then. And certainly, I can't ever see or use the word without thinking of the experience of that day, 25 August, rolling into Paris. We were bang behind the tanks. One just hoped that the tank drivers were sober! But they managed to keep the right balance of discipline and sheer joie de vivre. People came out onto the streets, great crowds of them, cheering, throwing flowers, hugging every soldier they could see and, suddenly, discovering that we were English, transferring their affections to us quite as much as to the French. And I fear that we were sufficiently young and gullible as to hang our tin hats out of the ambulances so they could see what we were. It was a brilliantly sunny morning and the French ladies looked magnificent – the widows in black looking motherly; the young ladies so beautiful – where had they got their lovely dresses from? We lifted them up into the tanks and ambulances until a German sniper opened up, then out they would go and it was on with the tin hats and into action in case there were wounded. It was enormous fun, a great outpouring of joy and relief and everything else fell into what seemed the right perspective on that wonderful day. We slept that night in our ambulances in the streets of Paris, with the local Parisiennes absolutely marvellous in their hospitality and welcome.

The next day we walked to the Arc de Triomphe up the Champs Elysées. I had my hair cut because the barber insisted on cutting the hair of 'the first Englishman in Paris', and that night we danced with Anne and Monique, the daughters of a Count whose name I have forgotten.

Yes, we were the first lot in, apart from the British Secret Service. We were in fact the only ones to make a public entry because the Americans had given the Division the honour of liberating Paris. So it was the 2nd Division and these thirty conscientious objectors who rolled in on that splendid day. Indeed, that very day, one of the local papers had the headline 'Duke Mann – First Englishman into Paris!' It had conflated two of our chaps, Marcus Dukes and Raymond Mann. I could go on talking about that journey into Paris for a week! It was a great revelation of the human spirit and astonishing that, in a sense, it required a war to produce it.

There were other similar moments, never quite as spectacular. But let me tell you of another precious moment a long time and several battles after, when we were in the Alsace area, billeted in the house of a family with three little girls. I remember that we were peeling potatoes at the sink and the little girls were singing the carol 'Stille nacht.' Two of us joined in, and I still remember the complete astonishment of the little girls that we knew the same carols. Here were these people coming out from a life underground, where they had suffered endless bombardment and suddenly finding in the midst of all this horror two people who didn't speak their language but could sing the same carols. It was a very moving moment. I went back a few years ago and went into the café asking after the family and was told 'Yes, Mimi lives there.' I went to the house and there was this widow looking very old indeed, not the little girl I remembered. We fell into each other's arms and the first thing she said to me was 'Away in a manger' which we had taught them in English.

There were uglier moments too. I think I felt slightly disappointed in myself seeing women having their heads shaved and doing nothing about it. Yet who were we to interfere in situations we couldn't begin to understand. We made contact with some Quakers in Paris and got to know them well. They obviously were finding their line extraordinarily difficult to keep to. They wished to be friendly to the Germans and they were no less friendly to the French who needed their help; but taking this line, short of being a collaborator, was very difficult. There is no doubt that our turning up in khaki uniforms, and piling into meetings for worship, did more to rescue the Quakers in local esteem than anything else. I remember the meeting when we laid side by side our witness and their witness as Quakers, realising what an astonishing range it was. Their witness, under occupation, was far more challenging than we'd had in attempting to give a witness. It wasn't clear whether some of them thought we'd compromised ourselves unpardonably. I'm sure some felt this, but the younger ones didn't and I think I fell in love for the umpteenth time in my life with a French Quakeress, but I lived to tell the tale...

It was whilst we were in Paris that we had one of our several meetings about medals. The French were very intent on giving us medals and it was desperately difficult to know what Quakers ought to do about it. I know those operating with the First Division had the same dilemma. At the time we came to the conclusion that we would refuse them individually, but we wouldn't mind if a citation and some recognition to us in general was made. In the end it was left in good old Quaker fashion to everybody's individual conscience. But I don't think anybody in our group refused a medal. I got the Croix de Guerre, which I must say, as a conscientious objector, gives me a perverse satisfaction. I accepted it for two reasons: I knew my mother would be so pleased and it seemed that perhaps I ought to please her; then I thought it would be a good thing to have up one's sleeve if ever one was accused of being a CO for cowardly reasons. It was such a nice name too! I have never actually claimed my medal. I still have the rather scruffy citation and the ribbon. Nor have I ever used it apart from those occasions when people ask for 'Honours and Decorations' when it seems quite nice to remind the world that one does have one.

Paris might have been liberated, but the war was far from ending and there were many more hard-fought battles experienced before the Division moved out of France into Germany. On September 8, the Division left Paris to guard the southern flank of the U.S. 3rd Army in its drive to Nancy and Metz. Stiff Panzer opposition was encountered as the drive on Epinal started, and this is when two FAU members, Humphrey Waterfield and Ray Birkett, were captured and imprisoned in Strasbourg until the relief of that city. Meanwhile the battles raged around Damas, Vittel and Dompaire with heavy French, German and civilian casualties. After this, with the onset of rain and mud of late autumn, the German counter-attack slackened for a while and the pattern then became a mix of intensive activity with occasional interludes of doing nothing. Demoralisation set in during these quiet periods, just as it had with those operating with the 1st Division. At the end of October Metz was taken. Then, on 19 November, the advance on the Saverne Gap started, for the final objective, Strasbourg. It was during the battle for Strasbourg that Denis Frazer was killed, whilst rescuing a seriously wounded man. He was twenty-two and had been in the FAU since 1941.

The next objective was to move south to link up with the First Division as it drove north to Belfort. But when Von Runstedt began his offensive in the north, the Division was switched back to block the breakthrough. In the area of Sarreguemines, wounded were evacuated under extremely difficult conditions of snow, ice and mud. It was at this time that Denis Woodcock suffered a serious leg injury and was repatriated. After further fierce fighting north of Strasbourg which, once more, was vulnerable to German attack, the position was stabilised and the Division was able to resume its objective of linking up with the First Division. Between them lay a small pocket of bitter fighting at Neuf Brisach. Every man in the sector had his share of narrow escapes, but here at Neuf Brisach the section suffered its second fatal casualty when John Bough – who had gone out searching for wounded – was shelled and killed. He was found the next day grimly clutching the steering wheel of his ambulance. [2] *Soon that pocket was cleared and the great moment came when the 1st and 2nd Division joined hands and France was free, apart from a few pockets of frantic German resistance. The final battle was dealing with the German stand at Royan. This was a bitterly fought last engagement when for thirty-six hours the rescue and treatment of wounded continued non-stop.*

At this time, General LeClerc wrote a letter of appreciation to the Unit's headquarters in London:

> '...attached to the Third Medical Company, wherein they constituted the entire group of ambulance and nursing personnel. They have contrived in their thankless and obscure work to show themselves worthy of their pacifist ideal in the very centre of the vast machine of war, on every type of road or terrain, in all weathers, by night, by day and very often in forward posts under a fire deadly enough to unsettle the composure of the fighting man. They have displayed the finest qualities of selflessness and charity in order to fulfil this service to their Friends.'

Bill Spray:

After Royan, we advanced into Germany. We weren't fighting there, in fact there was no action after Royan. I think we were just making our way to the part of the occupation that had been assigned to the French. It was a dismal business going into Germany: the air of desolation and a people whose spirit appeared to be broken, sullen and fearful – a nasty mixture. The sullenness may have been just fear. The first night in Germany we stayed in a workhouse and cooked our own food. The inmates were obviously interested in us. I think there was a spice of dislike behind the interest. One could understand why. We were identified with the French, and here they were coming in clearly as conquerors, with a lot to make up for.

This was our great problem as we went into Germany: how far were we going to find ourselves identified with French excesses of a kind which we couldn't possibly condone? A little later on we worked out a good system of spreading our influence so widely in the places in which we stopped that the French were prevented from doing anything incorrect. It soon became known that we stood for fair and proper treatment of the Germans and there was a great attempt to induce the French to think less emotively and uproariously about what they were about. So it was quite a testing time for us as individuals and human beings, even though we were no longer in any kind of mortal danger.

Before long the Division set up camp on the banks of the Ammersee, a blissful place. I remember we spread ourselves out over the village anticipating, correctly, that with our presence, the French would avoid their worst excesses. I turned up in a house in which the husband, an Englishman, and wife had obviously been key figures in the Nazi administration for all the reasons that one could understand. They were obviously targets of dislike from another faction in the village. The husband was clearly terrified as to what would happen when we withdrew. We represented a short period in their lives when they felt comparatively safe. I remember talking at length to him about developments in England. I had with me a copy of Laski's book about revolution and he begged me to leave it with him when I left, hoping that this would illustrate to those who were going to sit in judgement on him that he wasn't quite as bad as they made out. One felt desperately sad for them, and indeed for all of those who had made mistakes and were now going to cop it. We heard later that he had been imprisoned and that the family were living in fairly straightened circumstances. My main memories of Germany: gloom and despair and of a great wall which it was very difficult to get through.

I went through Paris on my way home and stayed with Quakers. The yearly meeting was in session and I remember speaking about the conditions that we had found in Germany, and the sort of attitudes I felt were going to be necessary, and the difficulties, not only in adopting the attitudes but making them effective. One of my few perorations of which I am still mildly proud.

Looking back on these war years, I think that we'd had a unique experience. All the different sections of the FAU had their own distinctive experience and aura of fame. The China Convoy members, as far as I was concerned, were the Gods of the Unit, but we were the people who had had to put up with danger of an extreme kind, and rather more of it than some other sections of the Unit.

REFERENCES:

(1) The other group, closely integrated with the British Army, was Field Surgical Unit Number 12, which served in Europe soon after D Day, landing in Normandy. See chapter 18.

(2) On 11 November 1997, a ceremony was held in the village of Algolsheim in Alsace to inaugurate a new war memorial. John Bough had been killed as he left the village in his ambulance. The villagers have placed a plaque next to the war memorial in his memory. Hamilton Mills and Derek Sayers attended the unveiling ceremony and laid a wreath on the monument.

CHAPTER 11

China Convoy: Trying to Live Extraordinary Lives

THE FALL OF BURMA

Chevrolet of G.M.C. from distant Rangoon
Flogging up the Burma Road in quite large groups
With a cargo of conchies,
Engine oil, and Bibles,
Matches and coffee and comforts for the troops.

Stately North West Convoy weaving out of Chengtu
Plugging north of Kokonor to the Kansu wells
With a cargo of tungsten,
Dynamite and concrete
And petrol and petrol and petrol smells.

Old and dirty coal cart with half blocked gas pipe
Fighting up the mountains and driven by the mugs
With a cargo of missionaries,
Mail bags, truck spares,
Rock salt, oranges, and possibly, drugs.

David Morris, Kutsing.

*J*UST WHEN SECTIONS *in North Africa were settling down to working with the Allied armies, an exciting opportunity opened in wartime China. The idea of helping the Chinese had been mooted as* *early as 1940 when a Joint China Committee, under the chairmanship of Dr. Gordon Thompson, was set up to direct FAU policy in cooperation with the British Relief Unit for China. In early July 1941, a small advance party consisting of Peter Tennant, Selby Clewer, Henry Rodwell and Theo Willis reached Rangoon.*

China had been at war with Japan since 1937. Although the Japanese controlled all the main Chinese cities, industries and communications in eastern China, vast inland areas still remained under Chinese jurisdiction with two main political factions forming the tenuous and short-lived 'United Front.' This consisted of the 'Liberated Areas' controlled by the Chinese Communists, the main base being Yenan in the north and 'Free China' ruled by the Kuomintang, Nationalist government, led by Chiang Kai Shek, based in Chungking. Isolated by the Japanese occupation of the eastern areas, Chungking's overseas links were through Burma. From Rangoon, the railway led up country to Mandalay, to the railhead at Lashio, whence the Burma Road coiled over the mountains through Yunnan province to Kunming in China. From Kunming, Chungking and other newly important cities – Kweiyang and Chengtu – could be reached.

In October 1941, after frustrating delays due to funding and lack of transport, the first major group of forty men – the 'Holy Forty', as they became known jokingly – left in small parties. They were about to participate in one of the greatest adventures and challenges faced by the Unit. Unit parties were still dribbling into Rangoon as late as mid-December. The seventh party, the last, turned up having escaped from Singapore just before the Japanese entered. By this time it had become increasingly clear that except for the five Unit doctors, the most useful function would be the transport of medical supplies and petrol throughout Free China. It was also agreed that the FAU should be affiliated to the International Red Cross (IRC) and take over its fleet, garage, equipment and transport commitments. In return the IRC would pay all operating expenses. The Executive Yuan (the executive arm of the Chinese Government) was to cover expenses incurred in the haulage of supplies for the National Health Administration (NHA). [1]

The 'China Convoy' was distinctive for many reasons: in the vastness of area covered by its activities and the great distance from home; in the huge need yet paucity of relief organisations there; in the degree of culture shock experienced and in the fact that, of all FAU sections, it

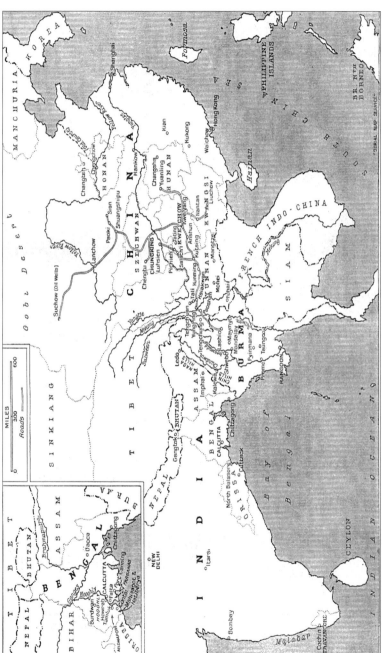

Map III – The Far East.

proved to be the most international. (2) From the start a very happy relationship developed with the American Friends Service Committee (AFSC) which had joined the American organisation United China Relief (UCR) in a joint board. Until late in the war UCR funds, paid through AFSC, were the chief source of income for the China Convoy. (3) Another very important input from across the pond came in the form of the Canadian surgeon Bob McClure:

Michael Harris:

Bob McClure, son of a Canadian mission family, was born in north China and grew up there. He went back to Canada and was then in Edinburgh for a time where he became a fellow of the Royal Society of Surgeons. He was brilliant and a great teacher and returned to China to go into what nowadays we'd call 'community health' – clean water, sanitation, hygiene, that sort of thing. He was working in north China when the war started and was very highly regarded. He went into the Red Cross and was then invited to lead the FAU. He was a committed Christian and very keen on family planning. He is rumoured to have performed one of the first vasectomy operations in China on himself with the aid of mirrors, to demonstrate how it could be done. He would draw the line at nothing. He always wore breeches and boots and a large Australian hat. He smoked filthy Chinese cigars and you could hear his voice from one province to another. He was a brilliant, tempestuous man with a terrible temper. He was very courageous, but hell to live with.

Duncan Wood:

I heard very much later that when word got around the missionary service in China that Robert McClure had been appointed head of a group of pacifists, everybody burst out laughing because although he knew the country like the back of his hand, he was a belligerent man who, at the time, toted a gun. So this relationship had to be sorted out and the first party to arrive got the brunt of it, especially Peter Tennant, the second in command. Eventually, this strange and mistaken appointment worked out very well; we established a modus vivendi with him and he became a very dear friend to us all. Much later, he was asked to write an article on 'the most amazing character I have ever met' for the Readers' Digest. He said 'I'm going to write an article on the forty most amazing characters I've met...'

The Unit's headquarters was initially based in Kweiyang, at first in a godown (warehouse) of the IRC. From early on, the Convoy had been keen to bring Chinese into the work. Contacts were made with the different universities in Chengtu to recruit Christian Chinese students and soon, in October 1941, the first eight arrived, the vanguard of many to serve with the FAU over the following years. At the start, with members of the various parties dribbling in or travelling between Rangoon and Kweiyang, there was a deal of confusion and rather low morale, largely due to the uncertainty of the war situation and the massive challenge the Unit was facing in setting up their operation in such an alien setting. But soon a convoy administration was formed and an Executive Committee set up to control the Unit under its chairman, Bob McClure. Peter Tennant was confirmed as his adjutant, Duncan Wood was appointed group leader, Selby Clewer as quartermaster, Peter Rowlands as manager of Garages and Gordon Keith as finance officer. A little later, after training, Tod Lawry became transport officer.

With the Japanese advance and threat to Burma, convoys began to dash back to bring up as much petrol as possible into China before the Japanese got to the oil wells. En route they dropped off members to set up depots on the trucking route, and new buildings in Kutsing, Paoshan and Hsiakwan. The other urgent task was to get supplies from Rangoon up to Lashio before the Japanese closed the port. Vehicles were unloaded from ships, assembled and driven up to Lashio; supplies were then rushed up the road – medical supplies, equipment, spare parts, engines and tyres – anything they could lay their hands on, even cannibalising the wrecks littering the route. During the month of February, the Unit had salvaged over £120,000 worth of supplies from Rangoon. Right up to the Japanese arrival Unit volunteers were risking yet more trips into Rangoon to see what else could be salvaged:

Tom Haley:

I had just been allotted to my job on transport in Kweiyang, when I was asked to go straight back down the way I'd come to pick up petrol supplies at Wanting.[4] When we reached Wanting there was a telegram telling us that Rangoon was about to be occupied by the Japanese, could we use our discretion about whether we could get the remaining medical supplies out. We had a meeting and decided that we'd try. We went like rockets back to Rangoon. As we got closer we met vast numbers of huge American vehicles careering out of Rangoon. You see, the American Army didn't have enough drivers to get them out before the Japanese arrived, so they gave half-an-hour instruction to anyone willing to get them away. With such limited training and the hazards of the Burma Road, the carnage was dreadful: some had gone straight off the side of the road at bends, others turned over on their sides or upside down and the gorges were littered with wreckage. When you think that those we passed had the Gokteik gorge ahead, I imagine that very few got out and there must have been hundreds of casualties.

We got into Rangoon at midnight having driven 300 difficult miles that day. The next day we located the medical supplies we were after on the docks, loaded them up as quickly as possible and got out. We risked the Pegu road – this was nearer the Japanese advance but the shorter route – and managed to get right out and back to Kweiyang. Another team of seven volunteers, including Bill Brough, went in after us and got more stuff out – they were with the last convoy out of Rangoon.

Bill Brough:

We had returned to Rangoon in a desperate bid to get our remaining trucks out. These were still in their crates but we managed to assemble them and to our surprise, the engines started so we loaded them with medicines and X-ray equipment and left on 7 March in mid-afternoon. The Japanese entered at 7pm the same day. We left with the remnant of a Cameronian battalion, escorted by a motor bike despatch rider called 'Shite' Sweeney who sort of adopted us. Rangoon at that time was a wild, desperate city about to fall to the Japanese: the prisons and mental hospitals had

The Burma Road – You're on your own, Chaps!

been opened and the inmates left to do as they would. Dogs, horses and cattle were also left to fend for themselves. We got caught on the way out, twenty-one miles north of Rangoon at a fork in the road. We were told that the Japanese had cut both roads. The Gloucester tanks went up to see if they could clear the road block to the oil wells in Yenanyaung. We had to be ready to drive out at a minute's notice and get out before Japanese reinforcements got through. We got through. The Gloucesters did valiantly there.

Sometime after daybreak the next day we drove through a Burmese village and I remember, as if it were today, a young woman who brought a jug of water from her house to the edge of the road where we had stopped for a moment. This gesture seemed the ultimate in kindness. It was symbolic, almost biblical – cold clear water, one of the fundamentals of life, given with kindness, another fundamental of life, to a total stranger in need. We drove our new vehicles and equipment back into China.

With the retreat from Rangoon and salving of supplies, work in Burma was not over. Teams were formed in China to provide surgical aid in the raided towns of Burma and for Chinese military casualties.

These worked with Dr. Norman Seagrave's Mobile Surgical Unit serving mainly with the Chinese 5th Army; and with the FAU Mobile Surgical Team, number 1 (MST1) led by Dr. Handley Laycock.

Tom Haley:

. . . Off we went to Sagaing, expecting the Burma road to be cut at any moment. We just kept going, praying that we'd get through. We drove day and night and got through to Sagaing, crossing the Ava bridge just before it was blown up by the retreating army. Into Sagaing we went where we met Major Seagrave and his team.

We quickly realised that we were working with a retreating, not a fighting army.

There were two main groups: one was part of the British Army taking a more northerly route over the Naga Hills into Dimapur and India, the other taking a more southerly route with the Americans. We seven, in Handley Laycock's MST1, were with the northerly route group. [5] The FAU had a council of war and decided that because there was no medical aid of any kind, we should keep as far back as possible, but just ahead of the Japs. We passed through Shwebo just before it was bombed, so we knew how close they were. You see, they would bomb immediately in front of their advancing army. The next stop was Kinu with its huge ammunition dumps; we were there during a huge bombing raid, everything burning and exploding. There were so many casualties, we just had to stay and do whatever was necessary, however close the Japs were.

We got the operating table, the steriliser and all the equipment off the trucks, boiled up the water, sterilised the instruments, got the dressings out, and within half an hour we'd started operating on our first casualty. We operated for nine hours continuously. We worked until the Japanese were within minutes of our position. It was hectic. Those who hadn't survived had to be buried. We had to wash down, clear up, repack and reload and then get on to our next place as quickly as we could before the Japanese caught up with us. Then we'd start all over again.

The difficulty of post-operative cases was insurmountable. We didn't have enough transport to take people out, nor enough men to give post-operative treatment. There were men who were very badly injured and were going to die. What could we do for them? We had to use our own discretion since there was no way in which we could leave them for the Japanese to bayonet. This was a terrible dilemma, a dreadful compromise position that everybody finds themselves in in wartime: wanting desperately to do the right thing, but being forced to do something which is abhorrent to them, having no alternative in the circumstances. As a pacifist, this was the most horrible and distressing thing for me in the whole of the war and it has lived with me ever since. I backed up the doctor and surgeon, I was in a cleft stick which there was no escape from: there was no way in which I could reconcile what was necessary to help these men die with dignity with what was in accordance with my belief as a pacifist in the sacredness of human life.

It was a physically exhausting time. You just had to get on and work, work, work as hard and fast as you possibly could. We didn't stop for food even if there was some available. If an injured man has to be cared for, you don't stop for a ham sandwich sort of business.

The journey was a nightmare: the terrain was dreadful but our driving on the Burma Road stood us in good stead. We passed lots of trucks completely stuck. I think the truck which I was driving was one of the very few, if not the only one, to have got out of that Burma campaign. It later did noble work in famine relief in India – a fitting end to the career of a good old workhorse. I remember crossing the Chindwin river by raft and on landing, setting up in a place where the Indians and Burmese were fighting it out, firing at each other over a grain store. But we eventually made it over the Naga Hills and through Imphal to the Dimapur railhead and safety.

The morale of the soldiers we were working with was one of hopelessness – they didn't stand much of a chance, and knew it. They were all on foot. Most of them realised they weren't going to make it and didn't expect any mercy from the Japanese. I think we were the only medical group in that area. We heard that the RAMC had been there but had got out at the beginning of the retreat. Certainly we never saw another medical service. This is what made us determined in wanting to keep back as far as we could. We had wanted to be where the action was and we were there. But at the time it was the last thing you thought of, it was just a case of getting on with the job.

George Parsons:

Those of us left in Burma after the fall of Rangoon were wondering what we were going to do. By this time the Chinese had sent three armies to defend Burma – the 5th, 6th and the 38th Divisions. This seemed a wonderful opportunity for worthwhile work; just what we had come out to do! It took a bit of time and negotiating to set it up, but eventually we were told about Dr. Gordon Seagrave's mobile medical unit which was in need of transport. Dr. Seagrave was an American missionary doctor who had established a hospital at Namkham, in the far north of Burma near the Chinese border. When war started, he offered his services to the US Army, and was asked to set up a mobile medical team with about half of his nurses, which was then working behind the lines dealing with battle casualties. About six of us set off to join Seagrave.

We arrived at Dr Seagrave's base at Pyinmana. There had been a battle on that front and they had been busy with casualties. We were ushered into his presence. He was sitting with another American Army doctor drinking a cup of coffee, both completely exhausted. We were introduced and he said 'Hi fellows, glad to have a bit of extra help.' He was a strange sort of man really – a black-and-white person: everything was either marvellous or terrible. But he got things done. He seemed to take to the FAU straight away and we became very good friends.

Our job was taking our lorries which were serving as ambulances to the front, picking up casualties and taking them back to the mobile surgical unit where Seagrave and his team would operate and care for them. When there was a big battle, and there were many, there would be great pressure of work and Seagrave and his two assistants and nurses would be working for twenty-four hours at a stretch. He used to work in just a pair of shorts and a rubber apron because of the heat. The nurses could act as anaesthetists and could also do simple operations like removing bullets and shrapnel. They were absolutely marvellous, and whenever they had a spare moment they sang the hymns Seagrave had taught them as well as their lovely Burmese songs. They adored Seagrave and called him 'Daddy.'

The exhausting nature of the work wasn't helped by the fact that the front was moving steadily northwards. So every few days we had to pack up, load the lorries and move on. Tom Owen was my particular friend all through the war. We were mostly working with the Chinese 5th Army. This was a very poorly trained, rather bewildered outfit. The Chinese 6th Army, which operated in the east of Burma in the Shan states, was much the same. But the Chinese 38th Division – although we didn't meet them until we reached India – was a very different matter, well trained and equipped.

On one of our missions down to the front we noticed dozens and dozens of Chinese lorries moving northward. It seemed obvious that this was the Chinese Army in retreat. We thought we ought to tell General Stilwell in case he didn't know. We went to the American headquarters asking to see him. We were told 'Sure, just knock at the door along there.' We weren't exactly pictures of elegance: we were absolutely filthy and Tom was wearing a very short pair of shorts with some rather grey looking underpants hanging down below the legs, socks all round his ankles and a big tear in his shirt. I wasn't much better. Stilwell was sitting behind a desk – an elderly chap with spiky grey hair and steel-rimmed specs. Tom said 'General, the Chinese Army's retreating!' And Stilwell said 'Goddammit, they wouldn't do that, would they? Anyway I'll have to find out and we'll have to move if they do. If so then I'll come and tell you.' And he actually came round himself to tell us much later that night, which I think speaks worlds for him. He was a great man.

Well, the retreat started over the vast Ava bridge – about to be blown up – which spanned the mighty Irrawaddy river. Once we had crossed this, there was no way back into China and no way out at all except India.

At this stage we were being strafed and bombed, and suffered serious casualties. We formed up into quite a large convoy just outside the Shwebo with the American HQ people. Stilwell was in his staff car and at that stage the rest of us were in lorries. As we travelled north, the tarmac road soon gave out, we continued on earth roads and tracks through Wuntho hoping to get onto trains, but no chance. At Mansi, the next town, the road petered out altogether so we just had to head through the jungle in the general direction of India, several hundreds of miles away. We drove through the trees and kept going all night. We'd stop to eat and refuel – we carried fuel in drums – but there was never time to sleep. The driving got more and more difficult – it was a question of finding our way around trees yet heading in the same direction.

We pressed on through the jungle. Then on the fourth day we drove into a clearing where all the lorries were assembled and were told that we had come to a river that we just couldn't get across. Stilwell gathered us all together – there were about a hundred altogether and I think he was rather taken aback to see the size to which his party had grown. It consisted of: American soldiers including Major Merrill who later formed a commando unit on the Burmese/Chinese border, known as 'Merrill's Marauders'; American civilians; a British Army contingent; a few missionaries, a war correspondent; some Chinese Army personnel, mechanics and mess servants; then the Seagrave Unit which included by then seven FAU: Peter Tennant, Martin Davies, Bill Duncan, Ken Grant, Eric Inchboard, Tom Owen and me; there were also a few refugees our FAU section had picked up.

Stilwell gave us a pep talk about how we now had to walk a very, very long and difficult journey. That we would take it easy and we wouldn't carry anything that wasn't strictly essential. I remember him saying 'If anyone falls and hurts his ankle, it's going to be just too bad for them.' Stilwell could have left us at Shwebo; he could have got to Myitkyina before the railways stopped working and be flown out to India, as might well be expected of a senior officer. But he chose to stay with us and do his best to see that we all got out, which is some measure of the man. Moreover, he was putting himself at great risk because, not only was he the senior American officer in that part of the world, he was Chiang Kai Shek's Chief of Staff, Commander of the Chinese Army in Burma, a huge prize for the Japanese who were, no doubt, making every effort to find us and take him prisoner. We had no idea where the Japanese were: Stilwell thought they might even be ahead of us because we still had to make our way across the Chindwin river some distance off. It seemed likely that the Japanese would make their way up the river and head us off there.

We disabled the lorries and set off. Stilwell was a fairly slight figure who always wore a boy-scout sort of hat; at that time he was approaching sixty. But he was as tough as old boots. He strode out ahead of us all telling us that we had to do 105 paces a minute, but that became impossible once we started. He was said to be very anti-British but I never saw any evidence of that. I don't think I ever saw him smile: he was always very serious and could be very cutting. His acidic personality was the reason he was called 'Vinegar Joe.' But there is no doubt that he was the moving spirit of the party.

Even at that stage at the beginning of the march, we were absolutely shattered, but we staggered off through the jungle and walked about fifteen miles that day, stopping at night in a deserted village where I bedded down in a field. We had reached the banks of a river which we followed for some way, often walking in the river because the jungle was so thick on the banks. We made rough rafts on which to pull the sick. There was always the problem of getting left behind. If this happened Stilwell would say 'What kept you?' and was none too pleased. We were very short of food but our Burmese nurses would go off into the jungle to gather roots, berries and edible plants with which they would make strange-tasting stews when we stopped at night. At last we came to a village on the banks of a larger river. Stilwell had known about this and had sent a couple of chaps ahead to arrange the building of rafts on which we floated down to reach the Chindwin. We made bamboo shelters on them. One went ahead as a kind of armed guard party in case we ran into the Japs. These rafts were about 100' long and 50' wide and were quite comfortable. The depth of the river varied which made things difficult: in some places too deep for our poles to reach the bottom, other times so shallow that we went aground. There were all sorts of underwater snags, like tree trunks. I remember one caught Seagrave in a very vulnerable spot 'Oh goddammit all to hell!' he yelled, 'we'll all be ruined!' By about the second day we saw mountains looming ahead; they obviously lay in our path and had to be crossed before we made it into India.

I remember one very beautiful moment on this river journey. We had been sleeping in the shelter with two of our number on lookout duty. We were all huddled uncomfortably together and one of the nurses and I got up and walked over the sleeping figures into the open. This was a part of the river which was particularly calm and deep and we were passing through some steep banks. In the east the sky was just beginning to lighten and above us hung an old moon with little bits of mist rising and drifting through the trees lining the banks. Others began to stir, and one of the girls came out to join us, walked to the edge of the raft, looked into the water and then turned slowly towards us with the rising sun on her face, and she began to sing a Karen song in such a pure, sweet voice. She was a Karen and her song was full of longing for home and people. It was so beautiful, and I think it is one of the moments which will always be in my memory from that journey out of Burma into India.

The first indication that we were nearing the Chindwin was coming round a bend in the river and seeing the strange sight of an American sitting on a rock in the river to warn us to get out as the Japanese might be ahead. So we left the rafts and proceeded warily on foot into a large, deserted village where we spent the night. The next morning it had been raining quite heavily. This was another hazard we had to face – the monsoon breaking. During the night canoes had been hired and we all walked off towards the Chindwin river. It was rather like crossing the Sahara, endless sand dunes with no sight of a river. Then suddenly, there it was, this huge river. When it came our turn to cross, I was in the middle of three canoes, clutching the sides of the next canoe and getting terrible cramp in the process. This was our Rubicon: once across we were much safer from the Japanese as they were hardly in a position then to cut us off. But when we looked ahead, the hills rising sheer ahead of us looked very daunting. There was still a long way to go.

We set off immediately, climbing steep ascents thick with trees in which we could hear the chattering of monkeys. As we got higher so the trees thinned out but it was still very hard going. The skies were getting darker and we had the occasional shower. After a while we came upon a pretty well-defined track which took us to the top of the ridge. It was depressing looking back – it didn't seem that we had made much progress at all. Would we ever make it into India? Then we had the problems of ulcers on legs. Eric Inchboard's legs were badly affected, so were Seagrave's which were badly infected with the pus which had run down while he was operating in underpants or shorts. He determined to carry on walking, despite the great pain he must have been suffering. I remember the bliss of coming to this pure mountain stream and can still see George Barton swinging his head back with water trickling through his beard saying 'I wouldn't swop this for all the beer in the world!' When the rain became heavier, so the leeches came out. I remember waking up one morning with my back bleeding profusely; quite a big area of skin had been removed. There was no chance of a change of clothing and my shirt remained stiff with blood. The girls' slip-slops had worn out and they were walking barefoot squelching in the rain. I still had my old Coop shoes – what an advert!

After we had been walking for about a week, we met a party of men who had been sent out to look for the General. Search parties had evidently been sent out over many different routes. This one was headed by Tim Sharp, a government officer. I have the feeling that rather like Stilwell's earlier reaction, he was taken aback at the size of the march because although he had brought some food, it didn't go far between the hundred or so of us. We were now in Naga territory, forbidden territory before the war. The Nagas were originally head-hunters and as we approached their villages, we would see strings of skulls around the trees. Every time we entered a village, the General would be fêted in local style. Occasionally we got a bit of rice from the Naga villages to supplement our jungle diet.

We plodded on, eventually arriving in Manipur state where we bumped into two Americans in a jeep, who organised a convoy of ambulances to take us to Imphal, twenty miles across the plain. We had made it. This was due in great part to Stilwell: his encouragement, his exhortations – he willed us to keep on walking, kept us together and brought his party out intact. This is a very great tribute to him and it is not an exaggeration to say that I owe my life to him.

Peter Tennant, who had joined us at the start of the retreat, returned to China, but it was agreed that we others should stay with Seagrave who was setting up a hospital on the frontier to deal with the refugees streaming out of Burma. So off we went through

Kohima to Dimapur and on to Gauhati where the hospital was set up. When I look back at the time we spent in Gauhati, the deepest impression was the Indian and other refugees and the tragic way so many died having reached the end of their journey. Paul Green and I had the task of removing their corpses to a makeshift mortuary. It was heartbreaking work and we somehow had to erect a façade of macabre humour to get through. Paul said 'We'll call ourselves The Morticians Union – ten stiffs a day, and we get more pay!' That was just surface bravado, we were both deeply affected underneath, and I began to think: the war is going on an on and all this suffering is being caused. Am I doing the right thing? Surely I have to do something to help end it. I don't think this was very conscious at the time, but looking back, I was beginning to re-think my pacifist position.[6]

FAU work continued in Assam until the autumn of 1942. Dr. Seagrave's team having worked in Gauhati then went on to Ramgargh providing a medical service for the Chinese 38th Division. Handley Laycocks' team had stayed on in Ledo to care for the 5,000 Chinese soldiers and civilians who had staggered out of Burma with their sick and wounded on the great retreat.

With the fall of Burma, the life-line to China had been cut. Other routes were explored, even one through Tibet, but in the event, the air route from India over 'The Hump' to Kunming bore the whole burden until the war in the Far East ended.

TRANSPORT – EXHILARATION AT A PRICE

THE OLD REFRAIN

They say there's a diesel that's leaving Kweiyang
Bound for old Kutsingfu
Heavily laden with worn out old men
Who know just what they're going to do.
Now there's many a man who has finished his time
There's many a twerp signing on.
There's no recreation this side of creation
So cheer up my lads, bless 'em all.

Bless 'em all, bless 'em all
Bless Murphey and Esmor and Paul,
Bless all the diesel boys: Parry and Chris,
Condick and Parsons, but remember this:
That there's never no rest, none at all,
As back to the garage they crawl,
There's no recreation this side of creation
So cheer up my lads, bless 'em all.

Various authors, tune 'Bless 'em All.'

WITH THE BURMA episode over all efforts could be concentrated on China. Gradually, the men who had retreated into India flew back over the Hump to Kunming (with the exception of a few who had resigned from the FAU in order to continue working with Dr. Seagrave). By late autumn of 1942 the whole section was back in China. By this time, Kutsing had replaced Kweiyang in importance as it lay at the junction of what had been established as the Unit's main routes, and the Unit HQ was moved there in August 1942. Unit members were delighted to find their newly-built hostel which provided, for the first time in China, a clean, comfortable base – their home. Kweiyang remained the main centre for major repairs and overhauls.

In the interim, the system of Unit democracy had been worked out, and the pattern of work had been established which, although modified over the years, persisted to the end. In 1942 the two main contributions made by the China Convoy were: transport and Mobile Medical Teams. Later, in 1944, with the war nearing its end, its third contribution to war-torn China started – rehabilitation and reconstruction.

'China Convoy' embraced all these activities, as Duncan Wood explained 'Some of us were never entirely happy with 'convoy' but the name derived from the fact that the first overseas operation was the Finnish Convoy which was indeed a convoy of ambulances. But in our case 'Convoy' referred to the whole operation, the whole group, including those who went off on small groups of solitary projects, for instance, members seconded to Chinese cooperatives, and Laurie Baker who went off to work with a leper colony.' Because of the array of needs in China and the willingness of convoy members to do anything in their power to help, the motto GADA – Go Anywhere, Do Anything – was coined and was soon adopted by the whole FAU Unit.

The loss of the main sources of liquid fuel was a devastating blow to the Convoy. Despite great efforts to get oil out before the Japanese advanced, supplies were now finite. There had also been the disaster of the loss of 200 drums of petrol which had been moved from Lashio and left inside the Chinese border. A convoy had gone down to move it to Paoshan, only to be refused permission by the Chinese General Yo Fei Peng. In all forty tons were lost in this frustrating episode.

Twelve precious trucks had also been lost in Burma. There were now thirty trucks in all: eleven belonged to the IRC, ten to the Executive Yuan, the remaining nine were FAU. Of the thirty, five were Hercules diesels, three were Sentinels which already ran on charcoal gas. The urgent job was converting the twenty-two petrol-driven trucks to charcoal. Over the years, these trucks – diesel and charcoal and other fuels – had to be kept in service by every contraption and resource which could be devised. The roads themselves presented a formidable challenge: the terrain over which the FAU operated consisted of plains, hills and valleys and mountains. When roads left the plains they climbed steeply up to the top of plateaus often with many switch-backs to be manoeuvred – 'The Twenty-Four

Between Kutsing and Kweiyang: It's enough to drive you round the bend!

Bends' and the 'Seventy-Two Bends' being the best remembered. Often bends were so sharp that drivers had to back up several times to get around to continue their slow crawl to the top. The scenery was awe-inspiring: as well as the twisting ribbons of bends there were sights such as the rocky pass 10,000 feet above sea level in the Kweichow Hills, known as 'The Hill that Claws to Heaven,' the P'an Kiang gorge and the waterfall in Huang Kuo Shu which was reputedly a rival in height to Niagara.

In January 1943, Robert Arthur with a Chinese crew set off on the longest journey of all, 3,000 miles which took them three and a half months. This was through Paoki and Sian, where medical supplies were dropped off, then along the Old Silk Road, past the Great Wall, across the Yellow River and fringes of the Gobi Desert to the oil wells of Suchow where petrol of a low octane rating could be obtained. Later trips were made, some in very bad conditions, but drivers returned to Kutsing full of the wonders of northern China and with drums full of the precious fuel, so vital for starting the charcoal burners and for work on the steeper hills.

All these challenges on the roads of free China resulted in one of the most demanding transport tasks imaginable in terms of mechanical and improvisation skills, strong nerves and saintly patience.

Tony Reynolds:

I had the job of repairing trucks and converting them to charcoal. We ultimately became very expert on these. Michael Fox, in his truck 'Anne Boleyn,' was one of our best drivers and fixed her up most effectively – she was called 'Anne Boleyn' because once we decided to increase the pressure ratio of the truck so much that she lost her head! I took over this truck at one time and it was on 'Anne Boleyn' that I did the fastest run of two and a half days, Chungking to Kweiyang, running on charcoal, with a return cargo of salt.

When you were running well, you could reckon on an hour, hour and a half preparation in the morning – stoking up, cleaning filters, checking tyres, springs and suchlike. On average, we could reckon on doing 100 kilometres a day. The slowest trip was done by Bill Kerr who took six weeks to do 400 kilometres on an experimental truck. We'd bargain for and buy stick charcoal by the

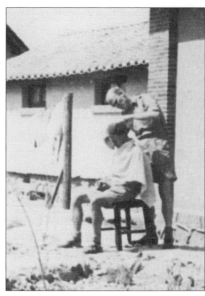

Short back and sides: FAU hostel at Kutsing.

roadside and break it into suitable pieces to feed into the system. In general one carried about a quarter of a ton of spares with one so that we could do anything that was needed on the road. We were very self-sufficient. I found the charcoal experience very interesting. Some very ingenious engineering took place because all these tubes and pieces needed for the burners were by and large beaten out of petrol drums by our tin smiths. We became very good at it.[7]

David Morris:

During my time on the road with the China Convoy (1942-1944) we used diesel lorries on the road from Kutsing to Chengdu via Luhsien on the Yangtse. For the most part charcoal burning lorries were used on the route from Kutsing to Kweiyang and up to Chungking. These lorries were mainly mass-produced American Dodges and Chevs which had never been intended to be used for such prolonged periods and in the conditions they were subjected to on the Chinese roads, particularly as they had been converted for use with charcoal. The roads themselves were exhilarating in the extreme – provided one's truck was moving! They passed through magnificent country but were nothing like the roads we are used to in the West, and they subjected the lorries to severe joltings and bumps so that it was necessary daily to tighten nuts and bolts on springs. The problem with charcoal was that it produced a very weak power. It also meant that particles of charcoal were passed through into the engine and the abrasive effect meant that the engines wore out very quickly. The end result was that only comparatively small loads could be carried and at very slow speeds. There were frequent breakdowns which took hours, sometimes days, to fix.

Some of us had driven in the north of England on snow and ice and that helped a good deal with the difficult Chinese roads. So far as the mechanical side was concerned, quite a few of our members were extremely skilful mechanics; I certainly wasn't one of those. But those of us without that competence who spent their time on the road usually managed, with the help of our often very able Chinese mechanics, to cope somehow or other, especially if we'd come across the situation before.

Before the China Convoy started, the IRC had been responsible for distributing drugs, but once we set up, from then on, I think the only medical supplies being moved around in China were being moved by us. At this time inflation was increasing and reached a crescendo after I left in 1944, but even before that the Chinese staff were being paid in rice, and drugs were becoming extremely valuable. I think the fact that the FAU had responsibility for distributing the drugs had a lot to do with their value. We were trusted.

To give some idea of how a convoy worked: we'd go off in anything from one truck to three or four in convoy. Depending upon the estimated length of the journey, the person in charge would be given a certain amount of Chinese dollars and he was expected to feed the rest and make payments for fuel – mainly stick charcoal – and food on the journey, keeping a log of what was spent. We would usually buy the 'Koufan' or guest-meal at a Chinese roadside fandien – this consists of one dish for each person and rice and tea. So if there were two or three of you, you would have, depending on where you were, perhaps a bit of Chinese cabbage, a bowl of soup, perhaps something which was a cross between an omelette and scrambled egg or you might get a little bit of meat with some onion. You'd have that twice a day. In the morning you might have a bit of bread or some bean curd milk and strips of batter; or if you were extremely unlucky, you might have a bowl of revolting wet rice called 'sheefan.' So far as our personal money was concerned, we got about £1 a month which doesn't sound very much, but there wasn't much to spend it on. Some of us bought Chinese cigarettes which were ghastly. We were well clothed, and able to buy adequate food which was excellent to taste but often gave us dysentery. We were in the prime of life having the good luck to be travelling around a fascinating country and all being paid for. We were having a free ride!

I thought China absolutely marvellous, especially Yunnan. The name means 'south of the clouds' and it has an exhilarating climate. It starts at 6,000 feet and although it doesn't very often rain there, it's never dry and barren. It is just superb and beautiful. It was thrilling to be there and moving around in it. I can envisage myself travelling along a road, its surface consisting of red beaten earth and not much wider than a truck, twisting down a series of hairpin bends with mountains of different shades of blue across the valley, and on each side one would see terraces of rice, with the emerald green water shining in the sun, and the dust flying behind one, and down in the valley you'd see the walls of a small city as it might have been two or three thousand years ago. If one arrived late at night, the gates would usually be shut but by then in west China there had grown up a street full of eating houses where the lorries stopped – sometimes it could be more reassuring to be within the walls of the city. So there was this tremendous visual excitement and beauty on the one hand, and on the other intense poverty and disease.

It's really difficult to convey the depths of the poverty: the way people were dressed in rags, the way you'd see them staggering up mountain paths with colossal weights, the sweat dripping off them. The poverty of the wayside inns and the flies crawling over every morsel of food available. Then there was the disease: possibly three out of four people you'd see had these enormous goitres and the eye disease of trachoma was everywhere.

Perhaps the best way to describe it is to give you the example of an occasion when I broke down and was stranded with my Chinese mechanic for some days. We were given hospitality, for which we paid, in a peasant's hut about ten miles from the nearest town. I remember that the only food we were given was rice and cabbage. There was a block of salt on which we rubbed our chopsticks to get a bit of flavour on the cabbage. There were chickens but no eggs because the peasants had to sell their eggs in order to trade for other necessities. So providing we didn't break down and were able to get to a village and have the kind of meal I've described earlier, you can see that we were living at a far far higher rate than the peasants of the countryside through which we were passing, although not at as high a rate as those feasting in the restaurants.

We had a general and continuing problem with theft. There was thieving from our hostels, there was thieving from the lorries and there were thefts from our garages. This meant that we had to sleep in our lorries with the cargoes, and once when I was in charge of a garage for a time, we had to establish watches. Thinking of this, I remember the lengthy discussions which took place about what on earth we were going to do with these chaps if we caught them – I can't remember the result, if ever we got that far, but the discussions went on and on. You see, we believed that if we reported a potential criminal to the Chinese authorities then terrible things would happen to him immediately, or he might be sent to prison. Prisons were awful. I had actually visited one in Kweiyang with a doctor and I had found it a very upsetting experience. I recollect a series of barracks in which prisoners were roaming free. There was a huge disparity between them in appearance: one or two had quite roomy accommodation and rather smarter clothes – better even than ours. They were smoking cigarettes and seemed to be well fed, and chatted to us in a fairly comfortable, even arrogant way. A few yards away, in another room – I can still see this – there were these skeleton-like bodies, two or three to a bed with perhaps one thin blanket over them and looking like the photos which one later saw of people in Belsen and Auschwitz. I realised that it was really a microcosm of Chinese society and that it wasn't so very long ago that the debtors' prison in England bought service and food for the privileged.

Apart from the general problem of theft which was obviously connected with poverty, there were also what the Chinese described as 'tufei', bandits. Driving along the road one day we saw a man's head suspended from a bush by the wayside. 'That's a bandit,' we were told. And often, when travelling, some friendly peasant would warn us that there were tufei around. One of the first trips I did in China was to bring Tom Thompson, whose arm had been slashed by a bandit's sword, down from Kweiyang to Kutsing. But the danger of bandits was nothing like the actual danger of the roads themselves – the poor condition and the crazy way in which other drivers drove. Bandits were probably poor people who'd taken to the hills trying to pick off the odd bit of plunder here and there.

Could I just say that although I think we were privileged young men seeing some of the most interesting parts of China with all expenses paid, and although we were very grateful for the exhilaration which being there brought, we did pay a price. We were escaping from the bombing, we usually had food to eat, but we supped full, I think, on distressing sights which we couldn't ignore because we were living there right alongside them, not separated by some compound walls. So our experience of this fascinating and beautiful country was counterbalanced on the other side by the impact of the poverty and disease and indeed on frequent occasions by one's own illness. I think it's interesting to point out that although we were very fortunate compared with service personnel who were risking their lives in much more hazardous circumstances, and the civilian population at home which was being bombed, so far as disease was concerned our situation was not quite so fortunate. Most of us were ill one day out of three, usually with some form of tummy bug or dysentery which considerably affected one's enjoyment of the place. My own introduction to China was being hospitalised twice within a comparatively short time with fever. Even in the early months of the convoy two men had died: John Briggs on 9 June 1942 with typhus and Douglas Hardy on 11 June of dysentery and typhus. Their deaths brought us face to face with the reality of China and risks to our health.[8]

I don't think the Chinese we mixed with had the faintest idea of what we were and why we were there but we were very low down the ladder, very small fry. One or two of our leaders met some important Chinese in Chungking and they might have understood us more, but we were just lorry drivers moving along the road. We were still, even in wartime free China, sufficiently an oddity to attract a crowd wherever we stopped; and when we ate, crowds would watch us. It could be rather trying if you had dysentery or something else which made you a bit off-form. In the streets the children would call one of the three names they reserve for shouting at foreigners: 'wei gwo jen', the polite one which means 'outside countryman; 'yang gwei tze' or 'foreign devil'; or 'da bi tze' which means 'big nose.' One only has to be alone with a Chinese mechanic stranded in a Chinese village for many weeks to become extremely conscious of the size of one's nose! At the time I wrote something which shows how our attitude towards the Chinese had two facets:

When you are well and the sun is bright
And the breeze is cool
When the bare bottomed children are playing in the dust
And old men are smoking long pipes
The fans flicking and fluttering
The coolies resting in the shade
Drink tea beneath the trees on the thin bench
And watch the scraggy chickens pecking in the spittle:
Wipe the sweat from your face and crunch a peach.
And women are spinning, cooking, making shoes,
And men are talking, dangling a baby;
When the rice is heaped in the bowls and the dishes are various,
When the food is rich and the cook ingenious,
Then is the country good and the land enjoyable.
But when you are sick, in heart or bowel,
When the body is in fever,
Those inquisitive eyes are maddening,
The children are noisy;
The sun is hotter and the wind colder,
The food is greasy,
The open sewers stink in the streets,
The flies darken the meat in the market place,
The fleas and lice are emboldened
And all is hateful.
O for a familiar face, a wholesome smell, a homely taste,
For an escape.

I have read a fair amount of the history of China, and the role of the whites, and gained the impression that they had not dirtied their hands. I think some Roman Catholic fathers and nuns had got very close to the Chinese way of life but as a general principle I think it was a novelty to see white people lying on their backs underneath trucks in the mud, with grease and mud all over them, trying to cope with getting the trucks running instead of just standing by and telling somebody else what to do.

What difference did we make? We were in China, trying to do something to help and I think we did do a little. It's difficult to understand just how little that was, but when you consider the millions and millions living in free China and the fact that we were just a couple of hundred people at the most, and that drugs had to be flown over the Hump by the American air force in planes which had to be carrying their own payload of fuel to get back, and that whatever drugs were being brought over were only a small proportion of the total load which included food for the Americans and all the myriad other war supplies, when you consider that this small band of people with a bunch of battered old cheap production line three-ton trucks were trying to move these drugs over mountains to mission hospitals and front-line medical teams and central distribution depots with worn-out engines, inadequate spare parts and fuels which covered fourteen different kinds, the principal ones of diesel and charcoal, you can see that the nature of roads was such, the age of the vehicles was such, the wear and tear of the fuels being used was such, that an extraordinarily large proportion of time was spent on repairing and cannibalising trucks and getting them to move. You got them out of the garage and they'd go hundreds of miles down the road and then break down. They'd not uncommonly roll off the road and have to be dragged back, sometimes in pieces and reassembled. You can see that in terms of material help it was all totally pitiful and inadequate in comparison with the vast need for drugs by this enormous population. But I don't know who would be doing it if we hadn't been there. I think we all felt that we were doing something useful even though it was on a very tiny scale in comparison with the need. We were ordinary human beings trying to live extraordinary lives in China.

FAU MEDICAL SECTIONS – CONDITIONS
LIKE THE CRIMEAN WAR

'The zeal and energy which they put into their work under extremely dangerous conditions, never complaining of their own hardships, with practically no rations and very little equipment or clothing, won the wholehearted respect of the Chinese and American personnel serving with them.'
Citation received by FAU Mobile Surgical Team 3,
from the American Army, 1944.

AS THE MEDICAL sections with Dr. Seagrave and Handley Laycock were retreating into India, another Mobile Surgical Team, MST2, was set up in Kweiyang, for work with the Chinese 71st Army at the front which had then become stabilised on the Salween. Michael Harris was part of the team:

Michael Harris:

We were based in a Chinese hospital in Paoshan, about fifty kilometres from the Salween River which was the front line. Our team consisted of two doctors – Hank Louderbough, an American, and Terry Darling – and four other British people, and four Chinese. We worked very hard. I stayed there for about a year and was one of the anaesthetists. I'd had no training but learnt as I went along. We used mainly ether at that time, the rag and bottle method. I also turned my hand to lots of other jobs too. There was very little actual fighting; the front lines were more or less static until the Japanese advance of 1944. But we did have some wounded and we dealt with a serious outbreak of cholera which involved inoculations of civilians as well as soldiers; there were a lot of other medical cases and quite a few accidents, planes crashing, that sort of thing. And now and again one was called out to rescue those from planes shot down nearby. This is when we got to know the terrain in the mountain areas well. I remember one plane which had a lot of American congressmen on board flying to China on an official visit. Well, the engine failed and it crashed. Bob McClure knew that part of the country and he and I went out in an old Dakota to the crash. He was an experienced parachutist, unlike me, but I dropped with him and helped to get the survivors back, some of whom were badly wounded. In all I went out for about eight or nine drops – really you had to be Jack-of-all-trades in that situation.

I also went on about three trips behind the enemy lines with Bob and others. The work was assorted; but the main basic work was the surgery in the hospital. I worked a lot with McClure. Working as we did in the outback, it was very difficult to achieve sterile conditions. So he did what many other surgeons did during the war – operate out of doors in the sun, under trees, anywhere they could fix up a table, maybe just an old kitchen table. Often we'd use an old temple. He made do, as they say. He made do.

As for the hospital, it had no facilities: no beds, appalling food, the soldiers were very often in the last stages of emaciation. Cholera and plague were rampant – really, the lot of the ordinary Kuomintang soldier was appalling, they had been fighting for years with terrible equipment, if they had anything at all, and there was no concern at all for their welfare; once a soldier fell ill, there would be no expectation on the part of the Chinese Army that he'd get well. He was finished. And the corruption of the officer class was terrible. We ran de-lousing stations and the cholera ward as well. So we had a very difficult uphill job there.

The Kuomintang soldiers were hated because they lived off the land. If they misbehaved they were shot. We had this one awful incident whilst we were in this hospital in Paoshan where our rooms were broken into and stuff taken. The military commander of the hospital lost face: it was terrible that the foreigners, his guests, had been robbed. Two days later a very high ranking military officer appeared and said 'Ah, we have found the thieves that stole your goods and if you will come down to military headquarters, we will return them to you.' In all innocence we went, and outside the barracks square, there were a lot of soldiers with some digging a big trench. We still didn't realise what was happening and we were given beer to drink and chairs to sit on and we looked at the countryside and chatted with the Army people making polite conversation. Then, suddenly a voice called out 'stop! finish!' and the diggers all laid down their tools, and before we could do anything, a high ranking Army officer strode along and shot eight people through the backs of their heads and they fell forward into the trench. 'There you are' said the General, full of smiles, waiting for our congratulations, 'the people who burgled your house have now suffered for their sins.' His face had been regained.

In the summer of 1942, as Handley Laycock's MST1 team arrived back from India, a commando raid was being planned on Hong Kong for December of that year. Eager for more work, MST1 set off for Waichow, fifty miles from Hong Kong. Although the area was not under Japanese control, it was being heavily bombed so there were many casualties and refugees to be cared for as well as the guerrillas fighting nearby. The raid never took place but the team remained until April 1943. Although there were trips into the guerrilla country with the Chinese Army, the team found they were mainly working with civilians in the Outpatients Department which it had set up in the hospital. As Duncan Wood explained 'The Hong Kong adventure, or misadventure, was rather typical: we would hear of the possible fronts or fighting zones where medical assistance would be needed, then the teams would set off – miles and miles from our base, in this case – and find that they would immediately be involved with civilian medical work and often the military need never properly materialised.' The MST teams quickly learned that they had to be sufficiently flexible to deal with whatever need arose rather than insisting on being a strictly medical or surgical team. It was this flexibility that made the FAU MSTs so effective.

Three more teams – MST3, MST4, MST5 – were formed in May 1943 for work under the CRC, to operate with the Chinese forces in Yunnan in readiness for the drive into Burma. The offensive did not begin until April 1944 and to fill in time, the three teams kept occupied with medical work before the military activity began: MST3 working in Hsiakwan; MST4 down on the Indo-China border near Yenshan; and MST5, working with the BRC, in Tsiao Chien and later in Tengchung.

Teams by this time approximated to Bob McClure's ideal of about eight people of mixed nationality: two doctors, two nurses, an administrator, a laboratory technician who would look after equipment and vehicles. Given the hilly, forested, semi-jungle and roadless country the teams worked in, equipment, although comprehensive, was kept as light as

possible, especially in those areas where motorised vehicles were not pos-
sible and mules the main means of transport. Teams therefore became
small self-sufficient groups, living off the country, and setting up in a
variety of places ranging from temples (often with the Gods watching
over them) to tents or clearings in the forests.

As the drive into Burma began, in April 1944, a new team, led by
Pat Barr*, an American doctor, was sent to an area between the Red
River and the Mekong. In July 1944, Pat Barr left Mohai, where the
team was based, with Dr. Pat Rawlence in charge, and took a small team
– MST7 – across the Mekong to Fuhai near the Burma border, to work
with troops in the area.

Pat Rawlence:

There was a certain amount of uncertainty at this time. We
were supposed to be going down as a military unit, as the Japanese
were expected to attack through Burma. That didn't occur.
Negotiations then started with the Yunnan Health Authority to
switch our team over to civilian work. It was known that several
types of malaria were decimating lots of villages down there. We
had a two-week walk over the mountains with three horseloads of
drugs and surgical equipment. As we were preparing to go our
Chinese members looked with dismay at our army boots and said
'You'll never do it in those.' 'What are we supposed to do then?'
Pat Barr asked. 'Ah, straw sandals!' So each one of us had two pairs
of these wonderful straw sandals made to measure and they took
us all the way there – we used them for ever after that. It was an
incredibly primitive life-style on that walk but eventually we reached
the Red River which we crossed by chain bridge – trying not to look
down – and it was on to Mohai, a salt-mining place where the feudal
landlord, Colonel Jang, told us we were going to stay. I still don't
fully understand the conditions under which we stayed there as all
the negotiations were between Pat Barr, the interpreter and Colonel
Jang, but looking back it is clear that he wanted a medical service

---

* Arthur Barr, known as 'Pat'; not to be confused with Patrick Barr, the
  British actor.

and we were the people on the spot and there was little chance of
going on, even if we had wanted to.

There was a hospital of sorts which had been a clinic in the past
run by an old Chinese doctor who had gone away. The problem
was that there was no communication with the FAU in Kutsing.
Postal runners could do the run in ten or twelve days but it still
meant a month before we got a reply. It was all very dodgy, but
there was work to do and we stayed and settled into Mohai and set
up our clinic. Pat Barr stayed a month and then left us to it.

Colonel Jang was extremely friendly to us, he gave us everything he could, we were feasted and taken to enormous parties and
really became part of the community there. He was greatly
respected and was a good man in his own way. I would describe
him as a warlord as he had his own soldiers and militia, but a benef-
icent one. I suspect his position was used largely for protecting the
opium trade. Opium smoking was normal. When you went into
someone's house you'd be asked 'would you like a cup of tea or a
pipe of opium?' I invariably chose tea and became addicted to this!
We ate all sorts of things: very good fish, elephant trunks, deer
tendons and every sort of grub – anything that creeps or crawls is
a 'chung' to be cooked and eaten. I remember the 'chung' out of
a bees nest, fried up – delicious!

We dealt with all sorts of awful diseases: malaria, relapsing fever,
dysentery, all sorts of horrible skin conditions and leg ulcers. We
had with us the latest thing of the day which was 'M and B'. It was
magic what you could do with people whose own antibodies were
pretty high having fought bacteria for a long time. We only had to
give them a few tablets for an ulcer of the leg and the whole thing
would clear up like magic. There was lots of innovation, had to be.
At first it was difficult to do surgery as there was nowhere to do it,
then Jang promised us that if we stayed he would build us a hospital, and he did. It was wonderful seeing them bring these great
timber logs down, adzing them into squares and getting it up ready
for this wonderful Chinese roof which finished it off.

It was really pretty basic GP work there: clinic in the morning
– anything up to ninety patients to see. Then people would ask for
home visits and I would do the rounds in the afternoon with an

interpreter, going into the mountains by horseback. I remember a fairly rich old man with a bad tummy ache sent for me. In the panic, the old lady who looked after him – number three wife, I think - had bound feet and had fallen over the dog and broken her leg. The Chinese medicine man had set her leg in a sticky rice mixture. After I had seen to the old man, I quizzed the medicine man who said this rice would set hard like a plaster and after six weeks her leg would be better. It all fitted in with orthopaedic practice. Although foot binding had been illegal since 1913, the practice was still being carried out in that remote area. As well as old ladies, we saw young girls with bound feet. What struck me was that not only the feet had been bound, but the whole of the lower leg was thin and wasted and the foot sort of curled up into a claw which meant they walked on the stumps of their toes. This meant they were very prone to ulcers and their very weak tibias meant lots of fractures. All our treatment was free, we insisted on that, and that's why we were so popular.

Our track went down to what was the French Indo-Chinese border. When the Japanese took over, the French troops escaped and came up our track with about fifty huge cavalry horses, the likes of which the Chinese had never seen before. It fell to my lot to be the interpreter between the French and Chinese. They were very weary and stayed a week before leaving for Kunming. That was the only sign of war I saw.

I had caught relapsing fever myself and was pretty ill; then when I started to get better, I began to get tummy aches, so had my appendix out in Mohai. Then it was time to go. It had been planned that we were to hand over to a Chinese team, but in the end we pulled out with nothing replacing us. Jang gave a tremendous feast to see us off and then half the place turned out and marched along with us as far as the bridge a mile or so out of the town, and then took a sad farewell. I think the impact we had in Mohai was absolutely staggering. There had been a total absence of medical facilities, and here we were offering them what were then the latest drugs and curing them of what had previously been incurable. They hadn't heard or seen anything like this before. That is why they took to us so.

It wasn't until years later that it dawned upon me that we hadn't been able to leave in the first place. I'm still not sure. I suspect that we had in fact been subjected to a bit of arm twisting to stay in Mohai. I wonder...

In June 1944, Margaret Matheson (Briggs), Connie Condick (Bull), Evelyn White (Dangerfield) and Elaine Bell (Conyers), the first 'women for China' had arrived. As with the initial admission of women into the FAU, this caused a lot of controversy, in London as well as China:

Elaine Bell:

I had been in the FAU since 1942, working first in various rest centres during the blitz and ending up working with the administration in the HQ in Gordon Square. I heard quite a bit about China from Tom Tanner, with whom I worked, and began to get very keen and I realised that I was in the perfect spot to do something about it. The FAU thought it wrong to send delicate women to foreign posts, but I became quite unpleasant in my pressure to get them to change. It wasn't just a question of the London HQ being so old-fashioned, the men in China were also opposed to women going out. They had become used to a very simple life-style and felt that if they had women they would have to put curtains up, and showers and to think twice about running naked from one spot to another, and to watch their language. They were really perturbed that things would have to change dramatically.

I would bring the subject up again and again, and after a lot of discussion in London and much correspondence back and forth, China agreed that it would try four of us – four women to the 150 men then there! That was enough for me because I was invited to be one of the four. That was the beginning of the end. It was never regretted on either side. It was really successful. I went out there as the only person who wasn't qualified as a driver/mechanic or medic – the only one to use my humble little skills of shorthand/typing and coordinating the office – at that time the London HQ, the Chinese HQ in Kutsing, and the Canadian HQ in Toronto. In the days when it could take over a month for letters to get around, the work could have its difficulties and often we'd make our decisions independently which could lead to a bit of friction. But this remoteness accounts, I think, for the extraordinary cohesion of the China group which we fitted in to.

Margaret Matheson:

I was nursing at the Queen Elizabeth Hospital in Birmingham when Michael Cadbury rang me one day saying 'We want you to go to China.' So there it was! I remember arriving in China having flown over The Hump, and looking down seeing all the people in blue running about on this brown plain. Then the FAU met us and put us on a train for Kutsing where we were taken to the hostel. As I walked in, it was just full of men and I thought 'Oh dear, oh dear!' Very alarming it was, very frightening at first. But they were very sweet and made us most welcome. They would come flocking around though if you gave them half a chance – we were such novelty value. They were slightly in awe of us because they hadn't seen women for so long. One of our worries was that knowing the tightly-knit group they had grown into, we didn't want to upset this. I went out of my way to avoid difficult situations. I had a strategy for this. I told myself firmly in the beginning 'I'm not going to get involved with any one man, I'm going to enjoy the friendship of them all' – my professional position was a help. Bob McClure started calling me 'the Matron' which made them all laugh; but it helped. Of course my good intentions went by the board when I fell in love with Al Matheson and we were married in Chengchow in 1946.

David Morris:

I regret that to my astonishment and amazement, I was much opposed to having women in the FAU, let alone China. Why? I didn't think there were enough to go round! Potentially, it was a pretty difficult situation. We were human beings whether we were conscientious objectors or not. We'd been away from home for a long time. We didn't have contact with the local women at all. In that sense I think perhaps we were different as a group from other groups. I personally have always found women very attractive and I didn't relish the idea of these women coming out and creating that sort of problem. In the event, there were no problems and one or two marriages came out of it. But that's my view at the time. It wasn't that I was opposed to them coming and doing the work at all, and I'm glad to say that I became friendly with them later.

The women were soon put to the test. For example, Evelyn White, on the seventh day after her arrival, was called on to help with victims of a very bad rail accident on the Yunnan – Szechwan railway where a troop train had become de-railed while negotiating a viaduct and had toppled off the steep gradient and dropped fifty feet into a stream:

Evelyn White:

It was bad, people were lying around, some dead, some badly injured. A lot were very young boys. Dr. Lonshore and I went around first of all sorting the living from the dead. The injured had to be given morphine and tetanus injections before we could begin to cope with their injuries and after we'd done this we'd write 'M' and 'T' on their foreheads. There was a farm nearby in which we began the work of dressing wounds and splinting fractures. We started early in the morning. Halfway though the day the Chinese Red Cross arrived but they left almost at once giving the reason that they didn't want us to lose face. So they were a complete loss. One little incident sticks in my mind: I was bending down dealing with a compacted fracture of a leg, when a little black pig came out of the farm and hopped over the leg. At this stage I was so tired and exhausted that I just sat back and laughed. It was a little bit of light relief in what was a pretty awful situation. What struck me vividly was that we in the medical team were binding up the wounded whilst over the other side of the embankment, the Chinese were sawing up wood, making coffins: we were dealing with the living, they with the dead. Macabre.

Towards the end of the day, we took the very badly injured back to a Chinese Army hospital in Kutsing by train, and those who could walk, we escorted to lorries. I couldn't sleep that night, I was so hyped up. So I went over to the Chinese Army hospital to help. They were very poorly equipped, they had medical orderlies but no trained nurses and very few highly qualified doctors. The conditions were like those in the Crimea during that war: beds would be wooden planks on a trestle or bricks, straw palliases for

It's better to give than to receive.

a mattress and they would be lucky to have a cotton blanket for covering. There was no running water, the floors were mud with bamboo walls and the place was infested with lice which brought with them relapsing fever, typhus and all types of malaria. A lot of men were lost because they were not nursed and cared for properly in that war. We found later that those we had rescued, whose wounds we had splinted and plastered, had torn the plaster off because they thought that if they died and entered the Chinese equivalent of heaven, their leg would not be there because it was bound in plaster. I can remember John Perry tearing his hair with frustration over this. This was the sort of frustration we'd meet from time to time.

It was a sort of diving in at the deep-end experience. A revelation to me. I had been nursing in the London blitz, it's true, but we had all the facilities there: hospital wards, blood plasma, the Civil Defence backing us up, ambulances for transport; here in the wilderness there was nothing, no back up: no ambulances, no blood plasma, very few medicines or splints. It was improvisation and those who survived were lucky. It was totally different, alien.

By this time, May 1944, the China Convoy took over complete responsibility for the work of the Huei Tien Hospital in Kutsing which had been founded by the Church Missionary Society. When the Unit first arrived in Kutsing, it had been staffed entirely by Chinese, but members soon became involved in both clinical and surgical work and when the Unit took it over, it became an important field of Unit work, providing new arrivals with a valuable introduction to medical work in China. This was known as MT10.

Meanwhile, a new MST5 consisting entirely of FAU members was set up and ran a hospital a few miles from the town of Paoshan. It was an Intermediate Hospital, consisting of huts, which received a heavy flow of casualties from the front. A section of MST5 went forward to deal with casualties on the spot. Evelyn White was part of the team, running a forty bed surgical ward in the hospital with Connie Condick working as a theatre sister. Margaret Matheson also worked in the Paoshan hospital:

Margaret Matheson:

I worked in the hospital at Kutsing for six months and then was sent off to Paoshan where I worked on the wards. There had been a lot of fighting down there and we dealt with the wounded soldiers who staggered in, usually in a terrible state, and with bits missing. We were really a field hospital, we did what we could and then passed them on. The FAU doctors were John Perry, John Wilkes, Eric Waddington with Bob McClure rushing in and out. Most FAU doctors were just through with their training, without very much experience. But they had to face very demanding cases, and coped wonderfully. I became very attached to Bob (McClure) both as a doctor and as a man. I often worked in the operating theatre with him and he was one on his own – incredible! His skill as a surgeon, brilliant. He could be extremely difficult, but I knew him as a surgeon, doctor, administrator and a super chap. I don't think the FAU could have managed without him. I could talk to the nurses enough to tell them what to do, but Chinese was his

71st Army Group Field Hospital at Paoshan.

second language and he could get things done. He'd buttonhole a top man in a way the FAU couldn't have done. He heard about Tengchung and off we went.

Tengchung is an ancient town on the China/Burma border which had been besieged three times: taken by the Japanese, won back by the Chinese, taken again by the Japanese and now just won back by the Chinese with their push against the Salween into Burma. One of our teams, MST3, worked outside the broken walls during the final battle for the town. When we arrived, it was a completely flattened city, with practically nothing standing. But there was a shell of an old temple and Bob said 'We'll turn that into our hospital.' Our men were so talented, they built a hospital on the ruins. It was a lovely place and I lived down there for about six months.

The local people started returning when they heard there was a hospital. We used to do amputations on those who had picked up shells and lost arms and legs, many of them children. We did a lot of medical work there. We had about thirty or forty beds in wards on two sides of a big courtyard and on two levels. The theatre was in the gate. The theatre became '*my* thing.' I became the surgeons' assistant as well as doing general theatre duties. Having no other doctor except the surgeon meant that I did things that normally young doctors would have done, like being across the table from the surgeon. In England, nurses don't assist the surgeon, so it was a most interesting medical experience for me. Apart from our medical work, a great deal of effort was put into clearing up and rebuilding the city because the Japanese had done so much damage. It was all very worthwhile and the beginning of a new phase of FAU work in China.

RECONSTRUCTION AND REHABILITATION – WE WERE NOT FORGOTTEN

When China lies far behind you
And you've sailed across the sea
What will there be to remind you
Of 1943?

If you haven't got any nice trinkets
Or pictures to hang on the wall,
Sing "Chao mi tan, kai shuei"
And then you'll remember it all....

We'll follow you sooner or later
And meet you in Leicester Square
If we can't afford the theatre
We'll go to a restaurant there –

When the waiter is taking our order
We'll holler as loud as we can:
"Yao chao mi tan, kai shuei,
A bowlful for every man".

Duncan Wood to his own tune.

(Chao mi tan, kai shuei is the morning street cry of the vendor of Chao Mi Tan breakfast.)

THE UNIT'S EXPERIENCE in the devastated city of Tengchung led to the recognition that with war nearing its end, it had to adapt to the changing situation. It was seen that as well as the continuing need for medical services for war-torn China there was a desperate need for help with rebuilding the devastation. This is where the final phase of the Convoy's contribution to China came in – that of reconstruction and rehabilitation.

After Tengchung, the Unit moved into the devastated cities of Nantan, Liuchow and Hankow, taking over hospitals vacated by the Japanese, and reorganising medical services. When war ended in August 1945 the question arose: what of the Unit's future in China? The FAU had been set up as a temporary wartime unit and soon the decision was made that the FAU should wind up its overseas commitments by June 1946. This did not mean that FAU members no longer had opportunities for service in China; they continued to serve but henceforth under the control of the full-time AFSC, with no appreciable change of personnel or administration on the spot.

The need of post-war China was formidable; after all the country had suffered civil war and war since the revolution of 1911, and the difficult decision had to be taken: where should the Convoy serve? Should it spread itself thinly and disperse its resources? Or concentrate on a large, single area? It didn't take long for the Unit to make up its mind. The northern province of Honan was in a desperate plight. It had suffered extensive fighting, its towns were in ruins, its railways destroyed. Floods, droughts and general neglect had devastated agriculture. On top of this, its strategic position as a junction of roads, rivers and railways meant that thousands of refugees were returning homeward through the province from the southwest. The city of Chengchow was selected as the main base and by the spring of 1946, the Convoy's headquarters at Chungking had moved there. Kutsing, the Unit's old home, was closed and its trucks and equipment moved north to Honan where its future now lay.

The initial task was to coordinate the work of all the various relief organisations and by the end of 1945, the Honan Relief Committee (later Honan International Relief Committee) was set up with the FAU providing its Secretary and Treasurer.

A medical team moved into the Hwa Mei Hospital in Chengchow and another team into Changte Hospital, two hundred miles to the north of Chengchow. Soon work started on repairing and re-opening other hospitals in the province and at a later stage, with financial help from UNRRA, a completely new hospital was designed and built by the Unit. As Doug Turner explained: 'We built it all ourselves, it had about forty beds. One of our members, Tony Reynolds, undertook the task of being architect and he worked exceedingly hard and did a wonderful job. We built it of local, handmade bricks, it was two-storey with a Nissen-hut shaped metal roof.'

The Convoy had long wanted to develop 'area projects' – medical, mechanical and relief – networking out over a relatively small region, so that resources could be coordinated and utilised to the full. In line with this, projects were put in hand to set up rural textile and agricultural processing industries. Also, by lending money to peasants for the purchase of animals, seed and machinery, a series of cooperatives was started.

Doug Turner:

We had provided sufficient resources for the villagers of Tung Hsi to purchase a number of animals. The scheme was functioning quite well when one morning one of the peasants appeared in my own village with a sad tale. During the night one of the oxen had been stolen. My immediate reaction was one of suspicion: what's behind all this? He hastened to assure me that this was a genuine theft and they were not looking for it to be replaced, but had felt it their duty to keep me informed and they had started looking for it. Anyway, towards the end of the day, they came over to say they had found the animal in a village about ten miles away. 'What happened?' I asked. 'Well, we went to this village and saw it tied up in the street, so we untied it and brought it back.' 'What about the thief?' I asked 'What did you do about discovering who took it?' They looked at me, and then at one another, then one turned round and said very quietly, 'Teng Hsien-Shen – that village is even poorer than ours.'..... Another moment of my biting the dust.

One of the most exciting times of my time in Honan was when, wandering through the small town of Chungmou, where I was working, I was called in by a mother to see her baby. As I looked at the baby, it became clear to me that it was in a severe state of dehydration. I had never seen a case of cholera before, but I had been taught the signs and it looked to me that this was a case, and if so, then it was pretty obvious it was going to spread in no time. It was one of the aspects of our training and thinking that we never left things to chance. I immediately contacted our headquarters in Chengchow, and in no time at all they had responded. A team was immediately sent down and we began to inoculate many thousands of people. As we did so a cholera epidemic broke out. Sometimes I compare this with the huge structures of today and wonder whether they would be able to cope in the way we coped at that very simple level?

We spent many long hours after that sitting up late into the night with patients being brought in; we dealt with many hundreds of cases. Following on from that we soon had a very healthy little clinic going in Chungmou with four peasant nurses. They were very good and showed themselves capable of coping with all sorts of emergencies. We employed two local Chinese doctors and instituted a very rigorous barefoot doctor campaign for many, many miles around. We also had our own medical teams going out on trek for four weeks on end. Later on the unit developed a very large kala-azar campaign, treating many, many thousands of cases of this terrible disease over the whole area of Honan.

One of the more delightful aspects of the work was the children who used to come along every morning to receive their glass of powdered milk. They would line up and we would weigh them at the beginning of the campaign, and then at monthly periods, and they began to put on weight and look well. We also taught them to clean their teeth and it was a great delight to see these lines of small children from three to four years of age busily brushing their teeth and then grinning as widely as they could to show their teeth to you.

Tony Gibson:

At Christmas we organised a nativity play in which Mrs. Fang was the landlady. 'No room at the inn' – that's something that always catches me; my voice changes when I think of that because it was *genuine*. It was a real donkey. Doug was Joseph; a Chinese nurse, Mary; and the whole thing came across. I operated a star which was a torch tied to a long willow branch. There was quality there and I think it was largely due to one or two people, mainly Doug Turner.

Work in the north brought the Unit in touch with the Communist-held territory. In January 1946, before the Unit headquarters had moved from Chungking, a small convoy had left for Yenan, the Communist capital, taking drugs and supplies for the hospitals there:

Tony Reynolds:

Throughout the war there had been a very uneasy truce between the Communists and Nationalists and when the war ended, the Americans were very keen to have a united China and to get Chiang Kai Shek and Mao to cooperate. But the position was that the Nationalists were blockading the liberated areas (areas the Communists controlled) and not allowing any medical supplies to go up. The UNRRA (United Nations Relief and Rehabilitation Association) Charter decreed that supplies had to be distributed without discrimination of race, sex, religion and politics. Clearly supplies were not getting to the liberated areas, so UNRRA gave the Nationalists an ultimatum: either you get the National Military Council to give a permit for at least some supplies to go up, or we cut supplies to the whole of China. Chiang Kai Shek reluctantly said 'yes.'

I was probably one of the more experienced convoy leaders and was asked to take the convoy up. At that time we were just getting twenty-odd Canadian built Dodge trucks, and the Americans had got their pipeline through from Assam to Kunming, so we were allowed petrol, oil and water facilities, which was wonderful. I remember the first time I drove one of those Dodge trucks. I drove up to a proper petrol pump and said 'Fill her up!' After years of driving charcoal burners or alcohol trucks – bliss!

Finally, the permit came through, so we loaded up and set off for Yenan on 21st January. The load included a generator, an X-ray set, and medical supplies and I had a very good Chinese crew with me including Henry (Yu Chin-lung). Now I was very apprehensive as to what sort of reception we'd get in Sian, which we had

Yenan in winter.

to pass through. We feared the Nationalist command there might have secret orders to stop us going through to the communist area. We had no worries about Yenan itself. Prior to our departure, a group of us had been entertained by no less than Zhou En Lai, his wife, and other high-ranking officials. They were very interested in the FAU, what we did, why we did it. So we knew we'd get a good reception in Yenan.

Off we set. We had not gone four kilometres when one of the drivers missed his gear-change going down a steep hill to the ferry, and pushed his truck over the edge where it rolled down into a paddy field. That was rescued and straightened out and off we set again. We took the northern route, meeting up with the old Imperial Highway, down to Chengdu. On January 30 we had reached Shaung-Shih-Pu, we then took the route to Pao-Chi where we hitched onto the night train to Sian. Throughout our drive, we kept a very low profile. The (communist) 8th Route Army had a liaison office in Sian where we obtained our road permit; they also sent one of their members with us on our route north. We then came to the blockade at the border and were allowed through. There was an immediate change: the children so much better clothed, troops looker much fitter and well clothed with far higher morale than the Nationalists. The driving became very difficult: the 8th Route Army had no trucks so the roads were not built for them but we managed and got through this barren landscape. The low temperatures gave us problems. We didn't have anti-freeze, but topped the radiators up with alcohol and in the mornings we'd light a bit of a fire under the gear box and put a blow lamp on the carburettor, that sort of thing.

On February 13, we reached Yenan itself. There was a welcome party with dancers and speeches. We delivered our loads at the Medical Headquarters and were put up in the State Guesthouse which, like most of the buildings in Yenan, was a cave built into the loess soil – very comfortable, warm in winter, cool in summer. We were servicing our trucks with stuff all over the courtyard when someone said 'Oh, Chairman Mao Tse Tung is coming. He wishes to see you.' We did a hurried clear-up, washed ourselves up and were then ushered along to the guest room. He'd been there some time seeing others, we were an afterthought. So while we were under our trucks working, he'd probably walked by and seen all our clutter. We had ten minutes with the Great Man. He thanked us for what we had done and I made a little speech in Chinese saying that we were merely doing our work, that sort of thing. He was a large man, wearing padded clothes, and I got the impression of quiet power. I saw him again three days later when we were invited to the Chinese opera. There was Mao and other leading Party members including Marshal Chu Te, laughing away at the good comic stuff.

We then had a proposition put to us which caused us a little trouble. 'Look,' they said 'You're going back to Chungking with empty trucks, would you be willing to take our technicians and staff down with you?' We knew they couldn't fly them down. 'I must think about this and consult my headquarters by telegram,' I said. This proved impossible, so Henry and I discussed it and agreed, providing they weren't armed.

When we visited the hospital, we were very impressed with what they had there; they had done a lot with very little, they'd made dental picks out of railway lines, things like that. When I asked what they'd had from Russia, they told me they'd received about five plane-loads in all during the war years, not much at all. They had also bought medical supplies in Shanghai and other towns and smuggled them through and used Chinese traditional medicines. But they were very short of everything.

We covered a distance of about 3,200 kilometres in a travelling time of thirty-two days on that journey and, apart from our initial crash, had no accidents or mechanical problems. On our return we were again entertained by the 8th Route Army and Chou En-lai personally thanked us for what we had done. Later we were invited to send medical teams up into the Border region working directly with the medical authorities there.

Elizabeth Hughes:

Eric and I had both served in the FAU during the war, we married at the end of the war and arrived in China in 1945. Under the auspices of Lady Cripps it was arranged that an FAU medical team of six people and many tons of medical supplies would be flown to Yenan, Mao's headquarters, by planes of the Marshall Peace Mission. Members of MT19 team were selected and I was chosen as the nurse of the team. [9] The idea was that we should go in to help the Communists establish a more westernised hospital. They'd had very few contacts with foreigners. Dr Bethune, a Canadian doctor, had been helping them but he had died from a septic finger a few years before we arrived. He was an enormous influence, when we told them anything they'd say 'Oh, but Doctor Bethune said to do it that way....'

We arrived in Yenan in December 1946 and were met at the airstrip by a crowd of very friendly people. We were taken to the Guesthouse where foreigners lived and given a splendid Christmas party, hosted by the American group there who were negotiating peace talks between the Communists and Nationalists. Many of the top Communists were there including Jiang Quing, Mao's wife, later the leader of the Gang of Four. She was then young and very beautiful. We had several other parties and receptions. Mao was always very aloof, Chou En-lai very friendly and Chu Te, the head of the 8th Route Army, fairly gregarious. Throughout our stay there we were treated as honoured guests.

Apart from delivering the supplies and equipment, we didn't really get round to anything that was of great value in Yenan because a new outbreak of civil war – the final one which eventually led to the Communist victory – started.

It was fairly early in March 1947 when things began to get very unstable. The Americans withdrew in February. Two of our members, Margaret Stanley and Frank Miles arrived just a couple of days before we moved out of Yenan. At first the plan was that we should establish a hospital about thirty miles from Yenan. We hadn't been in this place for long when we were told to move off again because of the risky military situation – the bombing of Yenan, we could hear, had already started. So off we set on what was going to be *our* 'Long March.'

Our Long March through Shenshi province lasted well over a year. Like the famous Long March of 1934, we travelled enormous distances, often back-tracking to avoid skirmishes and battles. On a good day we'd cover twenty miles, but often we'd only make no more than ten. We walked, wearing our Chinese cloth shoes, which were very comfortable; equipment was carried by mules and donkeys. We were a truly Mobile Hospital. Every time we moved into a village, people were asked to move out of their cave homes to make accommodation for all of us working with the hospital and for patients, as necessary. I never saw an argument about this although it meant them doubling up with other families. Occasionally they would come and with sign language ask if they could get something from their homes.

We started out with about thirty or forty nurses and other ancillary staff; then there was our group and three or four Chinese doctors came with us. We also had interpreters, of course. As we moved around, we gradually collected more people and in the end we had about a hundred staff. We also picked up patients along the way. Local people were recruited to carry patients and help carry the loads – they'd bring their pack animals along for this.

We used caves for wards and for the operating theatre. We'd hang a white sheet at the back to reflect light and another on the ceiling to stop dust falling on the operating table. Numbers of patients varied: we might have as many as two hundred at one time, but often far fewer. Many of the cases were gunshot wounds but

Caves at Yenan.

we used to get a lot of more serious ones, and were often faced with gangrenous limbs. We worked out a system of plastering. All this was done in the open air. The local bandages were very heavy and the plaster very inferior to anything used now; this meant that the result was very heavy. But it not only saved the limbs of the injured, but their lives too for without them being in plaster, the chance of reinfection would have been far greater. Really, the medical work done in those caves was an achievement of improvisation by the doctors, mechanics, anaesthetists and everyone involved.

This was about the worst time in history that I could have actually chosen to have a baby! I was very embarrassed when I discovered that I was pregnant and didn't let on for about four months, apart from our own FAU group. Eventually someone spotted that I was looking a bit fat, and it all came out. After that I was treated with velvet gloves. I still used to work in the operating theatre, particularly if Doug had a big operation. Fortunately, I felt well and was never worried having such excellent help around me. Somehow I never thought anything could go wrong even when I knew it would be a breech birth. The Communists showed such marvellous care, they even brought a cow that was in milk so that I could have a pint of milk every day. The padded clothes we wore were ideal – it was like taking your own upholstery around with you.

David was born in the village of Hsia Pei T'a on August 21st 1947. We had saved a little petrol so that we could have some Tilley lamps in the theatre during the delivery. Some of the villagers had poked little holes in the paper windows at the cave's entrance, to see what was happening to the foreign lady. It was a fairly long labour but I had no difficulties and David was a splendid baby. The Chinese made a lovely basket for him, an oval shaped one of the type they put their grain in and when he grew bigger they made a wooden sort of crate for him to be carried at the side of a donkey. Fortunately I had enough milk to feed him and he was a very easy, normal baby.

The journey was hazardous at times, especially when we had to cross the Yellow River. We crossed it a number of times, mostly by barge. These were very hefty and crewed by six oarsmen. They would pull the barges three or four miles up the river from where they wanted to land because the Yellow River flows so fast; really

Elizabeth, Eric and David Hughes.

it is a formidable river, full of silt. I remember crossing the river once by a bridge over a deep gorge. The bridge was very basic, made by three steel cables with boards put across with light chicken-wire stuff at the side – very swayey! The animals were blindfolded and led across. The boys carrying David in his cradle were very nervous, so I took the leading boy by the hand and led him across without trying to think about it.

I had a lot of respect for the Communists. When we stayed in the different villages, the peasants would come and talk to us through the interpreter, and we always got the impression that they were pleased to have the Communists who treated them decently and fairly. They compared them with the Kuomintang who had taxed them fifty years ahead, and we saw for ourselves when we were in Nationalist territory how the people dreaded the Kuomintang Army coming through because they took everything, while the Communists only took what they could pay for.

In 1948 we all felt it was time we were returning home. Eric, Doug and I were the last to go and we decided that we'd like to return to Yenan which by then was liberated, before we set off. When we returned, we found that during the Nationalist occupation, all the large buildings had been destroyed, burnt down, razed to the ground including the operating theatre at the hospital where we had briefly worked. It was real, wartime devastation, like the London bombing, very sad. But we were much fêted and David was considered a wonderful baby. When we left we were given some beautiful wolfskin gown linings and embroidery to take home; and the hospital staff went to enormous trouble to make a wonderful banner for us to commemorate the help foreign Friends had given to the Communists in the Border Region. This banner has since been returned to Yenan and is in the museum there today.

In 1978, I returned with Margaret Stanley and other FAU members, hosted by the Chinese Minister of Health. We were treated like honoured guests once more. We had a big party in Peking where they collected together anyone who had had anything to do with the FAU – it really did seem that we had made more impact than we imagined. In Yenan we were welcomed as old friends too. What was so wonderful was to find that they had followed up programmes like the kala-azar eradication that the FAU had started.

Duncan Wood:

When I think of what the FAU did in China, it's easy to dismiss it as a drop in the ocean, which of course it was. It's difficult to say that we saved a large number of lives, or how many we saved – and I think this was the feeling of other sections: in the end what is there to show for it in positive results? Yet, in China, we have evidence that the Unit is not forgotten, members have returned there over the years right up to 1996 when a group returned.[10] There were, and are, people whose eyes light up when you mention the Gung i jo hu dwey – the FAU. This is because we did travel a lot and had contacts in many different places and people would say 'Who are those foreigners, and what are they doing?' I think we showed the Chinese that there were some British people who were more ordinary and, dare I say it?, more worldly, than the missionaries, and more idealistic than the business community, and that we may have done something for the British image. So I think the memory they have of us is a positive one, and if you asked these people 'What was the Gung i jo hu dwey doing.' I think they would say 'They were trying to help.' That is all one can say: that's what we were and what we did was not forgotten.

The FAU continued its work after liberation and the last member left China in 1952.

REFERENCES:

[1] Under the terms of the Geneva Convention, personnel acting under the protection of the IRC were not free to use vehicles for other than medical purposes. This caused a dilemma for the FAU as, given the scarcity of fuel, no truck could afford to return empty from a delivery of medical supplies. The solution was agreed that those working on transport duties should give up their Red Cross protection.

[2] By the beginning of 1946, the convoy had grown to 172 members: 71 British, 58 Chinese, 18 Americans, 18 Canadians, 6 New Zealanders and 1 Indian. Of these 25 were women: 17 Chinese, 6 British, 1 American and 1 Canadian *(FAU Register 1938-46)*.

(3) In June 1941 the British Foreign Office offered a grant-in-aid of £50,000, primarily for FAU military medical services in China. The funds were channelled through the British Fund for the Relief of Distress in China.

(4) The town of Wanting is where Tom Haley man-handled petrol drums which had been set on fire by bombers, and prevented the total loss of the several acres of petrol drums. From Bill Brough's testimony.

(5) MST1 consisted of: Handley Laycock, Terry Darling, Quentin Boyd, Eric Westwood, Laurie Baker, Selby Clewer, and Tom Haley.

(6) See Chapter 19.

(7) Haulage figures on the main route from Kutsing via Kweiyang to Chungking: December 1942 the number of kilometre-tons (weight multiplied by distance) of medical supplies carried was 21,000; this went up to 33,771 by July 1943; in March 1944 it had reached 50,000 and was rising. Davies, A. Tegla *op. cit.* p.278.

(8) During the period of FAU service 1941-6, five men died in China. As well as Douglas Hardy and John Briggs, Quentin Boyd died in Calcutta after leaving China with a mental breakdown; Clement White died when he fell from a truck; Louis 'Pip' Rivett died of polio. Several members were repatriated due to sickness. Most serious was Sydney Bailey who returned with bilharzia (schistosomiasis) which debilitated him throughout his life. Margaret Matheson has drawn attention to the fact that the womens' health remained very good in China.

(9) MT19 consisted of: British doctor, Peter Early; New Zealand doctor, Doug Clifford; Canadian laboratory technician, Jack Dodds; British X-ray technician/anaesthetist, Eric Hughes; British nurse, Elizabeth Hughes; American nurse, Margaret Stanley; American engineer, Frank Miles.

(10) In May–June 1996 an 'FAU Old China Hands' trip took place, travelling over the routes used for delivery of medical supplies. They visited: Kungming, Chengdu, Chungking and Kweiyang. See *Reflections on a China Tour: Revisiting the Roads of West China*, May 1996, ed. Barber, C. B. and Mills, T. M., a privately published MS.

PART THREE

AIMS PURELY HUMANITARIAN

CHAPTER 12

Syria and Ethiopia: Atom Bombs and Spear-heads

The Ethiopians had their suspicions about us, as we were military. This why the FAU was so important and very useful. On one occasion, for instance, one of our Ethiopian assistants, when cleaning up, emptied a small amount of white powder into a clean jar thinking it was barium meal. Actually, it was arsenic – you see he couldn't read. Well, a bit later, one of the local chiefs who was suffering from stomach pains, was given this, seeming, barium meal for an X-ray and he died. This caused a furore because we had 'murdered' the local chief. This is where the FAU came in: because they had the confidence of the local chiefs, they were able to calm the local ill-feeling.

Harry Burbidge, RAMC doctor, Diredaua.

*C*IVILIAN MEDICAL WORK *was a very important strand of FAU overseas service in World War II. In China, it was performed as one of several activities, as was the case in India and Europe. In Syria and Ethiopia however, work in civilian clinics was the main concern of the Unit.*

SYRIA

Clinical work in Syria, as we have seen (chapter 9), started through the initiative of a member of the Hadfield Spears Unit, Nik Alderson who, with the support of Lady Spears and various agencies in the area, set up a series of mobile clinics to supplement medical services which were already in existence but mainly confined to the urban areas. When the main Hadfield Spears Hospital withdrew for its work in the desert campaigns, late 1941, two members were left to continue the work in the clinics.

By the end of February 1942, four more men had arrived and in August of that year, the clinic centre moved north from Damascus to Sednaya in order to eliminate long driving distances now that the number of villages being visited had risen to nineteen. In May 1942, a new clinic was based in the desert oasis of Palmyra from which teams left on long treks to visit Bedouin tribes. This clinic finally moved westwards to the swampy, malarial area of Selemeih where there was a more concentrated need. The clinic also expanded to Jezireh, first based in Hassetche, then moving up to Tel Tamer, which was a central point for Assyrians, Kurds, Armenians and Circassians as well as the Bedouins roaming the area. Finally, in September, a further centre was opened among the Alouites north of Latakia. By the end of 1942, as well as the expansion of clinic centres, the numbers of FAU members had gone up to ten, rising to twenty-four in the course of 1943, declining slightly until the autumn of 1944

Bedouins gather outside a mobile clinic.

when the handing over of the clinics brought further reductions of personnel. The last FAU member left in 1946. The Syrian clinics, now under the auspices of the FAU Middle East Command, were known as 'Spears Clinics.'

Stephen Verney:

I had elected to return to Beirut from Tobruk in 1942 where they were forming a little unit to work with the refugees in the Jezirah which was the part of Syria along the borders of Turkey between the Tigris and Euphrates. Freddie Temple and I went with an Armenian doctor. As well as the clinic, we set up a little hospital, the only one for a hundred miles, at Tel Tamer on the river Khabur.

It was a very beautiful place. The villagers had built little huts with domes which looked like beehives; and they had water wheels which splashed the water from the river Khabur over their gardens where they grew fruit and vegetables. They lived in great poverty but with wonderful hospitality – whenever you went to see them, they gave you lovely food. They still had their national costumes and used to dance and have festivities and keep their old culture going in the middle of the desert. These Assyrians were Christians living in a Muslim world. And they had a little church where they worshipped. I remember going on Easter Day to the worship, and when they announced 'Christ is risen!' they all clapped. That moved me a lot.

We had to do everything in the hospital and people came in with all sorts of illnesses. I was in charge of the dispensary, with almost no knowledge. I mean, I could have killed hundreds of people if I'd made a mistake, but I don't think I did. Then I was assisting in operations – quite skilled operations; and I was giving anaesthetics with almost no training. We did cataract operations, using my nail scissors to cut cataracts out of people's eyes. We had to do it. We were the only help they had. And we got through without any disasters, I think. Just. People used to come in from all around: Arabs, Kurds and Armenians – all sorts of people who lived in the area. They were very deeply grateful that we were there.

We were quite cut off but we used to go down to Beirut now and then to re-stock. I remember we once came back with a piano and put it in this little hut where we lived. And I remember a Kurd coming in and gazing at this amazing instrument. I invited him to touch it, and he touched one of the ivories and when the sound came out, he started with astonishment. So we were bringing quite an alien culture up there. And the way of western medicine was alien to most of those who attended our clinic. I remember a Mukhtar – a sort of head man – coming in from a village nearby. We gave him some medicine and then when I went to visit him, he opened a drawer and and pointed and said 'Well, I've been to many doctors, and they've given me all these medicines, but they've never healed me.' He had never swallowed any of them, but had the feeling that some kind of magic was at work by which he would be healed. He may have been right. He may have had a sounder idea about medicine than we have.

It was up there that one of the events occurred which made me change my mind about the war. Our hospital was very cold in winter. We had stoves but no wood. So I went to Hassetche, the nearby town, and saw the Mayor. I said 'I want some wood for my hospital.' And he made it quite clear that if I paid him a bribe, I would get the wood. And this made me very angry and I suddenly saw that unless I was tough, my patients would die of cold; that it was all very well smiling and being nice and loving and reasonable, but I was up against a corruption in the world which wouldn't respond to that. And I think it was that experience which began to open my mind. And from being a rather unrealistic young Englishman who'd grown up in a Stately Home, then gone to Harrow and Oxford, and had thought that if you were a Christian, God would give you everything on a plate....all that began to crumble in the middle of that stark desert.

Freddie Temple:

We would charge the wealthy sheiks so that we could treat the poor for nothing. There was always a nice session at the end of such a treatment when the sheik would say 'What do I owe you?' And we would say 'Oh, for you it has been honour and pleasure just to treat you.' 'No, what can I pay?' 'No, no, it has been such an honour, you've been a blessing on our house etc. etc.' And then finally of course they came out with far more than one would ever have suggested asking.

There was a tremendous need in the area of the Jezireh, indeed the whole of Syria and the Lebanon. Malaria was rife, so were eye diseases, the majority being the awful trachoma. There was a lot of dysentery, parasites, skin infections and deficiency diseases arising from a mix of poverty and ignorance. We used to drive out to new places and tell them about the clinic at Tel Tamer and what we were doing. You had to wait ages and put up with all the interminable hospitality rites. You'd hear a sheep being killed for the great meal which inevitably followed and finally it would appear and the old sheik would grub about in the middle of it with his dirty hands – they couldn't help this as water was scarce – and you would be offered the chief morsels. The major morsel to offer was the eye, and so one got used to eating eyes. Later I was chaplain to Archbishop Fisher and when we went on a visit to the Holy Land we had a meal with a sheik near Samaria. This was one of the few

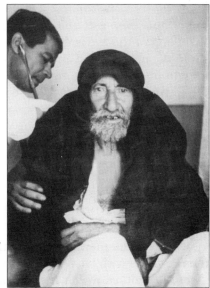

Old diseases – new cures.
An old shepherd with bronchial
asthma.

times I'd seen the Archbishop disconcerted, but this great dish came on and he whispered 'Freddie, I can't possibly eat the eye, you've got to do something to stop this.' Luckily, I remembered enough to be able to say 'Unfortunately His Grace has a very delicate stomach and I wonder if I could have the honour and privilege of receiving the eye on his behalf.'

One night Stephen and I stayed the night with a sheik. He spent the evening picking fleas from the head of one of his small sons and chatted and then went off to sleep and we lay down to sleep. Then I woke up in the middle of the night as a sheep appeared – there being a door in the tent – strolled up to where Stephen was sleeping and then performed right by his head. I have never seen Stephen wake more rapidly! We certainly got very close to the local community there!

One day Dr Shrijian prescribed three teaspoons of a certain medicine for a patient and told her to come back in a week if she wasn't better. The sheik brought this wife back saying that she was much worse, so the doctor increased the dose to a dessert spoon. They had wooden spoons. The next day the sheik came back and said 'the teaspoons she could manage but not the dessert spoons!' We presumed they had been sawn up and eaten. The major operation was the one for trachoma where the eyelashes were turned under the eye, and the rubbing of the eyelashes through the shrinking of the eye is what causes the blindness. We had to cut a slit in the upper eyelid and then take a sliver of skin from the lower lip and insert that into the eyelid and it turned the eyelashes out. Dr Shrijian said one day 'We could get far more of these done Freddie if you took on the sewing up of the lips,' and I agreed. The first patient I had was someone who had quite a large moustache and when I was mopping up the blood I found that I had sewn his lip into his moustache. The doctor looked down without saying anything. So I slit it open and sewed it up again. I would visit the poor man in the hospital each day, asking with trepidation 'How is your lip?' 'Quite alright, quite alright.' And his lip apparently recovered quite well.

Most of the men wouldn't let their wives be in the operating theatre alone with us. So they would huddle in the corner in their dirty old clothes which made it difficult to get good anti-septic conditions. I remember once there was a poor wife under local anaesthetic, she wasn't being badly hurt but just couldn't keep still. So finally we had to say to the husband 'Could you persuade your wife to keep still?' And the persuasion was to step forward and give her some hearty slaps. Some patients were frightened of beds and you would find them sleeping under, rather than on them.

When the piano arrived it wouldn't fit the front door so we just had to hack away a bit around the door to get it in and fill it in again, and we could add another room quite simply. We'd look out in the morning and see a cortege of camels coming across the desert and wonder what that was. Then you'd realise that the wealthy sheik you had in the hospital was just changing wives. We couldn't provide any cooking, so someone had to do this and after a while he'd feel like a change and the new wife would come in and the old one go back. We loved living in our little mud house. It was a good, simple way of living.

Roy Ridgway:

I was with the HSU in Tunis. At that time there was no action but we had been leading a very unQuakerish kind of life there and I decided, along with two others, to join the Spears Clinics in Syria. We drove over the Sinai desert to Palestine and then to Beirut. I was sent to Latakia where we had our ambulance-clinic and from Latakia we'd drive out to the little villages in the area. The patients would come in from miles around and we'd treat them for all sorts of diseases.I remember giving one patient 'M and B' to clear his pneumonia – penicillin hadn't come in then – and said 'This cured Churchill.' 'Who is Churchill?' he said. I helped a little girl who also had pneumonia and her father said to the doctor 'Would this young man like the girl in appreciation for what he has done?' She was offered as a gift. Women were less important than animals. You would see men on donkeys with their wives trailing behind. We used to get a bit fed up at times, it was hot and uncomfortable in the ambulance with all those sticky medicines.

From the start Spears Clinics had set itself two main aims: to reduce the suffering of the peoples of Syria and the Lebanon from disease by curative and preventative medicine and to strive for better health services for the future. Also, by living and working among peoples of many races and religions to play a part in increasing mutual understanding and respect. How far were these aims achieved?

During the 1940s, Syria and the Lebanon contained between them about 5,000 villages; Spears Clinics covered no more than a hundred, therefore they only touched on the vast need of the area. But in the areas they covered, they provided a valuable service, and often the only service, not only with direct medical aid, but also contributing to rural health and hygiene. Health conditions in the villages were appalling: water was usually contaminated, rubbish and excrement littered the streets attracting flies and vermin. Stagnant pools around living areas attracted mosquitoes and it was the custom to take animals into the windowless huts at night. Ignorance was widespread, as schools were few, and the prevailing fatalistic attitude, where Allah's Will decided all, meant that it was an uphill task persuading the inhabitants of the value of hygiene and of accepting medications other than local ones which included treatments such as infusions of horse urine or dog excrement for dysentery.

Hugo Powell:

I worked in the Bekaa Valley area and the countryside around Damascus. It was a most extraordinarily interesting and enlivening part of my life. But it was often so difficult because the people were very suspicious: 'Who are these people? Why are they taking an interest in us?' I remember one village in the Bekaa Valley where two-thirds of the people were suffering from malaria. It was a problem which had gone on indefinitely, and the reason was clear enough: there was a large swamp close to the village, full of mosquitoes. We tried to persuade the head man to drain the swamp and get rid of the mosquitoes, and how this would be better than loads of quinine. He made every excuse imaginable to avoid doing this although he had the means to do it easily. Eventually it turned out that he thought we were after the ground so that we could run a military road through – that was the sort of suspicion we were constantly up against. There was also a lot of corruption. We spent some time distributing wheat given by Australia and this was just disappearing into the black market. So we would take it to a village, with guards to protect it, and have the entire village out in the square and arrange to put it into the pans of each family. It was the only way to ensure that it got to those who needed it.

Gradually the teams won the confidence of the populace. An important factor was that, unlike the usual quacks who disappeared after making their profits, the Spears ambulances would appear regularly. In this way the work became routine and accepted. More serious cases would be loaded into the ambulance and taken off to the nearest hospital. Tel Tamer Clinic ran its own hospital, as Stephen Verney has described, and in the year ending May 1943 coped with 407 admissions. Chtaura and Sednaya used hospitals in Beirut and Damascus respectively. In all, over 45,000 cases were treated during the year ending June 1943, and in 1945 it was reported that over 4,000 patients were being examined monthly. [1] *Vaccinations were given against smallpox and inoculations against typhoid when epidemics threatened. In January 1943, the Latkia Clinic staff vaccinated over 2,600 people in four days when typhus broke out. The biggest anti-typhoid campaign happened in the first two months of 1944 when staff at Selemieh inoculated 6,800 people.*

When the time came to leave, in 1944, recognition of Spears Clinics' work by the Syrian and Lebanese authorities meant there was real hope that their work would be continued. Arrangements for handing over to local bodies were therefore far more positive than was the case in Ethiopia.

ETHIOPIA

When the Emperor of Ethiopia (Abyssinia) returned to his recently liberated country, in 1941, he found the place ravaged by two military campaigns: the Italian occupation of 1935 and the British liberation of 1941. A huge effort was required to rebuild the national life and establish social services. Wary of yet more foreign political influence, yet desperately needing outside assistance, the Emperor agreed to accept the offer of the FAU to send forty men to assist with medical work and the development of medical and social services. His very acceptance was a tribute to the Society of Friends: he had known Quakers whilst living in lonely exile in Bristol and knew that the FAU was not part of the military or political establishments and that their aims were purely humanitarian.

After a period of training in tropical medicine at Livingstone College in London, and in the Amharic language, the party of forty left in five groups. Although the first group had left in April 1942, it wasn't until November 1942 that all forty, converging from different directions and with some dramatic travelling experiences, arrived in Addis Ababa. Richard 'Richie' Mounsey was the Commandant and Michael Vaizey the senior Medical Officer. By this time, the British Army had been withdrawn except from certain reserved areas with only a small Military Mission left behind to train the Ethiopian Army.

The Italians had built up a very good medical service in the country during the occupation, but with their defeat the whole system had collapsed. About twenty-five Italian doctors were left behind. There were twelve British Military Mission doctors, mainly Palestinians whose main concern was with the Ethiopian Army, and three British Red Cross doctors who ran an Addis Ababa hospital. Initially, the FAU sent two doctors: Michael Vaizey (who was not actually a Unit member) and Anthony Husband. Later, in 1943 five more doctors arrived bringing the numbers up to seven – the highest proportion of doctors to men experienced in the FAU. They were certainly needed: although the Unit had always realised it would have to bear a great deal of responsibility, when it arrived it found that it was in fact to become well over half the official medical services of the whole country.

FAU service in Ethiopia consisted of five main contributions: hospital administration; developing and working in clinics in the Shoa and other provinces; providing a system for training Ethiopian dressers (nurses); improvements in public health; and educational work, part and full-time.

The geographical area covered by the Unit was vast and consisted of three main regions: the hospital and clinics of Addis Ababa itself, and the Shoa clinics which lay within an eighty mile radius of Addis Ababa; the provinces of Wollamo, Sidamo and Borana situated in the far south; and in the far north the towns of Gondar and Adua. By 1944, the Unit had built up a network of hospitals and clinics providing regular treatment to many thousands of people who would otherwise have had nothing. In 1945, before the Unit withdrew, it was responsible for the treatment of some 17,000 out-patients and 900 in-patients every month. [2]

Norman Pollitt:

The first to arrive were the six of us who had travelled on a small freight steamer which, in the course of the voyage, we discovered was loaded with explosives. We had earnest discussions whether, as pacifists, we should accept this as well as the protection of the anti-aircraft guns the freighter carried. But it was pointed out that if we didn't continue on that ship, then we couldn't get there anyway. Most of us accepted that in wartime you had to accept this kind of situation and, as we weren't asked to take our turn on the gun, it became an academic point. We eventually arrived in Addis and after a short while we began to go out to the clinics dotted around the country.

Usually we went in groups of two or three, but ultimately we'd often find that only one was needed. I went to Ambo, one of the Shoa clinics. I can't remember how many months I was there alone, but I know it seemed a very long time because weeks would go by before I'd see anyone. Communication was poor: there was a telephone service of sorts and quite a good bus service which ran more or less throughout the country, but it was erratic. We had to rely on commercial transport a lot as we didn't have a Unit transport system as such although we had a couple of cars in Addis. One was very much out on a limb.

Ethiopia sits on a great plateau and although it's virtually on the Equator, because it's about 8,000 feet above sea level it was a climate any European could fit into quite happily. The people there were very interesting: when you see the TV pictures today, they don't look any different now than how they looked forty years ago. Everyone went around draped in a "shamma" – they were, and are, a very primitive people. The interesting thing is that the same troubles we witness today were there in our time. In the north particularly, there were always tales coming down of brigands, highway robbers and inter-tribal warfare. The one difference is that we never saw any severe hunger or famine – perhaps the odd case of undernourishment, but nothing more severe.

I first went to Ambo with Dr. Husband, and he would sit in with me in the clinics, seeing the sorts of things I'd have to treat, and when he was happy that I could cope, he left me to it and went

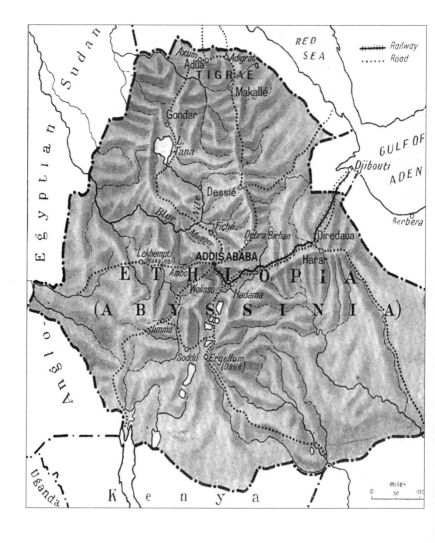

Map IV – Ethiopia.

off somewhere else. From time to time he'd visit and I'd line things up for him which required his surgical skills. I remember we operated successfully on the local headmaster's son on my dining table. I gave the anaesthetic and Tony did the operation on the sinuses.

Our training had prepared us to expect a lot of disease, and this was certainly the case as the whole place was disease-ridden: there were eye diseases of all kinds, many of which were caused or complicated by the venereal diseases which were widely prevalent. Malaria was rife in the south, there were wounds by accidents, skin diseases, chest diseases, tropical ulcers, digestive diseases, lots of tapeworm and dysentery. There were also outbreaks of smallpox and relapsing fever in some areas and leprosy and typhus too. Michael Vaizey took it upon himself to see that we had adequate further training while we were in Ethiopia. As for our own health, we were relatively lucky given that we were exposed to some pretty dangerous things. I went down badly with infectious hepatitis, now known as hepatitis 'A'. I managed to get a lift on a lorry returning to Addis and weighed in at about five stone.

The life and work in Ambo was pretty demanding. I was constantly coming up against the limitations of my medical knowledge. But then I would tell myself that, however limited, what I knew was one hundred per cent more than the chief Ethiopians knew. We had been taught to think that way. We were open for twelve hours a day. The clinic would be manned by the chief Ethiopian dresser and subsidiary dressers who were good at diagnosing certain basic things and treating them. I would go over in the morning and afternoon to deal with things they hadn't been able to treat and occasionally I would be called to an emergency case. So there was a good deal of spare time which would be filled with home visits to those too sick to attend the clinic. One would take one's little bag and trot off and hopefully would make the right diagnoses and give the right treatments. I also taught the dressers something of artificial respiration as drowning was not uncommon in the fast-flowing river there.

I had quite a nice house to live in and you could say that, with three servants, a houseboy, a cook and handyman, I lived a life of relative luxury – although the surroundings were certainly not luxurious. I slept on a camp bed and had matchwood-type furniture.

*Emperor Haile Selassie and
Alex 'Jock' Reid at Ambo,
Ethiopia.*

Old newspapers would be sent from London and generally it was a wonderful opportunity for reading, we all found this. But it was the lonely life of a missionary, and visitors coming to my door would be beggars, lepers and people with ghastly syphilitic lesions.

One of the most interesting things that happened to me in Ambo was a visit by the Emperor. He would occasionally make visits around the country with his retinue of bodyguards and servants and two huge great dogs. I'd heard that he was coming our way to see the Governor of Ambo and I put the word in that it might be a good thing if the Emperor came to see our clinic. On the day he was due to come we spruced the place up, tidied up the dressers and lined the patients up ready for him to see. A car arrived and this little man got out. The first things I saw were these two huge dogs leaping out; they were well trained and with the right instruction from him, they came to heel. Haile Selassie was only knee-high to a grasshopper but he was very impressive, a wonderful presence. He came into the clinic, I bowed, and we spoke French. He asked questions and then thanked me before he left.

I think he *needed* those dogs: he did live rather splendidly and the people were desperately poor and there were signs of revolution. He was very proud of being head of the only African independent state, but he could have done more to help his people: the poverty and living conditions were truly appalling. They treated their prisoners badly too. Occasionally, I would be called into the prison at Ambo. The prisoners were chained up like animals in one big room. 'Do they have to be chained?' I asked the Governor, 'They are making this chap's ulcers so much worse.' 'Orders.' he said. The conditions in some of the hospitals we took over were equally appalling: you'd see patients lying two to a bed which consisted just of an iron bed and mattress, the rest lying on the floor. I think the Emperor had the independence of his people more to heart than their social welfare.

I wouldn't describe it as an enjoyable life but one felt one was doing something reasonably useful. Looking back, in retrospect, I might have been better occupied, on an ethical basis, if I had gone to work with the HSU in North Africa. I think the China and Ethiopian Convoys were rather out on a limb, but we were doing some kind of good and if that's what the Christian witness is all about, then that's OK. So not enjoyment as such, rather a job to do. I did feel very early on: if only I knew more about this, I could do more for these people. One always had the feeling: this is second best. The idea of doing medicine when I got back home came to me in Ethiopia; this was reinforced by more sampling of the medical world when I went on to do relief work in north-west Europe after leaving Ethiopia.

Ted Dunn:

After some training in the Menelik Hospital, I was asked to go down south to Soddu. This was a pretty, idyllic sort of place with thatched homes, a market square and a mountain in the background. The prestige of the British was very high as they had liberated the country and I was basking in their glory as the people felt I was representing the British Government!

I was on my own for the first two or three months apart from one Ethiopian boy I took with me. I made contact with the

Government representative there and he was very friendly. I was invited to a feast. They brought in all this raw meat and were most insistent that I should eat some. Fortunately, I was a vegetarian so could quite honestly say I didn't eat meat, but I had to put some on my plate to show willing.

There were absolutely no medical facilities there at all. They gave me some buildings which the Italians had put up. After the Italians left they had been occupied by Amharas who had blocked out all the windows and lit fires in the middle of the floors. I spent all my time cleaning and repairing these buildings with some local help. One building became the Outpatients Department; another, which had been destined to be the Fascist Headquarters, became my hospital where eventually I had twenty beds, and the offices next to it became my living area.

I was thrown in at the deep end, but it was wonderful. There was no other public health service. I was *it*. I worked myself to death just over the excitement of it. One of my first patients was a relative of the Governor. I gave him the full works and this increased my standing no end. Patients would appear not just from the village but from the countryside around. I dealt with most of the common diseases: rheumatism, tropical sores, syphilis, eye diseases, tapeworms. Once a man came in who had been mutilated by an animal which had got under his house and mauled him. [3]

Before leaving for Ethiopia, I went round the medical section of Foyles bookshop in London and picked up a good selection of medical books together with a nature-cure book. These came in very useful. One of the first cases I operated on, which took me all morning, was an injury caused by a hand-grenade going off in this chap's hand – all his fingers had gone. I had to give an anaesthetic – chloroform – it worked on the principle that I just gave him enough to put him to sleep and when he woke up gave little bit more and so on. I tried to do a bit of a graft, taking skin from one part to another, but that wasn't successful.

I also did a caesarean operation which surprised everybody. I had never seen this done, but I had my book. It was very unusual for a woman to come to hospital for childbirth, but this woman had been in labour for a very long time and came in. I kept an eye on her but her temperature started to rise and still nothing was happening. So I looked up 'Caesarean operations' in my book and thought: well, either I have a go, or else she'll die. So I put her under anaesthetic and had a go. I was surprised how straightforward the operation was: the uterus was very, very thick and I was trying to hack my way through it very carefully in case I ruptured some blood vessels. Getting into the uterus and taking the baby out was quite straightforward really, there didn't seem to be any vital organs in the way. I had been concerned all the while for the mother, so I took the baby out and put it down, and carried on looking after the woman, and the assistant said 'Look, the baby's moving!' But it died.

We all did operations. I got a letter from my nearest neighbour, Hugh Brown, in which he said there were a lot of bandits in the town near him and somebody got a bullet in the head and the brain was coming out. Well, he pushed it back in and the man recovered. We did have great responsibility. It was really a case of looking at a patient and saying: am I going to do more harm than good? If on balance you thought you could improve things, you did it, and in most cases you did improve things.

After a couple of months, Paul Wakelin came to help and stayed for two or three months. He was brilliant on the academic side, very good at diagnoses. He taught me a lot. I was more practically minded. Dr. Vaizey also came for a few weeks. But I was on my own for about eighteen months and things did get me down a bit. Life was really just bed and work. We did get some horses later on which meant I could go out on home visits. This was interesting as I really got to know people in their own homes. These were very basic straw places, dark inside, sometimes you couldn't see anything; then as your eyes became accustomed you'd see a child lying in the corner. You'd see pot-bellied children but this would be more because of the wrong sort of food, not starvation. These visits gave me insights into the country which few would get.

It was difficult keeping in touch with Addis. A lorry would come every few months or so, then I had to nobble the drivers to take something or bring something I needed. It was a bit dodgy. Sometimes it was months before I got news from home. That was the hardest thing really, not being in touch with what was going on as I had no radio. I did get to Addis a couple of times, this did me good and made me see things in perspective.

I had problems with the bureaucracy, especially with money. The local Finance Office consisted of one little room in a building where you'd see hundreds of people milling around all wanting money. When I first went there, the money came quite quickly from Addis to pay wages and other expenses, but after a while they began to realise that I had no power apart from my medical work, so they took less and less notice of me. It was always 'ishi naga' – don't worry me now, tomorrow will do. The lack of money created problems for me. I was using a lot of M and B tablets for gonorrhoea which was rife, so I started charging a small amount for each tablet for a while to keep the hospital going. When I ran out of tablets, my money source dried up. This went against the grain as our principle was that treatment should be free. Really, the Government couldn't care less about the people. It was disheartening because when we came out of Ethiopia, we gave plenty of notice but they made no attempt to try to replace us, so when I left the thing just folded up and the talents of the Ethiopians we had trained were wasted. This robbed me of all satisfaction.

Eric Jones:

When the Italians were defeated they had left well-equipped hospitals and a wonderful road system which, sadly, soon fell into decay. When you consider how brutal the Italians had been in their attack, it was surprising how well they got on with the people. They didn't have superior attitudes towards them as the British had with their subject peoples, and a number of Italians married Ethiopians. Yet we heard all sorts of stories of their brutality when they first went in and how they shot every chief in every village because their main aim was to eliminate all authority. This explained why there was such a need of trained personnel.

I was sent down to Ergellum in the far south, near the Kenyan border, to relieve one of our chaps who had been working there on his own for some time. I was there alone for about ten days and then another chap came and joined me. I was amazed how he'd got this hospital going. It was very well organised and had about fifteen beds, with out-patients travelling anything up to three days to get to me – I saw about sixty to eighty every day. It was wonderful what our men did; Ted Dunn, for instance, once removed somebody's eye; he said if he didn't do it, the infection would spread and the man die. Before the war he was a furniture salesman.

There was a great need for surgery as there were many foolish accidents. When the lorries came up the main road you would get the Ethiopians travelling on the top. I remember one instance when a man was swept off by a wire stretched across the road. He was brought into hospital with a fractured skull. After a bit of care and some rest, he walked out again. People were always being burnt, terrible burns. One man was brought in in a dreadful state. The Shiftas (bandits) had gone into this village and asked this head man for money, which he refused to give them, and they just threw him on the fire. Apart from a whole range of diseases, we also treated spear wounds. Here was the world producing the Atom Bomb and people were brought in to us with spear wounds which we'd stitch up.

The childbirth situation was bad. All the midwives were native. Our own doctor was called out once to an Ethiopian Army officer's wife who was long overdue. Our doc wanted to use forceps but he wasn't allowed to, and the baby and mother died. This was quite typical of the backwardness, although this officer was relatively well educated. They would take our drugs though, and do anything for a 'Murfi'(injection). I never heard of addiction though, it was just the treatment they loved. There was some resistance: people would sit begging on the roadside with these enormous tropical ulcers, all the flesh eaten away to the bone. It was uphill work getting them to come in for treatment because, once cured, their income was gone.

The British Army's relationship with the populace was very different from ours, they had very few contacts with civilians compared with our direct involvement. There were lots of deaths in the nearby hills. Douglas Lister and I were asked to go out and investigate: the Army didn't want to be involved and the only other person was an Italian doctor who didn't think it safe to be out in the hills. So we went off and found just the tail-end of a meningitis epidemic. We did what we could but we arrived almost as it was over. The officials were very antagonistic and we found very little cooperation between the villages. We wanted to help but the bossy officials were more interested in frustrating than helping. There was an awful lot of corruption – they were almost like bandits themselves.

On the lighter side, when I worked in Dessié, I used to play tennis with the Emperor's son; his name meant 'son of the bedchamber.' He had learnt the game in Italy when he'd been a prisoner there. He would occasionally have parties and we'd be invited. He was a weak character in many ways but was very pleasant and nice to us. When I left the country, I happened to be passing through a town with another member and we had nowhere to sleep; somebody told us the Crown Prince was staying there so we went round, wrote a note on the back of a cigarette packet. He invited us in, we had a meal and they found us beds for the night. Next morning at breakfast, one of his officials came to us and gave us a piece of Ethiopian gold. It was thin and soft so it must have been pure, about six or eight inches long. When I was in Italy and short of money, I foolishly sold mine.

The FAU made all the difference in the world to Ethiopia then; without us they would have been in a very bad state indeed.

It was a great pity that our work couldn't be carried on when we left, there was no organisation to take it over compared with China. We had nothing like the glamour of the China Convoy with News Chronicle headlines 'Brave young Britons on the Burma Road.' Ethiopia was just continuous hard work and depressing in that you never felt that you were getting on top of it. We were so often alone…

Tom Barnsley:

When we first arrived at the Hammanuel Hospital in Addis, it was only a shell with inadequate beds, mattresses, no drugs, sanitation appalling and people just congregating there to die. There was one very good Italian doctor who was battling as best he could but with no back up, and he wouldn't have the temerity to approach the medical authorities because he was a 'wretched Italian.' So he welcomed the arrival of a unit of men who were able to speak their mind and make direct application for funds, if need be, to the Emperor himself. This was a major task but we at first had great success in getting what we needed, also we had brought equipment out with us from the UK. Our young doctors and surgeons did wonderful operations there.

I worked as the medical orderly in charge in the Tekla Haimanot clinic, which was a satellite clinic of the Hammanuel Hospital. This was the main Outpatients Department for the hospital. That worked very well except the hospital became so full that I had to have about twenty beds in the clinic itself. There were half a dozen dressers – three men, and three women who looked after the women's privacy. We dealt with the usual run of diseases and during my time there I became a bit of an expert on the diagnosis of leprosy.

I did this clinic in the mornings from eight until midday. Then in the afternoons I went to the leprosy camp some fifteen miles outside the city. That was basically my job plus being in charge of all the medical supplies arriving from Britain and keeping the out-lying clinics supplied with them.

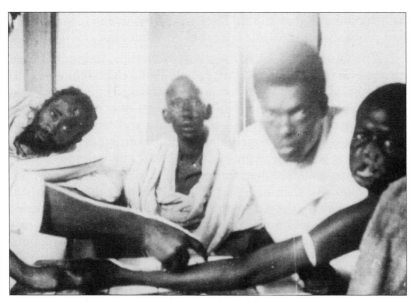

Syphilis and leprosy clinic.

The leprosy camp was built around a medical block and then hundreds, literally hundreds of these little round thatch huts. The patients lived in these and came for treatment to the hospital. There was a big communal kitchen for those who were in such an advanced state of the disease that they couldn't feed themselves. Orderlies prepared this basic food which the Government supplied.

Medical supplies were fairly primitive and had been left mainly by the Italians when they were forced out. The medical treatment at that stage was the famous chaulmoogra oil which, until modern methods, was the only treatment throughout the world for leprosy. So patients were given injections twice a week either by me or the Ethiopian orderlies. Apart from giving them these injections and feeding them, there wasn't much else you could do – this was only a slowing down of the disease. They had little plots of land, and we gave them seeds and encouraged them to grow some of their fruit and vegetables. We also tried to evolve some sort of camp democracy by getting them to elect their own representatives.

They were treated very much as outcasts by the local community because there was still a hangover from the old biblical times: leper, unclean. That is why when a man or woman suspected they had the disease, they hid it. They would be outcasts. I suspect it had probably got the same stigma as Aids has now.

When we arrived, there must have been three to four hundred men in the camp with their wives and about eighty children. We quickly saw that some of the children had already got leprosy and there wasn't much we could do about them. But there were some very young children with no signs of leprosy, and certainly the newborn ones were clear. Segregation clearly was important and we decided that we would segregate the healthy children into a separate building not more than three or four hundred yards away from the hospital. We then had the task of persuading their parents to release their non-affected children, and told them they would grow into normal people but if they stayed they were ninety per cent certain of becoming lepers. They saw the logic of that. So we put the children in this house – about forty or fifty in the end. Parents could go up and see their children through the big barbed wire fence we erected. As long as they could see them, they were happy to release them, and pleased, I think, that they weren't going to get leprosy. It was a very tricky situation when two of the children died (not of leprosy) and for a time the parents were demanding their children back, but we managed to persuade them that they should remain. I think that segregating these children was probably the most constructive thing that happened in that leprosy camp. I was very pleased that one of the nursing staff from the British Medical Missionary Organisation took the camp over when I left. I had meanwhile been made deputy commandant, taking over from Jack Frazer when he left for the Middle East, and went into mainly administrative work.

One of our greatest battles which was carried out mainly by our commandant, Richie Mounsey, was getting the Minister of the Interior to allocate more funds for the hospitals, clinics and training. This was so frustrating with promises 'Yes, it's on the way,' but nothing turning up. So we were getting screams and requests from our outlying clinics where letters took weeks. People were getting more and more frustrated. On several occasions, our commandant made direct appeals to the Emperor himself. I certainly had to make

Admissions tent at Hamannel Hospital.

a personal application to the Empress on behalf of the lepers who were going without food at one stage. I said that although I didn't see starvation, these lepers could do nothing for themselves and were totally dependent upon the food sent and that the headman had told me that unless they got food, they were all going to march on the palace. Loads of food arrived within a day or two. The Empress herself came up and displayed succour. She left a lot of dollars with local people.

I remember on another occasion our commandant complained officially to Haile Selassie about public executions. On this occasion there'd been a bomb explosion which had killed several people. They had captured the six alleged perpetrators and there was a public hanging of them. Gibbets were erected and the men were strung up one after the other – one of them literally outside my clinic at Tekla Haimanot. Our commandant, who was a pretty outspoken sort of chap, said what a great regret it was that a country that had been liberated from barbarism had to adopt such a barbaric way of justice. He got pretty short shrift, but he spoke up for all in the Unit.

Haile Selassie knew we were pacifists – that is one of the reasons we were asked to go in the first place – being the dead opposite of the military. But outside that, the local population had no idea of what we were: we were dressed in khaki, wearing the Red Cross, and they thought we were all hakims (doctors). Some of them associated us with the missionaries who were there before the Italian occupation. I think we were not recognised as anything other than kindly doctors who were giving them treatment.

Given the number of diseases rife in the country, it wasn't surprising that we went down with different things. Several of us got malaria and relapsing fever. I succumbed too. The health of those in Addis really was good because it was supervised by our doctors who were there. But the hospitals and clinics outside were very primitive and in their effort to do their work, several of my colleagues neglected their own health. One man in the south, who qualified as a brilliant doctor after the war, was very young, couldn't have been more than nineteen or twenty; well he neglected his health and we were very concerned about him and sent somebody down to make sure he did look after himself. That chap died in his forties. I think it is significant that of the total of seven or eight doctors we had in Ethiopia, all of whom were young men, only about three are still alive. In fact about a third of the entire group has died which is a higher percentage I think than of any other section.

We paid a lot of attention to education, recognising that in the end everything depended on this. Our members built and maintained schools and several devoted their full energies to education, becoming directors of schools – the Asafa Wossen Model School for Boys in Addis, for example. Others, like Bartie Knight in Hadama would, apart from their normal duties, devote time every day for teaching. I think it's true to say that wherever you had the FAU presence, there would be some involvement with education. We also placed high importance on education about sanitation and public health. In fact, looking back on it, I would think probably our most valuable medical work was education in public health; impressing the locals that they could do a lot to help themselves by cleanliness and general hygiene. Although that was less romantic than saving somebody's life, in the long term it was probably our biggest contribution.

Bernard Fisher:

I'd picked up malaria when I first arrived in Addis and it was whilst I was recovering from this that I organised a scheme for public health education – what's the use of running clinics, if one doesn't train people in normal health hazards, I thought. This is when the Education Adviser discovered that I was a trained teacher. 'Good heavens!' he said 'What on earth are you doing going out to a clinic! Take over a school here in Addis Ababa. So I took over an orphan school. What an experience! Unbelievable! When I arrived there were kids as young as five and up to men with beards. All orphans. Evidently, it was part of Italian policy to split families up. A village would be destroyed and the men, women and kids sent off to different places. So they became orphans.

The first thing was to whittle out these extremes of age, and somehow I got rid of the the nineteen and twenty-year olds – you couldn't really run things like that. Numbers were over a hundred and the teachers were mainly Egyptian Coptic Christians. I did some teaching which I found fascinating, but my main job was to run the place. The kids clamoured to get into the school. In fact the most severe punishment you could deal out was to stop somebody coming to lessons for two or three days – imagine that working in England! They were marvellous kids, and so keen to learn; maybe they saw education as the main hope of advancement; but there was genuine interest too.

One of the first things we did was attend a memorial service for Princess Tshai who had died in childbirth. It was most extraordinarily eerie – a mix of the Middle Ages and Old Testament with priests beating their drums and dancing around in this gloomy church. There were always rebellions going on: the rebel chiefs would march down to Addis with their armies, they would be caught and executions would follow. 'Where is everybody?' I asked as I went into school one morning 'Oh, they've gone off to watch the executions' I was told. Although I got on well with my kids, they would never walk level with me, always a few paces behind; and for me to carry anything in my hands – impossible!

When I first arrived at this school, the kids were in rags and in a pretty poor condition. In fact, during the first fortnight there was a typhus epidemic and six kids died – they all took it as a matter of course. Eventually, I managed to get an issue of a horsehair blanket for each kid, and an outfit which was a vest, jacket, shorts and a forage cap. They looked like little soldiers and were thrilled to bits. I remember going round the dorm at night and saying to the warden 'Where are their clothes?' 'Oh, they're wearing them,' he said 'they're not letting them out of their sight.'

There were various things I had to get used to, like foreign time and Ethiopian time. 'When do you begin your day?' they would ask, and you would feel foolish saying 'in the middle of the night.' Their day began at sunrise – very sensible too, for them. And their calender had twelve equal months and one short month. One day I talked about the earth going round the sun, and when I saw some of the kids looking out of the window, I said 'What's the problem?' 'We can see it going round the earth' they replied. That was quite a challenge. Another day, talking about telling the time and writing it down, I said 'It's very useful for time-tables.' 'Time-tables?' they said, puzzled. 'Yes,' I said, 'trains running underground every two minutes, for example. 'Underground? How do you get to trains under there?' 'A lift.' 'What's a lift?'

Strange things went on. When it rained, a field looking like a bare concrete playground was shortly full of greenery and flowers – amazing! I had taken some seeds with me and started a school garden. Here is an example of how easily one can adopt Empire attitudes: one day a boy came to me and said 'There's a big thing growing in the garden, what is it?' 'Bring me one,' I said. After a few minutes there was a gefuffle in the doorway and one or two of them were struggling through carrying what looked like a young bush at the bottom of which was this huge bulbous thing, the size of a baby's head. It was a radish! Another day the kids were banging tin cans making a great racket. 'Have you gone mad?' I shouted. 'No, locusts' they replied, and sure enough a huge swarm came over. I remember that when the guard answered the telephone to somebody important, he'd take his hat off. Another thing was that those kids knew far more than we supposed. I remember one lad was diagnosed with leprosy, and I thought 'Oh God, how am I going to tell the others without scaring them stiff?' And I was told by my interpreter 'Oh, they've known for three or four weeks and they been quarantining him already.' Another thing I heard was that in the tertiary stages of syphilis, they would chain people up in the marshlands where there was a very good chance that they'd catch malaria – the idea being that fever therapy can be used for tertiary stages of the disease. So you can see that education was very much a two-way process.

Another member, who ran a school right down in the provinces in appalling conditions, heard one day that the Director of the province was coming round, and he thought 'Aha, this is a good opportunity to show him what the conditions are like.' So he took him into the lowest class and said 'Do you realise that in this one class there are a hundred children?' 'Really!' exclaimed the delighted Director, 'Oh, I must tell the Emperor, this must be the largest class in Ethiopia.'

For eight months of the year, the weather in Addis was that of a perfect English summer day; it was lovely, you could sleep out at night and you'd hear the noises of the natives in their huts and the jackels prowling around. And then the blaze of yellow flowers when the rains came. I left with feelings of regret rather than frustration. The school had been improved: at the start there was just a collection of ragged kids, no health, no organisation. In my two and a half years, they were well looked after. I enjoyed my job hugely and thought I was doing something worthwhile. I would have liked to have stayed on had the Ethiopian authorities been more reasonable. I hope it carried on. I just don't know....

The FAU in Ethiopia and Syria faced common problems of corruption, superstition, prejudice and suspicion. In both countries the confidence of the local peoples was achieved successfully. The main difference between the two fields of FAU service lay in the fact that throughout their three years of service, the 'Ethiops' were confronted with attitudes of indifference and lack of understanding on the part of government authorities, as well as continuous acts of obstruction. This led to extreme frustration which, added to the enormous demands placed on their medical and technical skills as well as their health and emotional well-being, robbed them of the satisfaction they might otherwise have gained. The responsibility placed on individual members was far greater in Ethiopia than in any other Unit field of service – a fact acknowledged by Tegla Davies. [4] *But perhaps the factor which caused the greatest disappointment and dismay was that, unlike Syria, there was no confidence that the services and improvements which they had so painfully and enthusiastically worked for would survive their departure.*

Tom Barnsley:

In the spring of 1945 people were being transferred: some going back to the UK, some off to the Middle East, others going into relief work in Europe. We had gone to Ethiopia as a wartime section and knew we would depart when the war ended, but we had hoped that the authorities would take over our services for the future. In the end I think we virtually had to pressurise the government into accepting that they had got to replace us and had no faith that this would happen. So it was in sadness that we started moving out. But I think the vast majority of us felt it had been a very interesting and stimulating part of our young lives, doing what by our standards was a lot or personal good. Many were stimulated to do medicine on their return – I suppose four or five did qualify as doctors. So, yes, some satisfaction but also concern that our work might not be continued. I think Richie Mounsey and I were the last FAU to go, that was in August 1945, after VE Day but before VJ Day.[5]

REFERENCES:

[1] FAU Yearly reports 1943, p.12, 1945 p.9.
[2] FAU Yearly Reports 1945, p.10.
[3] Between My 1943 and March 1945, over 50,000 people were treated in Outpatients and 365 nursed in the little hospital. Davies, T. *op. cit.* p.224.
[4] Davies, A. Tegla, *ibid* p.232.
[5] Some Unit members remained in Ethiopia under other auspices: Michael Vaizey became Director of the Menelik Hospital; Selby Clewer continued with the Ministry of Education; Norman Boyes, Ken Tipper and Victor Menage continued on educational or welfare work under the British Council or Ethiopian Government. Richie Mounsey kept a very strong personal relationship with Ethiopia until his death. He trained about six Ethiopian students at his own expense in the UK. Other members of the Unit did likewise. In most cases the students had been either orphans or paupers. Several of them became ministers in the Ethiopian government. A Charitable Trust he set up in 1978 is still in existence, its main concern today being to help in the education of young Kenyans.

CHAPTER 13

India: I like to Think We Did Make a Difference

'The band of fifteen young men and women from England and two Bengalis who comprise the FAU in India are doing a job of work in the Bengal famine out of all proportion to their numbers. Ever since they arrived in India just over a year ago, they have been helping in the relief of human suffering caused by cyclone, floods and cholera, and now they are directly and indirectly saving countless lives in famine areas...they are specialising on work for starving mothers and their pathetic children... hundreds of them are dying and hundreds more would die but for the milk and vegetables, medical aid, clothing and blankets which the Friends are providing in conjunction with the Indian Red Cross...'

News Chronicle, 6 November, 1943.

*I*T *WAS AFTER the fall of Burma, when the eastern seaboard of India was threatened with Japanese attack, that a small FAU section was sent out to Calcutta. Initially, the task was to help organise effective Air Raid Precaution facilities (ARP). The team, rather than being the usual mix of experienced and less mature members, were all experienced relief workers capable of doing specialised aspects of ARP. All overseas areas of service presented their idiosyncratic challenges for FAU sections; a unique dimension of Indian service related to the ongoing 'Quit India' campaign – the struggle between the British Government and Indian Nationalists. As with any effective relief work, it was clearly important to show disinterest, yet the section was necessarily going out under the auspices of the British Government which, it was realised,* *could well estrange it from the Indian Nationalists. Therefore, it was a delicate political situation the section entered. However, it went with open eyes:*

Michael Cadbury:

Yes, this job was political and one had no inhibitions about it being political. One of the things Quakers have always been very odd about is getting in on left-wing views. There was this wonderful Quaker, Horace Alexander, who had lived in India for a long time and was a friend of Gandhi and other Indian leaders, and who had been concerned with the stresses and strains on India for many years. Although he wasn't a Unit member, he agreed to lead the Indian section, which was a wonderful help. Agatha Harrison, who was then an elderly Quaker, also became involved. She had been a Quaker missionary, like Horace, and also knew Gandhi and a lot of other Indians.

Quakers, you see, worked along with the self-determination of the country in their quiet way – very off-beat by normal British standards – but *not* by Quaker standards. Here was an area where the Indian nation needed self-identification, and this was a Quaker role. When Krishna Menon came to London as Ambassador, he was picked up by Horace Alexander and Agatha Harrison, so when we wanted help in India, we went straight to him and made our case. He was a delightful man, an absolute rogue, but a great help.

Horace Alexander and his deputy, Richard Symonds, arrived in India in June 1942. (1) They were soon joined by five others from the UK: Pamela Bankart, Jean Horsfield (Cottle), Glan Davies, Ken Griffin and Brian Groves. Alec Horsfield was already in India. He had gone out with the 11th China convoy; stuck in India with the fall of Burma, he wasted no time and in true FAU style had established important British and Indian contacts which were to facilitate FAU work in Bengal. Contact was also quickly established with Indian Friends who became valued advisers to the section, and it wasn't long before Horace Alexander and Richard Symonds paid a visit to Gandhi who welcomed them and gave the section his blessing. Henceforth, Unit members were among those in India who were able to work on good terms with the British and Indians alike. For the winter of 1942, this small section of eight members carried on the work. By the end of 1943 their numbers had been brought up to twelve men and six women.

Based on experience gained at home in the blitz and other raids, the FAU section helped Indian local authorities to complete their preparations for every branch of ARP, and the care of the homeless after raids. The section surveyed and helped in Relief Centres, trained officials and volunteers in medical aid, helped improve air-raid shelters, organised fire-watching parties and post-raid information services, and organised a body of Indian women volunteers. Because the FAU was recognised to be a neutral body, not working under direction from the British Government, and having good links with respected Indian figures, they were welcomed by the Indian voluntary services, as well as groups and individuals anxious to help. The work was not confined to Calcutta, but was extended to other parts of Bengal and into Assam, where the section also helped organise camps for the refugees from Burma. Pamela Bankart worked mainly with Indian women:

Pamela Bankart:

My task was to encourage volunteers and to organise them. I've got a little air-letter which I wrote home in January 1943 saying 'I've started the organisation which I wanted. It's called "The Women's Emergency Volunteers." This has quite impressive representation of about thirty different societies or bodies. There are so many branches of work that it's a job to contact them all and arrange everything. All the authorities are very pleasant but I'm having a bit of a battle at the moment regarding the "proper" functions of a women's organisation. There is great reluctance to allow women to go out in raids, but I hope I shall get my way soon...'

Yes, it was very sensitive dealing with Indian women. But our principal volunteers were the very young Indian students from the universities – quite independent-minded, well educated and keen to take part and help. The greatest problem was not the women themselves, but the authorities who didn't want their women exposed to danger. But the fact that we'd been working during the

London blitz and had been exposed to danger and coped, carried some weight. It proved that we could help women and children.

British women, other than missionaries and their workers, didn't really want to know. They were out there supporting their husbands, very much of the 'old school.' They didn't really believe in mixing with the natives. When I told one English woman that I was attempting to organise the local Women's Emergency Volunteer organisation, she said 'Well, you will never get the Indian women to come out and cooperate for social work, or cooperate with you at all.' I didn't say very much except 'Well, I'm going to try.' But already I had a number of women working and cooperating with me. They were only too happy to come along and contribute. But English women, no.

Of course there were problems such as the system of purdah.[2] This was not too important in Calcutta which is mainly a Hindu area. In Dacca district – now Bangladesh – this was more serious and significant. I remember arriving in one village where the village elders were very welcoming and kind, and the leader of them said 'I do want you to meet my wife and daughters, they would love to meet you.' And I remember the wife saying to me 'Well, I must say we do rather envy you. Perhaps our men will see the light one day. We would love to have the freedom you have, but we have a long way to go yet.'

In fact, there were not a significant number of air raids, although they were expected in the winter of 1942. I remember writing in a letter home that we were a bit scornful of the Japanese bombs which weren't anything like those dropped on London. They were more anti-personnel bombs which spattered where they fell. I can't recall that they did great damage. I don't remember any significant casualties. Later, Kohima was the crucial moment of danger. If that had fallen there was nothing to stop the Japanese sweeping through as the terrain was flat and not defendable. But one put it into the back on one's mind and didn't think about it.

Alec Horsfield:

The early raids concentrated mainly on the docks and very few planes took part. But on Christmas Eve 1942 they deliberately sent larger forces over because of the Christian holiday and then they came into the heart of the city and some of the ARP buildings were hit and two or three people killed. But the exodus of labour was the most serious result. You see all the labour in Calcutta was the male element of village families whose homes were under the bamboos in little plots of land outside the city, and at any disaster at all, labour got up and with bundles on its head, streamed back to the villages. Army movements were hampered by these fleeing streams up the Grand Trunk Road. It meant that trams stopped, refuse collection stopped and there was turmoil in the city. The rescue and ambulance services came out but they found that the reality was nothing like the training they'd experienced. And the training – such as with a broken leg – consisted of wrapping bandages around the leg. Nothing like a splint. So really, they didn't stand up very well under pressure because they'd very little real experience on the job.

We in the FAU did what we could: I had written a report for the Government on the ARP set-up in the UK which was published as a White Paper. Brian Groves had meanwhile set up an Information Service in air-raid conditions similar to what the CAB had done in this country. Jean was totally involved in first aid centres, Pamela was organising her women's organisations and Ken Griffin had organised a mobile dispensary which went up the Grand Trunk Road dealing with those who fell by the wayside, and some emergency feeding. Glan Davies was involved with training in the first aid posts and visited ARP depots and hospitals in the area. But before the air raids had really started, the cyclone struck.

In Calcutta on 16 October, we had a tremendous wind and torrential rain – the streets were flooded to eighteen inches deep in a very short period indeed, and giant trees crashed. The calm returned the following morning, but a few days later we heard rumours of a disaster down towards the sea. It was confirmed that a cyclone had indeed brought a tidal wave up and a large area of land had been flooded and 30,000 people had perished. A measure of relief was organised by the Revenue Secretary, B. R. Sen, and a couple of days later we had a launch with three lighters of food supplies and things such as lime which was used for cleansing water supplies. So the three of us – Richard, Jean and I, together with an

*Jean Horsfield giving glucose injections
for cholera victims.*

Indian doctor and his two dispensers, and an Indian judge –
boarded the craft. Another team had gone off to the area nearest
the sea, we were in the second party.

It was a very difficult journey as we could only move when the
tide was going downstream. We spent the first night on board and
reached the land that had been flooded on the second night, where
we were transferred to a country boat and man-hauled up a long
canal in the dark to our destination, a local Rajah's palace in
Mahishadal. There we saw the palace guest house standing blue in
a setting of stately palms, water-lilied pools and the moon's full
light. By the dim light of a clay lamp, we had a midnight meal, and
sank into undisturbed silence.

In the morning we started to make an assessment of the people
huddled in the grounds of the palace. We inoculated scores of them,
including lepers, only to hear the pitiful cry: 'Why save us from
cholera, yet let us die for want of food?' The three lighters of food
had been distributed to a wider area and that was totally out of our
control. It was only later that we heard disappointing news about
those supplies – that each barge had to serve a different area, and

that took time. In one area, for instance, the food had taken sixteen days to get there and when it did arrive, then the fifteen district councils of the area had to draw up lists of deserving families – there was no urgency about it at all... We were able to take much more urgent action.

We set off for the villages, long walks in the sun through stinking mud and water. As we approached people melted away. We stood alone in deserted villages. Gradually they came to trust us. From dwelling to dwelling we walked and waded, inoculated, walked, waded and inoculated again. Dogs and jackals howled and fought over putrid flesh and bone, packs of monkeys bounced angrily through the bamboos. We went where Europeans hadn't been before. Jean tended the purdah women, banished from the eyes of men. Her fame spread, men and women alike demanded her painless needle – she became a symbol. In their tragedy we felt the warmth of friendship. Yes, tragedy there was: houses demolished, crops ruined, cattle drowned, water polluted and food stores swept away. Cholera broke out on a minor scale. In the wreckage of homes, by day and night, by electric torch and clay lamps as old as civilisation itself, the struggle between life and death went on. Glucose and saline, collapsed veins and clotting blood, mosquitoes and cramp, hope and helplessness – that was how it was. The cholera demon spread fear and the people fought back in the only way they knew. To our weapons of syringe and flask they added eerie processions in the dark with the discords of conch-shell, cymbal and drum and the call of prayer.

We met the Rajah and his brother – two enormous mountains of flesh, and talked of cameras and Kodachrome. Various ministers made inspections and said 'How fine' and 'How noble' and returned to their cars. On a road, hard by a hospital, by police and by food, a man lay sick for four days and nobody heeded. He died on the fifth; he was left to rot in the sun. We played merry hell. Ten thousand were dead; amongst the seven hundred and fifty thousand who remained a handful of Indians and we carried on. In all we did 1,548 inoculations. Of the twenty-one actual cholera cases, only five died – a record of which our doctor was proud. I was there for about three weeks and returned to Calcutta where famine was beginning to show its terrible signs.

Pamela Bankart:

Reasons for the famine? I would say not really the cyclone at all. Primarily it was transport because all transport had been more or less commandeered for army supplies to Burma, so it was difficult to get food supplies down into the province. Burma was a very important source of rice on which Bengal depended and that was now cut off. There was in fact rice available in the province, but once shortage appeared you had hoarding and some of the go-downs (warehouses) were known to be stacked with rice – the merchants were hoarding it for the price to go up, and when it did it was to levels the mass of people couldn't afford. Then, in their wisdom, the Government imported wheat from the Punjab which was disastrous for Bengalis because, if you are unaccustomed to wheat at the best of times, and then starving, your system isn't strong enough to digest it. So it didn't help them at all. In fact I think many of them had more severe diarrhoea than they otherwise

Ken Griffin bringing supplies in a boat.

would have had. Eventually some rice came in, I can't remember exactly when but it was after General Wavell came down when he was Viceroy. The situation certainly eased after his visit.

Some of our section were working down in Midnapore district. Jean had asked the Government to build an extension of the hospital in Contai for babies, and she manned it until her health gave out, then other Unit members went down to carry on. The Friends, being a very wise organisation, looked around and said 'What is not being done? What part of the population is not being catered for?' By then the relief kitchens which had been organised for the raids sprang into action, but there was nothing specifically for children. So we started milk canteens in Calcutta and the villages for babies, children up to five years and nursing mothers. That initiative was in fact backed by an appeal – the News Chronicle was particularly good – and funds came pouring in and supplies from the United States; eventually the milk distribution scheme was taken over by the Indian Red Cross. We had somebody working with them

Midnapore milk canteen, India.

for a time and, from just a thousand or so children, eventually two or three millions were being fed. So then we went one further and said 'Right, what about children over six years?' And we then started these little canteens which served kicheri – rice and lentils. Some of the locals said this was very dangerous, that we would kill the children because it was so rich, that it was only served at festivals. We said 'No, it is very nutritious, they'll be perfectly alright.' And indeed they were.

Something like three millions died in the famine, they say. I think it scarred a future generation quite badly. They were dying in the streets, they were dying in the villages. You would walk past bodies all the time. As I said in one of my letters home 'You become quite hardened to it, because it's a kind of self-defence; you can't feel emotion at everything you see otherwise you wouldn't be able to take it – you'd have a nervous breakdown.' You know...you'd see bones and carrion. One would always have warning because the jackels and vultures used to fight each other over the carrion. It was horrendous.

Alec Horsfield:

When famine struck in the villages, they had less to go on than the city, and so there was an influx from the villages and one of our relief kitchens which had been organised for the raids quickly opened to serve 500 meals a day, then we sprang into action and opened the lot. There were lots of other charities, Hindu and Muslim, that wanted to contribute to feeding their own and they appealed to the Government for supplies, and it ended up that my seven kitchens, plus help from other missions, got up to something like 100,000 meals a day in one period in the city as a whole. It was a grim time, women and children were dying on the streets and the shortage of wood meant bodies couldn't be burnt...it was terrible...all a mistaken policy. The Bengal Government and Indian Civil Service should have anticipated the influx of population from the countryside into the city, and satellite kitchens should have been set up around the city instead of being concentrated in the centre. In that way the famine would have had less consequence and many lives saved.

Eventually the Government did open relief food centres outside the city to draw villagers away from the increasingly sordid and insanitary conditions of the city. By early 1944 the Unit, then reinforced with more members, had opened and was running canteens in 24-Parganas, Howrah, Dacca and Burdwan, feeding a total of 6,700 children.

In October 1943, the Governor launched the Bengal Central Relief Fund, appointing his ADC, John Irwin, and Alec Horsfield as joint secretaries. The New Statesman reported 26 March 1944 that more than 1,600,000 famine victims had received gifts of blankets or clothing in addition to all the medical and food supplies. As well as organising and distributing clothes and blankets, organising its own canteens and helping with the scheme of milk distribution, members of the Unit also worked officially on behalf of the Bengal Government. John Burtt and his wife, Mary, for instance, took on a variety of tasks. As well as undertaking the inspection of Government and voluntary canteens, they responded to the plight of the thousands of destitute orphans with John becoming a Zonal Officer for Orphanages and Mary directing four children's homes which provided education as well as care.

Throughout its time in India, the Unit concerned itself with Government policy. The appointment of a Relief Commissioner to coordinate the work of the many agencies working in Bengal owed much to FAU pressure, as did the system of special famine-relief hospitals throughout the province. Funds were derived from a variety of sources, not least the AFSC and Horace Alexander, who had returned to Britain in 1943. (3) Such funds enabled the Unit to extend its work to Travancore and Malabar, in south India.

As the effects of the famine developed, the Unit became aware of the growing numbers of beggars and the dangers of a dependency culture developing. Along with other agencies they had urged the Government to invest in rehabilitation of the devastated areas and their populations. Rehabilitation centres, organised by the Unit, were open at Mahisagot, Falta and Bashirat in Mindapore. Spinning and weaving, traditional village crafts, became the main work of the centres; pottery and vegetable production were also undertaken. Goods were sold with the proceeds going to cover costs, buy materials and pay wages. At the time of the Japanese threat, all boats had been confiscated. After the threat had passed, a boatyard was set up at Chittagong and the FAU initiated a scheme under which loans were provided for the replacement of boats. In a few months

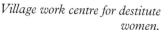

Village work centre for destitute women.

several hundred boats had been supplied. There were many other schemes concerned with reconstruction of villages. The main aim of all these schemes was to boost morale and get people standing on their own feet again:

Pamela Bankart:

There were many destitute women with children in tow. It's a biological fact that women survive longer than men – for the future of the species depends on women, so they are tougher. So I had an appointment with the Government of Bengal with the very delightful title of Special Office for the Rehabilitation of Destitute Women – rather a mouthful! My task was to try to find some future for these women because, in Hindu society, if the husband dies before the woman, she is nothing. So these unfortunate women were outcasts from their villages. We set up little village work centres – 'Industrial Centres' we called them, rather pompously. This sounded better than 'work centres' which sounded too much like 'workhouses' – although I doubt that Indians would have the same link.

We set about organising weaving and we encouraged the surviving men to go back to being craftsmen and the women to help the men. Their looms and everything else had been sold during the famine, so the Government provided looms and we paid them a daily allowance. The women would spin, and prepare the warps so that the men could get on with their job of weaving and earn. So men had the skill and women provided the back-up. Normally the men would have done everything themselves, but we managed to persuade them that it was a sensible division of labour. In the Chittagong area, we actually got a few of them making suitcases which was quite an achievement as they weren't too happy about working with leather, but they did it very well. But weaving was the main local village industry we concentrated on. It helped the women a lot: by working in these little industrial centres, they did get some sort of position, and were accepted back as being co-workers for the men. It was so much better than leaving them in some camp indefinitely. Our industrial centres went well, we had them in almost every district and they had some future and continued after independence.

Throughout FAU service in India, the Unit's position, in a political sense, was a very delicate one: yet, working as they were with both Indian and Government authorities, they gained the satisfaction of achieving good cooperation between official and unofficial agencies in a situation of exceptional tension and complexity. But it was a far from straightforward role and dilemmas abounded:

Richard Symonds:

In 1944 the Governor of Bengal, then R.G.Casey, asked me to join the Government to coordinate its relief and rehabilitation measures. By now Gandhi had been released and I visited him in Sevagram to seek his advice. He told me that I must follow my own conscience but that I would not find it easy to be a Government official. Fortunately my Welsh colleague, Glan Davies, was with me on this occasion, for quite without notice we were called upon to sing 'Lead Kindly Light'...Gandhi, I recollect, laughingly told Glan that he was excluded from having to quit India because he had married Sujarta, a Bengali.(4)

Alec Horsfield:

When we started work in 1942, Calcutta was choc-a-block with British and Indian troops and the political situation was very tense. There were 'Quit India' signs scrawled on walls and a very hostile attitude amongst those with any political leanings. There was a great deal of Japanese propaganda coming over the radio into India, encouraging Indian non-cooperation with the war effort and promising them freedom if they followed that course. The Lord Haw-Haw of India – Subhas Chandra Bose – was broadcasting from Japan stirring things up too. It wasn't long after Horace had gone to meet Gandhi that Gandhi was arrested and went on hunger strike. That produced riots in Bombay on a tremendous scale and in Calcutta cars were wrecked and tramcars attacked, and there was general rioting – but nothing like Bombay.

We moved in a very small circle of Indian people generally, mainly those Horace had known from past visits. Once we got into our own house we had some very distinguished visitors. Luckni Pandit, Nehru's sister, came and spent an evening with us; other leading Congress members came as well as the Muslim leaders. I remember too that after the cyclone a professor at Calcutta University asked me if I'd go and talk about what was happening in the devastated area, namely the burning of the police stations and police/army reaction, and that sort of business. I agreed and was taken in a totally enclosed gharry on a long drive through the streets of Calcutta, into a building, up stairs into a room full of Indian men who asked me many questions. Then a chap came in from a side door – a little man with a beard – who asked more questions. These seemed innocuous enough and I answered them all. But I was pretty certain he was a leader whom the police and the British Army would have loved to have caught. It was first-hand information he wanted.

Soon after that I was asked to go to Government House. Sir John Herbert was also concerned for the people and the general position and invited my comments. I said a halt should be called to the wasteful tit-for-tat situation of Congress supporters burning down the police stations, and the police, protected by the army, burning suspected homes. He responded that he wanted peace not a truce and that was unlikely whilst Gandhi encouraged civil disobedience.

We were not entirely neutral. No. We all looked to Sir Stafford Cripps back in Westminster to speed India's independence. We knew the time was ripe for India to gain its independence. It could have come sooner but for the war. I think that Horace Alexander was desperately trying to be a neutral broker between the Indians and the Government. I have a note in my diary here: 'Horace in contact with Stafford Cripps and India Office to see if could persuade Viceroy to have private meeting with Gandhi...' People came into our building who would have been aware of our sympathy towards the Indian cause, and newspapers were aware of Horace's position. Horace was an innocent, wasn't he? Anything he said off the record, wasn't off the record at all... He had an invitation from Sir John Herbert, the Governor, to go home anytime he wanted to, and indeed the Unit might follow him!

As for the army, they were just biding their time, in a holding situation for action in Bengal should the invasion occur, and after that it would be up to the front in Burma. So, given the very tense political situation, they had very little to do with the people themselves; but they did have the unpleasant task of protecting the police from Congress action when the police burned down dwellings suspected of sabotage.

During the cyclone time, one day I cycled out along the canal to the extremity of the area we were serving, to Terrafakia. There was an army base there of the 8th Punjabis, under English officers. They heard that we had a girl amongst us who would soon be left on her own. So they moved their HQ to our base. They commandeered Jean's bedroom which was immediately over the Tiger's cage – yes, with the Tiger in it – and we doubled up in the rest of the accommodation. They were good neighbours and hated the job they were at times required to do, and they helped a great deal when Jean was left down there alone, and acted as hosts to her in their mess. Jock Braidwood, a Lieutenant, fell in love with her and made me very jealous.[5] He was later killed in an ambush on the Burma front. He was a kind and caring person and a gentleman.

Pamela Bankart:

The political situation certainly made problems for us when we were trying to organise famine and post-famine relief because the village leaders, who would normally have organised things in their villages, were in jail. The people we relied on were the communists – they were trusted by the Government because Russia was in the war and they were accepted, unlike the Congress people. The Indian communists were idealist and very honest, and what we gave them to distribute, they did honestly and quickly. Some were village doctors, but the majority were schoolmasters. They were very nice to deal with and we always felt confident that they wouldn't abscond with the money. Other societies weren't so honest: one would check and find that the food was not being distributed quite as one had expected, some finding its way on to the black market – the temptation was too great and they hadn't got the idealism of the communists.

Later, in 1946, the political situation became very violent. I was still there when the Hindus and Muslims went for each other. There was appalling killing throughout the province. In Calcutta mobs would be running up and down the streets. If a Muslim saw a Hindu, he would probably stab him. I was working partly in the Government office, and the clerk would come to work and never knew when he left if his family would still be there, or whether they'd been caught up in it. He wouldn't even be sure that he'd get back. It was a desperately nerve-wracking time. I seem to remember at one moment driving a truck in Calcutta trying to get supplies to some refugee centre. I was going through one of the violent streets. The truck was big enough to prevent them from stopping me and overturning it – they would have done this with a car. I remember it very clearly, seeing those mobs lined up against each other – it was most terrifying.

I also remember getting temporarily trapped in a small hotel on Chowringhee, with a mob raging down the street and everybody desperately holding doors to stop them getting into the hotel.

It was a Muslim mob on that occasions after Hindus. That gave a taste of what you would endure if you were a Hindu. Risk to me as an Englishwoman? I suppose I might have got caught if I was in the way. I never really thought about it. It was like the air raids in Britain, you lived with it. That was the time when a communist friend said that if ever I was in trouble with mobs, to get a message to him and he'd come and get me out. That was nice to feel that somebody would help if I were trapped. By then one knew a lot of people in various organisations, political or otherwise, who would have come to our aid. Those riots of 1946 were almost like a rehearsal for 1947. They always said that Bengal was ahead of the rest of India as a hotbed of insurrection. By the time the main riots of 1947 came, Bengal had played itself out. They were virtually split by then, east Pakistan had divided off and it was a fairly clean division. I left in August 1947, at the time of independence. By then I had left the FAU and gone into the Bengal Government as a Special Officer.

As well as the explosive political context, another distinctive feature of the Indian section was the way, in practice, they all turned out to work as individuals with their own specialised task, each taking a great deal of individual responsibility. Like those in China, Ethiopia and Syria, most experienced health problems. Jean Horsfield, who worked in the most primitive conditions, seems to have suffered most. As Alec Horsfield explained 'she had to have frequent rest periods, and every rest period turned into hospital periods as well – it was exhaustion, it was anaemia, sandfly fever, dysentery – we all had it. It was a very sapping humid climate, but we enjoyed tremendously our short breaks in the hills, a world apart.'

As the war drew to a close, the Indian section, like other sections, was realising that its role as a wartime Unit was drawing to a close. Yet there was still vital work to be done, including the rehabilitation schemes which were getting under way. In the event, by the end of 1945, the bulk of work in Bengal was taken over jointly by the AFSC and FSC, with some FAU members switching to these in order to complete their particular work. Others, like Pamela Bankart, as we have seen, undertook work for the Bengal Government. The AFSC and FSC continued to develop solid and good relationships with the Indian leadership as the country moved into an independent state. The ground work for this was laid by three years of FAU service during which the Unit was accepted by the Indians in a situation of civil disobedience to the British Government. Sujarta Davies, who worked with the FAU on their various relief schemes from the start, and became an Associate Unit member on her marriage to Glan Davies, explained:

Sujarta Davies (Lukherji):

We realised in our interchange of ideas that they were pacifists and humanitarians, and had nothing to do with the British Government. We found them friendly and sympathetic...they had concern only for the welfare of people who were in distress and their activities such as the village rehabilitation training centres became models for the Indian government's cooperative societies. They certainly left their mark.[6]

Pamela Bankart:

...They would say 'The Quakers are our friends. The Quakers were friendly and helped Gandhi-ji when he went to England and Gandhi-ji had a very high regard for his Quaker friends. We are pleased to cooperate with you.' All the Indians I met would say 'We have no quarrel with the British people as such, it is the British Government that we have our quarrel with – they have taken our country into war without consultation and Gandhi-ji and Nehru are very angry...' The Bengal Government, in fact, found we were quite useful as a point of contact with the population. I know after cholera had broken out after the cyclone, there was a shortage of doctors. Bengali doctors were not permitted to go into Midnapore, except if the FAU sent one representative with them to ensure they didn't take part in political activities. We spoke with them and the doctors said 'Of course we won't take part in politics, this is an emergency.' and so that's what happened, an FAU member would go with them and the situation would be eased.

As for remaining a-political, I recall one occasion in Delhi when I was asked to accompany Mrs. Luckni Pandit to a meeting of the All-India Women's Conference in the Town Hall. Driving along, she asked, no *told*, me that I was going to speak. I'd had no time to prepare but got up and started talking about the famine. I'm afraid I got rather carried away. Travelling back to Calcutta on the train, I started to read the local Delhi paper I'd picked up and was appalled to read what I had said. Carried away as I had been, I had strayed into the political and dreaded the reaction of my FAU colleagues in Calcutta. But the local Delhi papers hadn't reached that area, and they hadn't seen it. I breathed a deep sigh of relief...

How important was our contribution? I think we *did* make a difference. Yes, I like to think so. I don't think the ARP side was particularly significant because in the end it wasn't really needed, but it had value in that relief kitchens were fortunately there when famine struck, we also got to know people in government and got to work with Indian people for the first time. So that enabled us to help when it came to general relief work such as in the Midnapore cyclone. The ARP emergency arrangements meant that we already knew these doctors, so we could talk to them and say 'Will you come on a team with us to Mindapore?' So that facilitated our contacts. I think we did help in a small way in the cyclone, and in the famine. It was an FAU initiative which started the milk distribution which was taken over by others. And I think the British canteens to feed the children was a contribution and those in time turned into small industrial centres. And our industrial centres continued as a post-war development scheme funded by the Indian Government, so they must have thought it had some value...Yes, I like to think we did make a difference.

REFERENCES:

[1]   Richard Symonds took over the leadership when Horace Alexander left India in August, 1943.

[2]   Purdah is the custom in mainly Muslim and some Hindu communities of keeping women in seclusion, with clothing which conceals their bodies completely when they go out.

[3]   Horace Alexander raised funds in Britain and the USA to support famine relief. In a letter to *The Times* he was able to counter a statement by the Secretary of State for India, Leo Amery that funds were not required. Quoted in Symonds, R. *Recollections of Horace Alexander and Gandhi, Indo-British Review* vol. XIV, no. 2, p.6 Madras, 1988.

(4) Symonds, R., p.6, *ibid.*

(5) Jean Cottle and Alec Horsfield were married in Calcutta during the war.

(6) Sujarta Davies, letter to Lyn Smith, 3/10/97.

CHAPTER 14

Civilian Relief in Europe 1943-45
Into Areas of Need

SICILY, ITALY AND THE MIDDLE EAST

*A*S THE TIDE *of war changed, so Unit members drew on their knowledge of FAU history in the First World War, recognising the vast civilian need which would have to be faced in the newly liberated countries. Civilian relief in Europe was, in fact, to be the last arena of FAU service and when sections entered Dunkirk in 1945 it had come full circle; for it was there that the Unit had started its work among the wounded French soldiers in 1914, and it was still remembered when it returned in the later war. From 1943 FAU medical units with the Allied armies worked their way through Sicily and Italy; then, after D Day, through northern France, the low countries and into Germany; and through the Balkans. Close on their heels, and sometimes in tandem, came the relief units.*

By the time the challenge came, the FAU had developed into a highly experienced and very flexible unit, not only those experienced in the field, but also those serving in the London Headquarters who had the difficult task of dealing with the interminable negotiations with Allied military and civilian authorities for access to the liberated areas.

It was the Civil Affairs Branch of the Allied Armies which had the initial responsibility and control for relief work in the liberated areas. The Council of British Societies for Relief Abroad (CBSRA), of which the Unit was a member, was responsible for negotiating agreements with the Army's Civilian Affair Branch (later with UNRRA), all of which took up a considerable amount of time and effort before relief work could actually begin. Eventually, a directive was issued whereby the FAU was officially attached to Allied Military Government (AMG) and the Allied Control Commission (ACC) which meant that the Unit was then entitled to rations, fuel and accommodation. Robin Whitworth was appointed Executive Officer for FAU Overseas Relief and Michael Barrett Brown was sent out to Cairo as Relief Officer to follow up investigating opportunities for working with Greek and Polish refugees in the Middle East. (1)

Meanwhile, the FAU had collaborated with the Friends Service Council, and Friends War Relief Service (later Friends Relief Service, FRS) in opening an Emergency Relief Training Centre, Mount Waltham, in London, which provided thirteen week courses in all branches of relief at a basic level.

The Unit, with its members immediately available and trained, was well suited to act as the spearhead of the voluntary societies and was keen to get into areas of need. By 1943, it had built up a very good reputation with the Allied forces but it was obliged to accept official machinery and had to work with the Red Cross which, in effect, served as an intermediary between the army and the Unit. Given the sheer chaos and confusion reigning in any liberated area, the Unit soon became frustrated with time wasted in bureaucratic planning while civilians were suffering. This was when the Unit's organisational strength and flexibility was vividly demonstrated and especially its ability, based on considerable experience, to quickly establish needs, set up its own relationships, cutting or by-passing red tape – often by some rather un-Quakerly means! – and getting into areas in which urgent jobs needed to be done. Thus, the Unit offered something different in style from other civilian relief organisations. While these settled down to long-term programmes of relief, the FAU's business was primarily immediate relief. It followed as closely as possible behind the occupying troops, doing the job at hand quickly and decisively and then withdrawing to the next urgent task, after handing over any work of lasting value.

On 10 July 1943, Allied troops landed in Sicily for the start of what was to be the liberation of Europe. In September 1943, the first FAU members arrived initially engaged on Red Cross stores work, but were soon attached to the ACC to assist with civilian relief work. The thirty-eight day war had aggravated the dire conditions already existing, and one of the most urgent needs was the rehabilitation of the hospitals of Catánia which had been destroyed or damaged in the fighting and to

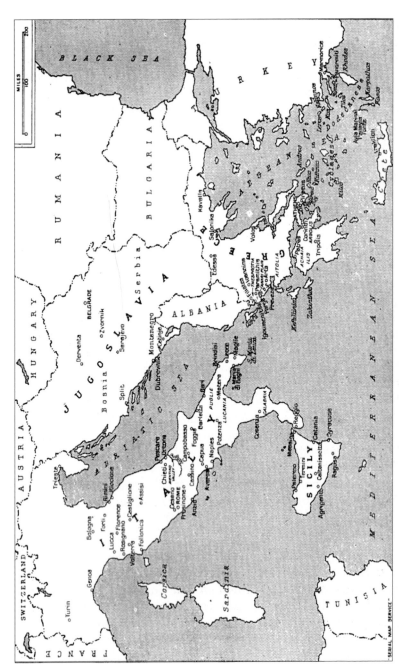

Map V – Southern Europe.

obtain medical and food supplies for the patients. Norman Barnes and Leo Davies set to work; by January 1944, three more members had arrived which made it possible to tackle the problems more systematically. By March 1944 a report had been produced outlining the various urgent needs and stressing the importance of having public support and responsibility to ensure continuity after the ACC left. A Commission was established and organisation set up to deal with the problems identified. As work on hospital rehabilitation got underway, more and more responsibility was handed over to the Italians themselves with the Unit continuing to provide support services.

By April 1944, with streams of refugees arriving from Cassino and other battle areas around the Gustav Line, three members were transferred to help with the clothing, feeding and general welfare of these mainland refugees in the transit camps set up: Peter Bamford to Palermo, Colin Giffard in Agrigento and Tony Gibson for Ragusa:

Tony Gibson:

I spent a lot of my time trying to get the refugees organised. They were from the mainland and were treated very roughly. I got a ration for each refugee and managed to get some industry going. I got the nuns to help and went around the Allied garrisons scrounging transport – really, it was much the sort of thing we did in Stepney with the bombed out people. I used the same amount of bluff there as in Stepney and got through to officialdom – the mayor, clergy, and Allied military organisations – by being bold. I managed to get hold of all the protocol numbers that referred to the rights of refugees. I printed it and circulated it to all of them so that they could quote it in case there was some rascal about who was saying 'Oh, this isn't very practical; we can't do this.' They could. The refugees had the protocol to prove it.

As 1944 advanced, the refugees, mainly peasants, became very restless wanting to return to what was left of their homes and to plant their fields for the next harvest. It wasn't until the winter of 1944/45 that repatriation took place on any scale; meanwhile the Unit, reinforced by another two members in November, had to cope as best they could with the range of problems arising. But by February 1945, the main work was over and the FAU section moved off to join the sections dealing with pressing needs on the mainland of Italy.

In the autumn of 1943, Peter Gibson had set up a Unit office in Naples. Although the Italians had surrendered in September 1943, the Germans were still in control of two-thirds of Italy. The Allied push north and stiff German resistance until the surrender of 29 April 1945 meant large waves of refugees fleeing from the fighting zones in desperate need of food and shelter.

Added to the Italians, there were also Yugoslavian refugees needing care and attention: 30,000 were passed through Italy to the Middle East by the end of 1944, leaving 12,000 in Italy who were placed in holding camps, the two main ones based in villas given over to them at Santa Maria di Leuca and Maria di Bagni. Seven Unit members, who had initially arrived to deal with a typhus epidemic in Naples, worked in two nearby hospitals helping with nursing and clerical work as well as acting as quartermasters.

It is impossible to detail every job done by the FAU in Italy. The vast and varied needs of the situation called for flexible responses and quick transference of members to places of immediate need. Essentially, the work consisted of assisting refugees and displaced foreign nationals (DPs), including Jews; helping to provide shelter, food and helping them to provide their own organisation; working in hospitals, giving a hand with whatever need arose, be it nursing or clerical; and running a rehabilitation scheme in part of what had been the Sangro river battle zone – the Aventino valley. Colledimacine ('the hill of the grind-stones) had been blown up by the retreating Germans on 23 November 1943:

David Thackeray:

....Reconstruction was begun in the summer of 1944 on a small scale by the peasants themselves...At the end of April 1945 a combined AFSC–FAU group arrived on the scene with three trucks, later expanded to five...Colledimacine stands on bare rolling slopes to the east of the river Aventino...most of the peasants till the soil by hand, reaping and threshing too are extensively carried out by primitive manual methods. The peasants lost nearly all their livestock during the war, and to them this means more than half their existence. If one was lucky enough to have saved a cow, it could easily be exchanged for the labour and materials required for a new house. But many prefer to begin their reconstruction by building a stall for the their cattle rather than rehouse themselves... Take Torelli Filomena. She works as a field labourer for another family who provide her with board and lodging. The 'lodging' consists of a hovel entered by an aperture two-foot square from the covered pigsty. The pig has the better of it. She owns a destroyed house but has little prospect of being able to rebuild without financial help to pay the labour.

But not all have a destroyed house. If you go into the cemetery you will find a one-room shack full of smoke from the chimneyless wood fire. Here on the stone floor sleep a hunch-back, his seventy-year-old mother, wife and six children, together with a widower friend...the barefoot children, whom you can hear singing happily outside in the fields, will have dim memories of their existence before the war came to the Aventino...the only hope for such property-less families lies in communal action to house them in Case Popolari which are now appearing in some areas.

Let us look at another type of family where our transport can be most aptly added to reconstruction needs. There is a subterranean hovel which shelters ten people belonging to two families. One of them, Di Stefano Giuseppe, owned three houses. Two are completely destroyed, while the third, formerly used as a stall, has four walls standing. He and his two elder sons will supply manual labour, but it will be necessary to employ a mason (costing about 400 lire – £1, per day). The material can be obtained on a credit system, the cost being deducted from the eventual war damage claim that is paid by the Government to those who have reconstructed their houses. If we deliver the goods and the house-owner does the job he can not only get back his house but retain a little in pocket after settlement of the war damage claim.

...Strenuous efforts throughout the building season in Colledimacine have produced forty houses repaired, thirty-five totally reconstructed and another thirteen in process of reconstruction. Perhaps one-eighth of the total damage has been made good in seven months, damage that was done in twenty-four hours as a war tactic which produced innumerable such stories of long-term suffering. With such bitter memories of the near past,

Devastation in Palena, Aventino valley.

conditions are unfavourable to spreading a Quaker or any specifically pacifist message. The barren rocky countryside has bred a hardy peasant type which easily takes to guerrilla warfare and it is with some pride that certain spots are pointed out to the visitor: 'Here two Germans were shot by ...' or 'in that house a sniper was found dead by the window, he's buried out there.' The idea that any member of our group should leave the Aventino Valley to do reconstruction work in Germany is received with shocked surprise. It is easy enough for our uniforms and trucks to give the impression that we are just one more foreign invader doing a military job. But the work brings us into close personal contact with a large proportion of the villagers...It has been made clear that the 'Americani–Inglese' are there to help them get back their homes, and that if we have any favourites we will choose from among the very poor.⁽²⁾

Meanwhile the 30,000 Yugoslavs who had arrived in the Middle East were placed in camps administered by the army in the Canal Zone, at El Shatt, Khatatba and Tolumbat. By the spring of 1944 eighty FAU members had arrived in the Middle East eager for relief work in the Balkan countries. After some training in Maadi camp just outside Cairo, and during the months of waiting for the fighting to cease and the call to come, they worked alongside members of other voluntary societies in the Yugoslav refugee camps as well as in the camps set up in Nuseirat in Palestine and Moses Wells in the Sinai peninsula for Greek refugees. Although a measure of frustration was felt at the delay in getting into the field, all admit that the work was worthwhile and prepared them for what was to follow in Greece, the Dodecanese and Yugoslavia.

Angela Sinclair-Loutit:

I was sent to Khatatba in the Canal Zone of Egypt, to work with Yugsolav refugees. The army was in charge of the camp and we had a few difficulties at first as a number of their people were suspicious of the FAU men, although friendly to the women. For the first few weeks there weren't any refugees so it was difficult to know what we should be doing and the army had their tasks. This only lasted for a couple of weeks but it did made for a difficult start as we tended to divide like oil and water.

The refugees arrived in trucks looking tired and confused. The first thing was to take their names and give them a number which was fastened around their wrists. There were lots of language problems due to the shortage of interpreters. This is when I learnt Serbo-Croat. There were about 6,000 in our camp, consisting mainly of women and children but with a few elderly men. At one time some partisan soldiers who were amputees arrived, they looked very bitter indeed. They must have been through surgery in Italy and then sent on to the refugee camps on crutches. Once the refugees had received their bracelet number, they were taken to a place where they were stripped of their clothes and taken through showers. Their clothes were thrown over a partition and steamed free of lice. Really, there were echoes of concentration camps – although the showers really were showers – but it must have been a dreadful welcome for them. I had to put paraffin on everybody's hair to kill lice. Naturally the women didn't like having to undo their plaits and have this nasty stuff put on. I remember the first words I learnt were 'only a little' – 'samo malo'.

They immediately demanded their own organisation, and made their committee in, I suppose, a very communist way. From then on we had to be careful to allow the committee to run the camp. Given the language problem, this was convenient for the administration. Teams were soon formed to work in the kitchen, in the sewers, on general drainage, that sort of thing. It seemed important to get to know the committee members, these were men in their forties and fifties. My memory of the first meeting we had with the committee is very clear. We were trying to be helpful and the interpreter was doing his best, but we were struck by the fact that his face didn't match the sullen, sulky looks on the faces of the committee. That's when I decided I had to learn the language and did this through a Yugoslav who spoke Latin. We had no dictionaries of any kind. In fact I never saw a Serbo-Croat book until I found an army phrase book a year later which contained phrases such as 'Walk in front of me with your hands over your head' which didn't seem very useful...

Our tasks were sometimes clear and often quite vague. I remember doing something like social work trying to help. I also tried to organise literacy classes and got about thirty or forty peasants who came, probably out of boredom. There was a child health worker who tried to teach the mothers some hygiene and child care – I think she was from Save the Children Fund.

It was hard to walk with bare feet on the hot sand. We were given 2,000 pairs of army boots which were tipped into a huge mountain in the sand because, apart from the men, they didn't fit anybody. Then one day a rich Egyptian lady came who owned a shoe factory, and she sent a great consignment of children's sandals. Everyone was thrilled until they found out how cheap and badly made they were. Then an American came from the Red Cross with a consignment of clothes. I tried to organise this in a suitable way – I had some experience then of running the clothing store – but she had other ideas and went to the camp commandant and got a building and arranged it all, and had a great big American flag fluttering over it to advertise where it had come from. The refugees were all very excited and when the store opened started pushing and scrambling outside the door. A lot fainted. Most of it was inappropriate. Yugoslavs are on the whole stockily built, and the clothes were very small sizes with ridiculous little boleros and other useless things which caused a lot of disappointment.

One useful thing that happened in that camp: I was able to get a small sum of money with which I bought cloth and embroidery silk. They could have done with dark glasses in the glare, but there was nothing like that – simple things could have made life much easier. The army can't be blamed but I don't think they thought of the refugees as anything but a lot of animals to be fed and kept alive. But they produced some beautiful embroidery with the small amount of material I could buy.

I remember a measles epidemic in the camp. We had a little hospital and the children were taken there, but the mothers were not allowed in. When people are feverish, they are not given food, and the mothers thought their children were being starved and were frantic and tried to get into the hospital – then surrounded with barbed wire – with bread and onions for their children. When the children died, as some did, the news spread like wildfire and you'd get all the women wailing around the hospital. It was a terrifying sound to hear. This situation was not kindly dealt with. It might have been better had there been no hospital.

There were only about six FAU in the camp. I remember spending most of my time with the Yugoslav committee and not having much to do with others in the Unit.

There were quite a few Egyptians around the camp. One day I saw an Arab sitting in the street. He was covered with sores and with a wound on his knee, black with flies. I took him into the quartermaster's store and washed and dressed his wound. The captain of the quartermaster's store was furious and said in a very nasty way 'I suppose you wash your hands afterwards?' And I said 'Yes, and I wash my hands before I touch his knee as well...'

One day one of my FAU friends from Cairo came with a bunch of roses. The look and smell of those roses was so fantastic. In the desert one got really hungry to see anything green. They would only last the day because of the heat and because I never stayed in the tent, I took them down to the committee who, like me, thought them fantastic. A few years later, in Yugoslavia, I met up with a lovely lady who was on the committee and asked her: 'Did we do anything to help you?' And she said 'Oh yes, a bit; you know what helped most – the bunch of roses!' I found this rather sad because I had put a lot of effort into the work I did for them. But you learn later in life that it's not the things that cost the most effort that are most helpful.

The partisans would talk of the fighting in the forests. There was one man who had been a cobbler in Split and had bad frost-bite whilst fighting the Germans. He looked pale and ill but wasn't disabled by Yugoslav standards. He told me of the hardship of the fighting. I also heard about a woman who used to take supplies to the partisans by hiding bombs under her baby in the pram – think of the risk! They did understand our pacifism. There was a Tolstoyan sect in Dalmatia, a few people with pacifist ideas, so they did understand in a vague sort of way.

Their singing was quite fantastic. After a time they gave a camp concert. They invited the army and the rest of us and sang partisan songs. I think we were all expecting something like a production in an English village hall, but it was more like the Russian army choirs, unaccompanied at times. In the open night air it was quite fantastic. Even the army were impressed.

We left when the UNRRA people started arriving -the arrival of the American 'experts' – they seemed so remote from it all with their typewriters and money and they went out a lot. Quite a lot of bad feeling developed. And I discovered that you can be very happy without having much so long as you're not besides people who have a whole lot more. Also, they treated us like coolies. But we had one thing that they had not, and that was transport. They had lots of baggage and the FAU were told that we were to carry these people and their baggage to Port Said. I remember one of these Americans, an older man, telling me to pick up his trunks and things as if I were a porter. So rude. One man though was very nice – the man I later married. Then for me it was Italy and eventually, into Yugoslavia.

Donald Swann:

I was sent to a refugee camp called Nuseirat, just south of Gaza, to work with a whole host of Greek refugees from the islands. These were people who had left their German-occupied Dodecanese islands – Kos, Rhodes, Kárpathos, Sími, Kásos – because there was no food and they had tracked their way through Turkey and Syria and eventually into Palestine where the British Mandate was looking after them until they could be returned home. They had been scarred by the occupation.. yes, yes. Lots had been bullied and pushed around or lost members of their families. They'd had a pretty poor war and we were learning about it all the time.

I see it all so vividly that I am re-living it: we're now on the Mediterranean coast in very desert-like country – not quite sand, but nearly, with this big Arab town, Gaza, to the north. The camp is enormous – mostly canvas with some huts, in about three fairly large sections – one by the sea and the others more inland. So there is plenty of room for these two or three thousand refugees, mostly living in family units, but with several single men and women.

There is a large cooking and eating place for the refugees, and the military and our group eat separately. The army is responsible for the general administration of the place and for security, and the voluntary workers, including the FAU, are responsible for the welfare and really getting on with what needs doing – cooking, registration. Certainly those of us who had learnt to dig latrines at last get their chance! So practical people get on with that sort of thing. We have been trained more or less for this and it is marvellous really being able to meet the circumstances.

We manage to get along reasonably well with the army. Our section leader is the one to go and see the Major or Captain and sort out any disciplinary problems. We have a few moments... for instance, we are supposed to salute them and most of us do it, but some of the chaps just can't do it, or they do it so badly that they are told off. We do look a bit raggety at times – just not good enough to be in such a disciplined place. Then one day a group of chaps refuse to stand up and sing the National Anthem. And they are sent away until they apologise. Do they?... I have no problem with this. These days, you do stand up for the National Anthem. So, if you don't, especially in our army context, it seems like an insult. A friend of mine who is a section leader and has more dealings with the army, has a more difficult time. But I am sheltered from it.

It is a thrilling experience for me. I am able to speak a fair amount of Greek and I suddenly realise what a wonderful thing has happened to me: I can talk to them and learn what they are thinking, and what they need. I run workshops for a while. You see there are all these women and they don't know what to do. So I go off to Gaza and buy needles and thread and some of the very efficient Greek women start them off making dresses and things.

I am a registration officer as well as welfare officer. That means that it is my job to know exactly who they are and how they'd come there. I am the one to know that they have come from Rhodes and that they are to be repatriated there. It is more than just registering them, it is more like social work. I am the one to say 'This man is the grandfather, he is Mr. Kalamanzakis; he is a civil servant on his island and he needs a little bit extra to eat, to build him up...' I think I get to know them very well. I get hooked into their religion – Greek Orthodoxy – with tents made into little churches. It's a mystery to me why I don't marry a Greek girl because they are so beautifully attractive, singing and dancing around. I have some very interesting experiences. Their music pervades my whole system...I even go to Jerusalem and buy a piano. I am given a hundred Palestinian pounds to pay for it and bring it back on the truck. Here I am at the piano again, music is coming back to me: folk music, camp music, silly ditties, songs from the troops – Knees Up Mother Brown. Add to this the Sinai desert with camels moving in the distance, and the stars so close to the horizon. It is pure magic. Quakers in the Unit hold silent meetings for worship in the desert. Sometimes I attend: it is quite wonderful to sit in the quiet of such a timeless place where so many religions have been formed. Isn't it amazing? Why am I here? It's basically Hitler's gun, isn't it? Here am I pushed out of England after tribunals and so on. And where have I arrived? Well, in a most extraordinary place, where the dividends are piling up right, left and centre.

And I feel deeply reaffirmed. There is so much to do in this big camp. It is a world of great need. Outside the camp there are a lot of hapless Arabs wandering around with almost as many diseases as the Egyptians we had seen earlier in Cairo. It seems to us that there is a very big war against want that we are fighting. We are on a new battle. True, what is a relief worker? Very small fry in the business of helping people. I haven't got money or anything like that. But my service is to them. But their service to me is infinitely greater, and is to change my life completely. I think I am meeting one of the best of human paradoxes – or super-human paradoxes – all in one thing.

But to come down to earth: sometimes there is torrential rain and they're all swept away; and then all the practical people run around and try to sweep out the mud and straighten things up. And people go down with illnesses and our young doctor and nurses look after them. Often there is burdensome responsibility. One day there is an enormous clothes distribution. Bales of clothes arrive and I'm responsible for handing them out. And they are all squeezing into a huge crowd and grabbing at the things they want with quite a chance that it will develop into a riot. They're all politicians, every one of them – you can imagine!....And every man is a leader. They are generally recognised to be disorganised. This is why you can't get them to queue. It was only on my way home after four years of war that I saw a queue and broke down in tears. I had forgotten what it was that people should queue up for anything.

The men are encouraged to run the camps – the general administration of their affairs, but it seems to us that they are only too pleased to let us get on with it. I am told by colleagues who were working with the Yugoslavs in Italy, that it was exactly the opposite. Everything was worked out to a 'T'. And every place had its own Yugoslav leader and it was working like a brigade. Whereas with the Greeks, it is each one working for himself in some way.

I find it hard to concentrate on speaking of the practical things we do because somehow I've fallen in love with all of them. I've just gone overboard. It seems that I've met the real world. That I've been in a fairy-tale world before. And of course they are talking of the sea and boats and here they are surrounded by wire fences. I begin to dream of these islands myself. Soon our time is up, all this magic comes to an end but I am to see some of them go back to their islands, and to visit them there, safe back in their homes.

GREECE AND THE DODECANESE

Planning for relief in the Balkans and Dodecanese had started in 1943. This was under the auspices of a sub-committee of the Cairo Council of Voluntary Societies, under the chairmanship of Michael Barratt Brown. After discussions with FAU London and other voluntary organisations, the pattern was decided. Teams were to be formed on the following lines: Mobile Hygiene and First Aid Units (MHFAU) for the emergency organisation of medical facilities in newly liberated areas; Relief and Refugee Units (RRU) for general civilian relief and the administration of refugee camps; Field Bacteriological Units (FBU) for emergency public health work; and Medical Supply and Transport Units (MSTU). In the main, members would be drawn from a range of British voluntary societies including FAU members filling in their time with work in Cairo and in the refugee camps.

British troops landed in Greece early in October 1944. On 13 October Lewis Waddilove, who by this time had replaced Michael Barrett Brown as chief relief officer, and Jack Eglon arrived with two representatives of other voluntary societies to reconnoitre. Back came the news that help was urgently needed, but with Greece being on the cusp of civil war, delay was inevitable. However, on 23 October, Harold Dromard, Sydney Carter and Paul Townsend landed at Piraeus as an advance party of the MSTU. [3]

Sydney Carter:

When we landed, in the south, the Germans were still in the other end of the country. It was a very, very complicated political situation as civil war had already broken out. But it was wonderful landing in Piraeus. We had to march, you know, under banners saying 'Welcome sons of Byron!' Everyone was clapping, and you saw all kinds of slogans in blue paint on the walls: 'The Jitterbugs of Athens are waiting to welcome the Yankees' was one. Then a lower one 'Greater Greece' – this showed about half of Turkey and was what they were hoping to get back after the war. It was all very strange – white dust everywhere.

We went on a sort of underground train from Piraeus to Athens. There was the Acropolis! Then a weird thing happened. We got into Omonio Square and we were with a couple of soldiers who'd been told to look after the armoury. They said 'Look, we want to get out and have a beer. Do you mind looking after this lot for us?' We said we would.

I then worked in a warehouse in Athens unshipping medical supplies and stacking them up. Our transport sections would then distribute drugs in the Attica region and deliver shipments bound for other regions to the docks. We wanted to set up a system which the Greeks themselves could take over, and this happened early in 1946, with UNRRA still holding some responsibility. We were then sent to other parts of Greece to do the same thing.

Paul Townsend:

After working in the warehouse in Athens, Sydney and I were sent off in a Wellington bomber and dumped down in Patras where Sydney stayed organising and distributing medicines, and I went off by caique from Patras up to Préveza alone. Once there, I made contact with the people in the Special Force who had been parachuted in during the fighting, and worked in the medical stores with their doctor and other ranks. I also did a bit of distribution, although my memory of this is vague. Then came the first rumblings of the civil war. It wasn't the final blow-up, that came a bit later. But there was trouble between the left-wing and right-wing forces in the area, and all British personnel were evacuated. I was taken to Corfu on a tank landing craft where I disembarked with about fifty crates of medicines which I had to organise. Somehow or other I got these into a large old *pension* called Mon Repos and, with the help of other people around, began distributing drugs in Corfu.

At that point, I had been the only Unit member in Ipiros and now the only one in Corfu. Then one day a whole lot more Unit people arrived from Italy and we set up the section to do what we could for the islanders. I was enormously pleased to see the others arrive because by then I'd had enough of being on my own. I knew quite a bit of Greek by then and was befriended by a Greek doctor and his family on Corfu, so I was not unhappy. But it was good to see them. We weren't there long before the call came that we could return to the mainland to begin the major relief work.

Theo Cadoux:

I had served some time in Athens mainly transporting the doctor and nurses to and from the hospital. Eventually a group of us were sent to Corfu. The situation we faced was not only the need of the indigenous population, but a large number of civilians of right-wing persuasion who had fled across to Corfu by boat after a show-down with the communist-controlled group. They were short of clothing and living miserably, often in need of medical attention.

As well as helping with clothing distribution, I also went out to one of the villages to see the people and how they were living. We were entertained by the EDES right-wing Greek guerrilla leader, Zervas, who like most of the Greek guerrilla leaders had grown an enormous black beard and had a very fierce expression and snorted like a war-horse at us. They provided us with a meal and we drank a lot of wine and toasted each other. And he gave me his photograph with 'to my ally Cadoux' written on the back. Most of us had rather left-wing views at that time, so our sympathies were with the partisans who'd apparently done all the fighting against the Germans and against the right-wing Government imposed by the British.

As well as sorting and distributing a shipment of clothing sent from America, and conducting surveys for estimating need, the FAU's mobile clinics visited the villages of both indigenous islanders and the refugees. The hygiene section quickly set to work, disinfesting refugees' huts and conducting anti-malarial surveys. It was time well spent, but the Unit were keen to get to their main destination which was Ipiros. On May 8 the call came.

Always a very poor and neglected area of Greece, the province of Ipiros had been totally ravaged by the war, first by the Italian campaign of 1940-41, then by the Germans as well as hordes of Turko-Albanians who claimed the northern areas as theirs. The war in Greece was marked by appalling suffering and great heroism and Ipiros was one of the most affected areas. Under the German occupation, a long period of guerrilla warfare began. Instead of the longed for peace with the German withdrawal in late summer 1944, the latent civil war between EAM-ELAS and Colonel Zervas's EDES erupted. The end of a war left Ipiros totally devastated: denuded of produce and cattle, with burnt villages, a poverty-stricken, dispersed population and run-down or destroyed towns overflowing with the refugees pouring in from the ruined countryside. Given the total lack of medical supplies, disease was rife. This was the situation the FAU confronted as it set to work.

Theo Cadoux:

We made our headquarters in Ioánnina, the capital, and had sub-stations in Préveza and Igoumenitsa. Donald Pitcher, who was in charge of our section, an interpreter and I went around Ioánnina looking for suitable places to store the enormous quantity of clothing bales we had gathered by then. Eventually we settled on a very fine building in the castle which had been a barracks belonging to Ali Pasha of Tepelenë, a famous character who comes into all the history books. It was a two-storey building with a very large hall on the second storey and it suited us well. It had been used for stabling, and cleaning it was a bit like the Herculean task of cleansing the Augean stables, but eventually we were able to store our clothing there and start distribution to Préveza and Arta and Igoumenitsa.

We had decided to make a proper survey of the whole of Ipiros to find out which villages had been most damaged. Whenever a German soldier had been killed by guerrilla activity, they would go to the nearest village and burn it, first making the inhabitants leave, taking just what they could carry, then driving the livestock away and burning the houses and contents. Villages which had suffered in this way were desperately short of everything. I circulated a letter and it went to every village saying that a representative of UNRRA would be calling shortly to find out in detail the condition of the village and what was most needed in the way of drugs, food, clothing etc. I did some village visiting myself. Two or three of us went up to the extreme north near the Albanian border. We stayed at Kónitsa. We heard that some of the ELAS guerrillas were still about in the area committing acts of atrocity under a certain 'Ares' – he had taken the name of the ancient Greek god of war. 'He was in Kónitsa yesterday, but moved away when he heard you were coming' we were told. This rather surprised us because we were unarmed and perfectly harmless. The boys of the household in which we stayed wouldn't sleep in the house at night for fear of a night attack, but would run into the hills. In the end the National Army came and cornered Ares and his band and their heads were cut off and displayed on poles to show that they had in fact been killed.

Don Pitcher entering Greek village.

Each woman is carrying 90lbs of wheat, over 30 miles of impossible track.

From Kónitsa I went to remote villages to assess their needs – the actual distribution was left to others – then I moved to Arta for a month and then to Igoumenitsa organising the clothing distribution of the area of Thesprotia, listing the villages hardest hit, and seeing to the distribution itself.

The clothing came mostly from America. Some was totally unsuitable for village women who tended to be rather thick-set. They have enormous feet and are big, broad and well-muscled and not used to wearing the underwear of the sort that townswomen used. Some of these articles were held up by laughing men who said 'We shall never be able to keep our wives once they get these things on.'

We tried to apply egalitarian principles but were often defeated. For instance, regarding grain deliveries, the villagers preferred wheat. One month the the supply for Igoumenitsa came in the form of maize and the mayor refused it saying that they were a town and therefore entitled to wheat, so he sent the shipment back to Corfu from where it had come. Our man in charge was furious. He got on the phone to Athens and asked UNRRA to insist that this maize be accepted, and they agreed. But then they heard that the maize had been left out in the boat and exposed to rain and some had sprouted, and the Greeks had got a doctor to declare that it was unfit for human consumption. So in the end they had to be given wheat which upset the whole pattern of supply.

Then, when the time for the clothing distribution for Igoumenitsa arrived, a deputation from some of the professional people of the town arrived, again headed by the mayor, asking that we should take into account the needs of professional people who needed to be better clothed than the rank and file in order to maintain their professional status – I suppose this wasn't unreasonable in a way, but we treated it with utter indignation and more or less sent them away with a flea in their ear. We said we could make no discrimination and that they really ought to consider first the basic needs of warmth and decency and the professional appearance of people next.

I began to get stale towards the end of my stay in Greece. I got to the state of mind in which I found the Greeks very charming as individuals to meeting socially, but very difficult to deal with on a practical basis because of their deep-rooted feeling that if you make a personal appeal to an official you can get more than you're entitled to. It got on my nerves more as time went on and I probably became unsuitable for future work as a result. I was no longer capable of acting in a completely impartial and humane manner. For instance on the very last day that I was in Igoumenitsa we were preparing to go to Athens in our truck and had quite a lot of people to take and stores and things. Before we set off an enormous crowd of Greeks had gathered outside our lodging house with bundles, all seeking to be carried to Athens for free. I appeared on the balcony – a bit like Mussolini – 'What are you all waiting for? You aren't all going to get on the truck. It's no good waiting here.' Donald Swann rebuked me. 'Easy on' he said 'this isn't the right way to behave, you're talking like a dictator.' This was November 1945, the war had been over, even in Japan by that time and I was anxious to get back to my civilian work. Some people in the FAU had found themselves in relief work and wanted to stay in it and joined UNRRA. But my stock of patience for dealing with people in that sort of depressed condition had run down…I thought I had done my bit, in a manner of speaking, in that I had separated myself off from my fellow citizens for a period of six years during which time my career had been completely delayed. What I'd derived was a certain amount of human experience but I ended the war completely penniless and six years older than when I started it. I didn't feel that was a big sacrifice to make in comparison with some of those who'd lost their lives or their limbs, or been in much greater danger than me, but I didn't feel that I had been completely selfish.

Meanwhile the FAU FBU, arriving in Athens in January 1945, had found plenty of need for their services. Water purification work was undertaken first with IVSP in Athens and then with UNRRA in Patras. By November 1945, sixty-one towns and villages had been surveyed and water purification improvements started. A public health service was set up for the city of Patras and Wilfred Dally's contribution recognised when a public health laboratory set up to serve the region was named after him. Relief work had also spread to Macedonia and to one of the most beautiful, delightful and satisfying areas of service ever to be experienced by the FAU – the Dodecanese islands.

Although the Dodecanese had been under direct Italian control since 1912, the population was mainly Greek. [5] *In 1941, soon after Italy entered the war, the British blockaded the islands. Conditions deteriorated to such an extent that in the winter of 1944/45 desperate refugees poured out of the larger islands, including Rhodes, landing on the Turkish coast where they were in the main unwelcome. Many, as we have seen, had tracked their way to the camps in Palestine, others trickled back to the islands.*

In January 1945, a group of five Unit men, under Fulque Agnew, arrived on the small island of Simi to find a refugee camp overflowing with refugees in a most pitiful condition. They had arrived, and continued to arrive, from the Turkish coast in caiques which lacked even the most basic facilities of food, water and sanitation. All were filthy, emaciated and exhausted, some even too weak to walk. Work was immediately started on organising and caring for as many as possible on Simi, and organising and escorting the transport of others sent on to Kásos and Kárpathos – two small islands lying between Rhodes and Crete – some in transit camps until they could be returned to their home islands, others returning to their homes. Eventually, the FAU undertook full responsibility for the organisation and running of refugee camps on these islands and had the satisfaction of seeing the job through to the final stage when all had been returned to their homes.

Donald Swann:

I was greatly impressed with the beauty of Kásos when I first approached the island and was moved to write a poem about it. But a greater poet, Homer, also spoke of Kásos as an island surrounded by foam. I fell in love with it and it has haunted me for the rest of my life.

Kásos

Far, far off in a distant southern sea
There is an island on which breakers fling,
Throwing gigantic waves against the scree,
Encircling the island with a ring
Of surging foam.

I see it now and wish my memory would grasp it tight
And let me be that foam, that surge;
Swim like a fish within that shimmering water;
And forget whatever else I've learned
Through all the years – my study, poetry, music,
Let them die.
Forget attainments and those lost in tears
And seek with them beneath that water.
Why?
So as to rise, my soul refreshed and bright
And learn the lessons I was taught last night.

                                    Donald Swann

The British army had for a few months fed the entire population, and this is still remembered. Now relief workers were coming and I was one. The main problems we dealt with were not too dissimilar to those of the camp in Palestine. As interpreter and registration officer, I'd go round with the section leader and explain what people were saying, or requesting. Often it was the case that several houses had collapsed, so they needed bricks and materials to prop them up. Sometimes it was a question of food. How much had they got? What could we distribute? Who would get it? Were the children in special need? There are hardly any roads on Kásos so there wasn't a great need for motor transport, but ships were a different matter. Would they come? Would there be enough supplies?

Most people had suffered from the German occupation: they would tell of the murder of the mayor, or the time when the Germans shot a whole village. But, generally, the Dodecanese islands had not been through the same traumas of the mainland. Mainly it was hunger that drove the islanders away in their tiny caiques. Also, it seemed that they didn't want to dwell on the bad times; they were trying to discover what could be salvaged and how to go forward. There was an extraordinary feeling of relief. People were excited and pleased to be home.

Camps were set up for those who were waiting to return to other islands and the day-to-day work was much the same as in any other refugee camp: getting them organised, sorting out the medical and hygiene situation, the distribution of food and other essentials, settling fights and disputes, dealing with black market goings-on.

I was only on Kásos for ten days, then I was sent to Kárpathos, the bigger island nearby. As Kásos was coping with the overflow from Sími, so Kárpathos, in turn, had the overflow from Kásos. The first thing I did was to bury somebody. I remember too the clothing distribution. These came from the West, all sorts of things, some useful, others not, but everything seemed welcome to people who had nothing. Kárpathos had roads and eventually a big tented camp was erected in Effialti Bay which accommodated something in the order of 4,000–5,000 refugees.

After a few months in Kárpathos I went to Rhodes – this was the Unit's final phase of relief on the islands. Rhodes is the biggest island with all the wonderful crusader castles. There I became a hospital almoner and got the chance to meet the patients as they arrived. I would watch these beautiful people coming in. I remember one girl came in with a tiny baby, and she looked just like a madonna, a perfect image.

I loved being on these islands. The beautiful hills leading down to the sea, something to look at almost every hour of the day. People were living out in the open. I remember we took one old man back to his home in an ambulance. When we asked him where he wanted to be dropped off, he said 'Under the tree, under the tree.' That's where he lived. Of course, with the wonderful climate in Greece, it is possible to live under a tree. It's not quite the same as sleeping rough in Stepney or Waterloo.

The people were singing folk-songs of great interest and depth: wedding-songs, work-songs and laments. Even now I have a printed book of the songs.[6] Later at Oxford I was to study modern Greek folk-song and discover the influence of Ancient and Byzantine Greece on them. A lot of the songs were extremely violent: they would sing anti-Turkish songs telling of how they cut Turk's heads off and stuck them on poles, in 1821. It seemed terrible to me to have war stories rejoiced and feasted over. Most of their songs were to do with war and fighting. I'd say to them 'Why can't you relax? You got rid of the Turks; now you've got rid of the Germans and your job is to make friends with other nations and see if you can make peace as well as war.

I was still on Rhodes when the war ended, and was in a camp called Efialtis, which is the Greek for nightmare, when I heard about the atom bomb. I was as far away from Nagasaki and Hiroshima mentally as I've ever been in my life. More immediate to me was the sight of my first banana for years. I took a boat out to a Turkish ship in the bay. The sailor gave me a banana. I was overawed. Our war had ended. I remember feeling that somewhere a long way off statesmen were trying to work out the peace.

In the early post-war period I moved from the Dodecanese to join another FAU unit in north Greece. But now, as the FAU were beginning to pull their people out, I came under the wing of UNRRA. It was exactly the same work but I changed my uniform from khaki to blue and got a bit of money in the process. The sojourn in Igoumenitsa lasted a year and was enthralling. I was immersed in the language, the surrounding hills, the people and the music.

How did it all end? One day, as I visited the Albanian border with some people from the UN, I flung my arms wide embracing the countryside around me which had been home to so many different races – Albanians, Greeks, Turks, Bulgars, Romanians, Vlachs – and exclaimed 'What a beautiful thing it would be if this were all one country! Surely we all are one!' This remark was taken down by a Greek soldier and sent to headquarters. A note was sent to UNRRA saying 'Mr Donald Swann is a corrupting influence and is making dangerous remarks and ought to be relieved of his post.' Was this the end of my war service, pitched out for believing that the world was one? At this moment Albanians are crossing the same frontier, in the same place, and uttering the same remarks.

YUGOSLAVIA

If political conditions had proved difficult in Greece, then they were doubly so in the case of Yugoslavia. Those who had worked with Yugoslav refugees, in the camps of Italy and the Middle East, had gained enormous respect for the independence, sense of orderliness and community among the Yugoslavs, and were keen to accompany them back to their homeland and continue assistance.

Although the Allies had switched support from the Yugoslavian regular army colonel, Draza Mihailovic to the communist partisan leader Tito during the war, with the cessation of hostilities Tito was hostile to the West and feared intervention in favour of a royal counter-revolution on the Greek pattern. He was also incensed by the Allied occupation of Trieste and its hinterland which left Yugsolavian troops in occupation of only a part of the area it claimed from Italy.

Another complicating factor was the large numbers of Chetniks who had fled out of Yugoslavia into Austria and had landed up and were being held in Allied DP camps in Carinthia. All this led to foreigners, whatever their good intentions, being regarding with deep suspicion, with inevitable long and frustrating delays. Eventually in March 1945 two teams consisting of an MSTU and FBU were allowed in. Passes had to be obtained, not only to enter the country, but to travel from place to place, and as the FAU's success depended on its mobility, this was to prove irksome and, given the trigger-happy nature of the partisans, at times dangerous.

The six FAU members of the MSTU who had arrived in March 1945 began their task of delivering supplies from the two ports of Split and Dubrovnik. Numbers had reached seventeen after two months. Stores were established in both ports and trucks ran the supplies of clothing, canned food, tinned milk, potatoes, drugs, vaccines and Red Cross stores to provincial centres under instructions from the Yugoslav authorities, eventually extending their distribution to Cetinje in Montenegro, Šibenik in the north, travelling through Mostar, Sarajevo and Zvornik to Belgrade with supplies for Serbia and Montenegro. Working first under UNRRA auspices, and then under the Yugoslav Red Cross, the FAU was the only foreign group in the country providing direct service to the Yugoslavs who were without transport and drivers in the early post-war period.

Driving conditions were as hazardous as any encountered by the Unit but by the beginning of July 1945, they had carried 800 tons of material over a 65,000 mile distance.

Working under a communist system, there was firm control by the authorities, but the positive side of this was the obvious sense of purpose and community among a proudly independent people who had liberated themselves from the Axis yoke. This gave the Unit confidence that whatever they had set in motion would be continued by the Yugoslavs when they departed. In the event a training scheme set up for Yugoslav drivers had quick effect which meant that all the FAU trucks were handed over with a few members staying on to give whatever assistance was needed until early December 1944, when the MSTU work came to an end.

Angela Sinclair-Loutit was the only woman member to work in Yugoslavia. She had been seconded to the Health Division of UNRRA in Belgrade throughout the summer of 1945 and was transferred to work with the Yugoslav Red Cross at the same time as the MSTU:

Angela Sinclair-Loutit:

I went to Yugoslavia as an unpaid member of UNRRA. The Chief of Missions had gone first to discuss where we should be set up. My husband-to-be went first, then cabled back that he had fixed up some arrangements for me to pick up some guinea pigs for the Pasteur Institute in Belgrade, and off I went. I was thrilled to be on Yugoslav soil. There were lots of partisans walking about with red stars in their hats. I felt that I wanted to greet everybody I met, and was very hurt at how cold they were. They didn't want foreigners there and were very suspicious of us and why we were there. The only friendly people were the older, formerly richer people who gave lovely teas with beautiful china and glass, and feared what would happen to them.

Tito was very much in control. We had a photograph for some time of Churchill shaking hands with him. I went to the trial of Mihailovic and heard evidence against him by some partisans. I heard him confess in court that he moved his troops by train, and since you couldn't have got on a train without a German pass, it meant that he must have moved his troops with German permission. The trial was public and there was a lot of publicity in the English newspapers. I don't know how I managed to get in because there were a lot of Yugoslavs who wanted to get in and wanted him punished. I certainly heard one peasant woman tell a story which others said later wasn't true – that a Chetnik soldier had cut the hands off a baby in a cradle. The peasants around the courtyard were shouting for revenge but the atmosphere within was silent and intense. Mihailovic was very pale, but looked well fed and wore spectacles and behaved with dignity, but I don't think he was able to give chapter and verse about his resistance to the Germans. He blamed the lack of arms from the Allies.[7]

I also went to one of the first Yugoslav elections. You were given a little ball which you had to drop into one box or another, with a picture of the representative on each. This was done privately in a little cubicle. But a Yugoslav told me it could be heard which box the ball dropped into. I remember thinking how difficult it was to make unquestioned elections because if people believed they could be heard, then it could influence the vote and be unfair. Ninety per cent voted for Tito which wasn't the impression I gained during my time there. But in the beginning people were grateful for the liberation. Also Tito changed: I remember seeing him march in the Victory Parade – a thin man with his troops in a motley of uniforms. But as the years went by he got plumper and plumper and began to look like Goering and moved into the King's Palace. I remember seeing him on another, interesting, occasion. Tito had always promised the wounded and disabled partisans, many of whom had not had proper treatment, that he would do his best to get them the best treatment possible after the war. UNRRA was anxious to help, and they managed to get a very well known plastic surgeon to come out and do some facial surgery. He was a very kindly, charming and sympathetic man. Tito went to the hospital to see a plastic surgery operation, and this brave general, who hadn't flinched from anything during the war, when he saw the plastic surgeon at work, the colour just drained from his face and he had to leave the operating room.

When I heard that the FAU had managed to send people to Yugoslavia, I did feel disloyal in having stepped sideways into UNRRA. So I felt divided, but preferred to be with the FAU. I worked with UNRRA for three months, because I owed something to them, then I went back to the FAU and was sent to Split to join the group working there.

In Split we were driving trucks of medical supplies which had been brought in by Liberty ships from the coast to Belgrade and other places. Distribution throughout the country was a tremendous problem because the roads were so poor and so many of the bridges over rivers had been blown up. Emergency bridges were eventually put up, but the whole transport system was not functioning and trains weren't running at all.

We lived in a little house with no windows – the glass had been blown out. It was very cold and we tacked sacking over the spaces which made it very dark. I remember trying to do the maintenance of our trucks on a muddy patch of ground. Then two German prisoners were sent to work with us. They were shy and quiet people. I remember one day asking them to sing some German songs and they sang Lilli Marlene. A Yugoslav came in, very cross, completely horrified first that we should be talking to them at all and then that we should be listening to war songs.

Although I had passed my army maintenance by one mark, I wasn't at all confident, and there weren't any garages about if you broke down – there was only you. So I was very grateful to have this young prisoner to help on my truck as this got very tough wear and tear over the dreadful roads. I don't know how many times I made the journey from Split to Belgrade; it's a long way and took two days then, stopping on the way. One journey I shan't forget. I set off in autumn weather, very wet. Going over a lot of fallen leaves on this little country lane, going round the bend, suddenly the truck skidded. The truck went off the side of the road into a deep ditch. So I had two wheels in this deep ditch and nobody in sight, miles from anywhere. There was a steep hill beside me on which somebody had stacked up firewood. I knew all about digging out trucks because we used to do that in Egypt when they got stuck in the sand. So I collected this firewood, putting pieces of wood in front of the wheel, making a little ramp, and managed to get it back on the road and went on. Then I reached a river which was in flood with the main bridge broken down. There was an emergency ferry, planks of wood on chains. They wouldn't take my truck because it was too big. So I set off for Sarajevo where there was a bridge and, passing the place where I had skidded off, saw another truck which had done the same. But the driver was worse off than I had been because he had hit a telegraph pole which had broken his radiator. It was driven by a Russian captain who was quite amazed to discover I was English. So I towed him back to Sarajevo – quite a job on the bad roads – and got to Sarajevo about five in the evening. Then foolishly really, I set off again for Belgrade along another route. I then started to have trouble with the truck. The first thing was that the bonnet catch broke and I had to wire it down. Every time I went over a bump I'd have to wire it down again. Then the petrol lead to the carburettor gave trouble, and the only way I could get petrol through was to take the lead off the carburettor and suck it through. I had to do this about a dozen times and it took a great effort. On one of these occasions a young boy of about ten years asked if he could come with me. He was evidently homeless and thought he might have a relative in Belgrade. So I took him and it was nice to have a companion. But he made me more nervous when it started to get dark because he said I mustn't stop as the woods were full of brigands and they would get me if I stopped. But when the truck broke down again, I had to stop and there were no brigands.

When I reached the suspension bridge, I was terrified because it went down in the middle, and was very narrow. There was no alternative but to drive extremely slowly, I felt almost sure that the truck would stop in the dip in the middle, but we just made it. At last we made the flatter ground near Belgrade. Then the radiator draining trap fell off leaving a big gap about an inch across. I had nothing to block it with – it was too big for soap or chewing gum. Then, looking around, I saw fields of maize. So I loaded maize cobs onto the back of the truck and jammed one in, just keeping enough water in the radiator to go two or three miles, then replaced it. I went on for some time like this. I arrived in Belgrade completely filthy.

My pacifism certainly came under test in the Yugoslav situation. One had to realise that there was no choice for a Yugoslav: you would either have to be extremely brave to oppose the Germans and be a hero, or be a villain and collaborate. And I don't think one could say how one would have behaved. Certainly the hardships the Yugoslavs endured seemed almost intolerable: just living in the cold forests was heroism in itself. So I didn't talk about pacifism. I was always ready to believe in work. I felt you had to live your pacifism rather than talk about it.

It wasn't until the war in Europe had ended, in August 1945, that the FAU FBU unit was allowed into Yugoslavia, being based first in Sarajevo attached to the local Hygiene Institute helping to build up an effective laboratory system for use of the newly introduced penicillin and other innovative techniques, thence to Derventa, a rural area some 150 miles from Sarajevo where it dealt with epidemics of typhus, typhoid and dysentery, and set up a system of water sterilisation in the contaminated wells there.

During the spring of 1946, the same question and dilemma faced the Yugoslav section as faced the Unit in Italy, Greece and other parts of the world, and the same solution was found: discussions with UNRRA and indigenous authorities led to FAU work being taken over and continued as the Unit sections were withdrawn. The Unit had entered all these countries actively searching out urgent needs, by-passing the relief authorities in London or Washington – getting on with the job, 'going anywhere, doing anything.'

As the FAU was officially withdrawing from Italy and Greece the Yugoslavs took over and on 10 June 1946 responsibility finally transferred with every hope that FAU work would be continued. Yugoslavian service, despite the frustrations and delays in getting started, had proved to be a brief, but worthwhile field of FAU relief service but it was by no means the end of the Unit's connection with Yugoslavs. For this, we need travel over the Yugoslav/Austrian border into the province of Carinthia where events were unfolding which haunt and involve FAU members to this day.

AUSTRIA

On VE Day, 8 May 1945, V Corps, Eighth Army crossed from Italy into Carinthia, the southern province of Austria where it occupied a huge slice of territory, some 120 miles by fifty, stretching from beyond Lienz in the west to the zonal boundary with the Red Army in the east, and from the Yugoslav frontier to the neighbourhood of St. Veit. It was a situation of confusion with different national groups, many of them enemies of each other, flooding into Carinthia from all directions, seeking the protection of the British who gathered them into segregated camps.

The political situation was sensitive in the extreme: Tito claimed Carinthia and Venezia Giulia as part of 'Greater Yugoslavia' and his partisans were much in evidence, occupying key points, brandishing weapons and posting up provocative proclamations. There were a few minor incidents relating mainly to preventing the fiery partisans from looting and harassing villagers, but heat was taken out of the situation when Tito, under Allied pressure, on 19 May, withdrew his partisans across the frontier and abandoned Carinthia. Among those who had surrendered to the British were two special groups: anti-communist Russians called, somewhat loosely, 'the Cossacks' by the British, who had been fighting under German command against Tito, and more than 30,000 anti-Tito Yugoslavs including thousands of women and children with their horses and cartloads of salvaged possessions. They had trekked across the mountains from Slovenia in a long column crossing the Drau where they met up with British troops who escorted them to camp in fields round the village of Viktring, south of Klagenfurt.

In his books Victims of Yalta *and* The Minister and the Massacres, *Count Nikolai Tolstoy has described the fate of Russians and Yugoslavs who were repatriated by the British, some by being tricked into thinking they were moving on to other camps, others forcibly at gunpoint.* [8] *John Corsellis's experience concerned the Yugoslavs:*

Camping in open fields.

John Corsellis:

I had been working in Italy in a refugee camp for about 900 Italian refugees who had been evacuated from North Africa when, towards the end of May 1945, a group of us were ordered to go to Austria. We went by truck, pausing a bit at Udine, waiting for permission to enter. Clearly the authorities wanted things to settle down a bit before they were prepared to let more civilians into the country.

I was sent at once to Klagenfurt, the capital of Carinthia, close to the border with Yugoslavia. At first I worked in a refugee camp for Volksdeutsche – refugees of German ethnic origin. Almost as soon as I arrived I was attached for half of each day to the refugee camp at Viktring a few miles south of Klagenfurt towards the Yugoslav border, where there were 6,000 Slovene civilians, mostly camping in open fields. They had only recently escaped over the border from Yugoslavia. During the war against the Germans, there was also another war on-going between the communists, the Titoists, and the anti-communists, including the Slovene refugees who felt, with good reason, that they were in danger of being massacred when the Partisans took over in Slovenia. Therefore many of them escaped across the border to the safety of British protection.

The camp was in the hands of the army, then there were two British Red Cross sisters and myself. At that time there would have been eighteen BRC and twenty-five FAU working in Carinthia. I was the only FAU member in Viktring, attached to the Red Cross, and very much a junior member of the team.

Slovenia was economically more advanced than Dalmatia at the time – a more sophisticated society. There was a substantial proportion of the intelligentsia among the Slovenes. Very soon schools were set up: nursery, primary and secondary – the Slovenes were very quick at trying to get back to some kind of normal community life. So far as they were allowed to, they ran the camp themselves. They were mainly Catholic and their priests were very much in evidence, involved in education and youth work. The fact that they were able to get back to some kind of normal life so quickly depended on the fact that they often arrived with the mayor or burgermeister of their village, and to a great extent they trusted the people they had chosen as their spokesmen and were prepared to accept their authority and accept the decisions that they had internally and democratically arrived at. They were a very socially cohesive group and there was a strong feeling of them pulling together.. Conditions were very basic and primitive as it was only a very temporary situation, some hadn't even tents to sleep in. It was clear that the authorities would have to move them on to somewhere more long-term, otherwise they would have suffered heavily from sickness.

I was primarily concerned with hygiene as one of the most urgent needs was to avoid the spread of sickness. I encouraged and helped organise the refugees in digging latrines, getting supplies of hessian and wooden posts for the construction, and generally liaising with the refugee team that was running the camp. I also tried to encourage, or bullied, the Slovenes to move their horses farther away from themselves as that wasn't helping the hygiene of the camp!

I spoke only a limited amount of Serbo-Croat but my contacts were mainly with the intelligentsia and they spoke either German or Italian and I had adequate command of both. I found that being able to communicate direct with the refugees was of vital importance. I'd very soon experienced how much influence the interpreters had, and how they could make use of and abuse the influence they gained from this – the scope for intrigue and forms of corruption on the part of interpreters was very considerable indeed. It was noticeable how the army administration was in the hands of the interpreters, who were able to manipulate things in the interests of themselves and their own small circle of friends. I resolved very early on not to become dependent on interpreters, and at the very least to know enough of the language to be able to spot when the interpreter was misinterpreting me!

I know now that by the time I had arrived in the area, repatriation of the Russians and other groups was underway. But I wasn't aware at all of this at the time, nor for that matter was I aware of what was happening to the Slovenes. But after being there for only a comparatively few days, I heard that units of the so-called Slovene Home Guard, or Domobranci, who were based in a neighbouring field to the 6,000 Slovene civilians, were being transported away. We didn't know where to at the start; we were told they were being moved to Italy, in camps of greater security and safety.

Then the refugees received reports from one or two members of the Domobranci who had escaped and returned over the border that in fact the men were not being sent to refugee camps in northern Italy, but in fact were sent straight across the frontier into Yugoslavia where they were handed over to the Yugoslav authorities. The escapees were warning the Slovenes of what was happening: how several deportees had managed to kill themselves on the trains when they realised that the train was heading into Yugoslavia and not Italy as promised; and how some were massacred by Tito's partisans immediately upon arrival by the most brutal methods, while others were force-marched to a forest near Kočevje where they were stripped, bound and flung into a vast pit where thousands died from bullets, grenades or asphyxiation. It was the few who managed to crawl out and get back into Austria that gave the warning. The representatives of the Slovene civilians refused to believe this and dismissed these reports to start with, saying that the men spreading such stories were just trouble makers and couldn't be relied on. It was only after two or three collaborative reports came in that they began to believe it.

I couldn't believe it was possible that these men were being encouraged to get onto the trains by a trick, by lies. Like the Slovenes, it was only after an accumulation of evidence that I was prepared to believe it, and it only gradually sunk in what was happening. I was deeply shocked. Then, of course, there was great horror and consternation and I remember vividly how their attitudes changed towards us from being open and trusting, realising that it was the British who had been sending them back into the hands of the Yugoslav authorities. And there was an undercurrent of bitterness and a great degree of despair among them. The refugees held a kind of funeral and commemorative service which I attended, where there was great emotion and deep sorrow. The whole community was in a state of shock. It was a confusing and bewildering time.

The two Red Cross sisters, who were working all day in the camp, knew of the instructions that once the last of the Slovene soldiers had been sent back, then the civilians would also be returned. There was a Slovene medical doctor, Dr Valentine Meršol, who spoke fluent English, and he was accepted as the spokesman for the Slovene refugees. He went to the Camp Commandant, a Canadian called Major Barre, who told him that he had received instructions that the civilians should be moved. Meršol told him of the reports they had received about the massacres. Fortunately Major Barre, being a Canadian, was not so inclined to accept orders from above unquestioningly. So he went with Dr Meršol to the English officer concerned and vigorously challenged the order. At first the English officer told him 'These are orders, you must do as you're told.' But when Major Barre would not accept this, he had to refer back to higher authority and eventually the order was countermanded. If this hadn't happened, the entire 6,000 Slovene civilians would have been sent back to Slovenia, almost certainly to suffer the same fate as the soldiers.

There were some important behind-the-scenes activities also ongoing which played a central role and explain the speedy reversal of this particular order. Selby-Bigge, the British Red Cross officer responsible for the team workers in Carinthia, together with David Pearson, our section leader, also went to the army authorities and told them that if the forcible repatriation of the civilians was not stopped, the Red Cross, including the FAU members who had protested, would have to withdraw from Austria, because they would be a party to what was happening. He wrote in his memoirs 'My workers got increasingly restless; one of my Supervisors threatened to resign; the head of the FAU said his team would not continue to work under these conditions...From our point of view, the position was untenable.'[9]

This is the only occasion of which I am aware, where the threat of a strike by a team of civilian relief workers – half of whom were conscientious objectors – in conjunction with the protests of the refugees themselves, succeeded in persuading the all-powerful army to cancel elaborate plans it had made to send the refugees back – not just the 6,000 at Viktring, this reversal was to affect all Yugoslav refugees in Austria, Italy and possibly Germany. Before the order was cancelled, 26,339 Yugoslavs in uniform and several hundred civilians were repatriated and the great majority brutally massacred. [10]

Recognition must be given to the enlightened army policy of accepting civilian workers in a war zone immediately after hostilities. Because of this a restraining civilian conscience was introduced into a situation which otherwise would have been dominated by military expediency. Another important consideration was the protests made by officers and men within the British Army which reinforced those made by relief workers and refugees.

A couple of weeks later the camp at Viktring was closed down and the Slovenes moved to two or three other camps further to the west. I was fortunate enough to be sent, at my urgent request, to Lienz, the camp where the largest number of Slovenes were held. After the immediate crisis had passed, for the next two years at least, there was always the very considerable fear on the part of individual refugees that they might be picked off by the Yugoslav authorities and sent back. I became increasingly conscious of this and, young and junior as I was, I tried to do something to alert people of influence in England to the danger. I wrote a memorandum and sent copies of this to a fair number of Members of Parliament who I thought might be sympathetic, including Winston Churchill, then Leader of the Opposition – in fact the memorandum was acknowledged in a friendly way by his secretary.

This came to a crisis about a year later when I was back in England. I received a letter from the wife of a Yugoslav refugee, Joze Jancar, who had acted as my interpreter at Viktring and with whom I had kept in touch, saying that he had been arrested by the Field Security Service in Austria where he was being held with the possibility of being sent back to Yugoslavia. This was a great shock. I sent the facts to our local MP who happened to be an old friend of my father's and asked him to intervene with the Foreign Office. This he did and got back an intending-to-be-reassuring comment. Then a few weeks later a telegram came from the refugee's wife saying he had been released and expressing their great relief. It was a very worrying time: one had a feeling of great helplessness.

I found out much later that, only a week before we arrived in Lienz where the Slovenes were now encamped, the Cossacks had

been sent back from there and handed over to the Russian authorities, where again they were massacred. In fact a small number of
the Cossacks smelt a rat, or in some cases may even have been
warned by sympathetic British officers, and had hidden in the
woods when the forcible repatriation took place, emerging when
the danger was over. I worked with them for some months in Lienz
– but I've only learned of the full story since the publication of
Nicholas Bethell's and Count Tolstoy's books.[11]

*As John Corsellis has mentioned, it was the intervention by Selby-
Bigge and David Pearson that was to have such an important effect on
the reversal of the repatriation decision pertaining to the Yugoslavs. An
FAU report sent to London HQ on 11 July 1945 shows that similar
protests were made on behalf of the 'Cossacks.'*

...BRCS/FAU workers were on the territory several days ahead
of Military Government. They discovered many camps housing
Displaced Persons, Todt workers, ex-Internees, ex-POWs etc...the
situation was not made easier by the presence of the Yugoslav Army
of National Liberation who at that time were claiming Karnten
(Carinthia) and as was to be expected, a good deal of confusion
reigned. There is no doubt that during this period the untried relief
workers in the section won their spurs.

The confusion was not helped by the presence of a Cossack
Army which had been fighting with the Germans, and a horse-
drawn Hungarian Army of some 50,000 carrying with it wives and
children, manservants and maidservants, asses and oxen and a thorough biblical paraphernalia.

... Trainloads of Russians were dispatched to the Russian zone,
and in this connection it should be recorded how intervention by
BRC/FAU succeeded in remedying a serious official blunder and
a grave injustice.

It appears that in accordance with instructions issued prior to
entry into Karnten, the military were to send all civilian and military Russian personnel to the East. The fate that awaited many of
them (especially those suspected of collaboration with the Nazis)
can only be conjectured, but many were very unwilling to go.

In the early days of confusion numbers were sent against their will, including white Russians and others who had been in exile in Yugoslavia for many years. Families were split; sick women and children were evacuated from hospitals without medical approval, even non-Russians were sent. Force was used in a number of cases.

(David) Pearson and Miss Couper (BRC) promptly collected evidence and saw Selby-Bigge. As a result Selby-Bigge and Pearson went to HQ, 8th Army where they saw the Head of MG and the Army Chief of Staff (Sir Henry Floyd). The General was shocked by the evidence and forthwith issued orders that *no* sick people were to be moved and *no* DPs were to be repatriated against their will. Further, he rescinded an outrageous instruction that in cases of doubt refugees were to be classified as Soviet Nationals. In parentheses, a number of refugees had been rescued from evacuation by BRC/FAU workers who classified them as 'Polish Ukrainians' and similar categories.

For obvious reasons, this story should be treated as highly confidential, but it is an excellent example of successful intervention by voluntary societies to effect a highly desirable change in official policy. The greatest credit is due to Pearson for the way in which he took the matter up.[12]

Despite the resolve of the Head of MG and a letter of confirmation to Selby-Bigge from Major-General Sir Henry Floyd, 16 June 1945, instances of repatriation still occurred:

Dennis Conolly:

I remember a conversation with a British officer in Villach where I was working at the time, this must have been in the late autumn of 1945 at the earliest. He said that he had been ordered to round up various alleged Russians living in farms, with a view to pushing them back to the Russian authorities. He said that he didn't like the work; that he had not fought the Gestapo successfully in order to have to use their methods. I reported this conversation to someone in the FAU in London, but unfortunately all he wrote back was a letter thanking me for writing about 'conditions in

Austria.' I am afraid that I have always taken a poor view of that fellow since, although he is normally regarded as a very worthy person. I well know that various of my comrades took action to hide Russians, chiefly Ukrainians. One of them, Bryant, told me that there were a lot of Ukrainians in his area which I believe was Lienz. They would come in one door as Russian Ukrainians and go out the other having been registered as Polish Ukrainians.

I had one example of this myself. A man, apparently German, was shown into my office. He explained that he was one of a large number of Russians who had been found in Italy and who were being repatriated to Russia. Evidently a trainload of these men was at the West Station in Villach and it was delayed for twenty-four hours. He had left the train not wishing to go back to Russia. On asking him why, he said that he was what was known as a Volksdeutscher – although a Russian citizen, he was racially German. I gave him something to eat, then I asked him to put on the table every piece of paper which he had on him. I handed back to him two or three family photos which showed a peasant-like woman standing in a garden. I retained other papers including some identity document.

Having sent him out of the room I then telephoned a certain Captain Campbell of the Surrendered Enemy Personnel (SEP) camp where there were still a few hundred German soldiers. I made up a story that his unit was being transferred to Italy and he had been pushed out of their camp where he had been working in the cookhouse, and asked Campbell if he could add the fellow to the men he had in his charge. Thus the fellow would be looked after and be somehow 'legitimised.' Captain Campbell, who was well disposed towards me because I had sent some cigarettes to his German charges, readily agreed. There then remained the problem of the man's identity and origin. I can't remember what I did about his name. Presumably, I told him he could keep the one he had. But I got a map of Poland, and pointed to some little town in the Ukrainian part – his 'place of origin,' a part probably in dispute with which it would be impossible for the British Authorities to communicate. My driver then took him to Captain Campbell's camp. I never heard from him again and thought it tactful not to enquire of Captain Campbell, from whom I heard no more.

Several FAU members have maintained, or renewed, contact with the Yugoslavs they met in Austria. In 1995 John Marley and Dennis Conolly attended the special 50th anniversary remembrance service and reunion held by the Cossacks and White Russians in Austria. Similar services were held by the Slovenes in Viktring and Teinach which were attended by Dennis Conolly, and John and Ann Corsellis. As John Corsellis has written 'It was apparent that the FAU presence was greatly appreciated as a witness to there being Britons who were aware of and cared about the appalling tragedies for which Britain shared responsibility.'[13]

REFERENCES:

[1] Davies, A. Tëgla, *op. cit.* pp.352-53 for further details.

[2] FAU Chronicle No. 80, 2 February 1946.

[3] Military Liaison and UNRRA had direct responsibility over the FAU. Although working under UNRRA in a military area, the Unit was given complete freedom to organise its work in its own way. UNRRA also took over several Unit members and the relief work which they initiated, thus ensuring its continuation after the disbandment of the Unit in 1946.

The Greek situation after Liberation is a complex matter. During the Unit's service in the area, hostilities between the two main anti-German guerrilla forces – the communist-controlled National Liberation Front (EAM)/ National Popular Liberation Army (ELAS) and Colonel Zervas's right-wing Greek Democratic National Army (EDES) had erupted into civil war in Athens on 3 December 1944, which the British military intervened to suppress. The monarchy was restored first under George 11, and after his death Paul. But EDES had gone underground to emerge again in 1946 when a full-scale guerrilla war was re-opened. The civil war continued until 1949 when the defection of Yugoslavia from the Soviet bloc closed a vital stretch of Greece's northern border to the rebels.

[5] The Dodecanese were ceded to Greece by Italy under the peace treaty of February 1947 and were formally annexed in 1948.

[6] A CD and song book are being prepared.

[7] Colonel Draza Mihailovic, was leader of the Chetnik resistance group during the Second World War, was executed with other Chetniks condemned as collaborating with the Germans on 17 July 1947.

(8) Tolstoy N, Victims of Yalta. (London, Hodder and Stoughton 1977) Tolstoy N, The Minister and the Massacres. (London, Century Hutchinson, 1986.)

(9) Selby-Bigge J, Unpublished memoir, quoted in Corsellis J. Friends' Quarterly, October 1995, Friendly Persuasion: how 6,000 Refugees were saved in 1945 p.359.

(10) In all 26,339 Yugoslavs in uniform consisting of Croats, Slovenes, Serbs and Montenegrins listed by 5th Corps had been sent back to Yugoslavia before the cancellation of the order to send civilians. Corsellis, *ibid.* p.355.

(11) Bethell N The Last Secret (London, Andre Deutsch Ltd 1974) Tolstoy N, 1977, 1986, *op. cit.*

(12) Report John Rose, Peter Gibson, 11/7/45. 7.Rome FLG/FS.

(13) 'Peace: We Pray – We Forgive – We Hope.' Message prominently displayed by John Corsellis, John Marley and Dennis Conolly at the 50th anniversary remembrance services.

CHAPTER 15

Civilian Relief: Northwest Europe – the Reality of Nazism

Anhalter Bahnhof

There's little left now except the façade,
The buxom ladies and their timepiece
Put there when the trains would run like clockwork –
All's gone, demolished, platforms unroofed;
Beyond the station's throat the Wall
And wasteland stretches. But I recall
A winter's night, ice in the air,
We watched and stood here by the tracks
Surrounded by a brittle silence –
Or was it the hush of hundreds of human
Beings too cowed and cold to whisper?
What seemed a field of crosses in the moonlight
The upturned tow-bars of their handcarts,
Bundles and bodies, the refugees, die Fluchtlingern,
Just waiting, – waiting for the locked dark train,
Bored driver, chewing gum and diesel muttering,
To move them on, another place, another day...

Are they still waiting? – who can say:
Only ghosts will leave the station now
On a train that's bound for Nowhere.
Meanwhile we shall once more pass on;
As refugees our time has yet to come.

Ralph Arnold[1]

L IKE EVERY OTHER unit involved in the war, the FAU was training hard and waiting eagerly for the long-awaited opening of the Second Front in North/West Europe. Number 12 Forward Surgical Unit (FSU) actually set off with the landing forces for Normandy soon after D day, eventually to become fully integrated into an Army unit;* but the acceptance of relief units proved more complicated and it was not until September 1944, after the immediate crisis had passed, that permission was finally given. On 6 September, two sections, each of eleven men under the leadership of Richard Wainwright and Len Darling, with Gerald Gardiner in overall command, arrived in France.

Len Darling's Number 2 section was detailed for work in Belgium and Holland whilst Richard Wainwright's Number 1 remained in Normandy transporting civilian casualties from the Falaise battles back to their homes and distributing medical clothing and other essential supplies. It has to be remembered that a huge proportion of French manpower was imprisoned in German labour camps or serving in the Maquis; therefore this service was essential and in all 12,000 miles were covered in the section's five weeks service in Normandy. Number 1 section was just congratulating itself that it was providing worthwhile service when the urgent call came for refugee work in Holland with the 12th Corps Refugee Detachment. In the event few refugees were on the move but the section soon made itself useful transporting sick civilians from vulnerable towns, and dealing with civilian emergencies – for example, helping to deal with the entombment of 150 victims in Heusen Town Hall which had been blown up deliberately by retreating Germans.

Word of the Unit's effectiveness had reached the Civil Affairs Director of 21st Army Group, and in November a direct approach to Gerald Gardiner resulted in the quick despatch of five more sections which arrived on 31 December 1944 to provide each army corps with FAU assistance. At this stage the armies were relatively immobile, waiting for an improvement in weather conditions in order to start the push into Germany. Meanwhile, Antwerp, the Allies' main port in Belgium, had become a target for German flying bombs. Richard Wainwright arranged for three of the new sections to work as an ambulance service for the authorities there whilst the other two sections worked with refugees. Thus the start of 1945 found seven FAU sections serving the liberation of North West Europe.

* See Chapter 18.

Just behind the battle-front again: FAU Section 5 with Dutch refugees.

Owen Hardwicke and F. Nicholson talking with Army Civil Affairs officers.

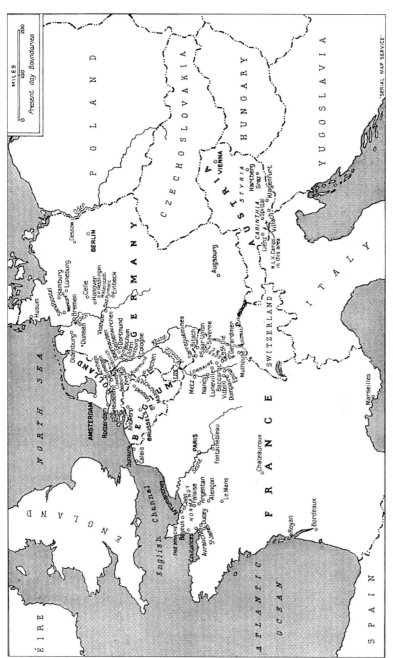

Map VI – Northwest Europe.

Once the advance of the Allied armies started, the FAU teams were kept busy assisting the care and evacuation of civilians caught up in the battle zones. Transit centres were set up near the front where refugees were registered and provided with accommodation, food and blankets; casualties and the sick were cared for and within twenty-four hours they were transported to safe areas. Earlier experience in the British blitzes proved invaluable and, in turn, methods evolved in the battle zones during the early months of 1945 enabled teams to cope with even greater demands when faced with the vast numbers of displaced persons (DPs) in Germany.

Robin Whitworth:

At this time I had the grand title of Executive Officer for Overseas Relief. Our sections were working in Normandy, Belgium and Holland under the aegis of the Red Cross. Now that our numbers had increased, a settled base was essential for the Unit and I had the task of sorting this out. So off I went to Brussels and found a hotel, part of which was a brothel. That didn't impinge on our lives very much and we set up our headquarters there with Gerald Gardiner in command and Richard Wainwright his second-in-command.

About this time, the Civil Affairs people of 21st Army Group were very worried about the advance across the Maas into Germany as they thought the Germans would flood a large part of Holland and Belgium, which would cause thousands of refugees to flee from the flood areas. The Red Cross had a representative there – Tommy Paddington, I think he was called – who asked me to help him negotiate with the army as to how we could help.

This was an extraordinary experience: Tommy and I met the Brigadier, who was Head of Civil Affairs, 21 Army Group, and one or two colonels, a major and several other army people, to see what the voluntary organisations could do. I made a couple of suggestions and the Brigadier said 'I don't think Whitworth understands our planning, could you explain to him what's going to happen.' And this chap got up and went with his stick to a map on the platform and said 'When the time comes, we shall advance across the Maas here, and go in this direction, and we fear that they will flood this area here, and the refugees will start streaming out at these points....' Really, it was most extraordinary that here was a conscientious objector, who might have been in prison, being told exactly where a most vital advance was going to take place and exactly what the plan was. It was the most extraordinary revelation of the reputation of the FAU. Evidently word had gone around the army: the FAU are to be relied on in any situation, you can trust them to get on with the job and do it well. This was no tribute to me personally: it was entirely due to the world-wide service of others who had built up this reputation. In the event, the anticipated flooding did not occur to the extent feared and British troops crossed the Rhine during the last week in March 1945. So here it was: Germany – perhaps the greatest challenge for any pacifist...

As the British crossed the Rhine on 23 March 1945, on their heels went four FAU teams to care for refugees. Apart from a team left to deal with refugees on the Dutch border, all FAU sections had moved into Germany by mid-April. Urgent work awaited one of the first teams which arrived in Bedburg just after it had been captured in February 1945. In extremely difficult circumstances, with fighting ongoing 300 yards away, they started their refugee work initially with 3,000 cowed and terrified refugees hidden in the cellars of a lunatic asylum without light and very little water; eventually this Refugee centre housed over 25,000 refugees in a huge tented camp with an FAU section remaining there until April.

The refugee work soon changed to working with the huge numbers of DPs. UNRRA had the main responsibility for DP work, but was not yet ready in the field. The need was urgent and the army quickly set to: it was fully prepared with transport, food and de-lousing resources and each army corps had an FAU section attached to it. At Kevelaer an FAU section set up a transit camp for DPs at Bislich which was followed by a series of camps between the Rhine and the Baltic. In many respects the tasks were similar to those experienced by workers in other fields: registration, de-lousing, catering and camp management. But there was an important difference: the Unit was now at the point of greatest wartime hatred and tension. They were not faced with grateful and friendly displaced families but with newly liberated forced labour workers of all nationalities, many of them surly and with feelings of enmity and bitterness towards each other. They were mostly young, burning with anger, many determined to avenge themselves on the German population for what they had suffered. In a situation of potential anarchy, speedy repatriation was essential. The army and its FAU teams did what they could, but often Unit members faced severe tests of their pacifism. None more so than when entering newly opened concentration camps:

Gerald Gardiner:

I was one of the first into Belsen concentration camp. We faced a situation where there were thousands of people in desperate need of hospitalisation, dying all over the place with huge piles of unburied corpses. All the army did was to provide two doctors and a few Alexandra nurses, and that was it. The first night I got there, I went into conference with the doctors to try to get some medical help. What it really needed was the services of the British General Hospital (BGH), which had all the staff required. I motored through the night and eventually found the General in charge of the 2nd Army who told me that the BGH was for the troops and not for civilians and he couldn't do anything about it at all. So I motored through the night to our Brussels HQ where I was the first person they had seen who had been to Belsen.

Belsen had been a terrible shock. We had seen other concentration camps but they were all relatively clean. Belsen, of course, was not an extermination centre at all. There were no gas chambers or anything like that. The people there were mainly British, French and Dutch – those the Nazis felt might be useful if they survived the war. It was just an end of the war cock-up: the food had run out, there was no water, no organisation. Our aircraft shot up the lorries taking food to the camp without having any idea of what they were doing and the inmates were all dying of starvation...It was a very upsetting sight. There was a nearby tank training school which had been evacuated by the Germans; as many as possible were moved into this. Graves were dug mainly by German women. It's a commentary on human nature that when they first started digging the graves, there were tears running down their faces. When we returned a week later, they were still at it, but all that had gone. There was nothing they could do about it, it wasn't their fault anyway. Yes, I was one of the first into Belsen and the first to report it to HQ.

Brian Cosford:

I was with Number 7 Relief Section, stationed near Celle. I shall never forget the first day when I saw the Belsen refugees. It was a hot May afternoon and those who could walk were sent down the seventeen miles to Celle. They were a pathetic sight in their ragged clothes, and in the heat of the afternoon you can imagine how they smelt.

Belsen was divided into two parts. Camp 1 was the 'horror' camp where piles of corpses were being buried. The SS guards had been working at the double, twelve hours a day, picking up bodies and putting them into trucks, taking them to the pits, and emptying them...Those who could be saved had their clothes burnt and were taken to the cleansing station, where they were stripped, deinfested and taken to hospital wrapped in a blanket. The hospital was set up in camp number 2, which wasn't so bad. When the British took the nurses from the hospital to the cleansing station, they protested. But when they saw the pitiful state of the people, they set to work. 500 entered the hospital every day, and it took eighty days to get through them all. The nurses worked from 7.45am to 10.30pm. There had been only 6,000 in the camp until February, but owing to Russian advances, many others were brought and consequently the camp became overcrowded. Typhus also came, and with it typhoid and dysentery...I visited Belsen one evening. It was an enormous place, and already they were burning part of camp 1 down. The whole hospital may have had 4,000 – 5,000 patients. German doctors and nurses were running the place under British supervision, and the organisation was excellent.Trying to find the entrance into the office of the typhus hospital, I blew into the maternity ward by mistake! On another occasion, when I had to transport three typhus cases to the hospital from Celle, I met a German doctor who could speak English well, and he knew about Quakers.

Clifford Barnard:

I was with FAU section number 2. We had landed in Normandy in September 1944 and had followed the British Army closely as it advanced into Belgium, Holland and Germany. The section

worked with the Dutch civilian medical authorities in Nijmegen
during the airborne battle of Arnhem, under constant artillery fire,
and later ran camps for DPs in the Ardennes as the British Army
repelled the final German advance of the war, and did the same
during the crossing of the Rhine. In April, 1945, we were then
attached to 205 Military Government Detachment (MGD) of 30
corps, located in the village of Holtzhausen, south of Bremen,
running a large tented camp for displaced persons of many nationalities. The war was drawing to a close and DPs, released from their
forced labour, were roaming the countryside and living on plunder,
only moving into official camps under pressure of hunger, bad
weather and rumours of homeward transport. Western nationals
were on their way home, but Russians, Poles, Czechs and Yugoslavs
were unable to go east due to the uncertain political situation. These
had to be housed and fed until arrangements could be made with
the Russian Army for their repatriation.

Our team was a young one: four in their thirties, four in their
twenties and four still in their nineteenth year. Despite this, we had
gained considerable experience in this work with DPs: arranging
sleeping accommodation, and foraging for food, giving medical
examinations and treatment, de-lousing, dealing with language
problems, transportation and many other things. Thousands had
passed through our camps. This was the work that other FAU Relief
Sections were doing in Germany and other parts of Europe.

This was the situation when intelligence of the Sandbostel concentration camp was received. 205 MGD with our Section were
given very short notice to prepare. The DP camp was taken over
by another Section, while further equipment and more army personnel arrived and a large convoy assembled.

It had been decided by higher authority that as Germans had
created a horror camp, then Germans should help clear it up. Some
sixty to seventy young German women including many high school
girls were ordered to report to the British Army in Delmenhorst,
a small town south of Bremen. They were well fed and had small
bundles of belongings with them, but they had been given very little
information and some feared they were destined for some form of
revenge, some kind of sex camp. The FAU were not very happy
with this but we felt we had no choice but to go along with the

arrangement as there was little time if lives were to be saved. Despite the strict non-fraternisation rules, one or two members were able to make contact with the women and gave some reassurance.

Before we departed Len Darling, our leader, hurriedly convened a meeting and advised of the exercise before us. The object was to move quickly and to save as many lives as possible. The army were to care for the prisoners of war and arrange for their return home, secure the German guards, bury the dead and finally destroy the camp. An RAMC unit, 168 Field Ambulance, were to take charge of the medical side and advise on the feeding. The FAU were to supervise the teams of German women in clearing up the camp, help care for the rescued inmates, take charge of the kitchen and feeding and generally assist wherever there was need.

The convoy moved off that afternoon...the conditions of the roads were very bad, bombing had left huge craters which had been roughly filled with rubble, bridges had been blown and in some places replaced with temporary Bailey bridges...The sound of gunfire and artillery flashes lit up the night sky...(the convoy) finally arrived during the day of May 1st...

The camp was fully entered early the following morning and the dreadful work was started. A fearful smell, impossible to describe, drifted everywhere. A huge pit had been dug in the centre of the compound by the Germans before they left into which row upon row of half-clothed or naked bodies had been thrown and lime scattered over them. There were some 8,000 political prisoners, all male, dying at the rate of twenty or thirty a day. At the gates of the concentration camp the rescuing personnel entered walking through a powder substance, and gloves, masks and overalls were issued. Hugh Jones, a member of our Section, has written: ' I shall never be able to eradicate from my memory the scenes and the stench. Behind barbed wire, thrusting their hands through in pleas for food were human skeletons, skin and bone, dressed or half-dressed, some with tops, some with bottoms, none with whole outfits, in pyjama-like filthy rags. They dribbled their incomprehensibly mouthed appeals which had to be turned down for they would have to be gradually weaned back from their starvation condition.'

The German women helped carry the dead bodies, more every hour, for placing in the pits. Two smaller pits had to be dug by the army. Inmates showing signs of life were transported to another compound created outside the perimeter of the main camp where 148 Field Ambulance were establishing a sort of hospital. Some FAU members supervised groups of German women in the 'human laundry'[2] and with the feeding.

Once the outside areas had been cleared the huts were entered. Mostly the men were lying in tiered bunks, without blankets, but many just lay on the wooden boards of the floor. The huts were deep in filth and excreta. It was dark, the smell unbearable and the RAMC doctors had to face the terrible job of deciding between the living and the dead. Amazingly, there were a few who could still walk. The work lasted several days and the rescue teams pressed on with little respite...Finally all the dead were buried. There were no means of identification and as far as I can remember, there was no form of religious service as the bodies were put into the pits. The pits were filled with earth and I believe the mounds were marked.

In the hospital compound anything that could be used as beds was brought into use: old doors, planks that sort of thing. Each inmate was laid out and thoroughly washed and as typhus had been found, any clothing they had worn was burnt. Two of our members with army personnel were given the task of seeking fresh clothing for the patients. A barge was discovered on the River Elbe that contained a great deal of clothing. This was commandeered and with the help of a Russian Army officer the clothing was transported to Sandbostel.

The FAU team was also asked to be responsible for organising the feed arrangements. Martin Southwood was put in charge of the kitchen.

Regretfully, communication with the German women was minimal and we never did discover how they felt. Clearly they were shocked by the experience and probably reluctant to express their mixed emotions. They slept in a section of segregated tents guarded by soldiers for their own protection...When some space in old German Army barracks became vacant as British Army personnel were withdrawn, it was allocated to the FAU, but we agreed that the women should have the accommodation, a decision the women found difficult to understand...

Due mainly to language problems we also had little communication with the internees, apart from their physical needs...they came from many nationalities. We did speak to some members of the Dutch Resistance who had some English, and from them we learnt most of what had happened. They had only been in the camp for about six weeks, brought there cramped into cattle trucks, dead and dying amongst them. None had expected to survive. Before they departed, two SS guards had fired at some internees who were raiding the kitchen for food, and many gunshot wounds found among the survivors testified to the truth of this.

During the time the FAU were at the camp, 1–16 May, the fighting in Europe ended on May 8. To celebrate the end of the war the officers' mess of 205 Military Government had a special evening meal to which the FAU were invited; even wine was served. It was a somewhat strange happening in the proximity of so much suffering...

After sixteen days the FAU section moved north to Cuxhaven, a virtually undamaged resort, for a week's rest by the sea. We had seen sights we hoped never to see again and indelible experiences were etched into our memories...It has been easy enough to describe the facts of what happened but far harder to explore our personal reactions. Every day somebody had stood in those wooden towers looking down on people dying, crying out for help. How, as conscientious objectors, could we reconcile those dreadful deeds? Personally, I was both profoundly shocked and very angry, and even contemplated returning home to join the army. I was quickly persuaded by my colleagues that at this very late stage of the war I was far more use where I was. So I stayed, and on reflection it was a decision I was glad of.[3]

David Rudd:

I had been transferred from Section 4 to Section 6 when the Allies advanced into Germany. We crossed the Rhine on D plus 4. We would drive our ambulances right up to the front line. I remember being holed up in a farmhouse in sight of enemy lines with our ambulances parked outside. Somebody – Roy Tyldesley, I think – had put an enormous red cross on the roof and we were hoping they wouldn't shell us. In the night there was a battle and we had military vehicles crawling past us, and our neighbourhood was shelled – that was the first time I was really frightened. We had a couple of chaps with us who had been in difficulties and sought shelter with us, and we had a sort of Edgar Allen Poe evening with them, with shells whizzing overhead. There were a lot of casualties half a mile up the road that night. The Allies won that battle. This was the sort of life we were living then, just after the Rhine crossing, moving about from place to place, billet to billet, setting up first aid posts, reorganising local hospitals as best we could, gathering nursing staff together.

I was the only one who rode a motor bike. Sometimes there were places that only a motor bike could reach and I used to take German speakers – Frank Edmead among them – to look for a doctor. In this way I got a real glimpse of war: shelling and all the accoutrements of war – the amount of ammunition used must have been terrific. Life was exciting and one was in the midst of it. I remember writing to my father 'I find this sort of thing terrifically exciting. Is that very bad?' And he replied 'No, it's quite natural that you should feel like that. You're young, and the Allies are advancing...'

Later on we took charge of what had been a concentration camp. We were told that we were to be in charge of this operation to repatriate DPs and ex-POWs, called 'PWXS'. Nobody knew exactly where it was, there was a great deal of confusion at that time. I was dispatched ahead to go to Corps HQ and find out where the front was. I did so and marched confidently through sentries to the tent where the battle was being directed by a Brigadier. I reported that I was from No 6, FAU, and where was the front? They told me there was a German contingent suspected of being on the way about half a mile away. So we went up an found this camp which was full of miserable people. Not as bad as Belsen or some of the other places, no heaps of bodies, but just very emaciated people. We got them out very quickly and turned the place into a reception place for DPs who had been released by the advancing troops. Most were slave labourers who flooded back in a disorganised way. We became one of the larger reception camps. There was a row of garages and we bashed holes through the connecting asbestos and made it into a reception area with different compartments for taking details, kit issue and delousing. I was in the last compartment and I had written in about seven languages 'Now give up your arms.' I didn't search them but gradually accumulated a huge pile of arms of all kinds.

The camp filled up. Five hundred would arrive at a time in a convoy: all ages, both sexes, POWs, DPs, women and children. Everybody stayed in camp until transport could be arranged. It was all very straightforward so far as the western Allies were concerned, they went back fairly quickly. So fairly soon we were left with eastern Europeans, Poles and Russians, with large numbers of Lithuanians, Latvians and Estonians. Some wanted to go home, some didn't. Life became more and more complex as we got more camps. My next camp was Sande, an enormous block of flats which had been commandeered to house DPs and PWXS, 5,000 in all. There was an extraordinary variation in morale. Part of this camp was in an appalling condition – I recall one block of flats with the excrement flowing down the stairs. Dreadful. Other areas were a bit better. The Russians and ex-POWs were an absolute menace. They went up to Wilhelmshaven once on a foray and got hold of some U boat fuel on which they got roaring drunk. And we had blindness and murders and a dreadful state of affairs for a while.

Something which sticks in my mind concerns delousing. We had a cylinder with a piston which we'd push up and down sleeves and trousers, with similar arrangements for the women. The army then produced air compressors and pneumatic lines which formed a sort of gun. So when you pressed the trigger, you could delouse a person in 15 seconds flat. We squirted hundreds and hundreds of people with these and we didn't get any of the diseases related to lice. Later on there was an argument about the harmful effects of DDT and the Mil. Gov. officer said that he didn't believe it harmful at all. So he ordered his batman to make some pancakes of DDT, not flour, and he ate several of them to prove that in the short-term there were no harmful effects. 'There you are, if you can eat it, it can't do you any harm.' So we continued with our DDT delousing. When my daughter was at school, one of her textbooks had a chapter on DDT and other pesticides and a footnote read 'There was an occasion when a Military Government officer had pancakes made with DDT and ate them.' I said 'Yes I remember, I was there.'

I was also involved in what was known as 'Operation Eagle.' This was a military operation laid on by the army for repatriating literally thousands of Poles, mostly DPs, from Lüneburg to Stettin where the Polish authorities took charge. It was a two day journey and we had to put them up for a night at Dessau in the Russian zone, where the FAU supervised the setting up of a camp for Mil. Gov. They came through in the early stages 1,000 at a time. I was there for three months, some of us for five. The route went right through the Russian zone, and our instructions were not to annoy the Russians. The roads were appalling with parts so grim that you couldn't drive fast. They were nearly all Poles. As well as supervising the camp, we also ran ambulances up and down the convoy. For some time I was the only person in the Section with mechanical training, so I spent time trying to keep the vehicles on the road rather than working on the ambulance route. One heard stories about those not wanting to go back...We used to get fed up with the camp and some evenings tried to have a walk, but you couldn't go far down the road before you were herded back. In a way we were like prisoners in Dessau.

We all wanted to go on leave, and when we went we'd pick up a FAU truck and drive behind a convoy. Les Barnes, one of our number got his leave order whilst on a convoy going east, meanwhile the convoy going west had gone. So he decided to catch it up and tore after it hoping to catch it before it went through the gates. He reached the gates but it had gone through. He was in trouble, the Russians didn't like it at all and they put him in a cell and kept him for a long time until they found someone who spoke English when he could explain himself. They were mystified that they couldn't find a watch when they searched him. They were amazed, they thought every British person had a watch. So a Russian took him into a room and opened a trunk which was full of watches and said 'Help yourself, Tovarich,' slapped him on the back, filled him with vodka, and Les went off with a beautiful watch. Another of our members, Roy Tyldesley, had a very frightening experience too.

Roy Tyldesley:

One day, with the permission of our Major, I took half-a-dozen Poles to the dentist in nearby Wusterhausen. We sat in the waiting room and the dentist had the first couple in. Soon Russian soldiers appeared with guns. I was in uniform, the Poles in civvies. I was asked what we were doing, what it was all about. Meanwhile, the Poles had just disappeared, merged into the countryside. The Russians took me to the local HQ and grilled me for a couple of hours in German, the common language. I was told to get into the truck and follow them. I was a bit apprehensive as we had heard awful stories about the Russians, although they were our Allies. We were about half-way back to the camp when the truck stopped, a Russian got out and got his gun out. 'Oh God, this is *it*' I thought. I'd heard stories of how they'd take you in a corner and shoot you in a ditch. But he'd seen a deer and just wanted a bit of free meat. He took a pot shot, missed and got back into the truck and back we went to the camp where he argued with the Major and I got a bit of a ticking off as if it were all my fault. But all those who disappeared from the dentist's turned up at the camp on their own two feet.

By August 1945, the FAU had eleven sections in Germany, spread widely over the British zone. Until June 1945, only male teams had been acceptable to military authorities in forward areas, but with the end of the war women members were included. The total number of voluntary workers in Germany in the summer of 1945 had risen to about 800; of these 150 were FAU who were spread widely over the British zone, including Berlin, Hamburg, and Husum on the Danish border. With the period of rapid advancement over, teams settled down to, relatively, more static conditions. The HQ had been moved from Brussels to Vlotho where the FAU shared a mess with the British Red Cross. In the autumn of 1946, Gerald Gardiner was replaced by Michael Rowntree, formerly of the HSU. Meanwhile the urge had been growing for undertaking welfare work among the German population and for rehabilitating German voluntary organisations. Contact was also renewed with German friends, German religious leaders, social service workers and educationalists. [4]

Stille Helfer – in war-torn Germany.

Hamburg – typical devastation amongst which the FAU worked.

Pip Turner:

Although there was plenty of work for us in Europe and the FAU were keen for us to go, the army wouldn't accept women until the fighting ceased. We went towards the end of June 1945, and I think the FAU were the first women to go into liberated Europe; we always went in mixed teams.

I was in Holland for a month or so and then moved into Germany. We drove in convoy, going over the Rhine very slowly in our trucks on a Bailey Bridge – very precarious. I remember the hordes of refugees on the road. Everyone walking, walking – the whole of Germany was just seething with people from all different countries, all on the move. It was chaotic. A non-fraternisation order had gone out and we all decided that we weren't going to have that. I'm sure that we all spoke to the German people. But when you said 'Guten morgen' they were likely not to answer. They felt hostility towards us. We didn't feel it because we hadn't been fighting in a war and we were all aware that some of the things we had done were as wicked as what the Germans did – the bursting of the Mohne Dam, for instance.

The Germans had *nothing:* no bandages, no soap – nothing. British troops took over German stores and we had the job of distributing sheets, blankets and medical supplies. I was in Section 126 and ended up in Bochum in the Ruhr. This was a desert of ruins with hardly anything standing. People were living underground in the cellars – often the only piece of a house standing, and you'd see an odd piece of corrugated tin with smoke coming out where they were trying to cook something. And the air raid shelters – or bunkers as they called them – were full of people living in the most primitive conditions and they were very short of food.

My job at first was writing reports on the medical services in Bochum. I had to report on what they were doing about infectious diseases and the state of hospitals, supplies of ambulances and drugs. They were very short of insulin, I remember, they only had fifteen or twenty per cent of their needs. Infant mortality was high. If the mothers weren't able to breastfeed, their babies simply died. We got great barrels of cod liver oil from the Red Cross, and we had the job of splitting it up and distributing it to infant welfare clinics. At one point I was asked to write a confidential report about the children: I remember a great deal of rickets and there was quite a lot of oedema – swollen stomachs. We selected the malnourished children and concentrated on them. We also started feeding schemes for children under school age, as school children were fed one meal at school. I went round the schools organising feeding schemes. We did cocoa and milk drinks, trying to get as much nourishment into one drink as we could. We had difficulties with some of the churches who always tried to get as much as they could for their own organisations. We strove to be fair to everybody.

We used to go past a camp for Hungarian boys. They were so wild and couldn't be controlled by anybody. There were so many groups of children wandering about by themselves, probably wanting to get home, but many didn't know where home was any more. It was all very sad.

Eric and I were married in Germany but we operated as single people in the Unit, and were only together during visits. One of these was to a youth club. It's interesting because it reveals something of the effect of war on Nazi children. We visited one which met in a large house in Bochum. It was perched high up in a wood and had been the pride and joy of the Natur-Freunde. It was taken over by the Hitler Youth during the war but had been taken back by the Natur-Freunde. They were very glad to have it back although the Nazis had deliberately smashed everything up: furniture, equipment and windows.

As soon as we entered the room we knew we'd enjoy ourselves because there were about sixty fresh-faced young girls and boys all singing at the tops of their voices. It could have been any English youth group – not quite as rowdy, but a slightly boisterous atmosphere of youngsters letting off steam. Eric said a few things in his halting German. Then they started asking him questions about English youth clubs, about boy scouts and youth hostels, what English youth thought about them and why it was that they were forbidden to talk about politics – all youth clubs started in the British zone were supposed to be non-political.One ernest boy asked me how a conscientious objector was treated in England, and how you could become one in Germany. They asked us the inevitable questions about rations and we tried to relate their conditions to world conditions. We were delighted that they were so enquiring and receptive after thirteen years of nationalist socialist education. So while work in the Ruhr was grim and a bit depressing, we really enjoyed this evening with these young people and we hoped they'd soon be able to build up their own democracy.

I also did a report on factory hygiene when I became very concerned for young apprentices aged between fourteen and eighteen. You see children who stayed at school had an additional meal which the apprentices didn't get. I agitated a lot about this and referred it to Mil. Gov. because they were working hard and needed the extra meal. I remember a sad story of someone in the factory telling me that this young boy had come home late one night and seen his sandwich ready for tomorrow's work and he was so ravenous that he ate it. So the next day he had to work the whole day with nothing to eat. If ever you went out for the evening in Germany, you had to take your own food and drink with you because they could never give you anything. We went into many German homes and made good friends. I think there was mute hostility when we first went into Germany, but we soon overcame that because we were so friendly to everybody. I think they probably regarded all us girls wearing the red cross as prostitutes at first because they had a lot of camp followers and judged us likewise. But after the first month or two it was much more friendly and settled.

This experience in north-west Europe confirmed my pacifism: war is such a dreadful thing. So many millions killed and so much misery. It took Europe years to recover.

Lilian Cadoux:

At Mount Waltham I had been qualified to boil up three hundred gallons of soup in a Field Kitchen for DPs. I could have deloused them; I could have built a very efficient shower bath made out of two old buckets and a length of string, but instead I arrived in this desperately bombed city of Bochum on the Ruhr to work in the Roundhouse which is the Town hall. By this time I was married to Harold Cadoux.

The German population were in a terrible state: very, *very* poverty stricken, mostly living in basements. You would drive through a totally blitzed area thinking no one could possibly live there, and your driver would say 'Oh no, we're going to call on one of these houses, as someone is living in the basement.' A little farther out there were some houses still standing. I remember our interpreter had quite a decent place but still the poverty and shortage of food hit him very forcibly. We were invited to coffee once, and it was absolutely horrible – poisonous tasting ground-up acorns. It was awful for them because the people of Westphalia are so hospitable. They are racially indistinguishable from the southern English. If someone had been dropped there by parachute, they might have thought they were in Kent: orchards, beautiful lilac and cherry blossom – the same faces and hair colouring. They made little biscuits for us. As they had no fat, they had little gadgets to crisp them out and make an acceptable looking cookie.

I remember once we were sent for to conduct a young couple and their premature baby to church to have the baby baptised. That baby weighed about three and a half pounds. The weather was still very cold and having been a nurse it horrified me that I was conducting that child through the streets to be baptised.

At one time we were asked if we would help with the feeding of the miners because their calorie ration was far too low for the manual work they had to do. Well, it was very difficult to get supplies for such a large number of people, but we thought we ought to investigate and went along to talk to a Major Coleman who was in charge. He was working in the Krupps mansion somewhere on the outskirts of Bochum which the army had requisitioned. Krupps had lived in such a grandiloquent style. He had bought an enormous tapestry – could it have been fifty feet long? All I can remember is that it hung from the ceiling of this great house down to the well of the staircase. Major Coleman explained that a terrible explosion had taken place down the mine and hundreds had been killed, so he couldn't allow us to go down. But we were allowed just inside the portals of the place to interview people in the canteen. I remember being met by a very overweight cook – she hadn't particularly kept herself short! She was very indignant about the shortage of food, and I said to her very coldly 'I hope you realise how the people of Belgium and Holland literally starved during the war.' I wasn't always reconciling. I sometimes felt they had to be made to understand.

What we could do was to feed the school children. That's what you always do in a relief situation – keep the younger generation nourished. It was done in a very extraordinary way. We collected supplies from wherever we could. The American forces had given us a huge consignment of what were called 'Pacific packs.' These had been prepared for the Far Eastern campaign. You had what looked like a large sardine tin and inside you had condensed rations for a whole day plus lavatory paper and two cigarettes. So we employed a lot of Germans unpacking these tins, removing the lavatory paper and cigarettes, and putting the food into a huge pile. This was taken off to some communal kitchen and made into a soup which we'd load onto our ambulances in much the same way as meals-on-wheels are loaded now. We would drive round the schools, stand in the playground and ladle it out into the children's containers. I can remember two very moving instances: once when a teacher greeted me with great delight saying 'Ah, I remember being fed by the Quakers after the last war.' I loved that feeling of continuity. The other when a teacher asked the children to sing a little thankyou song. When I think of it now, I want to weep...children singing...it brings back our common humanity. So one hopes that those particular children remember something about the Quakers.

Then, because Harold and I were one of the few married couples, we felt it incumbent upon us to accept all the evening invitations. The Mayor would ask us to the most boring concerts. After a hard day's work, sitting on a hard chair listening to chamber music, you'd nearly fall off your chair with fatigue and boredom. But you had to do it because they were holding out the hand of friendship, and we both spoke good German. I remember a Sunday afternoon concert in commemoration of some concentration camp victims where a woman recited a long poem which told about the shoes being left outside the gas ovens: "Kinderschuhe aus Leben". And of course we were always told by them that they had never known anything about the camps during the war, 'We never knew it, it was kept from us,' they would say; and probably in that area this was so because there weren't any there.

I want to tell you about Bielefeld. For some reason we had to drive over to visit this little epileptic colony. We spent the whole day there and I was very impressed and felt very privileged to meet the other sort of Germans. I felt a lot better. I hadn't felt too good before what with this grossly fat cook and those who were always saying 'We didn't know..' This place was like a small village, and they had their own bakery, post office, everything. And we were told that at one time Hitler had decided that he was going to exterminate the mentally ill. I don't quite know exactly how it was done, but the medical staff simply refused to let the SS through the gates. I have since been told that if you spoke with great authority and utter conviction, you could get away with it. It was wonderful to see some of these epileptic children, some with multiple handicaps, so lovingly cared for by these Evangelical nuns.

We worked very closely with the German relief organisations because the ethos of the FAU and FRS was that we must never go naively into a situation and start giving supplies away. They knew that they could get into the wrong hands and be sold for profit. So I often had to sit through really long and trying committee meetings with the representatives of the various churches and civil authorities.

I remember going to a Catholic orphanage and seeing the shocking sight of emaciated babies with arms and legs like sticks – they were the abandoned children of German girls who had been raped by the Russians. It was really tragic.

We had good relations with the FRS team in Cologne and with the Army of Occupation. We'd be invited to dinner by officers and I found them really charming and thoughtful men and far more compassionate than I had supposed military people could be. That was a learning situation as well, for both sides. I understood that they had a job to do according to their principles and I had a job to do according to mine. They never put unnecessary curbs on our activities nor stopped us travelling around in the way we did. They could have been awkward and made us observe some letter of the law to restrict our movements, but they never did

Helen and John Adamson were another FAU couple who worked in Germany. They left England in July 1945 and had worked on a survey of the living conditions and needs of British civilians living in France

during the war before leaving for Germany. They arrived in Berlin in August where they joined 135 relief Section who were living in a house in Ruhleben, situated between central Berlin and Spandau. Their arrival coincided with the mass expulsion of Germans westwards from the east of the Oder and Neisse rivers, territory which had been ceded to Poland and the USSR when the map of that area was re-drawn at Yalta. The refugees were mainly women, children and old men and some 18,000–20,000 were passing through Berlin every day.

There was nothing like sufficient stocks of food, clothing and other essentials to deal with such an emergency, so the Unit decided that the most useful thing they could do was to rapidly assess the facts and write a report which would set out the scale of the crisis. Information was gathered from the Military Government and any reliable printed information – English and German – that they could find and, importantly, from the section's own investigations.

John Adamson:

We went to the railway stations in daylight and at night and saw great crowds of refugees in endless queues. They might stand in line for up to thirty-six hours and then be squeezed into carriages with some travelling on the buffers and some on the roof. It was estimated that during July and August half a million refugees a month were pouring westwards through Berlin.

We visited a few of the forty-eight refugee camps which were said to be able to hold 30,000 people. Our school German suddenly had to cope with emotional conversation and new vocabulary. We were told that each refugee was entitled to stay at a transit camp for twenty-four hours only. During that time each person was given 100 grammes of bread (two slices) and three-quarters of a litre of soup. We saw sick and infirm people and some severely undernourished children. We remember a grandmother who had walked from Silesia with two grandchildren. She had large ulcers on her legs and the children were pot-bellied. In a refugee camp run by Sisters of the Good Shepherd we found a colony of orphan children...

After our first week in Berlin, I wrote a report on 29 August which aimed to set out the scale of the crisis, coordinating our section's findings and summarising what we had seen. Stunned by the suffering – and we had lived through six years of war – and with all the confidence of youth, we begged the Allied Powers to take action, including bringing in stocks of food and medical supplies to ensure minimum standards of nutrition and health of the civilian population, especially the refugees.

In the next few days, twenty copies of the report were typed out and sent to FAU headquarters in London and Vlotho, to the Foreign Secretary and other MPs, to Victor Gollancz and to leading members of churches and to newspapers. We heard later that the report had been used at meetings in Britain, had been quoted by at least one newspaper and in the House of Commons. Our aim was to confirm and add detail to the reports that were beginning to appear in British newspapers on the subject. We hoped to support those who believed that, whatever suffering the Nazis had caused in Europe, urgent action should be taken to avoid another major tragedy in the coming winter.

In our first months in Berlin our members began to help in a number of different ways. A few German POWs were housed in the Ruhleben barracks near our house. They were a pitiful crowd released by the Russians as unfit for work plus a few German soldiers released from hospital. I remember carrying in an ambulance four one-legged 'men' of whom one was aged fourteen and one fifteen. Hitler called up the Hitler Jugend in the last weeks of the war...Another 'casualty' of the war and subsequent occupation who came to our attention was a German woman we came to know, who had been raped by a Russian and was suffering from VD. We were able to organise treatment for her...

One of the effects of the non-fraternisation order was that VIPs visiting Germany from Britain, like the newspaper proprietor, Lord Layton, could not talk officially with leading Germans on military premises. This was why a number of important meetings took place at our FAU house. For example, in October, Helen helped to interpret for the Bishop of Chichester and the Dean of St. Paul's at a meeting with Pastor Gruber, a leader in the Evangelical Church in Berlin...

During the winter our Section dealt with some hundreds of Search Bureau enquiries. We found fifty to sixty per cent of the non-Jewish cases and sent back messages in reply. We found a few Jews who had been hidden and cared for by non-Jewish people for two or more years at risk to their own lives. It was moving to meet such people. In most of the Jewish cases the most we could do was to find someone who knew when the missing person was taken to the concentration camp and sometimes which one. These names were later checked against lists of surviving Jews. A few Jewish women survived because they were married to non-Jewish men who refused to divorce them...

Fortunately many people in Military Government were concerned for the inhabitants of Berlin as winter approached. Ambitious plans were made by the British authorities in collaboration with German officials, teachers and social workers to transport young children to country districts in the British Zone for the winter. This was called 'Aktion Storch' – Operation Stork, and altogether 25,000 Berlin children took part...It was a difficult decision for parents, usually just the mother, to agree to hand over their children who had survived the war, even though some teachers travelled with them. The scheme started at the beginning of October and ended in mid-November. Every day about fifty buses filled with children set off on the 120 miles journey through the Russian Zone. There were always two FAU ambulances with four members at the end of the convoy. We 'borrowed' two ambulances and drivers from another Section. Children aged four and five were accompanied by their mothers. On one occasion one of the mothers went into labour and the FAU ambulance had to leave the convoy and speed on to Helmstedt. Later, someone drew a cartoon of the ambulance speeding along and a stork with a baby trying to catch up with it. The children were cared for near the border town of Helmstedt by a relief team of Save the Children Fund who did a good job. They were then taken to country homes in areas like Schleswig-Holstein, which had a little more food than the big towns. In the spring the children and mothers were brought back to Berlin. By that time we were working with a Red Cross Child Welfare team. They reported that they could easily distinguish the Aktion Storch children from those who had spent the winter in Berlin...

Operation Stork – arrival in Oldenburg.

In February and March 1946, the FAU was also involved in Operation Waif – planned by the German Evangelical Church and the BRCS to take thousands of orphans out of Berlin to the British Zone. This time the transport was by rail. It was another example of cooperation between Mil. Gov., the FAU and German social welfare and church organisations. FAU members travelled with the children working together with German social workers, looking after the children on their journey through the Russian Zone.

How to sum up the work of 135 Section in Berlin? Unlike many FAU Sections in the British Zone of Germany we did not work mainly on one job and so could not count our success in thousands of DPs or refugees cared for. We sometimes wondered just what we were achieving. However, we were involved in many different kinds of useful work. Our presence was valuable for publicising the refugee situation, especially in the autumn of 1945. Over the months the FAU built up effective links with British Military Government and German churches and welfare workers. Although we had no large-scale supplies we did distribute limited relief

*1. Mütterchen horch
was klappert der Storch.*

*2. Im Stalle ruft
mit frohem "Muh"
zur guten Milch
die liebe Kuh.*

*3. Am warmen Ofen wird gesessen
zum reichlich guten Mittagessen.*

*4. Zur Schule geht ihr auch bei mir
und lernt genau so viel wie hier.*

*5. So soll ich sie so lang entbehren
und garnichts mehr von ihnen hören?*

*6. Das laß nur meine Sorge sein
ich bringe dir die Post herein.*

supplies from various sources to people in extreme need. We helped with some major schemes to aid children, such as Operation Stork and Operation Waif. Through Search Bureau work we were able to bring news of those separated by war. Our office also dealt with many individual enquiries from men and women in distress. FAU contacts with Berlin Quakers gave them some support which they appreciated and provided some continuity in Quaker work.[5]

Since the FRS, with its insistence on wearing Quaker grey, was unacceptable to the military authorities in NW Europe while hostilities lasted, it was the FAU that was the first to renew contact with Friends in various parts of NW Europe who had been cut off during the occupations. Renewed contacts with German Friends were particularly significant: they had been cut off for six years:

Douglas Scott:
One Sunday, one of the German Friends asked us to go to a meeting in Berlin. Although the centre had been very badly knocked about, the suburbs were virtually untouched and the Meeting House had been only slightly damaged. Gerald (Gardiner) and I turned up in FAU uniform and as we walked in a shudder went right through the meeting because they thought we were part of an army investigation. When they were told who we were and why we were there, everyone of them burst into tears. It was the most moving experience I've ever had.

There was another emotional meeting with Friends in Bad Pyrmont where the Quakerhouse was run by Leonhard and Mary Friedrich. Although their experience was an extreme one, it does illustrate the dangers and tensions Friends in occupied Europe lived under during the war. The Friedrichs and the small Quaker group around them in Bad Pyrmont had helped hundreds of persecuted people including Jews, many of whom they had helped to escape. This eventually led to the arrest of Leonhard and his internment in Buchenwald in May 1942. The Meeting House was commandeered and Mary, who was English by birth, now alone was forced to endure endless Gestapo interrogations and harrassment. Brenda, their only daughter, had been sent away to Sidcot school in England in 1933 to escape the intimidation her parents knew she would suffer had she stayed with them in Germany. Until August 1939 she had continued to visit Germany for holidays, but when war broke it was to be six years before she met up with them again, this time as a member of the FAU married to Sydney Bailey.

Brenda Bailey:

A week or so after Leonhard's release from Buchenwald, the FAU started their relief work in Germany. As the HQ in Vlotho was about forty miles away from Bad Pyrmont, members made it a habit of going to my parents for Sunday Meeting. They would take cans of food and Mary would cook Sunday lunch for them. This was really great for my parents because these young English men would listen to their talk about what they had endured and this helped them both enormously and pretty soon they were given a letter from me and we were in close contact again. Then, Diana McClelland (Close) and I were selected as the first women to join the FAU team working for displaced persons in the district of Einbeck....When the continental train eventually brought us to Vlotho on 23 October, I was very excited to learn that Mike Rowntree had arranged for me to spend the first five days with my parents in Pyrmont and that Deryck Moore was going to drive me there that same afternoon.

It was a very emotional experience to return to my home, after six years of separation and to find both my parents surprised to see me... Their dear familiar faces, their way of talking, their gestures were so reassuring, though they both seemed older and smaller than I had remembered when we had said goodbye in August 1939...We had supper at the kitchen table... My first shock came when I tried to eat the supper that Mary had prepared. We had a large plate of bread soup, made from bread crusts cooked with potatoes and put through a sieve, with some sour apple sauce in the centre for flavour. This was accompanied by herb tea. I could scarcely swallow it, though I knew this was the sort of food they had become used to. I was dreadfully sick and in the bathroom I found a bar of mud-coloured soap which produced no lather.

I enjoyed sleeping in my old creaky bed, and the following days passed happily, meeting Quakers and neighbours, strolling around the somewhat shabby town and parks, listening to each other's experiences and simply being together again...But the situation could not have been easy for them to accept. I had left home as a sixteen year-old school-girl and returned as an independent, twenty-two year-old married woman. We made great efforts to understand each other, but it was not easy because we had lived in such different worlds. They had become more German and I had become more English. It was very painful to hear them describe their suffering, though I had been able to imagine much of it. I could only listen to so much at a time...It was then only four months since Leonhard had been released from Buchenwald and he had not fully recovered...[6]

Deryck Moore:

I remember taking Brenda to her parents and on the way talking to her about what she would find: I think your mother will be the same, but I'm not so sure about your father after all his suffering. And when I met Leonhard – and I met him many times after this meeting – I became convinced that he was a different person, that Buchenwald had totally altered his outlook as a human being. When he went into Buchenwald, he aimed to follow his greater principles and was going to be kind to the next man. But he told me 'Within a week, I was grabbing for the food like the rest of them, my faith remained whole but it was purely individual.' His faith obviously had to take second place to staying alive. That was his one aim, to stay alive...I can only describe it as a man who was playing a tune before the war, and some of the chords were missing afterwards. I can dimly recall him visiting Brenda at school in England; he was never the complete Leonhard again. Something had altered him fundamentally so that he was always fighting back the urge to say 'that's mine, that's mine!' Yet, you still felt that he was such a saintly Christian man, and that he had done much more in the camp than he cared to admit...I think that if you had bumped into some of those he was with in the camp they would have said 'I don't know how he does it...' He lived to a ripe old age and led the Quaker Meeting in Bad Pyrmont for many years after his release.

Another FAU project concerned around 2,000 German evacuee children who had been evacuated to Austria from Berlin and the Ruhr when the heavy bombing raids on Germany started. The children were between the ages of eleven and fourteen years and, with their teachers, were stranded in small camps in Austria, the majority not knowing whether their parents were still alive or whether they had homes to return to. Unit members were selected for the task of camp supervisors. They were all German speakers, responsible for caring for the children and their teachers: getting supplies of food, clothing and fuel and evolving an educational programme to wean the children away from Nazi indoctrination and to teach them democracy. Meanwhile, efforts were made to trace their parents and eventually, with the help of an FRS Section in Germany, the majority of children had been escorted back to their homes in Berlin and the Ruhr by June 1946. The FAU was disbanded at that time and the few remaining evacuees came under the care of other relief organisations.

Frank Edmead:

The children had been gathered together from the scattered hotels throughout the mountains into some more manageable camps in the British zone of Austria. Six or seven of us in the FAU were asked to look after these camps until the children could return home. We were each given a group of camps to care for. Mine were fairly isolated: I lived in a camp with a classful of thirteen to four-teen year-old Volksschule boys from Berlin, and a few from an Adolf Hitlerschule – these were going to be the elite of the next genera-tion of Nazi leaders. I was also responsible for a hotel full of slightly older girls from Essen and Ruhrgebiet and another hotel full of boys from the same region who were situated in the next valley, whom I saw less often.

The students were delightful. One of the Hitlerschule boys said to me 'When we heard we were going to be looked after by the British, we were afraid that we would be treated brutally, but with you we've had the best time we've ever had in Austria.' The teachers caused far more trouble with the feuds they had among themselves.

The syllabus was more or less my responsibility. They learnt de-Nazified German history and I gave English and world history lessons. There was no sign of overt indoctrination in these children; they had the Berlin dialect and Berlin sense of humour and gave me a wonderful time. On my birthday, I came down to great piles of flowers and I was serenaded and given things they'd made in woodwork or had embroidered. Then in the afternoon they performed something they had been rehearsing in secret. This was Schiller's 'William Tell' which was considered a subversive play and had been prohibited by the Nazis – I remember the scenery was the natural scenery of the mountains.

In February 1946 the Rhineland children were sent back in a big special train which took us all across from Austria to the Ruhr. It was an extraordinary and horrible journey which took several days, as the train didn't go all the way to the Ruhr. We ended up at Lüneburg Heath one Sunday evening in freezing weather with no one about. Eventually, I found an old school with no heating in which we stayed during a freezing night. When I alerted the nearest authorities, we did the next stage of the journey to the Ruhr by bus. I then had to distribute the children to their homes. Most of them

Hugh Johnes with German refugees in Austria. Easter 1946.

hadn't been in contact with their parents and I wondered whether their parents would still be there and their homes still standing. But, extraordinarily, they all got home. Very often it seemed a miracle: a whole street of houses bombed and theirs still standing.

The Berlin children went back later in June. That was a still more extraordinary journey as we went across the Soviet zone. The railways lines had been taken off to Russia and we couldn't be sure how far we were going before another stop. At least it was sunny and warm weather. In Berlin the same thing happened: all the children's homes standing except for one boy who was adopted by a couple of teachers. I kept in touch with all the teachers until they died and the boys I'm still in touch with until this day.

Michael Rowntree:

Did the FAU bring something special to relief work in Germany? I would like to think that we did. Clearly our motivation as pacifists had an extra dimension, I think, from the natural inclination people have to help in such a situation. I think perhaps it also made us more inclined to forget the past and view the ordinary German population more charitably than some of the other voluntary organisations who perhaps were less inclined to overlook some of the atrocities that had gone on or perhaps were more inclined to ascribe blame to the whole population and not just to the individuals who had done this. So, I think there was a slight difference of emphasis. Whether that rubbed off on any of the other organisations, I wouldn't like to say. We did seek active reconciliation with individual Germans where we could, although one always had to bear in mind that you never knew who you were dealing with – the Nazis were quite good at dissembling about their past...

We had several advantages. I think it's true to say that the Unit, because it was operating throughout the war on a rather curious basis, had become accustomed to barging in where angels fear to tread, as it were. It was a very flexible organisation, perhaps less hierarchical than some of the others, and we were able to take decisions on the spot. By the time I got there – the autumn of 1946 – things had settled down to a degree and there was rather less scope for individual initiative – a structure had been set up, a bit of a chain of command, a control HQ run by the BRC, so opportunities for snap decisions were rather less than they had been in Gerald Gardiner's day. But fundamentally, the Unit has always been a body that has prided itself on being flexible and able to adapt itself to different circumstances. This was tested to the full in Northwest Europe, especially Germany.

REFERENCES:

(1) 'This poem was written (in 1986) after 40 years when the survivors of the FAU Berlin Section met for a reunion in that city. The cold war was at its height. The "viewing platform" at the Wilhelmstrasse over-looked the site of the Bunker: nobody told that to the tourists come to gawp at the Wall. The ruined Anhalter Bahnhof brought back the memory of the terrible winter of 1945/46.' Ralph Arnold, letter to Lyn Smith 12/1/94.

(2) This was the name given to the process of cleaning the patients so that they could enter the hospital for treatment. It is synonymous with the 'cleansing station' mentioned by Brian Cosford.

(3) *Two Weeks in May 1945: Sandbostel Camp and the FAU*, Clifford Barnard, unpublished memoir, January 1947.

(4) As the war ended other relief societies became involved in DP work under the auspices of the Red Cross. The FRS now came into its own in Europe: one team RS100, although still in Quaker grey, had been involved with the relief of Belsen. By March 1946 4 FRS sections were working in Germany, closely cooperating with the FAU, and with one transport section made up of FRS/FAU. When the FAU wound up in the summer of 1946, members continued working on FAU projects, but now under the aegis of FRS.

(5) Letter from John Adamson to Lyn Smith, November 1996.

(6) For more information on Mary and Leonhard Friedrich see Bailey, Brenda, *A Quaker Couple in Nazi Germany*. Sessions York, 1994. In 1996, Stille Helfe (Silent Helper), an exhibition honouring Quaker work in Germany after two world wars, was funded by the German government. Brenda Bailey, who was among the 14 British Friends invited to the exhibition's opening, gave a speech outlining FAU, FRS and AFSC work in Germany after the Second World War.

CHAPTER 16

FAU in Captivity

A tribute should be paid to our two Quakers (Michael Mounsey and Alan Dickinson) who arrived in Fort XV from Greece with the Australians. My memory tells me that their unit had been sent originally to Finland and, when that campaign fizzled out, they found themselves by some circuitous route in Greece. In spite of their non-combatant status they were treated by the Germans as prisoners and it was curious for them to find themselves in a camp of army personnel. But their ideals of service were respected by all.

David Wild.[1]

*A*S FAU UNITS *were entering NW Europe behind the invading Allied armies, several of their less fortunate comrades were sharing the fate of captured Allied troops in German POW camps. These were FAU POWs who had been captured in Greece in 1941, on the island of Kos in 1943, and in the borderlands of France and Germany, in 1944.*

The group of sixteen men, who had been captured in Kalamata in 1941, having endured many privations and an arduous journey through Corinth, Athens and Salonika, finally arrived in different groups, distributed in camps in Germany, Silesia and Poland.

In Stalag V111B, situated in Lamsdorf, Silesia, the group of seven men were soon officially recognised as 'protected personnel' which meant protection under the Geneva Convention as medical personnel. They were treated as such and received certain privileges such as not having to attend the tedious daily roll-calls. In May 1943, they were granted an interview with Gunnar Janssen of the Swedish YMCA, who gave them news of their comrades imprisoned in other parts of Europe as well as messages

347

of support from Friends in Geneva and Berlin. Working as they had been under the auspices of the Red Cross, these FAU captives were entitled to repatriation under the Geneva Convention. Despite vigorous efforts by Oswald Dick, on behalf of the entire captured group, nothing happened until October 1943 when three men returned home, followed by another three in 1944. The remainder were released by the British or Russian invading armies in 1945. Until then it was the daily routine of POW life they shared with the troops.

Martin Lidbetter, Stalag V111B:

On Friday, 15 October 1943, several thousand of us departed from the camp, two years and three days after the seven of us had arrived.

We entrained the same day for the journey to Sassnitz, a ferry port on the southern coast of the Baltic, some 400-500 miles to the north. The journey was slow but uneventful. There was a brief pause at Dresden station where we excited the interest of those waiting on the platforms, but it was a comfortable journey that in some ways was reminiscent of our journeys in Finland; there were no guards, and when the train stopped at wayside stations some of us walked up to the engine with tea leaves in our billy-cans into which near boiling water was poured!...We received a terrific Swedish welcome at Trelleborg where we arrive this evening by train ferry from Germany...It is almost like fairyland with Swedish Red Cross nurses serving us with apples and beer, sandwiches etc. ad infinitum...

When we arrived at Waterloo station there were long queues for telephones so I took a taxi home without warning my parents that I had arrived, so the first thing they knew of it was when I rang the front door bell. The taxi driver wanted to know where I had come from, and when I told him he refused any payment for the fare – another welcome home – nothing, however, to the welcome I received when the door bell was answered...[2]

Things did not always turn out so happily for other FAU POWs. Alan Dickinson, imprisoned in Fort XV with Michael Mounsey, suffered a mental breakdown in 1942. Although he was watched over day and night in the camp by his fellow POWs, he managed one day to break away and jumped from a window into a dry moat, suffering terrible injuries. The Germans took him to a nearby asylum where he soon died.

Michael Mounsey received perhaps one of the highest honours granted to a conscientious objector in wartime. The Camp leader of Fort XV had been replaced by the Germans by another man. This was not accepted by the men who claimed their right to choose their own Man of Confidence. An election duly took place in which the 700 Warrant Officers and NCOs and 150 Australians elected Michael Mounsey. He was a fluent German speaker and had built up a reputation for being tough, shrewd and scrupulously fair. 'I cannot imagine soldiers of any other army making such a choice,' wrote David Wild, a fellow POW.(3)

But Mounsey's POW experience was not without cost:

John Bailey:

Michael Mounsey had to be interpreter due to his fluent German and that experience etched into his soul so much. He was constantly having to interpret harsh statements coming from German officers. He hated it and suffered a lot translating insults to his pals. The result was that he hated the Germans like mad and wouldn't speak a word of German after that. Although he is a birthright Friend, that scar remained with him for many years. He did eventually live it down.

Lilian Cadoux:

My husband had been a POW for over four years. He still had time to serve when he was freed and the FAU offered him a place on one of the sections in Germany. It was up to Harold whether he accepted it or not. I always regarded it as rather noble of him to agree, so clearly he didn't blame individual Germans for his treatment in the camps. In fact you might almost say that he had more reason to feel more resentment against the RAF because of the High Command order for the saturation bombing of Dresden which was kept secret from us at the time. I think I would have cringed had I known of that whilst in Germany.

Harold at the time of the bombing of Dresden was in a POW camp not many miles away. Because he was medical personnel, he was sent to the raid to clear up. I didn't hear of those experiences for fifteen years because they were so traumatic that they were buried. Eventually he broke down mentally and had to go into hospital. After a length of time the doctors felt they weren't getting at the root of the problem and decided they had to give him what was called the 'truth drug' to get him to bring suppressed material from his subconscious. He then told this horrific story that it wasn't a case of going into the bunkers and carrying out the bodies, but of scraping them off the walls. That's why I say that he might have had more reason to feel resentful of our own High Command, because it had caused him to undergo frightful trauma.

Another group of men had been captured in the autumn of 1943 from the island of Kos, where they had arrived as an FAU advance party – No 12 Field Surgical Unit – for the abortive British attack on the Dodecanese in September/October 1943.

The team consisted of: Major Till, the surgeon, Captain Dornan, the anaesthetist, and two FAU men, Stephen Peet and Dennis Westbrook. They were setting up the Field Hospital on Kos when suddenly there was the noise of intense air activity and firing:

Stephen Peet:

What was happening? Then Dennis Westbrook leant out of the window above me and laconically shouted down 'enemy Friends have just arrived!'...Quite soon various wounded began to be brought in – British and German. A German doctor had arrived and at least one medical orderly and we all worked together in a very easy relationship. At one time I went out for a breath of fresh air into a sort of archway. There was a German soldier nearby and through the archway I could see an English soldier crouching down and creeping along. And the German picked up his rifle, took aim and shot him. He then slung his rifle over his shoulder and ran out – in some danger as there were bullets flying around – across this piece of ground, picked up the soldier he'd shot, slung him over his shoulder and brought him to us where he was taken straight into the operating theatre to have a bullet taken from his leg. The whole thing was like a film shot in one, sort of unbelievable as if it were fiction. Over the years I began to think I had just dreamt it. It was so absurd. Then I returned about fifteen years ago, saw the row of buildings and the archway and I knew the story was true. Very strange.

Although the invasion only lasted twenty-four hours, the medical staff continued to look after the wounded. Their work was hugely increased when vast numbers of wounded from the nearby battle of Leros started pouring in some time later.

Stephen Peet:

We had hopes of repatriation through Turkey in return for the medical work we had done. The German commander had written a letter of appreciation, but the papers didn't come through in time. However, it meant that Major Till, Captain Dornan and a couple of others were repatriated before the war ended as a result of the medical care given on Kos.

We had been sent off from Athens in mid-December 1943 on an eleven-day train journey still in tropical kit and a blanket. The whole thing was a bit of a nightmare and I began to realise what it must have been like for millions of others in much, much worse conditions. At some point we arrived in the dark and cold. All out, and into some camp right beside the railway line. And there I had the best meal I've *ever* had: two potatoes out of a barrel of hot water, still with mud on them but *hot*. I scoffed them down quickly and it was wonderful. This was a temporary transit camp and we each got issued with a Red Cross parcel. I knew – probably from reading Boys' Own paper – that after you've starved for a while, you mustn't eat a lot. But being unable to control myself, I did, and was very ill. Very soon we were sent off to another camp in a less cramped train with stoves in the middle of the trucks and we were issued with bread and tinned meat – food *and* warmth!

We arrived at a little village in Austria, on the Hungarian border. I remember marching in a long, long line of prisoners to a village which had a church with a double steeple and into a camp – Stalag 17A – where I stayed for three months. We were housed in a great building with three-layer platforms, and we slept on things about six foot square, three on each, three platforms one above another.

We had showers, our hair was shaved off – suddenly you can't recognise anyone! We were given warm clothes. Mine: wooden clogs, and foot cloths for winding round like socks, and a kind of Serbian uniform jacket. There was an exercise space at the end of the barrack and no work. No work meant, I suspect, that we were all medical corps, or a place where inmates were destined for work camps.

I remember very clearly, a day or two after being taken prisoner, suddenly feeling immensely relieved and light-headed. I knew where I was standing – or rather sitting! It must have been after the rush of looking after the wounded, and realising that 'I'm going to be housed, fed and watered and looked after, and be safe until the war's finished. I've got no property except a knife, fork and spoon and a blanket and no responsibilities except what I'm doing here.' Until then I had assumed I would be shot. This feeling of security wasn't logical really because as a prisoner in Germany I might well be bombed or shot at. So the feeling at first was relief, but it didn't last all that long...

But here I was in Stalag 17A. One half of the camp was for Russian prisoners. There was a double thickness of barbed wire and a roadway distance between us and them. Every day we would see corpses of those who had died being loaded onto a cart and taken out of the camp. They didn't receive Red Cross parcels and had very meagre rations. We attempted to get some of our own supplies to them without success. Sorry to say there was a Catholic priest in the camp who had special status and a room to himself, and he wouldn't help in any way. Occasionally we tried to throw food but that did more harm than good because they were so far gone with hunger that they fought for it and pushed themselves against the barbed wire. It was dreadful. Some time ago I was back in Austria and went to where this prison camp had been and was told it had 10,000 prisoners. I had no idea it was that big! I asked about the Russians and was told 'Oh, they would have been taken to the mass grave on the other side of the village.' We went over and saw where they had been taken. There was a whole field with a great monument saying 'Mass grave of Russian prisoners.' How many thousands in there? It was very upsetting. I picked three little dandelions and put them in my address book where they stayed for some months under the letter 'R'. It shocked the Austrian family I was with too. They had no idea...

Then one day, in April 1944, a group of us were put on another train to be part of a group of about forty medical orderlies of different sorts to staff a special camp. This was Stalag 4D Repatriation Camp, which was housed in a great big building, with big rooms which we used as wards. There were wooden barracks at the back in which we lived. It turned out to be the place where four lots of badly wounded, sick and mentally ill British and American prisoners were brought in to be returned to their countries in exchange for the same number of Germans who were being repatriated.

Four of these repatriations took place between April 1944 and the end of the war. The men came in, we looked after them until the Red Cross trains arrived and then took them away, then we had free time until another lot came. This was a way of sending news back to England surreptitiously. We also met a couple of FAU men who had been captured in 1941 in Greece, who were being repatriated.

The day before the repatriation, a list would go up on the notice board of those ten of the medical orderly staff chosen to go back with the repatriated. Four times this happened: before it went up you didn't know whether you'd be back home in a few days or whether you'd stay in the camp and perhaps never get back home. The first time was the worst. After that we got used to it: by the luck of the draw Dennis Westbrook and I were never on it. It was a trying time, everybody on the medical staff had the same difficulty, and those of us who had to remain felt very much drawn together. The business of being in the army or the FAU had disappeared completely by then. The issue of being a conscientious objector never cropped up. As for any difference in our outlook: I discovered that it wasn't only COs who did not think of Germans as enemies. There was a situation once on the train to Stalag 17A when the two boy-soldiers guarding us had dropped off to sleep near the stove. The train had stopped and the sliding door had been opened to give us some air. Without anybody saying 'Let's all run for it!' we woke them up, shook them, shoved their rifles in their hands and pushed them back against the door so that none of us would get into trouble when the officer came round to check all was well.

As for our status as conscientious objectors, I don't remember being given any information should I be taken prisoner before going abroad. I had a Red Cross card and number saying 'protected personnel.' Germans are very meticulous about such things, so I remember asking and being told that we were being treated the same as the Medical Corps. And that's how we were treated. Other FAU prisoners sought to get their status recognised and some did get repatriated on those conditions during the war.

The end came one day when I was out walking on some errand when I saw some German military staff cars rushing along with great speed into the camp 'The Russians are close.' the driver shouted. Then the Russians did arrive. The gates opened, they came in – mostly on bicycles – and the German guards disappeared. We heard that the dentist, who lived near the gates of the camp, had poisoned his wife and three or four children and then killed himself rather than be taken by the Russians. The anti-Russian propaganda was so enormous in the papers, they were scared stiff of them.

Then the gates were opened and the camp went a little bit wild. Some just wandered off although instructions were not to as the war was still going on down the road somewhere. We went out and walked around the town – a bit worrying going out of those gates, I didn't feel safe. There was a village green nearby and someone suggested an international football match, England v France. Now one of the camp guards, who was now disabled, was known to have been in a German team against England just pre-war. He was sought out. So the match went ahead. England v France with a German referee whose whistle was respected by both sides. It was a marvellous thing, and while we were watching in shorts, down the road in one direction huge crowds of Poles were travelling with horses and carts with a big Polish flag on top, they were making their way home. Streams were going the other way. The whole country was on the move with people trying to find their way back to their countries.

We were out walking one evening when we saw a cart approaching from one end of the village, it was travelling very slowly. As it got nearer, it was a terrible sight, some very, very ill men and boys, led by a Belgian who spoke English and explained that they were the remains of a working party from a concentration camp. A group had been rounded up and machine-gunned and these were some of the survivors. I escorted them to the camp which was now a hospital. There were about twelve or fourteen of them in a corpse-like state. A medical orderly and myself cleared a room for them and we got them into bunks. I then mixed up a jugful of very, very weak cocoa and gave each a little. The doctors came down to advise and we made it our job to look after them. One died at once, but we carried on and did what we could. Then three days later, out of the blue, came three American ambulances to fetch them – most mysterious, there must have been some radio communication somewhere. These Americans looked huge and over-fat and over-fed, but they were kindly men and lifted those who couldn't walk like babies in their arms and placed them into the ambulances. This was my one and only sight of concentration camp victims.

We were obliged to stay and run the hospital: every day there was a queue of German deserters coming out of the woods covered in mud and sores; we had Russian casualties and women from the village with sick babies – queues of people waiting to get treatment. There was a wonderful feeling of friendliness all round, an extraordinary feeling, no senior officials anywhere telling you what side you were on, who was supposed to be your enemy. War was over and it was a great feeling.

It was late in the war, September 1944, when Humphrey Waterfield and Ray Birkett were captured whilst they were serving with the 2nd French Armoured Division*. The drive on Epinal had started when the Division came up against a strong Panzer counter-attack during which they were captured as they were returning wounded from the battle, taken to a prison in Clomar where they stayed for five days, thence to Strasbourg where they were put into a cage already crowded with French and Americans. After two days of extreme discomfort, they were moved to an old French military hospital where they became resigned to POW life which by then had become one frighteningly long air-raid. As this was not an official camp, they were not able to receive letters or parcels. The food situation was desperate: one small loaf a week, a thin soup once a

---

* See Chapter 10.

day. Humphrey Waterfield told his friend Nancy Tennant that he couldn't stop himself thinking of food and dreamt nightly of plum cake. (4) Yet he was able to look on this experience positively.

Humphrey Waterfield:

I had Aeschylus, Ray had nothing. We were still a great deal better off than many people – prison after all is but a reduction ad absurdum of the military life – just one degree more intolerable to the free man. As a pacifist I was glad of the experience, glad to experience hunger, glad to pass through the looking glass, to find a world, oh so like our own, propaganda so exactly mirroring propaganda; only as is the way with mirrors, the image a tone or two lower than our own. If one did see, on occasion, the face that might have launched a thousand whips, it was pleasant to find from personal experience, what no propaganda now can shake, that there are far more bearing patiently, courageously, and with acts of kindness the experience that the folly of their government has unleashed upon them, an experience so like, only now so much worse, than our own.(5)

When the French arrived in early December, Humphrey Waterfield was asked by the Camp Commandant to arrange their surrender. Having tied a sheet onto a broom, he walked into Strasbourg, accompanied by the commandant – who evidently kept asking him to wave it harder – only to find they were being rescued by his own 2nd Armoured Division. He and Ray Birkett, both now in a very weakened state, were taken straight to hospital, but not before he had ensured that their erstwhile captors would be well treated. (6)

REFERENCES:

(1) Wild, David 1992, *Prisoner of Hope*, Book Guild, Lewes.
(2) Lidbetter, H.M. 1993, *op. cit.* pp.101, 106.
(3) Wild David, *op cit.* p.66.
(4) Interview Lyn Smith with Nancy Tennant. August 1997.
(5) *Chronicle* article, *Through the Looking Glass,* late 1944.
(6) Letter Nancy Tennant to Lyn Smith. August 10, 1997.

CHAPTER 17

France: Availability, Continuity and Intelligent Cooperation

*A*S SECTIONS WERE *moving forward with the invading Allies through Belgium, Holland and into Germany, opportunity for more worthwhile work opened in France. In January 1945, a section of ten men, led by Michael Cadbury, arrived in Paris with six four-ton lorries which they delivered to Entr'aide Française, the official French relief service, hoping to work under its auspices. At that time there were no FAU sections in France and news had filtered through to London HQ of the streams of French refugees returning to their villages which had been totally destroyed in the invasion fighting. To their disappointment and frustration the FAU section discovered on arrival in Paris that although the lorries were welcomed by the French, the men were not. Michael Cadbury then had the task, as he put it, 'of stumping around Paris, trying to find some organisation under which we could operate.' Eventually, a small group of the section left with two kitchen cars to provide meals for refugees returning to their villages and the rest found temporary work with Secours Quaker, the French Quakers' relief committee. Then a breakthrough came when news filtered through that a new organisation – American Relief for France (ARF) had been set up and supplies were piling up at the dockside in France with no personnel to distribute them. An offer to help was made by the FAU and readily accepted. Michael Cadbury became the ARF's Technical Director.*

Michael Cadbury:

The ARF which had access to the American war-chest had got a lot of money for resources and no way of distributing it; and we had means of distributing the resources. So from then on life became easy. We wore both badges – ARF and FAU – and we set up four centres where we distributed food and clothing to returning refugees as well as providing general help.

At one stage we had a fleet of a hundred lorries going up and down the roads of France; a lot from army stock – British and American – often battered six tonners, but they did the job.

The British Army supplies rounded up after Dunkirk by the Germans had all been impounded at Coutances and there seemed to be miles of trucks, rows of this and that: spares, engines, tyres, and all the records had been destroyed. These were no good to the Americans and there were no British Army vehicles in France at that time, so we used to write out order permissions and go and help ourselves to whatever we needed. We got all the spares we wanted as well as new vehicles and in this way we kept ourselves in business.

Fuel had been a problem with the French who wanted nothing to do with us. But as soon as we merged with the Americans – no problem. They laid oil pipelines from the channel ports to every part of France. All along the main roads there would be a pipeline running along with petrol stations dotted along and any credited vehicle could just fill up and on you go. Really, we had complete autonomy: with the ARF/FAU stamp on documents we could go anywhere we liked in France, buy stuff in the PX, have a meal, fill up with petrol – and off. It was *marvellous.*

It was a good relationship with the fighting forces being willing to acknowledge an outfit like us. We made real Quaker contact because they would say 'Who on earth are you odd people?' And we would spin a pacifist and conscientious story which would be quite monstrous to some of them, but others would say 'Oh, I wish I had taken that stand!' One or two of our people got our backs up because they went about proselytising but very soon they realised the importance of not overstepping the mark and played it quietly – 'by their deeds be recognised'. I think we did a useful pacifist propaganda job just by being there.

Many of the towns had been completely devastated by the retreating Germans. In April 1945, we were told to go to St Dié where, in November 1944, not a house was left standing; the cathedral museum, hospital and seven schools had also been systematically destroyed and all the bridges blown behind the retreating Germans, leaving 13,000 people refugees at the beginning of winter. The Germans as they were about to withdraw told the people 'Your house is going to be destroyed, you have six hours to get out.' and they systematically went through each street and every house putting in a charge of dynamite, and up they went. Now they were coming home. They had no food, no clothing, no household utensils – everything had been burned or looted by the Germans. We managed to get two vehicles down there. We were received by the Mayor who gave us a ruin as our HQ, where we could prepare food for the refugees as they came back. We were also able to get clothes and other supplies mainly through the AFSC at first and then once our relationship was formed, through the ARF. This was the first job we did in France: feeding the people and distributing clothes.

The team in St Dié was built up to half-a-dozen and they stayed on for two years and did a splendid job, coping with whatever was needed at any particular stage and soon they became very much part of the developing community. That's what happened to all the French sections: each one went in on an emergency basis and then moved into the community reacting to local needs. The devastation in this town was appalling. What they had to do was to build a new town. First they put up temporary wooden huts and the people came into the town into the huts, each intending to rebuild their own homes.

The second place was Coutances, out on the marsh on the Cherbourg peninsula. That had been destroyed by the British. It had been a very nice old-world fishing village and had been more or less flattened from the sea as the British troops moved down, and there was a bitter, bitter feeling at first which quickly changed when they realised that we had come to help them rebuild their village. There again, two of our food lorries went in, starting our relief with food. And we were able to get nets for the fishermen and motor engines for some of their boats, and helped with housing, food and clothing – the whole business of building up the community again. We had a good section of ten men there in the end, and they stayed for a couple of years. In fact one of our men married a local girl and settled there building up a boat-building business. So we integrated with the population in the best sense of the word.

Another place was Metz – in the north-eastern corner of France where the fighting had been very intense. Again, much the same picture: the place destroyed, the people coming back to homes which didn't exist and without even the basic fundamentals of life. So jobs like helping with drainage, finding timber, getting glass and clothing and food; and constantly feeding in supplies of food because the French system of distribution was a bit low. An awful lot was getting lost on the black market – the black market was also taking food out of the agricultural areas so for great sections of the population there was no food at all; a very difficult period for the whole of that year, 1945. The French Government was doing very little because it was too divided. You still had the two divisions: the Gaullists and the communists who all through the resistance had been fighting each other. And once de Gaulle was back, the others were sabotaging what was going on. So it was a very unsettled, irresolute, irregular Government and it was really local rather than national support that got things going. The country was in a dreadful state. We'd had our blitz, true, but France had suffered beyond belief in the destruction of its infrastructure, what with the occupation, the invasion and sabotage of key points.

Dunkirk was an area of sentimental concern to us. The Unit had worked there during the 1914-1918 war and many in the town remembered this. It was very badly damaged of course, being a potential invasion base. Our people did much the same thing as in the other destroyed places.

Our relationship with the Americans was very interesting and good. With their help we got the vehicles, and the supplies, and we had convoys going out from the centre in Paris to these four main points and then smaller vehicles on the spot to get to specific destinations. This was immensely satisfying – a very rewarding period. I was only a stooge in the office but the people in the front line were doing a wonderful job.

France at this time was a very sad place to be in: we were in Paris where probably the pressures were greater. The whole place was down at heel. The electricity would go off three or four times a day. You got stuck in lifts. Gas would suddenly go out, no warning.

Nothing worked. The water would suddenly be off. You had two classes: those who managed to get by and were doing very well, and others who didn't and were enduring great difficulties. There was an enormous black market and virtually no food in the shops. It was an embarrassing place to be driving around in a car and trying to distribute what we had in a fair kind of way. So it was a sad city, but a city that was beginning to shrug off the dreadful atmosphere of people enslaved. This was the hardest thing for us to grasp – the occupation atmosphere and that pervaded the whole of France in 1945 into 1946. It was something psychological: people were bitter and there was no trust. To see the few surviving Jews creep back – that sort of thing hurt enormously. One could understand the extreme hatred the French felt for the Germans; you could see this was justified by the things they had suffered. Collaborators were treated in a devastating way: women had their heads shaved, people were ostracised, beaten up, quite a few were killed. That sense of living hate was something horrible to see. Fortunately it died off fairly quickly. Because it was so intense, it just couldn't last.

During this time in France, my mind would go back to the original training camp when Stanley Mackintosh, the training officer, said the essence of relief work is: availability, continuity and intelligent cooperation.[1] Availability: it's no good being frightfully well organised if you're not there when the crises happen. You've got to be available whatever happens. Continuity: you've got to have your sources of supplies, you've got to be able to keep going once you start. But most important of all is intelligent cooperation: if you get in a situation, you can't do anything on your own, you've got to work with anyone else who's there. This may mean very difficult situations, very awkward people. Unless you cooperate intelligently, you've no hope of doing anything worthwhile. This is very good training for relief work, but the thing behind it is the caring spirit. What you've got to do is to put yourself in the place of the person. Can you get across to the person as an individual? Then, even if you can't do much for them, they feel a sense of caring. It's not always easy, people are often awkward and difficult when they are in painful distress. Be practical, yes, but have something behind it – *giving* rather than just serving out ham sandwiches. So, I think, the three plus a little bit of caring.

As the war in Europe drew to its close in the summer of 1945, planning regarding the future of the Unit had started. The assumption had been made – correctly as it turned out – that the release of conscientious objectors would, like the armed services, be based on age and length of service. The decision was made that FAU, World War II, should end on 30 June 1946. As we have seen from the experiences described above, there were closures of fields of activity, or continuity of service under the auspices of other relief organisations such as the FRS, UNRRA, AFSC, the BRC, or the ARF which offered such a satisfying field of service to Michael Cadbury's section.

But the vexed issue of conscription was still in place and who could tell just how long it would continue. One the one hand it was recognised that the Unit had not been set up to provide alternative services in peacetime, yet it seemed likely that the wartime National Services Act would continue to exist before any firm decision was taken on a peacetime policy. The question was asked and debated at length: should young pacifists who decided to take their stand in peacetime be given the same opportunities as Unit members had been offered during the war? Eventually the decision was made by the relevant committees that a provisional and distinct unit, the FAU Post-War Service (FAU/PWS), should be set up to cover the period of transition.

As the policy of continuing conscription consolidated with the onset of cold war, in 1948 the FAU/PWS was replaced by the FAU International Service (FAU/IS), which continued until the end of conscription in 1959. [2] *Deryck Moore was one of those whose experience straddled the transition from wartime FAU into PWS. It was July 1944 when he entered Manor Farm for initial training. After further training in Hammersmith Hospital during the flying bombs period, he was sent to Germany soon after VE Day to join the sections there. He stayed for a year looking after transport at HQ in Vlotho as well as helping other sections on the transport side.*

Deryck Moore:

It was during my time in Germany that what we laughingly called 'the true FAU' was coming to an end. Because conscription was still ongoing, it was decided to form the PWS bringing in new COs leaving school in a non-wartime situation. I was asked what I wanted to do: to transfer to the Red Cross or transfer to the PWS.

I was very happy to continue with FAU/PWS, my demob wasn't for another couple of years, so I went back home to Britain to train some PWS men on a six week course in mechanics. Towards the end of that time, there came an appeal from the Red Cross in Paris for some help.

Basically, the story is this: between the wars, an orphanage had been set up in Caen for war orphans. This had survived throughout the war in difficult circumstances until the Falaise Gap battles when the Germans wanted to fortify it for their own use and they had kicked all the kids out. The Germans offered no advice as to where they should go, other than to suggest that they should all go down a nearby mine. This was right in the middle of the war zone, and Father Charles Lavallois, who was in charge of the orphans, didn't think it wise to go there. So he gave every kid a white pillowcase to wave and said 'Right, we'll walk to Paris!' And those kids, caught up in the Falaise Gap battles, walked right through waving their pillowcases and got to Paris, where Lavallois went up to the Ministry

First PWS training camp – 1946 Manor Farm.

October 1946, Vauréal. Bill Boreland, Harold Dellar, Deryck Moore and Brian Priestman with the famous HGH 68 Bedford truck.

of Health people and said 'I've got 120 orphans. I want a home for them.'

The Minister said 'Sorry, there's not a chance anywhere.' So Lavallois said 'Well, they're in the streets outside, they're all yours!' and started to walk out. Twenty-four hours later he was given the château of Vauréal, one of the many homes of a French chocolate manufacturer.[3] This had been occupied by the Germans and then the Americans and everybody else had had a go at the place. Now it was totally empty and the kids were dumped there with Father Lavallois, his sister and a group of school mistresses, with sickness, illness and no money. They didn't know what to do for food. The French people they appealed to said their only hope was to contact one of the relief organisations. They went to the American Red Cross in Paris who said 'Look, we can't do anything, but there's an oddball organisation called the FAU in London, we'll phone them.' So we took on the problem and I was given three chaps, a truck, some French money and off we went and drove into this place one October night in 1946. I went in and met the Catholic Father. 'We're here to see what we can do to help' I said. 'We're a funny crowd of conchies, you can take us on our word. Let's see what we can do.' He couldn't believe that we would work for nothing, that we only wanted our keep. He thought we were pulling his leg.

We spent the first week going around the château to see what needed doing. There were structural and decorating problems. But the first problem was money. The only way we could get some was to sell wood from the trees which were greatly overgrown, so professional forresters were brought in and the priest saw to the endless negotiations, and that's what happened.

We set about getting the place sorted out: beds repaired so that the kids could sleep properly. Then in the winter of 1946/47 there was a fearful gastric flu epidemic, everyone was laid low with it, we were acting as nurses and cleaners. Father Lavallois got pneumonia. The doctor gave me injections to give him. It was quite extraordinary where my Hammersmith hospital training came back: cleanliness, sterility – all that.

Christmas was coming. 'Are you chaps going home for Christmas?' the priest asked. 'Not at all, we shall be with you,' we said. 'Well, let's try and devise a Catholic mass and a Quaker service' he said. It was quite extraordinary; they had their mass in this little chapel, then the priest took off his robes and we all sat in their chapel in the manner of Friends' worship. And I read the Christmas story in English and French – it was the most extraordinary, uplifting spiritual experience. To think that we had broken across the great barrier of Roman Catholicism! I think he would have been excommunicated if it were known that he had lowered his guard as it were, but he wanted to pay tribute to us. So we had a very impoverished but very happy Christmas and it made us think that we enjoyed it for the real spirit of Christ's birth, not because of presents and all the trimmings.

In the following January we were virtually out of food, so short that I got on my bike and went to the Red Cross in Paris and said 'What are you going to do? You've got to help me; I've got to get food.' And I couldn't believe it, this chap took me down into this lorry park and said 'There's a 'big Mac' truck there, it's just come in, solid with food – butter, margarine, meats, soups, everything....just take it!' 'What about the truck?' 'Oh, get it back to me sometime.' So I drove this left-hand, big six-wheeler truck back and made the mistake of taking it into the Champs Elysées, where no trucks were allowed. And this policeman nearly blew the pea out of his whistle trying to stop me. I put the brakes on and everything skidded and I was going straight for him and he ran for his life, and I drove out of the Champs Elysées and back to the orphanage, arriving like a saviour from heaven. This food lasted us for at least three weeks, and we're talking of eighty people at that time.

The children were divided into little family groups. Each one of our team adopted a group. I adopted the little nippers, and the girl who was a baby in my group came to stay with us when she was a teenager in 1955. She is now married with a family. They were getting a good education there, very practical: it was run as a school, and the lessons started from the word go. They had the August holiday off. Occasionally we took them out in the truck – a bit risky. I was never too happy with too many kids in the back. Once, we put on a huge carnival for the village who were dying to see what had happened to the orphanage. We charged them at the

M'an By's 'Little Tots' at Vauréal in 1947.

gate and put on all kinds of sideshows to get money for the orphanage, and they paid willingly.

We got into desperate situations: we had to cope with burglaries and people pinching wood. We used to have patrols and sticks to threaten the robbers with – I'm sorry, it might not sound pacific, but they were taking what amounted to our livelihood and we certainly weren't going to talk to them for long! The estate was huge, very much run-down but very beautiful. We bought a cow with a calf from money raised in England. So we started to farm with the help of a farmer. There were huge areas of arable land covered with brambles and rubbish. We lit huge bonfires and got rid of all this; we got a plough and ploughed it up and got the farm working. So we had our own vegetables. We over-planted tomatoes and got such a bumper crop in the summer of 1947 that we had tomatoes coming out of our ears!

I used to get in touch with London and say 'Two more carpenters please.' And they would send two lads who'd been good at carpentry at school to repair the chairs, beds and doorways. One of them was Bill Boreland, an ex-milk lorry driver from Belfast who had taken a pacifist stand. Bill and I were in a car one day when a cyclist came out of a side road and there was nothing Bill could do, and the cyclist was killed. Well, this put a complete blanket on us for a while. Until then we were looked at as the young team who were doing something for the orphanage, then we got these vibes of 'The military are there and they've killed my son.' Father Lavallois said 'Are you coming to the funeral?' 'Certainly' I said. 'Are you going to wear your uniform?' 'Yes.' And we went to this funeral and it was probably the most stressful thing I've ever experienced. I could feel that everybody in the room hated me. I couldn't let Bill go. Like everyone else, I had to make the sign of the cross over the coffin with the Holy Water. At the end of the mass, the priest, who was not Father Lavallois, said 'That's the funeral over, but we have reason to believe that it was the fault of the man in the coffin, not the driver, and we all know what a good job they've been doing there.' You could feel the atmosphere change, and everyone became friendly. But that was an awful half-hour.

What worried Father Lavallois and his staff more than anything was that we were four young healthy men, and apart from one boy, all the orphans were girls. I said 'Don't worry, they're all under my discipline, all will be well.' When we first arrived, he had invited us to eat with them in the main refectory. I said to our little team, as it then was, 'We'll put on our FAU uniform for the meal. We are going to be neat and smart, none of this old shoes and overalls for the meal. We'll show them that we are a disciplined force.' This was what I had learnt in Germany: if you're going into a situation, play and maintain the part. Throughout our time there we maintained this discipline.

But of course you can never do that sort of thing without having fun. It's the spirit that comes into community service, you get a lot of fellowship. It was a good time. I think under stress and pressure you get the best coming out of people and there were a lot of comedians amongst us and this got us through many a situation. We had to be careful that we weren't laughing at the French, many times we wanted to with their funny ways. Some of the locals would ask for a hand and we'd say 'You're not going to put that telegraph pole there are you?' 'Why not?' 'That's where your new road's going!'

I was twenty years old when I first went there and had my 21st birthday there. I had matured very quickly in Germany. It was only in later years that I realised that I had the hand of God guiding me in some way. I wouldn't want the responsibility I had then now. Jack Eglon, the commandant of PWS would come over occasionally to see what was happening, and we could struggle through to get a call to London if we wanted help and you'd get advice, but it took precious reserves and normally, in the FAU manner, we'd be told 'Look, you're the boss, you make your own decision, we'll back you even if your decision is wrong.' They accepted that only we knew the full circumstances.

So, the initial four of us went for six weeks and stayed for fifteen months with our numbers up to fifteen; and we finally got state-aided and very well established. I feel it was the FAU/PWS at its very best, able to give tremendous personal service in practical ways. Because we were doing that we developed a wonderful camaraderie with those French Catholics. When I was married, my wife, Anne, and I went back to see them on our honeymoon, and the links have continued.

REFERENCES:

[1] Like GADA, (Go Anywhere, Do Anything,) this became a Unit motto, A Unit wag (Paul Townsend) paraphrased it as 'Availability, contiguity and intelligent copulation.'

[2] For further details see Bush, R. *FAU. The Third Generation: The Friend's Ambulance Unit Post-War Service and International Service.* William Sessions, York, 1998.

[3] La Maison d'enfants du Clos, Vauréal, near Pontoise in Seine-et-Oise. Other PWS projects, with orphans were opened, for instance at the Château de Grouchy, Osny. See Bush, 1998, *ibid.* Ch. 3.

PART FOUR

TEST OF WAR

CHAPTER 18

The FAU: A New Set of Horizons

> Already for us who were its members, the Unit begins to recede
> into the past. Some day we may perhaps see it in its true per-
> spective, but in 1946 we, like the rest of mankind, are too close
> to the tremendous events of the war years to see aright the Unit's
> place in the pattern. Indeed it will never be possible for us who
> served in the Unit to view it dispassionately from without. It was
> not a mere interruption of a few years in our normal existence.
> The Unit has become woven into the fabric of our lives.
>
> A. Tegla Davies.[1]

*A*S THE WAR *was drawing to a close and with members
returning home from their overseas postings, Tegla Davies undertook the daunting task of compiling an 'official history' of the Unit's
wartime experience. Helped by a team of Unit members with experience
from all fields of service both at home and abroad, the history was published in 1947. Although fifty years is a mere blip in historical terms,
surviving Unit members feel that the time is ripe to take up Davies' challenge.*

*What then can be said about the FAU's role in the pattern of World
War Two? The vast range and sheer diversity of the Unit's experience is
certainly an important factor. Serving, as it did, on the Home Front and
on all fronts abroad from neighbouring France to far-flung countries such
as Ethiopia and China, we not only get reports of wartime activity in
these places, but we are also given a different perspective, with the war
being seen through the eyes of non-combatants who were relatively
detached from the war machine. Even with those in the thick of the fray,*

there is little sense of 'them' or 'us', no firm line between the 'right' or the 'wrong' side. The propaganda of both sides is generally discounted, and terms such as 'heroism,' 'sacrifice,' 'patriotism,' 'victory,' and 'defeat' have entirely different connotations from those usually accepted. True, the Unit formed only a tiny fragment of a whole world in turmoil. Nevertheless, the FAU story provides a valuable counterbalance to military accounts of the last war and deserves its place in World War II bibliographies.

The FAU story has also to be seen within the context of the overall pacifist/conscientious objection story of World War Two. All pacifists and conscientious objectors liable for conscription in the Second World War were brought up under the shadow of the Great War, and a very high proportion trace the roots of their beliefs back to the inhumane slaughter and subsequent disillusionment with that war. Fathers had been wounded and left unemployed, gassed uncles wheezed away their lives and many of their peers had been left fatherless. They had read the poetry of Wilfred Owen and Siegfried Sassoon, seen films about the war, heard first-hand stories of the trenches, and had grown up used to the sight of the maimed.

Tom Barnsley:

We'd taken on board the terrible, *terrible* 1914-1918 war and what seemed a totally needless loss of life in the ghastly conditions of the trenches. I suppose really that many of us were revolting against *that* war... plus the fact that after all the millions of deaths, the politicians, with the Versailles Treaty, led us from one terrible situation which was building up to another...

Another important legacy from the Great War was the example of the conscientious objectors in that war. Those who became pacifists in the Second World War realised that whatever they had to face in the war, their experience would not be as harsh. For it was the COs of the Great War who, enduring humiliations and abuses such as physical punishment, the loneliness of solitary confinement, and the exhausting 'cat and mouse' routine, had stood up for and tested the right of individual conscience against the state, and paved the way for their Second World War counterparts to make their witness against war and be received with greater understanding.

Michael Cadbury:

My two uncles were in the Great War and they went on ambulance trains to carry vast numbers of slaughtered men from the front back to base hospitals under shell fire. We didn't do much train work in World War Two, but the range of other things we did was enormous. Of course we were able to cash in on the status COs had gained because of their contribution to the First World War – those who went to prison, for example. Many Quakers spent years in prison in that war before the FAU was recognised and allowed to go in. That was the contribution that paved the way for our generation. We were able to build on top of a mountain which they had scaled on our behalf. Theirs was a less imaginative but a harder grind than ours because it was sheer slogging in the mud. We were able to do much more exciting work – just as dirty, just as risky but far, far more variety and interest. And our status was there from the beginning. This was entirely thanks to the First War conchies. We also had the magnanimity of government and public opinion which had been changed largely through those who went to prison in the First World War.

It wasn't only would-be COs who had gained from the Great War. As Neville Chamberlain said in May 1939 'We learned something about this (tenacity of COs) in the Great War, and I think we found that it was both a useless and exasperating waste of time and effort to force such people to act in a manner which is contrary to their principles.'[2] Neville Chamberlain had been a member of the Birmingham Tribunal during the Great War and was anxious when he became Prime Minister in 1939 that COs should be given a fair hearing. Tribunals had members appointed by a central government department and the representation on panels was changed, with no role given to military representatives as prosecutors, as had happened in the Great War, and ordinary people were brought in. The right of absolute exemption was also respected.

Tod Lawry:

I've thought a lot about this since I had my tribunal in Bristol in November 1939. I was given unconditional exemption which gave me a choice of any other occupation I wished to take up. It was an extraordinary thing, an astonishing, noble thing for a government to do. To allow young men – and there were hundreds of us – to put our principles into effect even though being a government at war they must have disagreed with the stance we were taking. Yet they granted us that freedom. I don't know of any other country that did such a thing with the possible exception of New Zealand...This had one particular effect on my life. In China during the war when we were on long distance convoys or during periods of enforced inactivity when you had time to read or think, I made the decision that if I survived the war I would devote the rest of my life to some form of national service. That I had an obligation to repay my country for the degree of freedom it had given me.[3]

Michael Harris:

Is it possible to be a patriot and a CO? Yes. Because you can contribute to your country in other ways than fighting. It's a matter of definition: to die for one's country is one thing, to support your country in other ways – in citizenship and working for society – is also patriotic. When you look at some of the good work the Unit did at home and all over the world, I think in a strange way that the FAU gave Britain a good name, not least because so many people admired Britain for taking that liberal attitude even at times like Dunkirk when we were really up against it. At such a time they were still prepared to give recognition to the consciences that dictated they should do otherwise than fight. That's really what Britain gained from the whole thing.

Most Unit members have appreciated the difficult job Tribunals faced. Tom Haley felt 'They had an impossible job to do. There was no way in which a Tribunal could infallibly say "This man or woman is sincere and deserves to be protected and not hounded and certainly not shot for his or her views." You can't look inside somebody's heart and head, so that's an impossible job but really they did their absolute best.' Others, paradoxically, felt that, despite the far greater psychological and physical suffering, it was easier to remain a CO in the Great War compared with the more accepting attitudes of the Second World War.

David Morris:

If I had been tortured, I would have been a coward and I would have soon given up my belief. But if I had been sent to prison I could have stood that alright, and I would have then said 'Damn that for a lark! I may or may not be right to be a conscientious objector but I'm not going to give up now they've put me in prison.' So it would have relieved me of the burden of having to continue to worry about the problem. That, I think, is certainly my case and I think the case of plenty of my friends and contemporaries who registered as COs. One of the reasons why we *did* change over and go into the forces was that we were continually exploring our beliefs in a way which we wouldn't have done if we had been persecuted.

As for public opinion: the media seems to have kept an interested eye on the Unit, publicising their various activities, especially the more far-flung and dramatic areas of service such as India, Burma and China. Members on the whole appreciated this coverage although often squirming at headlines such as one in the Sunday Pictorial, September 6, 1942 'Would you call them COWARDS?' then outlining in heroic terms FAU activities abroad and comparing them with the CO 'slackers' and 'miserable cowards' working on the home front.

Doug Turner:

We used to attract a fair share of press attention and often appreciated it and sometimes had a good laugh at how we were portrayed. But there were times when we felt pretty uncomfortable and embarrassed, especially when we were presented as paragons of virtue compared with other conchies doing work just as valuable but perhaps not so newsworthy.

Most FAU men, along with their fellow COs, suffered at some stage a degree of personal insult: 'yellow belly,' 'dirty conchie,' 'shirker,' and suchlike. Some recall incidents which upset them. Eric Jones recalls: 'The only really hurtful thing that happened to me was after the war at home. My friend who joined the Navy was killed very soon after war's outbreak on a minesweeper. I had grown up with him from a tiny tot...I used to send his mother a Christmas card and after the war I met her and said "Hello," and she said "Some folks come home, others hasn't," and just walked away. That hurt.' But public hostility was nothing like the prejudice and abuse endured by COs of the Great War and there were no white feathers handed out. Being in uniform sometimes helped, if only for their families' sake. Donald Swann remembers 'my father certainly bucked up when I walked down our street in my khaki uniform – smiles all round.' It was when first-hand cooperation with civilians increased with the blitz and other humanitarian service that relations warmed and genuine understanding of what the Unit was about was achieved. Margery Parker was working at the Hammersmith Hospital as a medical social worker during the flying bomb attacks in 1944.

Margery Parker:

...I began to realise that there were these young men around the casualty department who were wearing brown overalls with some kind of badge on them. These were described to me as Quakers who were conscientious objectors and they were training in the casualty department presumably in preparation for working with the medical services for the forces. They also did odd jobs, like taking messages around the hospital – that's how I met them because they would sometimes come into my office with a message from a doctor wanting to see me, that sort of thing.

Two things struck me: one was that they were well educated young men and were very much at home in the hospital atmosphere. The second was that they had very good relationships with the staff. I must say this surprised me at the time because I had the usual conventional picture of conscientious objectors as having a hard time. I had heard comments around me as a child like 'He's a conchie, disgusting!' – that sort of thing. But they seemed cheerful and friendly and very self-assured, and they were very popular with the general staff. Although many had contacts with the forces, and there were members of the forces coming in and out of the hospital all the time, nobody was making remarks about 'conchies' or commenting on the fact that these obviously strong and healthy, good-looking young men were not actually in the forces.

It struck me that there must be something very nice about them that they were so accepted. Partly, I think, because they were not in the least apologetic. You got the feeling that they were really quite

proud of their status, or certainly that they felt they were people
with an important point of view. Later, of course, I met the full
Quaker and conscientious experience when I married Tony...

*One of the greatest challenges the FAU faced in the Second World
War concerned the need to work closely with the fighting forces without
violating integrity of conscience. Often the Unit was criticised for its compromise by members of the Society of Friends, or absolutist COs. Within
the Unit itself, there was the worry about maintaining a separate identity and resisting being swallowed into a military system. On an individual level members often worried how they were going to be accepted?
It seems that FAU women had an advantage, as Marjorie Asquith
explained: 'I think it was much easier for us to get on with the troops. I
assume they felt it was acceptable for women not to be warlike. But I
think the men had a rather more awful time with the military. I never
saw anything directly because this wouldn't be done before a woman, but
I often sensed it.' Yet, although there were cases of mutual dislike and disapproval, and there was often bewilderment as to who exactly these odd-
bods were, as war progressed and interactions increased feelings of mutual
respect usually developed between the FAU and service personnel. Given
the nature of FAU service, it was the Army rather than the Navy or
RAF they served alongside.*

Derryck Hill:

When we worked with Number 1 Mobile Hospital for a while
as drivers, from the start the Lieutenant-Colonel in charge made
it clear that it didn't want the FAU. He saw us as 'yellow bellies'
and 'softies.' He made life very difficult for our section leader, Peter
Gibson, with his petty obstructions. That was something we'd never
met in our 15th CCS. In fact they made us feel that we were something special and took pride in us. When we were mentioned in the
7th Armoured Division dispatches as a unit involved in
Auchinleck's push...well, you should have heard the elation of the
troops!

Ronald Joynes:

The Sergeants were the backbone of the army. We had great
respect for them. When we arrived in Alex, we wondered what sort

of treatment we'd get as conchies. Would they regard us as effeminate? But no, we were immediately taken under their wing. We could play football and hockey, often better than the troops, and that helped – when we played soccer in Sweden, we won hands down because we had two 'Blues' in our midst. Of course the army did everything by number and we thought them inefficient in many ways, but we sometimes saw sense behind it. We heard stories of the odd looting or rape in Norway, and I would say that they drank more than we did, and every other word was of four letters. But I found some very good men in the army. I even had a sergeant dancing partner!

I have been told many times how the nearer Sections came to the war zones, the more tolerance and understanding was found. Many have spoken of the feelings of respect, sympathy and friendship they felt for the troops with whom they shared imprisonment, dangers, wounds and sometimes death, realising that their detestation of war was shared by many front-line soldiers. They were also constantly being reminded of their dependency on the armed forces, both for providing the opportunities they cherished for front-line service as well as the protection provided by them. As the liberation of occupied zones increased, they also appreciated the important role army personnel played in the humanitarian field. They were also conscious of their own privileged position as volunteers with a degree of choice denied those acting under military discipline and having to obey orders, however distasteful or terrifying the task.

Donald Swann:

During my spell of working with the army, far from thinking they were all bullies I'd learnt to respect many of them. I felt in a way that we had got a far better deal than the troops, that they were going to have a rougher time, and some would even be pitched into the front, whereas I would get to a place behind the front and never be allowed in a shooting area. I learned later, when meeting ex-servicemen at Oxford, that many had questioned their position and suffered crises of conscience and deep despair. There have been times in later years when I've felt that some of the most pacific people I know are in the forces. When you think about it, they are the ones who strive to keep the peace and are ready to suffer and die for it. In many circumstances they stand between warring factions. They seek a reasoned world where you can at least order people to do something, rather than the maniacal world of total anarchy. Indeed, paradoxically, some of them have worked very hard for the peace movement, especially in the nuclear age. Brigadier Michael Harbottle and the Generals for Peace movement is an example. During the cold war years of the past decade he drew the military from east and west together in a continuing dialogue. And how about ex-servicemen's Campaign Against Nuclear War?

This is not to suggest that there were no misunderstandings or tensions between the FAU and service personnel. Often these came to the fore when members were caring for wounded troops.

Brian Bone:

I went into the kitchen of a military ward at Gloucester to find a young wounded soldier there. He looked at me: 'Conchie?' 'Yes.' 'Why? Come on, I'll buy it.' What does one say to a wounded and shell-shocked soldier? I mumbled 'It depends how you interpret the Bible.' 'Listen', he said, 'I joined up under age and went to France. We went over the top. My pal was shot down as we ran. He clasped his belly and said 'Mother' – you always think of your mother. Then we were on the Dunkirk beaches. We found a German hiding, and held his face under the water till he drowned.' I stood still and heard him out. Then I picked up my meal tins and headed for the door. As I reached it he called out in a friendly voice 'So long mate', and I replied 'cheerio.' Was it because I listened?

Dilemmas abounded, and one which cropped up from the earliest campaign in Finland and lasted throughout the war was the argument concerning the transport of troops and war materials on the Red Cross lorries used by the FAU. With Jerry just over the hill and advancing quickly, how could they remain so obdurate in their refusal? In later years many members wondered and often agonised whether they had been petty and trivial arguing about issues which during the war had seemed so important. But the essential point was that one small compromise after another would have meant a gradual acceptance of war and an erosion of their pacifism.

Something which often led to arguments in front-line areas was the insistence of FAU in treating 'the enemy' wounded on an equal basis. Bill Spray, who worked in front-line zones with the Free French, often faced such problems. 'It was part of our creed that we were going to treat the German wounded equally. On the whole we carried the French with us on this, but I don't think they would have done it had we not been there. But we'd say to a doctor "Come on, there's this chap as well" and that encouraged him to do what he might have been diffident about doing.'

Many tributes have been paid to the FAU by the army personnel they worked alongside. We have seen that the first FAU men to land in north-west Europe after D Day, at Courselleus, on June 23, 1944 were the only Unit section to serve with the British Liberation Army as a Forward Surgical Unit – 12 FSU. They were continually on the move through France, Belgium, Holland and Germany, serving with various army medical units, including one under Major Clifford Brewer. They are noteworthy as being the FAU group most closely integrated with the British Army, as mentioned in a report to the FAU Executive Committee: '...I was surprised to find how very different was the attitude of those whom I saw to that of the relief sections. They seemed very involved in the army set-up and to take a very limited view of the Unit and its work. I think, however, that they were more or less holding their own as pacifists according to their lights...'(4)

Major Clifford Brewer:

It was somewhat disconcerting to find these pacifists posted to my FSU because at first I didn't know how to get on with people who were not really military: they were very informal, had no ranks, and called each other by their first names. But I quickly got their measure. The clerk for instance had been reporter on a local newspaper and would type the evacuation reports as fast as I could dictate, which was a huge advantage in the forward areas we served. The drivers too were fully trained in engineering and electronics and three of them were graduates. One of them found some discarded small German searchlights and mounted them to provide fantastic lighting for our mobile operating theatre. We probably treated some 2,000 casualties in three months and performed 600 operations. I would say our standard was higher than the normal FSUs. So instead of being difficult to work with, they were a crack unit of very high quality. I have nothing but praise for them.

Robin Whitworth:

Throughout the war the FAU had built up its reputation and the army came to understand our worth: they knew what we stood for, they knew we wanted to do all we could for humanitarian work, that although we would not assist the prosecution, we would not hinder the war. And that they respected – our purpose and integrity – and they trusted us with their secrets and gave us great freedom of action.

As for the Allied forces, one can only admire the way in which army officers accommodated units of men whom they often found bewildering, difficult and infuriating. In short, the FAU–military relationship in the Second World War is a tribute to both the Allied armies and the Unit. Of course, the FAU were not the only pacifists who undertook dangerous and risky front-line work with the armed forces in the war. (5) What distinguished the FAU was the high degree of Unit cohesion, and the efficiency of the FAU organisational back-up.

As with any oral history undertaking, asking FAU members to remember events of more than fifty years ago was fraught with problems of accuracy of recall; this was especially so when it came to recalling thoughts and emotions of the times. But all struggled, even agonised to get it 'right' – to separate out the then from the now; and to distinguish their more mature selves and judgments from the green youngsters they then were. However, when it came to reflecting on what the FAU had meant to them at the time, there was no hesitation. Practically everyone recalled the enormous sense of relief they felt at finding a wartime home. For many, and men in particular, especially those from non-supportive backgrounds, the decision to be a CO in the first place had been agonising, so to be fully accepted for what they were was 'a priceless gift' as one man put it. The FAU, as well as providing a home and training, gave them much else – a sense of identity, a context for personal growth, a sense of purpose and, as time went on, a degree of choice for really worthwhile humanitarian service at home or abroad. Importantly, it gave the chance to prove they were not cowards. As Tom Haley explained, 'thanks to the FAU I could express myself in action.' The Unit's journal, the FAU Chronicle, kept sections in touch with each other as well as the London base throughout the war, helping to maintain a sense of overall Unit cohesion. (6)

Paul Townsend:

The organisational side was amazingly good. I didn't think of this as a young man, but having attempted to organise some things later in my own life, I often think about it, and I pay tribute to those who started it off. Of course Paul Cadbury being a business man had lots of contacts, but even so it was amazing at that level to get the organisation initially accepted so that it could get into institutions, get onto boats and be sent to places all over the globe. Not only organisation in terms of institutional arrangements but in terms of making the contacts in a slightly hostile environment. It seems to me in retrospect that the people who took charge and organised it really did a very good job because most of our members weren't by definition natural heel-clickers and conformists. That the thing worked as smoothly as it did was a great testimony to the way in which it was organised.

Donald Swann:

To actually belong, to have a name and a place – this was something quite different from being the isolated individual puzzling about the rights and wrongs of it all. I remember the tremendous feeling of relief when I joined. We would discuss things and this helped enormously as previously I was made to feel very uncomfortable. I was certainly called a coward at times and accused of being utterly idealistic. So having this home was ever so comforting. Many of us were not Quakers, but there were enough always to keep the FAU 'Quaker', and we would have silent meetings for worship which I grew to love. When I think of it, these must have been held in some pretty odd places around the world, I certainly

remember ours, sometimes just ten minutes of sitting in the desert
– a place of pure magic for me – a good place for silent worship.

Michael Cadbury:

I think the FAU approach of being absolutely open with ourselves and knowing what our capacity was, and having endless optimism feeling there was something we could *do*, however desperate
the situation. *That* was the FAU spirit: the world is a bad place, but
we've got something to give it if only labour and enthusiasm. And
we found a way of using that urge. Given a team of devoted young
people with no inhibitions, you could get into any situation and do
something useful. We'd tread on a lot of toes and fall very hard on
our behinds, but I think we would achieve in almost any situation
something of worth. We had our failures, but very few. Flexibility
was our keynote. We often achieved the impossible simply by going
in not knowing it *was* impossible – ignorance was a wonderful ploy
for us.

*Flexibility was certainly a great strength of the Unit, summed up by
their motto GADA – Go Anywhere Do Anything. Although there has
been the odd murmur about 'weighty Quakers', it is generally agreed
that equality and democracy were very much part of the FAU ethos. In
the early days when the first men went to Finland, the Unit adopted what
Michael Rowntree has called 'a quasi military terminology with "officers" and "corporals" – and this sometimes continued mainly in sections
working with the army. But it was largely dropped; then there were just
section leaders and deputy section leaders.' Given the nature of such individualistic characters, it was not surprising that strong arguments
occurred. Several sections, as we have seen, had palace revolutions,
changing their leaders when they thought a change essential. Discipline
was accepted '..we had no hang-ups on that. We were not a collection of
anarchists wanting to rock boats. The awareness of group discipline was
very strong in us, and we therefore accepted other structures, such as hospital hierarchies. You need a disciplined structure in order to undertake
the GADA formula.'[7] Decisions, whether in the Headquarters in
Gordon Square or out in the field, were reached by consensus. Several
non-Quakers have expressed their initial frustration with such a time-
consuming process '...the interminable process of going over and over,*

and over yet again the same issues and problems with everyone having a say', but most felt that once the decision was reached, then it stuck and everyone pulled together to implement it. The pooled allowance, whatever the parental contributions, also served as an equalising factor.

Doug Turner:

I think the FAU was an almost perfect example of a truly democratic structure in which give and take existed. And if there were occasional tensions between personalities, well there was always an answer found by perhaps separating them and putting them into a group into which they could function more adequately. This was always accepted by everybody. I was deputy leader of our particular section in China. What that meant, I don't know – nobody ever took any notice of what I said! Things just worked. It was good, acceptable, mutual responsibility and it functioned. It was *our* Unit, we were part of this community – I would stress this community aspect rather than a collective. A collective is an 'it', a structure which people accept and belong to rather than share. Whereas community is something which is moving, it is spontaneous and is concerned with relationships and sharing. The FAU community was an I-thou relationship rather than the collectivist I-it.

As for social class, I think pacifism is something above and beyond class. I think there is an intellectual element, which may give the idea that an educated, middle class background gives rise to it. But I imagine that the working class pacifist – and there were a lot of us in the Unit – is a pacifist primarily because he has investigated and enquired further. He's reaching out, and in this growth meets others of different social classes so that in the end we do reflect a completely classless approach. I don't think one can really be a pacifist without also being wholly concerned with injustice and the breaking down of classes. There may be pacifists who don't take this approach. I can only hope that they're very, very rare.

With women, it was a division of labour as it was between the men. Clearly women came with their own training, primarily in the nursing field, and they carried on as any other member of the Unit. There was never any discrimination of any sort, not in China anyway, and if there was then it was purely at the humourous and facetious level. I suppose those women who were actually members of the Society of Friends continued to carry the tradition of Quaker women who are certainly *not* known to be unforthright in expressing their opinions and getting their way.

Elaine Bell:

The FAU! What would I have done without it? I really have no idea. I suppose I would have gone on the land, something like that. Certainly I wouldn't have joined the forces. The FAU was *very* important especially to the men. It was somewhere for their questioning minds to go. But it was important for women too. It was marvellous that it functioned so well and took in such a cross-section of the community. Provided you shared the basic tenets of the Society of Friends and the commitment to non-violence, then the door was open.

Deryck Moore:

When I arrived in Germany, I had the naivety of youth about me compared with the more experienced members like Michael Rowntree and Gerald Gardiner. They had enormous influence on how I operated at a later stage. I was an also-ran in that first year and always did what I was asked to do – asked but not instructed. That was very nice because you tended to do a bit more because of the way it was put over: 'What do you think about popping up to see them in Lüneburg?' 'Yes, sure, I'll go up tomorrow morning.' 'Fine.' Not, 'Get off there and do it.' It was a very happy organisation. I can honestly say that I can't remember a row. You would have differences because perhaps you would like to do something in a certain way. But it would all be worked out smoothly, with consensus, without argument.

At Vlotho, before Michael Rowntree arrived to take over from Gerald Gardiner, I was put in a room with Gerald. I must be the only one who can say that I've thrown hair brushes and socks at the Lord Chancellor of England because he would snore so. I can remember waking some mornings with his bed littered with my stuff. He didn't mind. He was a wonderful man and a great influence on me. The fact that he had given up what had to be a very lucrative career as a barrister to come and be amongst poor conchies, and to go out on a motor cycle in war-torn Europe just after D day to see how we could help – and when he must have been getting on for fifty years old!

Frank Edmead:

We weren't very much aware of the centre in Gordon Square but we had confidence in it. I never felt they were bureaucrats unaware of the real problems we were facing out in the field, and I always felt that I could approach them if there was a problem...I do think there was a very, very high standard of competence in the leadership of the FAU, the more so when you compare the Unit with the military – they could have taken a few lessons from the FAU.

Listening to the FAU, one is made vividly aware of what an important formative experience it was for members. Of course the majority of those involved in a situation of total war, whether service personnel, civilians or conscientious objectors, had their horizons broadened to some extent. But with the FAU, it was the responsibility thrust upon them and trust that they could cope in what were often extreme situations, that enabled so many to grow as individuals and achieve a potential far beyond their expectations: 'I did things that I never imagined possible and often thought: what would my mother say if she could see me coping in charge of this large medical ward?'[8] They were, as Chris Barber has explained 'ordinary people who performed extraordinarily.'[9] This was especially so for those isolated sections in China and Ethiopia. The bonding process, which for many had started in training camp, was also another very important factor. The fact that men were not separated by the rank system of the forces resulted in a far greater mix-up of different socio-economic backgrounds which added to the process of mutual learning and respect. Everyone I interviewed has mentioned this educative aspect of Unit life and given thanks for the deep and lasting friendships that were formed.

Tom Haley:

The more we went through, the more the sheer character of the men that I was working with was revealed, and the more it helped me to realise the way in which I had to live and the way in which I had to be able to direct my life. There were certain people too who were particularly good examples for me in that way – Peter Tennant and Robert Arthur, for instance – men with integrity and guts who tackled a situation in the way in which they wanted to live and have their being. This meant that I had learnt a great deal about how to live which was completely different to my initial upbringing and gave me a completely new set of horizons and new understanding altogether. Without doubt this set me off on a different course after the war. There is no doubt that my life was completely changed by belonging to the FAU, and living and working with those men I admired so.

Margaret Matheson:

The FAU affected my life in all ways. If I had remained a ward sister in Birmingham, what would I be now? I wouldn't have had much to look back on. It made an enormous difference. I've got a most wonderful collection of friends all round the world. The medical experience in China is something I wouldn't have missed for anything. And I met Al...

Tod Lawry:

Having decided to be a pacifist, I was immensely fortunate to spend World War II – five and a half years – with the type of men and women who were in the FAU, of whom only about a third were Quakers, but the rest with a firm conviction about Christian pacifism. I remember Beryl, my wife, saying when she first began to meet my FAU friends 'You know, everyone of ex-FAU people, not only China convoy, have done something worthwhile.' I think it's true. Some have achieved elevated levels – Gerald Gardiner, the former Lord Chancellor, for instance. We had several members of the peerage: Lord Hugh Russell was out in China. He dropped the 'Lord' out there. The FAU was an astonishing experience for any youngster, boy or girl. I think we were all a huge influence upon each other and this was one of the tremendous things about the FAU: practically everybody had been doing something constructive, purposeful...they were the kind of people among whom I made my friends and that I could talk anything over with. When it came to the question of marriage, I think we all shared with each other what the girl was like before we proposed.

David J. Morrish:

I thoroughly enjoyed my FAU/PWS experience. I learned from it the ability to react quickly to changing circumstances, in getting on and doing things that I never felt I had any aptitude for doing before...I'm not a great DIY type but what the FAU taught us was to make the best use of the skills we've got and to get on with others, working together. I do think the FAU was immensely important for me and when people say 'Well, it would be very useful these days if youngsters had conscription' I say: 'Satan get behind me quickly!' There's no doubt it did provide a welcome opportunity for me to get away and do things, meet people, totally divorced from the sausage-machine business of school, university, then into teaching...I do sometimes wish there was something like the FAU to get young people to work in hospitals, or with piles of smelly old clothes in warehouses, on forestry commission plantations, and not to do it for money but for the community where you are all working together and developing community loyalty. I certainly wouldn't have missed it. It was part of my education, part of my growing into manhood in a very important way. It was another kind of university in that sense, perhaps more useful in life skills than real university taught me. If I had to make the choice of FAU or university, I would say FAU first. I think I could have caught up through adult education into university, but there is no substitute for the FAU.

Anthony Perry:

I know that those six Unit years were for me an experience which I never forgot, and still talk about easily, given the slightest encouragement. I am sure of a pride in Unit activity, and that we were different from other units. I think that the experience led me into an ability to be content with my own company, for there were occasions when we had to move, or operate independently...We did work together, or travel together, most of the time. But there were also many times when we were on our own. So that whether it was a question of collecting petrol from the wells in the North-West (of China); or feeding a large and somewhat angry crowd of refugees on the move; of a journey with valuable medicines, or with petrol, over hundreds of miles alone; of addressing a public meeting, celebrating VJ Day in a packed Chungking suburb; or receiving the freedom of the city of Shantung during the post-war civil war period – all these contributed to building a self-reliance which has remained.[10]

Roy Ridgway:

The FAU was in the *reality* of war: you know how much one can do, how much one can't do, and how one's dreams are knocked on the head. But there are some good things that come out of it, and I think we did something worthwhile. And on the whole we didn't let the Quakers down. People still talk about what the FAU did including the post-war part in Europe helping the refugees. Those of us in the HSU were only a very small part of the whole FAU effort, but we were the people in the thick of things. We discovered how difficult it is to maintain one's values in the midst of war. We were the people who found out what war was really about. How people become degraded in a way by war. We were degraded as well, but being aware of that was something different, being able to express that, being able to talk to your friends about it and openly admitting it makes it a different kind of experience from the experience of the ordinary soldier somehow. We struggled with ourselves, and we didn't think we had won the battle. For us there was no 'victory.' There was just a terrific experience that was worth going through. It was *so* worthwhile. I still think how wonderful it was that it had happened to me. What a privilege! Yes, a *privilege* to have been in the FAU.

Duncan Wood:

We were all changed by our FAU experience. It's difficult to say precisely because most of our members joined at such a young age not to have had much of a career pre-war. So it's difficult to say how different it would have been if war hadn't happened. In some cases – Sydney Bailey is one – he would never have gone on to the kind of career he has had if not for the Unit experience. He left school at fourteen years and was a bank clerk before joining the Unit, but he has had a most distinguished career as a writer and journalist. This is entirely because in the Unit he was exposed to a quite different atmosphere and intellectual environment to anything he had experienced before, and so the FAU was a launching pad for him, as it has been for others. A large number of members went into social service of one sort or another. Several found work in UNICEF and several in OXFAM. The FAU concept of working with people in their contexts is fundamental to Oxfam philosophy. As Save the Children was a child of the First World War, Oxfam was a child of the Second. Both wars have produced the desire to meet the needs that have been unleashed by wartime experience.[11]

Given the formative nature of FAU service it is not surprising that so many members returned from the war with changed career expectations. This, of course, also happened with service personnel. What distinguished FAU members was the strong urge to continue the humanitarian service they had found so satisfying in wartime. Although they had to get back into the routine of working life and make independent lives for themselves and sometimes wives and families, generally material incentives were in the background; they were looking for socially constructive work above all. Not everyone found it possible to change tack, especially if it meant taking more time out for educational qualifications or lengthy periods of training, and this applied particularly to newly-married couples and those with young families. But even if socially constructive jobs were not possible, it would seem that most Unit members have succeeded in putting their FAU experience and ethos to good use whatever their work, as well as in voluntary activities in their communities. Two charities were set up by FAU members after the war which are staunchly supported to this day: the Laurie Baker Society, for hospital work in India; and the Richie Mounsey Charitable Trust which helps with the education of young Kenyans.[12]

Although FAU women in the main were busy setting up homes and starting their families, some were able to continue socially useful work. Angela Sinclair-Loutit became a social worker 'always with the same motivation of wanting to do what one could to relieve distress and not to cause it and to try to make the world a better place to live in.' In the

1980s, she did secretarial work for the London Centre for International Peacebuilding, run by Brigadier General Michael Harbottle. Although going out to work was not an option for many women, several like Pip Turner found worthwhile voluntary work.

Pip Turner:

The FAU did affect my life... very much so. I've worked voluntarily all my life: I did a lot of work for Save Europe Now – a famine relief organisation started by Victor Gollancz to feed Germany and other devastated European countries. I also worked for British Aid for German Workers, later on with Refugees for Peace, and about 1970 I started working for Wolverhampton Probation Department as a volunteer. The experience I had looking after families in deprived conditions in liberated Europe really helped me. Now I work with families who have members suffering, or have lost someone, from leukaemia. The FAU was a wonderful period of my life. We have made life-long friends, and of course I found my husband, Eric.

For those men who were able to fulfil their changed career ambitions, the medical world beckoned a high proportion of FAU members – unsurprising really considering how strongly medical work had featured in FAU service. Many of those who became doctors have mentioned the importance of the vast experience gained in areas like the 'clinical paradise' of Ethiopia. For Pat Rawlence, his experience in China '...helped me to cope with anything that came along...and I think that experience in Mohai – if you can get through that, you get through anything.' Ralph Arnold stresses the value of the menial portering jobs undertaken with the Unit in UK hospitals 'My friend Sam and I used to say that we were the only people who both stoked the hospital boilers and also took out appendixes.'

David Rowlands:

I am sure that seeing so much suffering gave me the desire to be a doctor. I felt that. I had been really pushed into my father's milling business without any sense of vocation for milling. I had no thoughts of becoming a doctor before the war because in any case my parents couldn't afford it. So, with the benefit of a grant after the war, and being largely with ex-service people at the London Hospital and medical teaching hospitals, one didn't feel so much a fish out of water as if one had been amongst a lot of younger people. The value of my war experience? I should say self confidence. Having worked in those front-line wartime conditions, and then to be working in better conditions, I think that helped a lot. I also think to have gone straight from school into medical college, one wouldn't have had much knowledge of the world of human nature. Certainly we had the rough edges rubbed off in the years with the HSU, and I value that and feel that possibly I may have been a better doctor because of that. I don't think my experience as a CO was ever held against me. In fact there was tremendous competition to get into medical school. I had a letter from Colonel Vernier which I dropped on to the table as I was leaving the interview. I'm sure that would have helped. I had made it quite clear that I had been a CO and it didn't seem to affect things.

Norman Pollitt:

I can't really be specific that I suddenly thought: right, I must do medicine when I get back home. But it came to me in Ethiopia...From that Ethiopian group, three of us decided to take up medicine – Paul Wakelin, Fred Wilson and myself. There were quite a number in the Unit as a whole who subsequently took up medicine. The FAU was a bit of a breeding ground because we did sample the medical world and associated with doctors. The work we did and the techniques we learned were very useful for medical training. In my case, it was a gradual decision to do it.

...There was only one instance where there had been any kind of prejudice. I remember once getting on very well indeed at an interview for a very nice practice in Staffordshire. Getting on fine with the senior partner. Went to lunch – delightful! At the end he said 'Well, Dr. Pollitt, you've been very helpful...I know my partners would like to have you here but there's one thing that bothers me. I don't know that your experience in the FAU and your history in the war of being a CO is really going to fit in here.'

Ted Dunn:

I considered medicine when I got home, but that meant starting at the bottom and doing courses before going on to medicine, and I didn't have that kind of brain or that kind of money to have paid for it. But if I could have done the same kind of work as I had done in Ethiopia, yes, I would have liked that. But at the end of the war Mr. Cadbury set up a sort of rehabilitation group which tried to put FAU members in touch with employers. He was thinking along the lines of agricultural work for me, so I worked for him on a probation basis on a strawberry growing venture. Then he died. I had no intention of returning to my old job as a furniture salesman – my FAU experience had given me more self confidence. I was not afraid in the sense of thinking: well, that's a professional job and beyond me. Professionalism can often be a veneer. Simple common sense goes a very long way. Eventually, I took advantage of a Government scheme and opened up my own little market garden.[13]

Bernard Fisher:

After my demob, I came back to Brighton and went back to my old school and started teaching again. I found it very difficult to settle down and saw an advertisement for teachers wanted for Service children in Germany. So I applied and got a teaching job there. My boss was John Trevelyan, later the film censor, an amazing, outstanding man. He interviewed me and instead of offering me a teaching post, offered me an administrative post. I think my conchie experience made me less ordinary. I don't know why. So I worked out there in this new venture. The Education Act was just out and was not implemented here yet, but it was in that outfit. The teachers were pretty good. It was rather like Ethiopia but not so isolated. But I had independence in running new schools, in new conditions – an enterprising and interesting job. Then I went back to Brighton teaching. My CO experience was never held against me, only bureaucratically, regarding the pension situation. The question: was FAU service war service or not? In the end the matter went to the Ministry of Education. The final interview was not going too well until someone looked through the papers again and said 'Oh, I see that in the 12th camp you were quartermaster, is that right?' So on the strength of my getting supplies organised into an FAU camp, my service was recognised as war service and I didn't lose my pension.

Few of those interviewed faced overt prejudice and discrimination when applying for posts, but several felt that the inclusion of FAU war service on their CVs might have worked against their chances. Some, like Theo Cadoux, were less fortunate than Bernard Fisher when it came to their occupational pensions:

Theo Cadoux:

After a year at home I got a job. It is possible that my CO stance was held against me. I went in for many jobs in the first year or so. I always used to put down that I had been in the FAU during the war. I don't think I was ever asked 'Does that mean you were a CO?' directly at an interview. I didn't conceal it but I didn't make a display of it. It may be that it was taken into account. I never got a fellowship at Oxford which was my ambition.

I suffered to the extent that my war service was never recognised by the University Grant Committee as qualifying for shortening of time in which I could obtain full pension rights. I had to do forty years actual teaching, carrying on until the age of seventy in order to acquire full pension rights. If I had been in the army, I would have received compensation for those lost years. But I don't complain considering I live in a country where it is possible to be a CO and not put up against a wall and shot.

Michael Cadbury:

I'd been away for six years and I wanted to get back to my family. I had been offered a post as senior traveller in Bournville. I was far too young really. I was thrown in at the deep end and learned from there. The FAU made you welcome challenges, there were a lot coming out of the FAU looking for that sort of challenge in civvie street. Many found it, some didn't and drifted back into dead-end jobs. But an enormous lot were fired to do all sorts of things: a lot became teachers, went to universities, a lot became doctors. The Unit taught a lot of ambitious young men that they had the stuff within themselves to make contributions and it is very remarkable looking back at what people have achieved and very largely through Unit training. When I was put in charge of twenty men all older than myself, I couldn't possibly have done that if I hadn't been in charge of Unit sections. One had learnt to be gentle and caring with people.

Tony Gibson:

I have had a very strong feeling about the FAU which I have had ever since...What I felt about the FAU, particularly in China, was that there was a mix of people of different backgrounds, different degrees of religious commitment, different socio-economic backgrounds who managed to tackle things together. I thought this formula worth pursuing. The notion that we're all in it together, we're not going to have too much of this top-down stuff, but we'll delegate, because the delegation is important...I wanted to see a way of involving people in practical things which had a shared motivation. That motivation I'm inclined to think is related to what makes sense in what you do. In that sense it's pragmatic – it's worth doing this because it's worth doing *in itself*...I thought that the interaction between people, the way people took each other down – I was taken down at various times – was good because people weren't looking over their shoulders all the time at some superior person, or some inferior person who was going to get your job. The GADA notion seemed to dispose of that...all my work in neighbourhood schemes is concerned with people having not just a say, but a *do* in what is decided in matters which affect them. That's why I made an abortive attempt to persuade the FAU to use the money that they had salted away to involve a new generation of youngsters both at home and abroad who are caught up in civil strife. And if there is not civil strife in some of the council estates I work in, then I don't know what it is...[14]

Doug Turner:

When I returned from the war, I began to explore the possibility of taking up leprosy work and eventually, in 1952, found myself sailing for the Gold Coast working within the government leprosy control scheme. Although I'd had no experience of leprosy, they seemed to think that my FAU experience had given me the right approach for the post.

I think there was a tendency for many in the Unit to look for something more socially worthwhile rather than return to their old jobs and what had been for some their old mediocre way of living. Thus it was that many went into teaching with the new opportunities opening up. Many went into the field of medicine. Usually I think most wanted to choose some kind of professional life which offered potential for creative development – yes, yes. I think that because the nature of peace demands a creative approach, it must express itself in a *positive* way. I think we see the results of this in many different fields: within local social work, for instance, I'm quite sure it's recognised the part the Pacifist Service Units played in laying down the foundations for the development of the Family Service Units; and how this, in turn, played a part in the future development of the children's services and social work as a whole perhaps may have moved on since then. I would hope that in general most pacifists take into their work a creative approach. We've seen it in the literary world, the worlds of art and music – Tippett and Britten, for example. And Donald Swann and Sydney Carter would be two good examples from the Unit with their anti-war songs, and songs for peace and reconciliation.

Donald Swann:

For me the importance and influence of my FAU years cannot be exaggerated. As well as having the opportunity for worthwhile humanitarian work in a war situation, it was crucial for my musical life. To begin with I learnt that music comes from *within*. The music I was going to compose was growing inside me. It was like an inner well. The Greek refugees struck this for me, their music became part of my whole system and fertilised my whole experience. After a bit it seemed that I was learning everything I wanted to know. I was forgetting that I'd ever been through Russian studies, or even been a piano player. It was just as if this whole life took over. Withdrawal from the musical culture that I had been brought up with gave me the key. And when I got to the islands the songs they were singing were the juiciest folk songs. I mean Cecil Sharp and Vaughan Williams would have given their right hands to be there.

They are incredibly complex, not 'Yours' or 'You Are My Sunshine' which is what we were singing at the time. It was the *real thing*.

I have since used my songs in the cause of peace. I've worked with friend Sydney Carter. He was also in the FAU. Perhaps I could tell you an anecdote about a song which I call 'The Pilgrims Hymn.' In 1964 I was on the way back from a performance tour of Australia and called into a Quaker school in Ramallah which was now a Jordanian Ramallah, not Palestinian as it had been when I was there with the FAU in 1944. Then, much later I went back again, and it was then Jewish. I looked at them all and they seemed to be the same children with the same idea of bringing peace and reconciliation. The Quakers trying to bring the Jewish and Arab children together. That gave me inspiration for this hymn. From time to time I use it at the end of concerts with a few trumpets, and I get people to join in.

> We ask that we live and we labour in peace, in peace
> Each Man shall be our neighbour in peace, in peace
> Distrust and hatred will turn to love,
> All the prisoners freed,
> And one only war will be the one
> Against all human need.
>
> We work for the end of disunion in truth, in truth
> That all may be one communion in truth, in truth
> We choose the road of peace and prayer
> Countless pilgrims trod,
> So that Hindu, Moslem, Christian, Jew
> We all can worship one God.
>
> We call to our friends and our brothers unite, unite!
> That all may live for others, unite, unite!
> And so the nations shall be as one,
> One flag unfurled,
> One law, one faith, one hope, one truth,
> One people and one world.

REFERENCES:

[1] A. Tegla Davies, *op. cit.* p.464.
[2] Neville Chamberlain, speaking during the reading of the Conscription Bill, House of Commons, 4/5/1939.

(3) Tod Lawry worked for the British Council until his retirement. He returned to China, working in Shanghai, Nanking and Peking 1946-1950.

(4) Report to Executive Committee by Robin Whitworth 10/12/1944. 12 FSU team: Roger Balkwill, Frank Bridge, Harold Brown, John Fleming, Reg Middleton, Ken Myers, Peter Gladstone-Smith, Brian Taylor, George Watson. It is interesting that George Watson has told me that at his Tribunal he refused to accept any form of non-combatant service 'and yet that is what I did (and happily) with the FAU'.

(5) For instance a group of COs known as the 'Red Cross Devils' accompanied the 6th Airborne Division's advance across Europe as part of the 3rd Parachute Brigade, dropping by parachute when necessary. Others worked in bomb disposal – this would normally be under non-combatant army status.

(6) FAU Chronicle was started in 1940 and ended in 1946.

(7) Interview, David J. Morrish.

(8) Interview, Eric Jones.

(9) Chris Barber's book *FAU Postscript: Some reflections of former Friends Ambulance Unit members on what their unit experience of 40 years earlier has meant to them.* Oxfam, 1984 p.30.

(10) Anthony Perry, unpublished manuscript, and letter to author, 5 January, 1994.

(11) Michael Rowntree's involvement with Oxfam started in 1950. He served as Chairman 1972/77 and is now Emeritus Chairman and a member of Oxfam Council. Chris Barber served as Chairman 1984/89. Michael Harris and Bernard Llewellyn have both served as Directors of Overseas Operations.

(12) The Laurie Baker Society was formed by ex China Convoy members as a charity to support the work Laurie Baker (FAU China) and his wife, an Indian doctor, did in hospitals, first on the Indo-China border and later in southern India.

(13) Ted Dunn has devoted much of his spare time to writing numerous booklets and books on peace and reconciliation, and regional peace and development. They include: *Alternatives to War and Violence,* ed. Dunn, T. James Clark Ltd 1963; *Foundations of Peace and Freedom,* ed. Dunn, T. Christopher Davies, Swansea 1976. The latter won the World Education Fellowship Award for 1976 as 'the book which made the greatest contribution towards promoting the social purposes of education.'

(14) Tony Gibson was awarded the OBE in 1996 for his neighbourhood-based work. He published *Power in Their Hands,* John Carpenter, Oxford 1996, 2nd edn 1997.

CHAPTER 19

Some Price to Pay

The emotional cost of war has, moreover, been heightened in this
century in a peculiarly excruciating way...

John Keegan[1]

*ALTHOUGH THE UNIT was renowned for the large degree
of support it gave members and the overwhelming reaction of
members has been one of affirmation, it should be apparent by now that
life in the FAU had its downside. Although the pay situation (pocket
money of 7/6d weekly) was largely accepted as adequate, fair and equi-
table, no doubt many were excluded from the FAU for financial reasons.
It also caused problems and some anguish for those within the Unit and
several members left for this reason – this was especially so for those with
dependants to support. Johnny Wiper left in 1941/42 because his firm
(an insurance company) which had originally made up his FAU
allowance to his old salary level, ceased to do so, leaving his widowed
mother without an income.*

Alfred White:

...Like most FAU members I looked forward to the time when
I would go overseas. I was very much choosy about the kind of
service that I would undertake. I let it be known that I wasn't willing
to work with the Free French, for instance, as I couldn't see much
difference between this and being in the Armed Services. China I
saw as a service I could undertake and with this in mind learned
to drive and undertook a three month course in motor mechanics

398

at Hackney Technical College and generally prepared myself for the call. Dicky Wainwright, then Personnel Office of the Unit, told me that I had been selected for the next convoy to China. But I told him that I couldn't accept because I must resign from the Unit.

This was because my father had to give up work in mid 1943 because of a serious heart condition. This was in the pre-Welfare State era and as both father and mother were dependant on his income, their finances were in a very parlous state. I felt I had to support them financially in whatever way I could and as the tribunal had given me teaching as well as FAU, I decided to leave the FAU and teach.

I saw Dicky and I think I must have been very reticent about explaining the predicament I was in. I realise with hindsight that had I done so means might have been found of making some payment towards the support of my parents. At the time I didn't think this possible and hence my resignation. It was then that Dicky told me I was on the next China convoy.

...I think I may truly say I've never got over the bitter disappointment of not taking part in the China adventure. I felt it as a great personal loss, a deprivation which nothing could replace. I think I have tried to replace it by subsequent service as a teacher and lecturer in Kenya and Malawi but my loss still rankles. I feel this very much at the reunions I've attended. On my name badge I feel that the lack of initials denoting FAU service overseas is something almost to be ashamed of – it's something that cuts me off from fellow FAU members...There's always pain there and despite the passage of time the pain and disappointment continue. I feel I've been a member of the FAU nominally but not intrinsically been a part of it. I stand at the sidelines, a spectator.[2]

Like returning service personnel, many FAU members found problems of adjustment to civilian life. This was particularly true of those who had served abroad in areas like China, had been very active in front-line service, or had found a satisfying wartime niche. Often the problem was compounded by the FAU pay situation and was particularly acute for women.

Lilian Cadoux:

Settling back to the UK? It was *terrible*. It was absolutely *terrible* because we'd lived in that communal situation with our team who shared our ideas and I really found it the most awful culture shock to come back to Britain and instantly to lose all of those friends. And I didn't much like hearing English people making remarks about how bad Germans were, implying that we had suffered and they hadn't...

One of the big problems we had when we left the FAU was associated with the housing shortage which was extreme, and neither Harold nor I had been resident previously in the town where he was working, and therefore had no points for a council house. Also, because of our pacifism and war experience, we had no money either. You couldn't save on 7/6d a week and he got no gratuity, not being a member of the forces, and he was only doing his apprenticeship at the factory. So we had to take a tiny cottage in a village nine miles from Rugby where he worked. I was shocked to find how behind the times people were there, having grown up in London and in my nursing training learnt all about public health and hygiene. We had no mod cons at all. People on either side didn't feel deprived, but I was like someone from another planet. Everything about us was wrong for them. I was middle class for them because of the way I spoke. If ever they knew that we'd been in anything like the FAU, that would have made us even stranger. So, all this added to the culture shock.

Although few women have complained about discrimination and prejudice whilst in the FAU, this did occur. FAU attitudes on the whole reflected the prevailing values of the time: women were treated equally, provided they were given tasks suitable for their traditional skills – secretarial, nursing, shelter work, welfare and relief work. When it came to service in the field, few women felt they suffered discrimination – men did their share of housework in the hostels, and if there was discrimination then it was usually positive, for instance women were often barred from cooking because it was felt the cooking pots were too heavy. Some resentment has been expressed about men's attitudes towards women entering hostels for the first time, which were 'suspicious and cold.' This was particularly so in the beginning when women were just appearing in the Unit. It was also the case that right from the start, when Tessa Cadbury and Gwendy Knight were given responsibility for setting up a women's section, men were always in control. Women had to fit in with the system as it was, with very little say about the overall administration.

Although nothing has been put on record, I have been told informally of the concern felt by those in the Gordon Square headquarters about potential sexual complications once women were admitted: here were young and attractive men and women thrown together, often in confined conditions and in novel and dangerous situations. Given the 'live for today' wartime ethos – wasn't this asking for trouble? Sexist attitudes were certainly there within sections. Many sections refused to accept women on the grounds that 'they weren't fit for the demands of the job' or 'we're happier without them.' Others feared the competition which would be generated: 'there's not enough to go around' or, more tactfully, 'they were at a premium romantically.' Nev Coates recalls his initial antagonism to having Hedy Hinton in his team and how he besought Richard Wainwright 'No women! They're nothing but trouble.' He soon changed his opinion when Hedy proved her worth as a valued member of the team but admits to being unsympathetic and a 'sort of bear' at the start.

David Rudd:

We had no women in our team in Germany. We were thorough male chauvinists, I'm afraid. Some FAU sections did, but we resisted the suggestion. We thought they were weak, feeble creatures and wouldn't be of any use, I'm ashamed to say. And we thought they would disrupt the camaraderie of the section and of course they do have a disturbing effect – I'm not saying a bad effect. But a group of men by themselves are not the same as a mixed group and you get into a way of life with just men which you can't repeat if there are only a few women. It makes for bad feeling among men, especially if the women are young and attractive. We used to say things like: 'the only place for a woman is in bed.' Not that any of us had put a woman in bed! But it was the way we talked...We mustn't forget that the feminist movement had hardly got off the ground. It was natural for women to regard themselves as inferior to men, and they didn't appear to want anything in the way of equality. They were content with their lot.

Not all FAU women were called to a tribunal and there was a range of reaction to this: many felt it very important to bear witness to their pacifism and felt deprived of the opportunity to express their peace witness. Others were grateful to be spared what they considered to be an ordeal. Those who did attend generally regard the experience as being signifi-cant. Women's attitudes to pacifism were just as deeply held as the men's and many had experienced personal struggles before the decision to be a CO was made. Yet it seems that women didn't face the same doubts and dilemmas as men during the war, although several have admitted a change in attitude since the war. All have expressed the opinion that it was far easier for women to be COs than men, given the stereotypes of women then existing – gentle, passive, caring. This is not to say that their pacifism wasn't put to the test: they too faced the reality of war. Those who worked in relief of war-torn Europe, for instance, have explained how they realised that pacifism had to be lived and worked through, not just held as a faith.

There were many romances within the Unit and a number of mar-riages – both within the Unit itself, and with Unit members of both sexes finding their partners through their wartime connections. David Rudd, for instance, married Inge, a young German woman he'd met during his service in Germany. Evelyn White met her husband-to-be on a troop-ship en route to China. However, several men have explained how they were dogged by a sense of emasculation during their time as COs, as Paul Townsend explained: 'I suspect for younger members, partly for doing something unpopular, partly by having a slight sense of insecurity, also having no money and various other things including the macho culture of the times, there was a sense in which a lot of us were taken out of sexual circulation.'

Donald Swann:

Of course, being COs, there was some price to pay regarding our emotional lives. In my own case it seemed that my conscience was taking up all my own emotions when I was in Palestine and Greece – that somehow there was a denial of an emotional life. It is possible that there is something arid about pacifism in my case – that it dried me out emotionally in a way that I haven't totally understood. I think there were people who were not affected by this at all and had perfectly straightforward emotional and sexual lives running through their pacifism and indeed there were many marriages. But for me, and others I know, it seemed that the war had eaten up what we would have done for our emotional lives, because it had given us another emotion. We were creatures of conviction rather than human love. The Greek girls were so beautiful and I admired my friends who could marry them and have happy emotional lives on that dimension…it seemed a thing that couldn't happen with me.

I was also interested to know if members had experienced any social disapprobation due to their wartime CO stance. Most, although never hiding the fact that they had been COs, didn't go out of their way to mention it. Several, like Bill Spray, mentioned dilemmas 'It is extraordinarily difficult: if you make a pugnacious business out of it, you tend to imply that other people were mistaken and I was never in a position to say that…' Sydney Carter and Donald Swann, although never evangelical, were always very open about their anti-war beliefs, imbuing many of their carols and songs with pacifist sentiments. Neither felt it was ever held against them professionally or socially although Swann did mention 'During our Flanders and Swann partnership years, Michael Flanders was awarded the OBE. I wasn't. I didn't shed any tears over this as I don't think much of the Honours system anyway. Michael always maintained it was because, being disabled, he had to work a bit harder than me. I wonder: did it have anything to do with my well-known pacifism and my FAU service in the war?' The situation was far more definite for David J. Morrish. He has stood as a Liberal parliamentary candidate in several general elections; 'during the last election campaign various telephone calls were coming into the Liberal Party headquarters asking "Which regiment did Mr. Morrish serve in? Is it true he is a pacifist?"'

Paul Townsend:

In social life I have sometimes felt that if it were known what my views about certain things were, this particular stand-up cocktail party would be rather different. And in a certain sense I think I might have participated in the local community more fully if I didn't feel that, in matters of real substance, I didn't go along with most of the people around me. This is not something that has affected my family life, or my intimate friendships or even my professional friendships. But in the wider acquaintanceships, or behaviour in the pub, the odd party – that sort of level – yes, I have felt a sort of constraint. There is this problem of how far you feel obliged to make plain to people your difference of opinion. I don't think there's any point whatsoever in parading difference of opinion when you're not going to influence anyone and immediately cause social embarrassment. On the other hand, there are moments when it becomes almost a matter of honesty to make something plain and I haven't always found it easy to decide whether I am being appropriately emollient in the situation and not being too awkward, or whether I am in actual fact failing to make something plain which I ought to make plain.

Michael Rowntree:

My position as a CO has never affected me professionally, but socially, yes. This would be occasionally when I've met people in social situations who have served in the war, or perhaps didn't like the position COs took in the war – then I have been conscious of disapproval. The only occasion when it was forcefully put to me was during the war when I met a man who was subsequently a member of Mrs Thatcher's cabinet – whom I will not name – he forcefully expressed to me his disapproval.

Given their special wartime status, COs were treated differently from service personnel regarding disability pensions. As we have seen, particularly with those serving in Third World countries such as China and Ethiopia the health toll was very high. Sydney Bailey, for example, contracted schistosomiasis in China and was so badly damaged that he was incapacitated for the rest of his life, unable to walk without a special apparatus. His wife, Brenda explained 'Sydney received no pension for his ill health. Had he been in the forces he would have received a nice pension for the rest of his life.' Eric Jones was another case:

Eric Jones:

When I returned from Ethiopia, my health had deteriorated. I had malaria and a duodenal ulcer which pulled me down. I was never quite the same again, it haunted me for the rest of my life until sorted out recently. This was typical of the Unit there, very few were as fit as when they first went out. The heat got you down and sometimes we lived in very high mountains. I remember a Russian lady living there was advised to spend three months in the valleys because of the strain on the heart. I lived for quite a while at 9,000 feet and it does tend to be a strain to move quickly. There's one of our chaps who looks twenty years older than he should – that could be the wear and tear of Ethiopia. I remember when I was diagnosed as having an ulcer this chap said 'If only you'd been in the army, you would have a pension, whereas because you were a CO, you won't get one.' Personally, I've never thought that way. I don't think the government owes me anything although it was probably the stress of Ethiopia that caused it.

Tod Lawry:

We were of course spread all over the world. We lost a higher proportion of our men in the war by war casualties, or illness or disease, than the armed services did. There were quite a number killed in North Africa, particularly outside Tobruk. We lost people in China. Although no one was actually shot, a couple of chaps were so badly maimed by sabre slashes that they almost bled to death, but were saved miraculously outside Pichieh by the German sisters there and had to be sent home. We lost other men from disease – Doug Hardy died from dysentery when actually out on a convoy. Johnny Briggs died from typhus, one of our doctors died from malaria. Quentin Boyd died of starvation. He was down on the war front and was an enormously highly principled Quaker – unfortunately too highly principled because he insisted that the FAU boys down at the war front should live on the same diet as the Chinese soldiers – rice and salt. Westerners can't do it. Quentin insisted on doing it and collapsed and had to be flown out to India and died in Calcutta.

Michael Cadbury:

It is difficult to get the figures regarding effects on health. Once we were separated, the statistics don't show…There were sad cases. When I was working in France I had to go south to sort out some trouble in the Unit near St Dié. Indeed there was trouble. A young lad had been taken off to a mental hospital. He had broken down under the strain of seeing all these hordes of people coming back homeless and only being able to do so much. This had affected his mind. You see, we were raw, innocent people to be faced with the sort of horror we were trying to deal with. It was more than he could take. I went to see him in the mental home. He didn't know where he was, or what it was all about, and we had to leave him there for a week during which time he deteriorated and died. This bore in on me, the enormous strain I was putting on these young lads who had great concern but who hadn't got the mental background to cope. It was a very sad case because he was a splendid chap who had done great work.

I have been told of other cases of mental breakdown. Also, how some members experienced events so traumatic that these were repressed at the time only to well up and haunt them for the rest of their lives – Harold Cadoux's experience of clearing up the scorched human remains after the Dresden bombing raid is a case in point. The sheer weight of responsibility placed on young shoulders, especially in situations of extreme isolation, often caused feelings of despair and anguish, as Eric Jones experienced in the outback of Ethiopia:

Eric Jones:

We had so much responsibility. Sometimes you felt that what you were doing just wasn't up to the problem. I remember one chap had obviously got stomach ulcers. I hadn't a clue how to operate on these so the only thing I could give him was an Italian medicine for acute indigestion. We gave him this and he died. And you felt so frustrated, and knew that if you could have got him to Addis there were surgeons there who could operate on him...it was that sort of thing which added to a sense of isolation and frustration.

Very few of those interviewed have admitted to staying complacent about their pacifist stance during the war and, although the majority stayed in the FAU, most were forced by the dilemmas of the moment to reappraise their stance; this was particularly so with men out in the field and was sometimes linked to the adage of 'war being mainly long periods of boredom punctuated by moments of acute terror.'

John Bailey:

When we worked in the CCS in the western desert, we were pushed around by the army, unwanted by them in several places. We were very busy during the retreat from Libya to Alex – plenty of wounded and stretcher bearing – but after the retreat, that's when lethargy and boredom set in. FAU chaps were very young and got very fed up 'What's the point of us being out here? We're helping the fighting part of the war and we don't like this.' Morale got *very* low. The war seemed so negative and we all wanted to do something far more constructive and positive. Really, we wanted to be in a largish group like the HSU with our own leaders telling us what to do, rather than split up as we were with the army. So a lot of frustration and it was at that stage that doubts emerged: were we helping the war effort? It was a low-grade pacifist situation to be in.

Derryck Hill:

Dilemmas? We lived in a daily sense of dilemma. Our situation was far from clear cut. For instance, one day when having to go in transit from the canal area (of Egypt) back to Tripoli in convoy, it was suggested that we should drive some of the lorries. Whilst we were happy to drive lorries with medical supplies, no way were we going to drive lorries with Army loads. As section leader I had six very vociferous members saying 'You go and spell it out' which I did. I suppose I explained the pacifist position to the officer-in-charge for well over an hour. You see the question which cropped up again and again was: where do you stop? Sometimes our leaders would accept things that other members wouldn't accept, and they said so clearly. Sometimes the most trivial things cropped up in daily decisions and we'd have endless arguments. Pacifists argue more than anyone else...It certainly kept pacifism alive.

As for staying neutral! There's no doubt that we backed the Allies and their successes. You can be impartial like that sitting here in my sitting room, but it's very different when you're with a fighting army. If we could move forward and finish the war, I was quite happy. The only way I could see it ending was either the Germans pushing us out of the western desert, or we doing the reverse. I wanted the latter. For some this was a terrible dilemma, not for me. I don't think in general that I was ever elated by war, but if I were ever in a position to witness in a tank battle an enemy tank being wiped out, I think it might be difficult to dissociate myself from a feeling of elation.

Deryck Moore:

Being in the thick of war – both with the victims of the V2s in London as well as those in Europe – we were all human enough to challenge our stand. There were many times when I questioned: is my pacifism right? Shouldn't you be going out with a gun to sort out this evil? So I had many doubts, and all the time...So, yes, we were challenged all the time about that. Anyone who says they weren't challenged must have been a magnificent person, so solid in their faith. But not me at the age of seventeen and a half!

Several members found the alienation from mainstream wartime society very hard to bear. Friends and family had gone off into the fighting forces and worthwhile though their FAU service may have been, they found, as Michael Harris put it, 'sometimes one felt out of tune with one's own kind.'

Sydney Carter:

I remember being nearly in tears on my thirtieth birthday, feeling I'd really cut myself off from everything. I was at a very low ebb you know...It was related to being a man in a way...yes. As a man you were expected to fight in the army. If you didn't there was something wrong with you. You'd set yourself up as being different, cut yourself out...If I listened to Vera Lynn singing 'Blue birds over the white cliffs of Dover' and all the war speeches, I felt 'that's me! A whole chunk of me is in there, and I'm cut off from it.' I wanted to belong *so* much and be able to sing those songs along with everybody else, and feel the warmth...I felt pulled in two directions, you know; that was the hardest part. People didn't give me white feathers or persecute me very much, it was this internal split which I found the hardest thing...I think a lot of us felt this way. Possibly

Quakers might not have felt it; possibly Jehovah's Witnesses brought up in their weird world might not have felt it, but somebody brought up in the ordinary world felt it. I think the tension really cracked some people. I think of two friends of mine who had breakdowns after the war. They went safely through the war, but felt knocked out by something – this tension which you'd been carrying inside yourself and then at the end of the war you tried to get back to normal. But you couldn't somehow.

It was whilst working in a refugee camp in Nuserat, Palestine where I nearly cracked up. We were living in a real camp society of people with their own language and making yogurt and dancing and talking. And I felt somehow outside it all. Terribly exposed... And suddenly I felt: look! I can't take being a conchie any more, I'm going to join the gang, you know join the army, join the world. And I said goodbye to the old Sydney.

So I said goodbye to all the officers who said 'Ah good chap!' Others said 'Goodbye Sydney, sorry to see you go.' And off I went across the Sinai desert to Bahb el Louk, the HQ in Cairo. I chatted to the FAU officials there who said 'Well, stick around for a day or two and think about it.' And I thought about it and I began to feel: Oh, I don't know, I like those people and places, I might as well stick with the people I know. Goodness knows where I shall end up if I join another lot. So back I went across the Sinai desert, back to all these people to whom I'd said goodbye. 'Oh, you're back again, glad to see you.' Everybody was very nice. Nothing to worry about at all. But it was a big thing for me.

...I always doubted. I had this theory that pacifism was a matter of vocation. Perhaps it was right for some people to be pacifists and some not to be pacifists. What I was never sure about was my own vocation. That's the trouble. Because my pacifism is rather like my Christianity: I can't believe in all the things you're supposed to, all the trimmings. Yes, I'm a doubter, a cheerful doubter in a way. A lot of people say you mustn't doubt, you must crush doubt. I never crush my doubt, I couldn't if I wanted to...I was doubtful right up until the last moment of my tribunal, and after it. People like me sometimes wonder what would have happened if they'd done the other, and how much you did was due to pride or wanting to be different? Or was it some kind of revenge or cowardice too? If you're in the army, you don't have to ask these questions all the while. I wrote a poem about doubt, it was about my religious doubt, but it goes for all my general doubts. It's called My Dancing Doubt:

> The prizes and the medals which I find,
>   turning the cupboard out, now seem to have
>   nothing to do with me.
>
> I can account for all the scars of shame
>   and horror that I carry; not for my
>   hope and hilarity.
>
> I wore the mask that nature handed out
>   of being English, old or young, a male
>   married or otherwise.
>
> Where was I really living all the while?
>   I played the conscientious hypocrite
>   and persecuted doubt
>
> Which flowered like a faith turned inside out,
>   dancing and lyrical, and made a mock
>   of all my history,
>
> Laughing at solemn Boy Scout promises,
>   badges and wedding rings by which I tried
>   but vainly to commit
>
> What cannot be committed. For the tail
>   can never wag the dog. My centre is
>   not where I thought it was.

Although most Unit members experienced doubt at some stage of their experience, many coped with this and remained confident that theirs was the right way, the only way for them; 'the standard of non-violence has to be upheld whatever the dilemma.'[3] Others, like Tom Haley, were caught in agonising dilemmas which tested their pacifism to the ultimate. We have seen how Tom had the choice of assisting in the mercy killing of fatally wounded soldiers on a China/Burma front retreat. He had entered the war 'to save lives, not to take them,' but he knew only too well the cruel and terrible fate of mortally wounded men falling into Japanese hands. *Yet after an anguished re-examination of his pacifism, which followed this crisis, he found it emerged reinforced and strengthened by the ghastliness of all-out warfare.* *

The knowledge of concentration and death camps seems to have been particularly traumatic, revealing as they did the full horrors of Nazism and raising the doubt: could Hitler have been coped with short of all-out war? Many with direct experience of concentration camp victims seriously doubted they could stay in the war as pacifists and would have left for the forces, yet looking at the worthwhile work they were doing on the humanitarian front and with the war coming to a close, decided to stay, albeit with an uneasy conscience. But there were others who doubted so strongly that they renounced their pacifist stance. In all about 8% left the Unit for the forces.

Stephen Verney:

My mind began to change whilst working in the Syrian desert when I began to be toughened up to the reality of things. And then, as rumours began to get through of Hitler's extermination of the Jews, one began to think: What am I doing just keeping my hands clean! And thinking that love and service are going to heal the world while other people suffer and die. And it was then that I decided that I must leave the FAU and join the army. I would describe it as a gradual disillusion which I've come to see is a very good thing. When people say to me 'I've been disillusioned,' I say to them 'Oh good, because do you want to be illusioned?' I think I had been living under an illusion. Everything was tough up there: there were locusts which swept over the countryside and ate up all the fruit and crops which my friends had grown so painstakingly. And I think the whole ruthlessness of the world began to impinge on me in a way which in the gentle climate of England it hadn't.

There was an incident which illustrated this particular kind of toughness which influenced me. There was this rich Arab merchant who was admitted to our hospital for treatment, and when he left we asked him to pay and he refused. There was an army sergeant living alongside us, and he got really tough with this Arab and told

* See Chapter 11.

him he would be in prison within twenty-four hours if he didn't pay up. So he paid. Later in Aleppo, I was walking in the souk and suddenly this man stood in front of me. And I thought: Goodness, now you'll murder me. But not at all. He was full of courtesy and smiles and took me back to his house and regaled me with food and treated me with great honour. This was because I had been tough with him. He respected that. And suddenly my eyes were opened to a whole new dimension.

Well I joined the Army and ended up in the Political Warfare Branch of the Intelligence Corps and was trained in sabotage, explosives and in the use of firearms and knives in preparation for being ferried into occupied Crete in 1944. My mission was to undermine the morale of the German forces there. It was known that there were a number of men in the German forces who were anti-Hitler, so if one could get at them, there was a reasonable hope that one could persuade them to capitulate or mutiny as they had at the end of the 1914-18 war.

I was called Stephanos Stephakis and became a 'zornpotod' – a buyer and seller of cattle. I built up a little network of anti-Hitler Germans and had many adventures and several narrow escapes. There is one story which is significant to my growth. We heard that someone was giving information about us to the Germans and we thought we knew who it was. So my gang went and captured him and brought him in front of me. He was very, very frightened. The boys said 'Let's beat him up.' I had absolute power over this man – the power of life and death. And I felt a desire rising up inside of me to smash him, to break him. It was really a terrifying feeling because it went against all my instincts as an English gentleman. It was a kind of cruelty surging up, a violence erupting out of the very depths of myself. And I came to realise that this was really Hitler in me. Although I was supposed to be fighting a war against Hitler, here he was hidden away inside me. And that became a very fundamental mind-changing thing for me. I suddenly knew that all the violence I was fighting against – the concentration camps, the torture and the sadism – was all boiling up inside my guts. That has been a profoundly important insight for my life – that one should recognise this darkness. I sometimes feel that if you become a total pacifist, the danger is that you begin to think you haven't got these things in you. You become very gentle and smiling, but underneath you're boiling away.

So I experienced a very big switch between being a pacifist and being a soldier in the thick of things. Because in Crete I had to use immoral means to carry out my work. I mean, I had to get prostitutes to try to get information out of soldiers and officers – I had to engage in lying and untruths.[4]

Duncan Wood:

Debates about pacifism weren't always to the fore in China when at work. It came to the fore when such questions as carrying troops on trucks came up; then one has to admit that on the long drive from Kutsing to Chungking, there would be many hours when the driver would be turning over in his mind: is this right? Am I doing the right thing? As trouble-shooter, I did indeed discuss with those who felt it their duty to quit and go off with the forces. There were a variety of feelings: that pacifism was irrelevant to the Chinese situation; those going into politics after the war couldn't see how politics could be successfully practised from the pacifist position for even if this doesn't imply taking up arms, you have to behave often in a very aggressive manner, fighting verbally if not physically. So one or two felt their expectations for the future incompatible with their pacifist position. Also, some felt war so awful that it was necessary to finish it as soon as possible. I always tried to persuade them to leave the decision for a week, not to jump too quickly to conclusions – to make sure it wasn't some passing phase, the result of perhaps a bad day or some kind of accident. I don't think I dissuaded anyone in the end, but at least I could assure myself this was not a snap decision. I was acting as a kind of tribunal judge in reverse.

I don't know to what extent it was China that challenged certain people's pacifism or whether it was the total war situation. Undoubtedly it was for some the realisation that in China people were still living in an era when personal violence could still occur and western pacifism hadn't found an answer. But those who persisted did come to see that although violence was around, Chinese civilisation had found a rough and ready check to violence and one of these is the concept of 'face.' This is respect for the individuality for the other person and limits to which you can dominate another person. You have to respect those limits in a society where people are living close together. The fact that they had found a way of living together despite all the problems is what fascinated us about China as a whole.

George Parsons:

I can't remember giving it much conscious thought. It was just a feeling which had grown on me, perhaps something had been there underground from the very beginning, but it had begun to take on some sort of shape during the Burma campaign of 1942. I began to realise that I was cheering our side on to myself, but then feeling that this was completely wrong: wasn't I supposed to be a pacifist? Then it arose: I can't be a pacifist if I feel like that. Somehow it bubbled up of its own accord. It wasn't a conscious decision I came to, it was something which was borne upon me, and it broke out finally: I can't stay with this, I've got to do something about it. I no longer felt neutral and indeed, looking back I wonder: did I ever feel neutral? I have an awful sort of feeling that the whole thing might have been there from the very beginning but didn't surface until 1943, and once it was out, I could think through things freely. I need no longer feel guilt about thinking this way. I suppose my views were never tested in any significant way in my tribunals, because it was just accepted that I had joined the FAU and that was the right thing for me. So I got off without being closely questioned on what I really believed...Of course there's nothing like experience, it's all very well to sit at home and theorise about what you might do and not do in certain circumstances, but until you're actually involved in it, there's no way of really telling. In the Burma campaign, I had been involved in the war in a very direct sort of way and I'm sure the change of mind – if indeed it was a change of mind – was spurred on by that, if not actually started by it.

I decided on the army, not the RAMC. I felt the RAMC would still be a compromise as really the FAU was a compromise. If I were to be absolutely honest then I had got to be prepared to do anything the army wanted me to do. I didn't want to compromise any more. I thought about bearing arms and having to kill...I think...I'm not sure how much was conscious logical reasoning or something which just appeared from within myself. I wasn't the only one. At about the same time several others took the same course as me. Duncan Wood never dissuaded me. When he had satisfied himself that I was quite sure in my own mind, he was extremely helpful. I had said that if possible I should like to stay in China. We had discovered that the British military mission in China were looking for a convoy officer, and Duncan kindly wrote a letter to the army authorities in which he spoke of my experience on convoy work. He commended me highly to them. I was then in the army with a direct commission as a Captain. After a few days I was sent back to Kunming in charge of a convoy of about a dozen vehicles in no better condition than the FAU vehicles but at least they ran on alcohol, not charcoal. I was later given some weapons training and had an enjoyable time shooting at targets. The life wasn't that different – not much army discipline in that outfit. But I did meet a frightening old soldier, General de Wiart who had one eye, one army, 'one of everything that matters.'

Bill Brough, who left the Unit to join the American Army, distinguished himself in the later Burma campaign. It was the American surgeon Dr Gordon Seagrave, with whom Brough had previously worked, who invited him to join the American Army in order that he could continue his medical work with the Chinese Army. Brough was awarded two Bronze Stars, the Silver Star for later service in the Office of Strategic Services (OSS), and the highest decoration given by the American government in time of war – the Medal of Merit. Yet he summed up his position '...in China I had become a conflicted and confused conscientious objector, then had changed to become a conflicted and confused soldier. I could never decide whether I had been both a failed conchie and a failed soldier, or whether to be a bit of both at the same time is the only real human condition.'

Doug Turner

China tested us physically – but that was no great hardship – certainly it tested our thinking – our pacifism, it tested that to the utmost. Many of us were pragmatic, recognising that being human beings we couldn't always live up to what we always like to pretend, but felt we still had something to offer, and we carried on. Some, like David Morris, were unable to, and decided that they were more fitted for the forces than trying to live under what they saw as false pretences.

David Morris:

...What finally triggered the move off was that I was on a journey back to Kweiyang from Chungking, where I had delivered a load of drugs to the home in Chungking of Madame Sun Yat-sen, and some way, about seventy or eighty kilometres out from Kweiyang, I stopped when I met an FAU truck going in the opposite direction. We stopped for a chat and then said goodbye. As I turned back to my truck, I saw that some members of the Chinese Army were climbing on board. We had a rule against this; it sounds a pretty unpleasant rule but of course the problem was that there were often groups of soldiers wandering along the Chinese roads and if you allowed one to come on board there was no reason to prevent others and that would eventually mean that your charcoal burning truck would find it even more difficult to move. Anyhow, that was our rule. I asked them to get off and I got involved in a scuffle with them and started shouting and screaming at them in a non-pacifist sort of way and they started throwing rocks at me. Eventually my Chinese mechanic managed to calm the situation down a bit and we went on. But for me that was the final trigger.

At this length of time I can't pretend to remember accurately exactly what the stages were which led me to leave the Unit. I think that one had these worries about the problem all the way through. I think one had always wanted to be fighting for one's country because one thought if ever there was a war which one ought to fight it was this one, so that one felt really that one was on the wrong side. I think what worried me was that I couldn't see anything to distinguish myself and some of my great friends in the Unit from the friends I'd known at school and university who were in the army. It didn't seem to me that we were any better than they were. We were no worse but I don't think that we were setting ourselves particularly high ideals. I don't want to give a false impression, probably the standard of our behaviour was higher than in some groups one would have encountered during the war, but it wasn't the standard of behaviour of a group of saints. We were fairly ordinary human beings who were doing a very interesting job of work in marvellous surroundings without much physical danger compared with a soldier in the fighting troops or a sailor at sea, or a member of the merchant service or a bomber pilot. There was no such risk at all.

Is there any logical position for a pacifist in a situation of total war? No. No, I don't think logic is everything but if one's trying to sort out in one's mind about whether you should do a certain thing because it assists the war effort, the fact of the matter is that next time it doesn't matter because we all go up in smoke. But last time it was a serious problem because really for the first time we were engaged in total war where every mouth to feed made a significant difference to the result. So that it could be said that if you wanted to be a CO in our country from 1939 onwards, if you didn't want to affect the war effort, you should have committed suicide, which is a curious result. Indeed, I did say this at the time. This was part of our dilemma: that whatever you did or didn't do was inevitably involved with the total war effort.

From what we've been talking about, you'll be aware that my dilemmas, like many others, were continuing from the time I registered as a CO. Indeed they were there before registration and have probably continued since the war ended. I suppose that what I wrote in Kutsing on 20 September 1943 does give some idea of what was going on in my mind at that stage:[5]

> White candle, marigolds, black clock,
> By darting night light I take stock
> Of four years mostly waste—
> Quote Eliot
> In his clerical rut—
> War years
> That went in haste
> And what's to show?
> Like Socrates I know that I don't know,
> But unlike him I know it and fret.
> I do not find it easy to forget
> That experience

Means loss of innocence
And youth.
Truth
Is as yet
Not beautiful.
The Twentieth Century Machines
Have made it hard to dream old dreams.
"Ancient, liberal, humane,"
I seek the cause but not the why of pain.
Efficient, modern and aseptic,
A man with bellyache is called dyspeptic,
I know ambition is a fraud,
Doubt the divinity of Our Lord,
And with no inner clear compulsion
I look at all things with revulsion,
Reluctant prophet of a brave new world
I much prefer to keep my banners furled.
I am an agnostic apostle of peace
Who rather dreads the day when wars will cease.

REFERENCES:

(1) John Keegan, BBC Reith Lectures, programme one, in *War and Our World*, Hutchinson, 1998.
(2) Letter to author from Alfred White, 7/10/96
(3) Douglas Turner, interview.
(4) Such feelings of violence were not unique. Others have mentioned 'upsurges of violence', 'awareness of a hidden well of savagery lurking within' which they managed to bury or sublimate in various ways.
(5) David Morris *China Changed My Mind*, Cassells, 1948.

CHAPTER 20

Fifty Years After – Would You Say That Still?

I'm not a great reunion person...But I decided to go along to the 1984 reunion – something attracted my eye to it. I found it quite a shock to the system. Suddenly I became aware of this thing from World War One onwards...Certainly it weighed in on me very heavily that we were part of something that traced its roots back to that time. And here we were, all in it together: there were some very old people who looked as if they hadn't long to live, some younger people than me; some doing very important things in life, some doing very humble jobs. Yet there was something that bound us all together. Also, although older and wiser, their faith wasn't shaken in it. I must admit that I came away from that first reunion feeling somewhat emotionally drained. In addition to that I enjoyed the reunion, and the last one too. But the first brought home to me the totality of the FAU experience over three generations.

David J. Morrish

*T*HE FAU, WORLD WAR I, had occasional reunions; indeed it was during the reunion of 1938 that the decision was taken to form a new organisation for the coming war. Reunions have also been held regularly since the Second World War and, more recently, have included members from the FRS and FAU/PWS/IS. As well as the usual renewal of old friendships from home and abroad (including many of those who had left the Unit in wartime), catching up with news and the reminiscing over old times, the content is always way beyond mere nostalgia. FAU reunions are dynamic and forward-looking, packed with *events, and characterised by an emphasis on continuing humanitarian concerns. From start to finish, one is aware of how fully and creatively the GADA spirit has been carried forward in organisations such as Oxfam, the Halo Trust, International Integrated Health, neighbourhood schemes and many other diverse areas of humanitarian involvement.* [1]

Reunions are also a time for questioning. Fifty years on: how do members stand on war and peace issues? These are men and women who have raised families, experienced life and work in diverse fields, have witnessed vast changes in world affairs, have watched the development and proliferation of nuclear weapons and missiles systems, and have seen other conflicts rise and fall. As older, wiser people far more aware of the complexities of issues – how fares their pacifism today? Has it survived? Been diluted? Given the same circumstances today – would they do it again?

John Bailey:

My pacifist convictions came slowly, and they were more developed at the end of the war. I was quite dismayed with some of the chaps who said 'Well, that's the end of being a conchie...' My feelings over the years as I got deeper into being a Quaker were that there are various grades of enlightenment, almost as in Buddhism. We had chosen not to fight, but there were Quakers who had decided to fight and put this man Hitler down. There is room for those two grades of people to be in unity. When Quakers go round with banners saying 'Quakers say no to all war' and we feel good, we ignore the person who feels he has to fight – his is as honest and tender a conscience as ours. It is over the years, sitting in the quiet as it were, that I have learned that the true Quaker witness is simply to say: our prime object must be the positive side, not the negative side saying 'What can we do to help bring the Kingdom of God into being on this earth?' And positive work, like relief work is what is important, to reconstruct the damage that has been done. But further than that, following the lead of Jesus simply to help each other on the spiritual road, not just the material. One of the lessons learnt in well over a hundred years of Quaker relief work is that when you take the bread to those in need, they are most thankful but especially if in addition to the bread, they get a bit of *you*, or your love for them as a fellow human being. In the Lord's Prayer we say 'Give us this day our daily bread.' This doesn't just mean give us a crust, we're hungry, it means feed us spiritually.

I try not to be depressed with what is going on in the world today. It doesn't help to entertain negative thoughts. It was the prophet Micah who said 'they shall beat their swords into ploughshares and nation shall not lift up a sword against nation' – that is engraved in the entrance hall to the United Nations building. And although some are predicting that the millennium of Armaggedon is nigh, I don't believe that things are moving so fast. The scale of bombing and destruction in Iraq (1991) has made many ordinary people say 'This is a ridiculous situation. It does no good.' I'm optimistic enough to think that war is ruling itself out as a useful way of solving disputes – there will still be minor wars, but I'm doubtful that we'll see another major war.

Marjorie Asquith:

I have certainly talked about pacifism since the war. I do say that war's terrible and a waste. But I would say that the *majority* feel like that now. I feel that most of the public want peace moves and don't want jingoism and waving of the flag. The Falklands (1982), now that was a nasty one. I didn't like it at all – especially the renewal of jingoism by the Prime Minister. I also didn't like the idea of the Argentinians just walking in...But I didn't like the war because it was possible to prevent it. You've got to get talking before it gets to that.

The thing is that soldiers *are* brave, and I can't help thinking there must be some other way of using that spirit. I don't think you can disband armies even now. It would be nice if there were a volunteer force in every country. It could be armed in case of having to defend against something really violent. But it could be trained as disaster teams, and there would still be opportunity for members to put their lives on the line. I still think there are enough people who want to do that. They would be sent to any part of the world where they'd be needed – it would be peacemaking and not just peacekeeping. I think in a way people do need a bit of adventure and perhaps some risks. Regiments could be kept and honours could be awarded say in an Armenian earthquake – something like that. They could be 'robust pacifists.' Soldiers sent out to kill in the Second World War turned out to be very good at looking after refugees and doing other peaceable things...

Michael Cadbury:

War simply made one more and more confirmed that it was never the way to settle anything. When one looks at history, no war has ever settled anything. The suffering after every war has been greater than the actual fighting at the time: the broken homes, the families destroyed when one breadwinner is killed. Everybody knows that war is a fearful disease, creating havoc wherever it has been. Yet we go on doing it. To see the actual results of war first-hand simply confirmed my view that this was no way to run a tuck-shop. War is going to damage more people than it is going to save and it makes the pacifist view realistic. Nothing could be worse than winning a war or losing a war. Why have a war? Why not put up with the suffering you would have by an occupation? If you're not resisting an occupation, they're going to want to live on good terms with you in order to get the most out of you. I think that's an argument which is sensible and logical, but very difficult to put into practice; unless enough people are willing to do that, then clearly it wouldn't work.

I'm a born optimist. Yes. I'm lucky always to see the cloud with a silver lining and ultimately I think mans' inhumanity to man is going to fade out. And I think ultimately it will become clear that war and violence is not the way to settle things – I think we still have a very long way to go, and I think nuclear weapons have helped. Causes of war are political and economic. Every major war one looks back on has actually been an economic war – 1914-18 was because Germany wanted colonies and wanted to get into a wider world role. The last war was because Germany was still fighting the Versailles Treaty and was terrified of Russia and wanted to get east. If you could get a better distribution of the world's goodies then people wouldn't want to go and fight. Until we think *globally*, we shall go on having wars. We have to change people's minds about war, then the rest will fall into shape.

Frank Edmead:

I ended the war as a pacifist, more so, and I've remained one ever since. I joined the Society of Friends in 1950. I never took an anti-war stance in my work with the *Guardian* saying 'All war is wrong.' But I opposed every specific war. The Guardian itself was opposed to the Suez expedition – in fact it was at that time that I was brought along to the leader-writers' corridor. But each subsequent war I opposed – not on pacifist lines specifically, but on political lines which to me is the same thing. All wars are bad politics.

Deryck Moore:

My wife and I went back one holiday to look at the First World War battle scenes. We were very moved to see what our fathers had been through. We sat in the lovely warm sunshine on Hill 60 and had a picnic with birds singing – nobody there but us. And you could look over and see the blasted trees as they had left them... and the trenches.....and we were both virtually moved to tears by seeing the Menin Gate, and the names of thousands they never found – men just buried somewhere in the mud. It made you realise that at the end of the day, the stand to do anything to prevent war *had* to be right. It convinced me beyond measure, as Churchill said 'Jaw-jaw is better than war-war.' I feel that stronger than ever now. Whether it's a local dispute, a strike – it doesn't matter what field you're talking about, talking is better than conflict. We also went on to Berlin and I was incensed with that war. What was it all about? Six years of war and Poland was as trapped as it had been at the start! Yes, I still consider myself a pacifist. It is a way of life for me.

Eric Jones:

Seeing the wounds of war reinforced my pacifism. There's no doubt about that. When I was working in a Blood Transfusion Unit in Italy, after Ethiopia, I remember one day a chap came in with his foot hanging on just by a little bit of skin. 'What do I do with this?' I asked the doctor. 'Get some scissors and cut it off.' As I did it I thought 'Good God!' The Germans had invented a very small anti-personnel mine made of wood, which had no metal in it so it couldn't be detected. You'd get seven or eight fellows coming in at a time with their feet blown off. It went on for days and you began to think 'My God! The world is going to be full of cripples when it's all over.' Some of the casualties were terrible. The thing that hit you was that generally you couldn't do much for civilians. We had parents of a little boy come to us one day, they knew we had penicillin and asked for some for their badly injured little son, and we couldn't give it – every tiny bit had to be recorded. It was that sort of thing more than anything else which made you realise the stupidity of it all.

Evelyn White:

If you are person to person with a soldier badly injured or a child with its hand blown off, you begin to think 'What a wicked waste!' Literally hundreds of thousands of Chinese died in that Salween push. It makes you think: what is it about people who make wars? It's not the average person. Do we choose the right people for our politicians and leaders? What is it that makes people so aggressive? And I think back to my father's experience in the Great War when the finest men of that generation were sacrificed. It makes you think that the man in the street isn't speaking up loudly enough and saying 'Hey, we're the ones who are going to be bayoneted, or blown up by the bombs, or radiated.' We must have our priorities wrong when we can cheerfully say 'We're going to war.' But then, on the other hand you say 'right, if we hadn't gone to war, Hitler would have invaded Britain and our country as we know it would no longer be here.' Basically all people – whether Russian, Chinese, Indian, German, British or American – we all have the same hopes and fears. We *all* want to live as long as God allows us, and we want our children to grow up and not be thrown into another war. So there is something missing in our make-up or leadership which makes nations go to war, or want to go to war. I don't know the answer... I wish I did.

David Rowlands:

Yes, I'm still a pacifist, as much as ever. In fact stronger now. Yes, *absolutely* – although I wavered at times. I have been involved in the CND and in local peace groups, even in Northleach. So I kept it up and again it's a matter of making a stand. In fact there is some opposition now to the peace group down in Northleach. We had a 'Bread not Bombs' demonstration in the square of

Northleach and we approached the local postmistress who sold bread 'We don't want to queer your pitch but would you mind if we did it?' And she said 'It's a stab in the back for my son who's a soldier in Northern Ireland.' So it's still there, isn't it? So is the need to make a stand.

Pat Rawlence:

Yes, yes, yes; I think more so. I don't think war solves *anything* only makes things worse. I'm still as convinced as before although it's difficult to say what I would have done in 1943 if I felt like I feel now. I might have gone into the RAMC – perhaps a little more compromise – but I certainly wouldn't have done firearms drill, that was one of my objections. I wouldn't be prepared to use a firearm against anybody in any circumstances. I'm not active today. I belong to the Medical Campaign Against Nuclear Warfare, but I'm not very active in it. I am a member of Greenpeace – green is all part of the way of thinking. Greens are not proclaimed pacifists but if you're going to be Green you can't let off enormous quantities of rocket or nuclear fuel, can you?

Eric Turner:

I still feel against war and violence, yes. But I'm less innocent about it. I feel it easy to understand why people feel they must resort to violence and I would not, I think, be able to say that under no circumstances would I be violent. I can think of circumstances where it would be difficult if not impossible for me to behave non-violently. I don't think this invalidates what is basically my own position. I can see a place in the world for an instrument of force such as the UN forces which attempt to arrest certain kinds of political behaviour before too much damage is done. One good thing that has come out of the Gulf affair (1991) is that it does seem to have enabled the UN idea to have a renaissance. I know that for many Quakers that falls far short of what our peace witness ought to be but that is the point I have reached. I still think that it leaves my central pacifist position intact. But it's easy to say that when you're seventy-two. My sympathies are with the young people who still have to consider what they must do if war came – a different kettle of fish...

Hugo Powell:

I have no involvement with the peace movement today. I do have the awareness of responsibility to speak out about certain things. I often shock nuclear disarmers because I think there is so much that is very weak about their arguments. They think I'm a terrible militarist because I don't think it's a matter of fixing on one particular weapon and a set of ideas. Peace is a lot more complex than that. I think that as a pacifist who wants to see war got rid of, it's best to put forward a lot of queries to the younger generation who have to think it all out the way I had to from one's experience, and leave them with a lot more to think about than to give some ready-made solutions. That's really the contribution I would try to make today – to play devil's advocate to young people and relate to the doubts and experiences I had in the last war. I don't lay down the law, but I think the best that people of my age can do is to query easy assumptions about how we achieve peace in the world – yes, I'm still a pacifist, basically a pacifist.

Duncan Wood:

I think for me that when the war ended I still felt satisfaction that I had maintained my pacifism through to the end in spite of the challenge of Belsen. When all that was uncovered and people said 'How *could* you have stood aside from the struggle to eradicate this appalling evil?' that was a very real challenge. I nevertheless felt I was glad I had kept up my witness that war is an evil and we have to eradicate it. We've got to maintain opposition to war as an institution. Subsequently, I did feel when working for the UN in Geneva that it was a great advantage talking about peace from a pacifist angle while at the same time understanding those who don't take the pacifist view but seek peace by other means. I have to say how impossible it would have been for me to have remained in a lone situation. I don't see how on my own I could have avoided the intrusion of questions in my mind without those to discuss them with.

When I view the future, I am neither optimistic nor pessimistic. Quakers are often accused of being over-optimistic about human nature. Now, we have to bear in mind the important distinction between optimism and hope. I think it's part of the Christian duty to maintain hope. This has been summed up by St. Paul in his Epistle to the Romans where he says: 'And not only so, but we glory in tribulations also, knowing that tribulation worketh patience, and patience experience, and experience hope.'

Spencer Cox:

...I think there have to be pacifists. *Somebody* has to keep the idea alive. And I can't say that I'm a hundred per cent certain that I'm right on this, but if nobody keeps the idea of non-violence and pacifism alive then society has lost a great deal. I also think that pacifists are put in an unfair position often by being asked to defend their position when somebody like Hitler comes along. If we had our way originally, then Hitler would not have *existed.* So we're asked to justify a position which looks untenable because of the way other people who run things have acted. I don't think it's quite fair for pacifists to be put on the defensive when the world is not of their making.

Norman Pollitt:

My experiences during the war didn't change my ideas of the futility of war but one of the first things we learnt about on coming back from Ethiopia was the concentration camps. We'd been very cut off before and when one realised how bestial the enemy could be, this made one wonder: where does pacifism fit into this? The Jews were pacifists – they had to be because they had no option, but it didn't keep them from the gas chambers. This is the worrying thing... I don't know whether I would do the same again. One or two left the Unit at the fall of France. They felt they couldn't go on being pacifists in view of what had happened to France. On the other hand some from the army came and joined us during the war. It's a circle you go round and round in the argument. There's a lot of difference in making up your mind theoretically and making up your mind in a practical way. In 1939 you had to make up your mind one way or the other, there was no middle course. From a personal point of view, if you regard each of your fellow men as having a spirit within him which emanates from God, then there is no way you can take life. I have no involvement with the peace movement today. I had a bit to do with CND when I was in practice in Newmarket. I was very anti-nuclear then – still am. I am still a PPU member, but have nothing to do with the pacifist movement at present. Perhaps if another war loomed up...

Derryck Hill:

Pacifism is a humbling experience. You get no chance to shine as a leader or anything like that. By and large the work is never glamorous. There was one stage at the end of the war when I seriously began to question my pacifism – this is when news of Belsen came out. I haven't even now resolved my position over that. Had we known about it at the war's outbreak? – that's the question! I know that George Fox said that 'neither princes nor principalities' would influence his faith...but, yes, my pacifism *has* changed – as a youth it was black and white and now it's shades of grey. I still think war is wrong and that it never solves anything and that it's a question of 'jaw-ing' not 'war-ing' if you want to solve anything. Even if you're victorious, what do you gain? Look at this country, what did we gain as a result of war? I don't belong to CND largely because it throws the wrong emphasis – the objection to nuclear weapons. My objection is to *all* war including nuclear, and all that war implies. But my pacifism is no longer black and white.

Lilian Cadoux:

I am deeply involved with CND and have been on many marches and demonstrations. I still feel very strongly indeed that I have to make *my* witness, what is right for me, but I want to make the distinction that I now don't think what is right for me is necessarily right for other people. I think that there are still so many hawks left in the Kremlin that it is quite likely that what the supporters of nuclear weapons are saying is true – it is quite likely that it acts as a deterrent. So I am ambivalent. There are lots of others like me who refuse to be holier-than-thou and say 'I am right and you are wrong.' I think this ambivalence is much healthier. CND is anti-nuclear, not anti-war which is more comfortable for somebody like me. I truly think there is a lot of real evil in the world...

powers of darkness which are manifested in us. I can see it in myself, but I consider myself fortunate to have been brought up by such decent parents, and to have gone to such a good school which instilled good principles in me. Without those two things, and, say, had I lived in Nazi Germany, I might have become a young Nazi...So, no, I'm not a wholehearted pacifist now. Had I known the full extent of the evil during the war, then I don't think I could have been a pacifist then.[2]

Tom Barnsley:

I think I'd answer your question by saying that I'm still pacifist in spirit. Whether I've got the strength of character to make the positive stand as we did then, I doubt.. I'm far less sure of the pacifist rightness... but what I'm equally sure about is that my own temperament and aspirations are still pacifist. That's not saying that pacifism can, as I once thought, cure most of the world's ills. In fact I doubt if it can. I think it becomes very much a highly personalised issue and on a personal basis, I am still a pacifist. If there's any solution to be found, then I'm equally sure now as I was then that military decisions are not going to solve the problems of the world. So I'm in limbo if you like.

Stephen Peet:

Pacifism today...I think so. I think it can only be measured in terms of being faced with a certain problem, or bit of behaviour, and then finding out what you'd do. In the present situation in the Gulf (1990) – strange, isn't it, how we point towards the television set? – I strongly hope they won't revert to war to solve it...It's abhorrent to think of all those people lined up in the desert, and plans being made to probably try to find some excuse to go to war. Therefore every headline I see and any news that points to negotiation, I'm happy to see. Anything else horrifies me. So *there's* an answer. But I'm sure that's the answer that most military people who are not bloodthirsty would say. However, there are small undertones and worries of the Munich Agreement – with hindsight, was that the right thing to do? Or, maybe they *are* doing the right thing in this case – that's my little worry...

Paul Townsend:

My pacifist position today? I find it increasingly complex and the contradictions more apparent. I don't know whether that is simply the result of brooding on it more or being seventy and no longer having to make decisions but having to mull things over. There are terrible problems, and one feels it very much at the moment with the war in Bosnia, and I find myself grasping at little bits of comfort like hearing members of the Red Cross saying that they always get on better if they don't have military escorts and I find myself pleased when I hear people on the ground plainly not wanting the air strikes. But I'm not sure that's not wanting people to go even half-way towards agreeing with what my view is...But the point is neither they nor I can solve the problem but when I hear it I feel a bit of moral support...What we're looking at now in some ways is particularly alarming because it suggests that people can indulge in a kind of communal badness, almost suggesting that people are predisposed to violence if they can find some outlet in violence, and I would like to think that humans aren't necessarily like that. I would like to think that some histories and cultures have encouraged that more than others – I don't think that would happen as easily in Britain as it has happened in the Balkans. I remember having this discussion recently with a friend as to what our pacifist position would have been in 19th century Greece with that extraordinary violent tradition in which the heroes were aggressive brigands. One can only hope that there is a process of education in which people no longer think that kind of assertiveness is good, or anything can be gained from it. But it's singularly disturbing that people who have managed to achieve some kind of symbiosis suddenly turn on each other, and not people who are economically deprived either.

Also, the last thing I want to say: it does raise the question, and a very big question, I think, for people who are or have been pacifists. It was fairly easy to be a pacifist for us. But would I if I was a Serb or Croat or Bosnian muslim of a certain age, have the courage to step aside there? ...I've always felt that somewhere along the line the ultimate of the pacifist position is some kind of crucifixion. I've never been pushed there – I mean, how easy it was to go before a comparatively tolerant tribunal and then to be allowed to do most useful things in a unit of Friends! But then, as St Thomas à Becket tells us in *Murder in the Cathedral,* it is not a good thing to seek martyrdom. But I suppose that out of the corner of one's eye, there is always this little question: would I, at a pinch, have the stuff of martyrdom?...Probably not.

Bernard Fisher:

I have changed my attitude. I am now an atheist. Today, of course it isn't a feasible question as to whether I would do it again as I am seventy-six. Any change has been very gradual and nothing to do with CND or anything like that. Is it a good or bad thing when people change their minds? When I go to some of the reunions, I find that people haven't changed their minds by a centimetre. I find that very hard to take. The thing I'm scared stiff about is developing a closed mind – whether politically, religiously or any other way. Good luck to them though. It takes all sorts to make the world. One wants the military people, the pacifists and the agitators...I keep an open mind on everything.

David Rudd:

I emerged from the war with my pacifism intact and went back to college with it intact. It is difficult to know when or why it began to weaken. I think the Nuremberg Trials began to have an effect. I hadn't realised what a terrible Holocaust it had been and although I thought that in some ways the trials were vindictive and very rough justice – I used to say: that's not *justice,* its vengeance! – nevertheless it was fairly clear that there had been awful evil in Germany...I never had any wish to face issues which were hypothetical; I never thought about issues in my life until they became real and then I drew on the philosophy I had in order to make a decision. I suppose when new facts came to light, and I had new experience of people, I began to realise that what I'd done wasn't a solution to the problem. What the solution was I still didn't know and don't know now. But I came to the conclusion that what I'd been taught – the elementary Christian type of approach – doesn't relate to people as they really are. A lot are extremely evil and the only way to deal with them is by force. So I haven't any coherent philosophy of life

which enables me to deal with these enormous problems and all
I've done is withdrawn my objection to participating in things with
a military flavour.

Theo Cadoux:

No, I am no longer a pacifist. I'm not sure how long I remained
one but it took some time for it to sink in. As you get older, you
get much less sympathetic to one's fellow men, feeling that a lot of
what they suffer is their own fault. And so much more aware of the
depths of wickedness that appear to exist in other people. There is
no doubt there was wickedness enough to know about at that time
in the behaviour of the Nazis towards the Jews and others in concentration camps. But one persuaded oneself at that time they could
be educated and brought round to another point of view if only you
had a chance to talk to them – that everyone had good in them
which could be brought out. But the longer I live, the more convinced I become that some people are completely wicked and unre-
deemable. And when I see some of the things that are done by
people all over the world as individuals and as members of political parties and groups of raiders, guerrillas and suchlike, I feel I
would have no compunction, if I were in a position to do so, to stop
them by forcible means and, if necessary, kill them. And I have
become a supporter of the death penalty among other things. So,
although I still go to FAU reunions and I like meeting the people
again and talking about our experiences, I don't really share their
ideals. I think some other members have changed as well. There
are some people who are saintly by nature, and Donald Swann is
one of them. I am not.

Donald Swann:

There is this whole idea of living with a conscience and that we
had to go on living with it. You know, I think I've lived with it ever
since. And it is a permanent partner: a little, quiet, second identity that goes along with you – a little conscience, a little box. And
I think I am a conchie for life...

REFERENCES:

(1) Roy Ridgway and his wife Dorothea set up a charity, the International Integrated Health Association, for helping sick children in Russia and organising exchange visits for English, Russian and Ukranian doctors and nurses.

(2) Lilian Cadoux was interviewed in 1989 prior to the end of the cold war.

Coda

Home is where one starts from. As we grow older
The world becomes stranger, the pattern more complicated
Of dead and living. Not the intense moment
Isolated, with no before and after,
But a lifetime burning in every moment
And not the lifetime of one man only
But of old stones that cannot be deciphered...

T. S. Eliot, East Coker.

Duncan Wood:

A POSITIVE SIDE to war? I'm rather sorry to say, yes. Yes, for this reason: I've mentioned the fact that a number of FAU colleagues went into various forms of social service and wouldn't have done perhaps if the war hadn't come along and made them face up to their position. Now for a long time when I was working for Friends in Geneva, we had colleagues sent over to us from Philadelphia who had had the American pacifist experience which was different from the British, but nevertheless they came out from the great reservoir of those who'd had this wartime experience and had been in a way 'baptised' by what they had gone through and from which one could draw a continuing series of volunteers. Now I sadly have to confess that in spite of the good work of Oxfam and Save the Children, the reservoir is beginning to dry up. There is no longer a group of people who have had a wartime experience. Is there a group of people who have inherited the concepts of voluntary service and the acceptance of the hardships of voluntary service in the same way as in the war? I'm afraid not. So is it therefore necessary to have war every generation in order to create a new reservoir of people who are going to do these jobs?

A story has just come to me, I can't vouch for its authorship but it was told to me by one of those who came out with Stilwell through the jungle to Assam. They experienced the jungle for the first time and in the course of their march came across places where battles had taken place and had left behind a number of corpses. And on occasions they found these corpses were covered with the most beautiful butterflies, presumably butterflies who were feeding on blood. Now, did this underline the horror of war – the corpse becoming the food of a kind of vulture? Or could it be that the beauty of the butterflies somehow overlaid the horror of the war and enabled one to see that from that slaughter there was something beautiful that survived? This puts me in mind of the collection of stories brought together by Victor Gollancz in the book *Above All Nations*, published very soon after the end of the war, in which were recorded acts of kindness from one enemy to another. These were just little incidents and don't give a picture of the war as a whole; just a few examples of how the men who had been taught to kill, taught probably to hate, taught to be fierce and aggressive, nevertheless had managed to preserve their human feelings and managed still to be able to recognise in the enemy a common member of the human race. As Gollancz himself said 'above all nations is humanity.'[1]

REFERENCES:

[1] *Above All Nations,* compiled by George Catlin, Vera Brittain and Sheila Hodges, with a foreword by Victor Gollancz. Gollancz, 1945.

Bibliography

Bailey, Brenda *A Quaker Couple in Nazi Germany: Leonhard Friedrich Survives Buchenwald.* William Sessions, York, 1994.

Barber, Christopher B. (ed.) *FAU Postscript: Some Reflections of Former FAU Members on what their Unit Experience of 40 Years Earlier Has Meant to them.* Oxfam Print Unit, 1984.

Barker, Rachel *Conscience, Government and War.* Routledge & Kegan Paul, London, 1982.

Braithwaite, Constance *Conscientious Objection to Compulsions Under the Law.* William Sessions, York, 1995.

Brock, Peter & Socknat, Thomas (eds.) *Challenge to Mars: Essays on Pacifism from 1918 to 1945.* Toronto University Press, 1998.

Brough, William *To Reason Why: Getting the Mind Around War.* At present in manuscript stage, with possibility of publishing by Brasseys US Inc. 1999.

Bush, Roger (ed.) *FAU The Third Generation: Friends Ambulance Unit Post-War Service and International Service, 1946-59.* William Sessions, York, 1998.

Cameron, Catriona *Go Anywhere Do Anything: New Zealanders in the Friends Ambulance Unit in China 1945-1951.* Beechtree Press, Wellington, New Zealand, 1996.

Corsellis, John *Friendly Persuasion: How 6,000 Refugees Were Saved in 1945.* Friends Quarterly, October, 1955.

Davies, A. Tegla *Friends Ambulance Unit: The Story of The FAU in the Second World War.* Allen and Unwin Ltd, 1947.

Keegan, John *War and Our World,* Hutchinson, 1998.

Lidbetter, Martin *Friends Ambulance Unit 1939-1943: Experiences in Finland, Norway, Sweden, Egypt, Greece and Germany.* Sessions Book Trust, York, 1993.

McClelland, Grigor *Embers of War.* I B Tauris Ltd, London, 1997.

Moorhead, Caroline *Troublesome People: Enemies of War 1916-1986.* Hamish Hamilton, London, 1987.

Morris, David *China Changed My Mind.* Cassells Company Ltd, 1948; Houghton Mifflin Company, Boston MA, 1949.

Smith, Lyn & Swann, Donald *Swann's Way: A Life in Song.* Heinemann, London, 1991.

Socknat, Thomas P. *The Canadian Contribution to the China Convoy, Quaker History,* 69, 1980.

Sykes, Marjorie *An Indian Tapestry: Quaker Threads in the History of India, Pakistan & Bangladesh.* Sessions Book Trust, 1997.

Tatham, Meaburn & Miles, James E. *The Friends Ambulance Unit 1914-1919: A Record.* Swarthmore Press Ltd, London, 1919.

White, Evelyn *South of the Clouds: Yunnan and the Salween Front 1944: Memories of a British Nursing Sister.* China Society, 1985.

Wild, David *Prisoner of Hope,* Book Guild, Lewes, 1992.

Wilson, Roger *Quaker Relief: An Account of the Relief Work of the Society of Friends, 1940-1948.* Allen and Unwin, London, 1952.

UNPUBLISHED MANUSCRIPTS

Aldous, Kenneth *Travel Journal.* 1993.
    Brief Encounter with 'Ba Lu'. 1947

Awmack, Joseph W. *In China with the Friends Ambulance Unit, 1945-1946,* a Family History booklet.

Barnard, Clifford *Two Weeks In May 1945: Sandbostel Camp and the Friends Ambulance Unit.*

Clark, Bronson P. *FAU – China Convoy,* taken from *Dear Daughters . . . A Memoir,* 1944.

Coates, R. Neville *The Friends Ambulance Unit in Berlin 1945-46.*

Coates, R. Neville *From the London Blitz to the Champs-Elysées: An account of the Friends Ambulance Unit 1940-45.*

Cosford, Brian *Diary Extracts, No. 7 Relief Section, N.W. Europe.*

Du Feu, Clifford *Journal of Clifford de Feu, December 1944 – January 1946 in Holland and Belgium and West Germany with the BAOR.*

Harkness, B. (ed.) *No Other Option: Experiences of New Zealand Conscientious Objectors and Supporters during World War 2.* Christian Pacifist Society, New Zealand, 1989.

Hinton, Arthur and Hedy *Friends Ambulance Unit,* 1996.

Keith, G. *Friends Ambulance Service, China (South East Haulage), Various Reports and Diaries.*

Locke, H. Brian *An Unimportant Member of the FAU.*

Morris, David *Unpublished Poems.*

Murphey, W. Rhoads (ed.) *A China Convoy Anthology*. Chunking, 1945.

Norton, Jack *1950-1959: Lavender Farm.*

Paul, Denis E. *War-time and Post-War Reminiscences.*

Parry, Dr S. C. *Some Medical Problems at a camp for Displaced Persons.*

Pritchard, Donald F. L. *The FAU in Europe: One Member's Personal Views.*

Rodwell, Henry H. *A Short History of China 1911-1986.* 1987.

Selby-Bigge, J. *Unpublished Memoir.*

West, Gordon *Celle 1945.*

Wood, Louise H. *Italy Programme (of AFSC) 1940-1940, 1944-1945.*

FAU PUBLICATIONS

Friends Ambulance Unit Reports 1939-1946.

FAU Chronicle 1940-1946.

FAU Information Bulletins 1945-46.

INTERVIEWS, IMPERIAL WAR MUSEUM SOUND ARCHIVE

Marjorie Asquith 10650/1989, Brenda Bailey 16901/1996, John Bailey 12034/1991, Pamela Bankart 17515/1997, Chris Barber 10352/1988, Tom Barnsley 10144/1988, Elaine Bell 13499/1993, Clifford Brewer 16480/1996, W. (Bill) Brough 12103/1991, Henry Burbidge 10773/1989, Tessa Cadbury 14205/1994, Rachel Cadbury 10038/1987, Michael Cadbury 10051/1987, Lilian Cadoux 10885/1989, Theo Cadoux 10738/ 1989, Sydney Carter 9218/1986, Dennis Conolly 10553/1988, John Corsellis 10458/1988, Jim Cottrell 12181/1991, Spencer Coxe 14206/ 1994, E. (Ted) Dunn 10355/1988, Frank Edmead 13658/1993, Bernard Fisher 10653/1989, Gerald Gardiner 10456/1988, A. (Tony) Gibson 12267/1991, Tom Haley 10143/1988, Michael Harris 9325/1986, Derryck Hill 9403/1986, Alex Horsfield 17516, Eric Jones 11487/1990, Elizabeth Hughes 9437/1986, Ronald Joynes 10652/1989, Gwendy Knight 10929/1989, R. E. (Tod) Lawry 17578/1997, Margaret Matheson 11531/1990, Deryck Moore 9941/1987, David Morris 9811/1987, David J. Morrish 10116/1998, George Parsons 9789/1987, Stephen Peet 11736/ 1990, Norman Pollitt 10353/1988, Hugo Powell 10351/1990, Pat Rawlence 10776/1989, Angela Sinclair-Loutit 10040/1987, A. (Tony) Reynolds 12223/1991, Roy Ridgway 10350/1987, David Rowlands 13631/1993, Michael Rowntree 10883/1989, David Rudd 11313/1990, W. (Bill) Spray 10551/1988, Donald Swann 9133/1985, Alan Taylor 13649/1993, Freddie Temple 12035/1991, Paul Townsend 13411/1993, Doug Turner 9338/1986, Roy Tyldesley 11530/1990, Stephen Verney 9832/1987, Evelyn White 10142/1988, Robin Whitworth 10265/1988, Duncan Wood 9371/1986.

Index

Abbreviations used: AFSC, American Friends Service Committee; ARF, American Relief for France; CO, conscientious objector; CSC, Civilian Service Corps; FRS, Friends Relief Service; HSU, Hadfield Spears Unit; MSU, mobile surgical unit; MST, mobile surgical team